Multicultural Perspectives in Working with Families

Second Edition

Elaine P. Congress, MSW, DSW, is Associate Dean and Professor at Fordham University Graduate School of Social Service in New York City. She has also served as Director of the Doctoral Program there. Dr. Congress has written extensively in the areas of cultural diversity, social work ethics, and social work education, including 3 books and over 30 professional journal articles and book chapters. She has presented on cultural diversity and social work ethics at national and international conferences in the United States, Europe, and Australia. She developed the *culturagram*, a tool for assessing and working with culturally diverse families. Dr. Congress serves on the United Nations (UN) Team for the International Federation of Social Workers (IFSW) and is a past president of the New York City chapter of the National Association of Social Workers (NASW). Before entering academia, she was a practitioner, supervisor, and administrator in a community mental health program.

Manny J. González, DSW, is an Assistant Professor and chair of the clinical concentration area at Fordham University Graduate School of Social Service. He has practiced in primary health care centers, teaching hospitals, school-based mental health clinics, child welfare agencies, and community mental health centers, providing clinical services to patients of various immigrant and ethnic/racial minority backgrounds. Dr. González has published articles and chapters on mental health practice with Hispanic immigrants and refugees, Hispanics and community health outreach, urban children, and evidence-based practice. He is co-editor (together with Gladys González-Ramos, PhD) of *Mental Health Care for New Hispanic Immigrants: Innovative Approaches in Contemporary Clinical Practice*, on the psychosocial treatment of new Hispanic immigrants and refugees in the United States. Dr. González's current research focuses on psychotherapy intervention with depressed Hispanic preadolescents and the mental health outcomes of abused and neglected children. He maintains a private practice in New York City.

Multicultural Perspectives in Working with Families

Second Edition

Elaine P. Congress, DSW
Manny J. Gonzalez, DSW
Editors

 Springer Publishing Company
 Social Work Series

Springer Publishing Company, Inc.
11 West 42nd Street
New York, NY 10036

Acquisitions Editors: Sheri W. Sussman and Lauren Dockett
Production Editor: Sara Yoo
Cover design by Joanne Honigman

05 06 07 08 09 / 5 4 3 2 1

Library of Congress Cataloging-in-Publication Data

Multicultural perspectives in working with families / Elaine Congress, Manny J. González, editors.— 2nd ed.
   p. cm. — (Springer series on social work)
   Includes bibliographical references and index.
   1. Family social work—United States.   2. Minorities—Services for—United States.   3. Ethnicity—United States.   4. Multiculturalism—United States.
   I. Congress, Elaine Piller.   II. González, Manny J.   III. Springer series on social work (Unnumbered)
      HV699.M85 1997
      362.82—dc22   2005004804

Printed in the United States of America by Sheridan Books, Inc.

To my husband, Robert T. Snyder, whose support and encouragement helped make Multicultural Perspectives in Working With Families (second edition) *a reality.*

–E.P.C.

To my wife, Mildred, whose support made the publication of this book possible and to my sons, Jeremy John and Elijah Gabriel.

–M.J.G.

Contents

SECTION FIVE
CONCLUSION

Contributors

Nuha Abudabbeh, PhD, has been a clinical psychologist since 1972. Born in Palestine, raised partly in Turkey, she attended college at American University in Beirut. Dr. Abudabbeh specializes in cross-cultural issues and forensic psychology and is currently consulting and offering workshops on these subjects.

Portia Adams, PhD, is an Assistant Professor at Fordham University Graduate School of Social Service. A student of African and Afro-American Studies and Politics, she served in the Peace Corps in Kenya and as a social worker in New York City for 13 years. At Fordham she teaches Clinical Practice, Social Work with Adolescents, and Methods of Group Intervention.

Valerie Borum, PhD, MSW, is an Assistant Professor at the Fordham University Graduate School of Social Service. Dr. Borum's research interests include African American families, Afrocentric social work practice and research, African American women, suicide and culture, disability and deafness, multicultural hearing families of deaf children, qualitative methods, prejudice reduction, and applied behavior analysis.

Patricia Brownell, PhD, CSW, is an Associate Professor at Fordham University Graduate School of Social Service. Dr. Brownell joined the Fordham faculty in 1995 after 26 years of service in the New York City Human Resources Administration. Her areas of research and practice include domestic violence, elder abuse, and gerontology. Dr. Brownell is a Hartford Foundation Geriatric Faculty Scholar, has served as the United Nations representative for the International Network on Elder Abuse, and is a member of the New York City Women, Welfare and Abuse Taskforce.

Robert Chazin, DSW, is a Professor at the Fordham University Graduate School of Social Service. He has served as a mental health consultant to various social service agencies and has trained clinicians working with Russian-speaking Jewish immigrants. His varied international experience includes service as coordinator and trainer in an Eastern European program addressing the psychosocial aftermath of the Chernobyl disaster.

Roslyn H. Chernesky, DSW, is Professor at the Fordham University Graduate School of Social Services. She teaches courses in the Masters and doctoral curriculum in management and administration, program and proposal development, and organizational theory. Her research, publications, and consultation focus on enhancing service delivery and building organizational capacity.

Carole B. Cox, PhD, is Professor of Social Work in the Graduate School of Social Service, Fordham University. She is the author of six books and numerous articles and chapters dealing with various aspects of aging. Her particular interests are grandparent caregivers and family caregiving for dementia relatives.

Susan Bair Egan, PhD, is the Assistant Dean for Student Services in the Graduate School of Social Service at Fordham University. Dr. Egan's research interests are women's issues. In addition to the needs of multiple role women, she has studied parenting skills for mothers in substance abuse recovery.

Irene A. Gutheil, DSW, is the Henry C. Ravazzin Professor of Gerontology and Director of the Ravazzin Center for Social Work Research in Aging at the Fordham University Graduate School of Social Service. A Fellow of the Gerontological Society of America, Dr. Gutheil has worked with older persons and their families in institutional and community settings and her publications address issues in aging and social work. Her most recent research examines the needs of older adults and their family caregivers, and end-of-life planning.

Meredith Hanson, DSW, is an Associate Professor and the Director of the Doctoral Program at Fordham University's Graduate School of Social Service. He has been a social worker in the field of substance abuse for over thirty years. Among his publications are chapters and articles on evidence-based practice, social work practice in substance abuse, and cross-national training of practitioners working with traumatized families and children.

Carmen Ortiz Hendricks, DSW, ACSW, is an Associate Professor at Hunter College School of Social Work of the City University of

New York. She has been on the school's faculty since 1980. Her research and publications have been in the area of culturally competent social work education and practice. They include *Learning to Teach—Teaching to Learn: A Guide for Social Work Field Education*, and the coedited text, *Intersecting Child Welfare, Substance Abuse, and Family Violence: Culturally Competent Approaches*. She was a principal contributor to NASW's "Standards for Cultural Competence in Social Work Practice."

Janna C. Heyman, PhD, is an Assistant Professor at the Fordham University Graduate School of Social Service and Assistant Director at the Ravazzin Center for Social Work Research and Aging. Dr. Heyman has been at Fordham since 1985. She currently works with the Ravazzin Center on end-of-life issues and is coinvestigator of Strengthening the Role of the Healthcare Agent: A Protocol for Use with Hispanic Elders. Dr. Heyman is also involved in intergenerational programs, the Westchester Millenium Aging Project, and spiritual studies.

Carol P. Kaplan, PhD, is an Associate Professor of Social Work at Fordham University Graduate School of Social Service. Dr. Kaplan worked for many years as a social worker in the child and adolescent divisions of a community mental health center. Her research has focused on Hispanic adolescent girls and she has published many articles and book chapters dealing with children and adolescents.

Eun Jeong Ko, MSW, CSW, has been a doctoral student at Fordham University Graduate School of Social Service with a concentration in gerontology. Ms. Ko came to the U.S. from South Korea in 1997, has worked as a medical social worker in a local hospital, and currently is a psychotherapist at a mental health clinic.

Winnie W. Kung, PhD, is an Associate Professor at Fordham University Graduate School of Social Service, and a former faculty member at the University of Southern California. Her research interests are in the areas of mental health and families, particularly the impact of culture among minority groups. Some of her past studies and publications include impacts of beliefs about burden among Chinese American caregivers of patients with schizophrenia, help-seeking behaviors of Chinese Americans on emotional problems, and sociocultural impact on the divorce experience of Chinese women in Hong Kong.

Edith A. Lewis, PhD, is an Associate Professor of Social Work and Adjunct Associate Professor of Women's Studies at the University of Michigan. Her areas of interest are women of color and international practice.

Maxine Lynn, PhD, is Assistant Dean at Adelphi University School of Social Work. She has presented at national and international conferences on the use of group intervention with children who have witnessed violence or have been traumatized. She is a former Vice Chairperson of the Association of Social Work with Groups.

Gerald P. Mallon, DSW, is an Associate Professor and Executive Director of The National Resource Center for Foster Care and Permanency Planning at the Hunter School of Social Work in New York City. Dr. Mallon is the author or editor of 12 books and lectures extensively on a variety of topics in child welfare. For over 29 years, Dr. Mallon has been a practitioner, researcher, and advocate for LGBT children, youth, and families.

Idalia Mapp, PhD, formerly of Fordham University, is taking time off from teaching to work on her research agenda in the area of parents of deaf children. She has published and presented widely on the topic of ethnic differences on stress and coping among parents of deaf children. Dr. Mapp has a private practice specializing in couples intervention, family intervention, and individual therapy.

Cynthia Cannon Poindexter, MSW, PhD, is an Associate Professor at Fordham University Graduate School of Social Service. A human services practitioner for 28 years, she has spent the last 17 years in the HIV field. Dr. Poindexter was the first social worker in the first AIDS Training Network, the Southeast AIDS Education and Training Center, the Midwest AIDS Training and Education Center, the New England AIDS Education and Training Center, the NASW HIV Spectrum Project, the Massachusetts Department of Public Health HIV Division, and the HIV/AIDS Service Administration of New York City. Dr. Poindexter has also been an associate with the National HIV Research Center and a board member of the National Association of HIV over Fifty.

Jessica Rosenberg, PhD, is an Assistant Professor of Social Work at Long Island University. She is the former Assistant Director of the

New York City Chapter of the National Association of Social Workers. Dr. Rosenberg is a bilingual, Spanish-speaking clinician who has provided mental health services to the Hispanic community for over 17 years.

Samuel Rosenberg, PhD, is an Associate Professor of Social Work and Sociology at Ramapo College of New Jersey. Dr. Rosenberg served for 10 years as Director of a community health center affiliated with South Beach Psychiatric Center, of the New York City Office of Mental Health. For the past 25 years Dr. Rosenberg has been involved as a scholar and practitioner in program development, and has provided clinical services for diverse and immigrant communities.

Yvette M. Sealy, PhD, is an Assistant Professor at the Fordham University Graduate School of Social Service. She has also worked in practice with children and adolescents with various developmental and psychiatric problems. Dr. Sealy regularly consults with New York City Department of Education schools, community-based organizations, and faith-based groups on matters pertaining to child and adolescent development, crisis intervention, stress management, bereavement, and culturally competent client/organizational practices. Dr. Sealy maintains an interest in the development of quality youth service programming to address the prevention of drug and alcohol abuse, teen pregnancy, and the transmission of HIV/AIDS.

Virginia C. Strand, DSW, is an Associate Professor and Director of the Children and Families Institute for Research, Support and Training (Children First) at Fordham University Graduate School of Social Service. An experienced educator, trainer, program evaluator, and clinician, Dr. Strand has published in the field of child welfare and children's mental health, particularly in the evaluation and treatment of child sexual abuse. Current projects include the implementation of standardized trauma assessment measures in community-based mental health services for children and adolescents.

Zulema E. Suárez, PhD, is an Associate Professor at Adelphi University in Garden City, New York. With 25 years in the field, she has practiced and taught clinical graduate work in the Midwest and in New York. She has published a number of chapters on culturally diverse practices, has led seminars on spirituality and social work, and is delighted to integrate both of those topics.

Sandra G. Turner, PhD, is Associate Dean of Fordham University Graduate School of Social Service. Her research interests include factors related to suicide attempts of adolescent Hispanic girls, prevention of adolescent substance abuse, depression and self-esteem of women alcoholics, and enhancing resilience in women and adolescents. She has written numerous chapters and articles on these topics.

Tatyana Ushakova, MSW, is a social worker in the Guild Care Department of the Jewish Guild for the Blind. She works with ethnically and culturally diverse individuals and groups with multiple diagnoses and psychosocial issues, including Russian-speaking Jewish immigrants.

Peter B. Vaughan, PhD, is Dean of the Graduate School of Social Service, Fordham University. His practice background includes ambulatory health and mental health with a special interest in adolescent health behaviors and well-being.

Foreword

Peter B. Vaughn

American society has witnessed drastic changes over the past 3 decades. Some of the changes are attributable to international events and others to national circumstances. Resulting from some of those changes has been the arrival of new immigrant and refugee groups. These groups frequently cluster in decaying cities that historically have accommodated persons arriving from other shores. Members of a number of these newly arrived groups have also moved into rural areas that heretofore were unaffected by mass migrations of persons born in other countries, many of whom do not speak English and are people of color. During this 30-year time span the traditional American nuclear family structure in many instances has given way to nontraditional families. Many social work professionals fail to understand these different family forms and lack both the practice skills and wisdom to work effectively with these families. There are also new institutional arrangements that have come about as accommodations, and in some instances nonaccommodations, to the changing economic, political, racial, and ethnic character of our nation—which unfortunately often leaves us feeling as if we are living in a nation divided. Major challenges for us as a nation are valuing the social and cultural differences that each of the groups who live here adds to the great American mosaic, and understanding the economic, political, and social forces of the society that either inhibit or enhance the opportunity structure of all those who inhabit this great land. A careful reading of this book will help the practitioner meet these challenges.

The book is arranged in such a way that each section builds on the preceding section. Throughout the book practice examples are used that help the reader appreciate the complexity of working within and across fields of practice with specific problem behaviors and conditions. The book begins with approaches to practice, and ends with a full consideration of ethical issues and future directions that should be taken by professional social workers as they engage clients from varied backgrounds in achieving better life chances. It features direct practice as well as indirect practice strategies and modalities. Illustrative of approaches to practice is the chapter on assessment by Congress and Kung, and Chernesky's chapter on managing agencies for multicultural services, that will enlighten the reader about using administrative practices to create a welcoming environment for a diverse clientele.

This text addresses a range of social problems of diverse cultural and ethnic groups across the life course. The problems of substance abuse, incest, and domestic violence are addressed respectively by Hanson and Sealy, Strand, and Brownell and Ko.

This book represents a good beginning for professional social workers and other human service providers who wish to practice in a more culturally sensitive manner. This will allow them not only to respect the diversity of clients, but help to celebrate the richness that cultural, racial, and ethnic diversity brings to our society, as so well portrayed by Suarez and Lewis in their chapter on spirituality and culturally diverse families. It also provides a platform from which practitioners can not only begin to understand the differences that are a part of the relationship between the social worker and the client from a different background, but it provides ways of approaching a mutually respectful helping relationship. Hopefully as a beginning it will give impetus to professional practitioners to explore each problem area and each group highlighted in the succeeding chapters in more depth than can be achieved in any single book chapter. As a text it assures that at completion of their studies, students will begin their journey in multicultural practice paces ahead of those of us who did not benefit from such readings in our own study.

Preface

Elaine P. Congress and
Manny J. González

*M*ulticultural Perspectives in Working With Families (2nd edition) includes "something old, and something new." The old has been significantly revised to include current knowledge and research to help practitioners work more effectively with culturally diverse families. For the most part the case examples and illustrations are new. One third of the chapters are completely new: chapter 5 focuses on group work with African American adolescents, chapter 8 looks at social work practice with immigrants and refugees, chapter 11 studies Arab American families, chapter 12 introduces an Afrocentric approach in working with African American families, chapter 13 looks at social work with the families of Hispanic deaf and hearing-impaired children, chapter 19 focuses on Hispanic adolescent girls who are suicidal, and chapter 20 examines spirituality among culturally diverse families.

As in the first edition of *Multicultural Perspectives in Working With Families*, culture is used as an umbrella term that includes ethnicity, race, national origin, and religion (Lum, 2004). Although religion and race are subsumed under culture, class is not. The practitioner must consider the socioeconomic class of the family in order to avoid inaccurate generalizations. Often families who have recently immigrated to the United States or have been the victims of generations of racism and discrimination are poor. Many of the families described in this book are poor, but certainly not all families from diverse cultural backgrounds are poor. Clinicians must be cognizant of the following factors when assessing families of diverse cultural backgrounds: degree of acculturation, poverty, history of oppression, language and the arts, racism and prejudice, sociopolitical factors, child-rearing practices, religious practices, family structure, and values and attitudes specific to life and help-seeking behaviors (Locke, 1992). Family therapists must also be aware of what financial resources are available to the family, as this may affect their functioning.

This second edition of *Multicultural Perspectives* addresses cutting edge issues in assessment and treatment of families from diverse cultural backgrounds. These chapters are not all-inclusive, but rather focus on some of the most important, emerging issues in multicultural practice with families. The second edition captures the three emerging elements in cross-cultural practice that must be incorporated into the effective psychosocial treatment of ethnic cultural groups: the client's worldview, language, and religion (González, 2002).

Section one looks at both micro and macro perspectives in work with families. Assessment of families begins simultaneously with the beginning of treatment. A good assessment should include an understanding of family boundaries, rules, roles, and structure. The Olson self-report assessment tool (Olson, Russell, & Sprenkle, 1989) looked at a family's reactions to situational stress in terms of flexibility and cohesion. The Beavers Model (Beavers & Hampson, 1993) and the McMaster's model (Epstein, Bishop, Ryan, Miller, & Keitner, 1993) have been used in assessing family functioning. The ecomap first developed by Hartman in 1978 looked at the relationship of the family to external resources (Hartman & Laird, 1983), while the genogram (McGoldrick, Gerson, & Schallenberg, 1999) helps the practitioner learn more about family relationships, both current and past.

A concern on which none of the existing family assessment instruments focused, understanding the cultural background of the family, led to the development of the culturagram (Congress, 1994) and its revision (Congress, 2002). The first chapter in the book looks at the culturagram as an assessment and treatment planning modality. Authors Congress and Kung use clinical examples from their extensive teaching and practice experience to illustrate different parts of the culturagram and how it can be used in assessment.

How do we make decisions about whether to see clients for group or family therapy? Chapter 2 focuses on similarities and differences between group and family work. Dr. Congress and Dr. Lynn discuss these issues by way of a timely case example of a Caribbean family that lost a family member in the 9-11 disaster.

Most people seek help because of family problems and are seen in family service or mental health agencies. No matter how skilled the clinician is, if agency context is not considered, then family engagement, assessment, and intervention may not be successful. Green (1999), for example, has noted multicultural skills and knowledge are not just for individual providers of psychosocial care. Human service organizations—the social systems in which most providers of care are employed—must also promote the delivery of culturally competent clinical services. In chapter 3, Dr. Roslyn Chernesky outlines how practitioners and administrators can "manage for diversity competence" within the workplace. She suggests that agency leaders must continually assess their cultural competence on all levels—board of directors, administrators, staff, policies, and programs.

The second section of the book focuses on work with families from diverse backgrounds across the life cycle. School is the primary place where children from very different cultures meet. In chapter 4, Dr. Carmen Ortiz Hendricks looks at the multicultural triangle of child, family, and school. She stresses the need to understand these differing cultures in order to work effectively with children and their families within the school system. She discusses the need for social workers to understand their own cultural backgrounds and to apply culturally competent standards in their work with diverse children and their families.

An important new addition to this edition of *Multicultural Perspectives in Working With Families* is the fifth chapter, that focuses on social work practice with African American adolescent girls. Based on her extensive practice and research in this area, Dr. Portia Adams discusses how African American adolescents experience this period differently than White American adolescents. One of the main issues may be that African American adolescent girls may not experience the loss of self-esteem that has recently been documented in studies of White adolescent girls. Group treatment illustrated through a case example is used to demonstrate effective family work with African American adolescents.

Older people are increasing in numbers globally as well as in the United States. More older people than ever before come from cultural backgrounds other than White. Drs. Irene Gutheil and Janna Heyman in chapter 6 point out important issues in social work with older people from diverse cultural backgrounds. Older people frequently encounter health problems, and great health disparities exist between White people and other cultural/ethnic/racial groups, possibly related to economic and educational differences. This chapter looks at important assessment issues, service utilization, and treatment approaches with older people and their families. The need for social workers to understand and work within the cultural background of older clients and their families is illustrated through a case example.

Grandparents raising grandchildren is an increasing phenomenon especially among communities of color. In chapter 7, Dr. Cox aptly describes the very successful use of an empowerment-training program to provide support and foster strength among grandparents from culturally diverse backgrounds.

Section three looks at selected culturally diverse populations. Recent immigrants to the United States, including legal immigrants, refugees, and undocumented immigrants are the focus of chapter 8, written by Dr. Manny González, Dr. Jessica Rosenberg, and Dr. Sam Rosenberg. The chapter also explores their mental health needs, access to services, and implications for social work practice. Although immigrants and refugees may be at increased risk for a host of psychological problems such as depression and traumatic stress, they are less likely to access treatment, because of financial inability, the lack of availability of culturally competent services, their own cultural prohibitions against participating in mental health care, and a general mistrust of government agencies. The importance of accurate assessment and culturally sensitive intervention is illustrated through case examples.

In recent years there has been a large influx of immigrants from the former Soviet Union. Although this immigrant group comes from a country with a very different language, political system, and culture, Russians have received little attention in professional literature. Dr. Robert Chazin and Tatyana Ushakova, MSW, focus on the diversity of immigrants who have come from different parts of Russia, in chapter 9. Issues of pre-immigration, transit, and resettlement in terms of changing expectations are addressed, as well as family conflicts related to immigration and lowered socioeconomic status. The chapter includes detailed case examples of assessment and intervention with Russian families who have immigrated to the United States.

In chapter 10, Dr. Gary Mellon addresses issues that gay and lesbian people face within their families. The psychosocial needs and risks of gay and lesbian people, clinical issues, as well as recommendations for working with this population are addressed.

An exciting new addition to this second edition is Dr. Nuha Abudabbeh's chapter focusing on Arab American families. This growing U.S. immigrant group is frequently misunderstood, especially post 9-11. Practitioners will learn more about differences among Arab countries, religious backgrounds of Arabs, their psychosocial needs, attitudes toward mental health, family relationships, and treatment issues.

An Afrocentric approach in working with African American families written by Dr. Valerie Borum is also new in this edition. Chapter 12 addresses the historical background of African Americans in the United States and the racism they encounter. The importance of adopting an Afrocentric framework, the use of language, spirituality, family relationships, and conceptions of mental health are all addressed in this chapter.

Children with disabilities present many challenges to families and chapter 13 looks at how Hispanic families cope with deaf and hearing-impaired children. Dr. Idalia Mapp looks at demographics of different Hispanic groups, especially in terms of disabilities. In this new chapter she explores the psychosocial risks and needs of this population, clinical assessment factors, and social work interventions. Case examples are used to increase understanding of Hispanic families with a disabled child.

Women often have multiple roles at home and at work. Dr. Susan Bair Egan in chapter 14 looks at women with three roles: students, employees, and parents. Chapter 14 examines how Hispanic and African American women cope with role strain and stress of multiple roles. Comments from these women demonstrate their skills and strengths in handling multiple roles.

Section four addresses challenging practice issues. HIV/AIDS continues to be a major health problem that has a serious debilitating impact on families from culturally diverse backgrounds. In chapter 15, Dr. Cynthia Poindexter looks at the negative effect HIV has on all families and then examines special stressors for African American and Hispanic families. Challenges caused by stigma are addressed, as well as continual crises, management of complicated treatment protocols, caregiver stress, handling multiple losses, and grief. The chapter concludes with a discussion of treatment interventions that have been helpful in working with HIV affected individuals and their families.

Evidence-based treatment is a major focus of current treatment interventions. In chapter 16, Dr. Meredith Hanson and Dr. Yvette Sealy look at the latest studies on effective marriage and family treatment with problem drinkers. Adopting an Evidence Based Practice (EBP) perspective, the authors present the case of a Puerto Rican family with an alcoholic member and how this approach can be used to engage and facilitate treatment.

An often neglected and victimized population are mothers in incest families. In chapter 17, Dr. Virginia Strand first looks at general issues for this group, who are frequently blamed for the sexual abuse of their children. She then focuses on special implications for culturally diverse families, including Hispanic, African American, and Asian families. Transference and countertransference reactions when the clinician is White and the client is not are also explored in this important chapter.

Domestic violence presents special problems in families from culturally diverse backgrounds. Chapter 18, by Dr. Patricia Brownell and Eun Jeong Ko, MSW, discusses the unique needs and challenges that many culturally diverse women who have been abused encounter in recognizing, seeking, and securing services. Special difficulties for non-documented women, as well as issues specific to Latina battered women, Asian battered women, and Southeast Asian battered women are discussed. Different types of treatment interventions as well as policies that affect the identification and treatment of battered women from culturally diverse backgrounds conclude this chapter.

Latinos are the fastest growing ethnic group in the United States and by mid-century 25% of adolescents will be of Hispanic background. A growing concern as outlined in Drs. Sandra Turner and Carol Kaplan's research is an increasing number of suicide attempts by adolescent Latinas. Chapter 19 describes strategies for prevention and intervention with Latina adolescents and their families. Treatment interventions are illustrated through a case example.

Section five concludes with a focus on spirituality and ethical issues. A new addition to *Multicultural Perspectives in Working With Families* is chapter 20, in which Dr. Zulema Suarez and Dr. Edith

Lewis describe the role of spirituality in culturally diverse families. Major religious trends in the United States, as well as the differences between religion and spirituality, are outlined. This chapter focuses on the relationship between cultural and religious views and the effects they have on psychological and interpersonal behavior. Implications for practice with culturally diverse families that recognize their religious beliefs and spirituality conclude the chapter.

The final chapter of the book looks at ethical issues and trends in family therapy. For many reasons family therapy often presents the most ethical challenges. Issues of countertransference, confidentiality, self-determination, and value differences in culturally diverse families are discussed. Managed care and evidence-based practice are seen as important current trends affecting the course of family therapy. The increasing diversity of clients, as well as their therapists, will affect the future course of family therapy.

REFERENCES

Beavers, W. R., & Hampson, R. B. (1993). Measuring family competence: The Beavers systems model. In F. Walsh (Ed.), *Normal family processes* (2nd ed., pp. 549–580). New York: Guilford Press.

Congress, E. (1994). The use of culturagrams to assess and empower culturally diverse families. *Families in Society, 75*(9), 531–540.

Congress, E. (2002). Using *culturagrams* with culturally diverse families. In A. Roberts & G. Greene (Eds.), *Social work desk reference* (pp. 57–61). New York: Oxford University Press.

Epstein, N. B., Bishop, D. S., Ryan, C., Miller, I., & Keitner, G. (1993). The McMaster model view of health family functioning. In F. Walsh (Ed.), *Normal family processes*. New York: Guilford Press.

González, M. J. (2002). Mental health intervention with Hispanic immigrants: Understanding the influence of client's worldview, language and religion. *Journal of Immigrant and Refugee Services, 1*(1), 81–92.

Green, J. (1999). *Cultural awareness in the human services: A multi-ethnic approach* (3rd ed.). Boston, MA: Allyn and Bacon.

Hartman, A., & Laird, J. (1983). *Family oriented treatment.* New York: Basic Books.

Locke, D. C. (1992). *Increasing multicultural understanding: A comprehensive model.* Newbury Park, CA: Sage.

Lum, D. (2004). *Social work practice and people of color.* Belmont, CA: Brooks-Cole.

McGoldrick, M., Gerson, R., & Schallenberg, S. (1999). *Genograms: Assessment and intervention.* New York: W. W. Norton.

Olson, D. H., Russell, C. S., & Sprenkle, D. H. (Eds.). (1989). *Circumplex model: Systemic assessment and treatment of families.* New York: Haworth Press.

Section One

Micro and Macro Approaches

CHAPTER 1

Using the Culturagram to Assess and Empower Culturally Diverse Families

Elaine P. Congress
Winnie W. Kung

The United States is becoming increasingly culturally diverse. It is estimated that by the year 2050 almost half (49.9%) of the population will be non-Caucasian (U.S. Census Bureau, 2000). In large metropolitan areas such as New York City the majority of the population now already come from various countries in Asia, South and Central America, and the Caribbean, and as much as 36% of its residents are foreign born (U.S. Census Bureau, 2000.) The presence of families from 125 nations in the area covered by one zip code attests to the increasing diversity of our country (National Geographic, 1998).

From the beginning of the social work profession social workers have stressed the importance of respect for clients from diverse backgrounds (Addams, 1911). In the most recent Code of Ethics social workers are advised to understand cultural differences among clients and to demonstrate competence in working with people from different cultures (National Association of Social Workers [NASW], 1999). The culturagram, a family assessment instrument discussed in this chapter, grew out of the recognition that families are becoming increasingly culturally diverse and that social workers must be able to understand cultural differences among families.

When attempting to understand diverse families, it is important to assess the family within a cultural context. Considering a family only in terms of a generic cultural identity, however, may lead to overgeneralization and stereotyping (Congress, 1994). A Puerto Rican family that has lived in the United States for 40 years is very different from a Mexican family that emigrated last month, although both families are Hispanic. Furthermore, it cannot be assumed that even within a particular cultural group all families are similar.

THE CULTURAGRAM

While the ecomap (Hartman & Laird, 1983) and genogram (McGoldrick, Gerson, & Schallenberg, 1999) are useful tools in assessing the family, they do not address the important role of culture in understanding the family. The culturagram was first developed (Congress, 1994, 1997) and revised (Congress, 2002) to help in understanding the role of culture in families. This tool has been applied to work with people of color (Lum, 2004), battered women (Brownell & Congress, 1998), children (Webb, 1996), older people (Brownell, 1997), and immigrant families (Congress, 2004).

The culturagram, a family assessment tool, represents an attempt to individualize culturally diverse families (Congress, 1994, 2002). Completing a culturagram on a family can help a clinician develop a better understanding of the sociocultural context of the family, which can shed light on appropriate interventions with the family. Revised in 2002, the culturagram (see Figure 1.1) examines the following 10 areas:

- Reasons for relocation
- Legal status
- Time in community
- Language spoken at home and in the community
- Health beliefs
- Crisis events

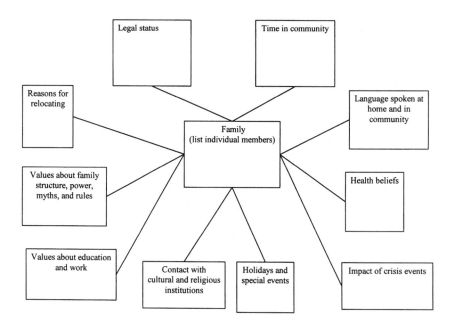

FIGURE 1.1 Culturagram.

- Holidays and special events
- Contact with cultural and religious institutions
- Values about education and work
- Values about family structure—power, hierarchy, rules, subsystems, and boundaries

Reasons for Relocation

Reasons for relocating to the United States vary among families. Many families come because of economic opportunities in the U.S., whereas others relocate because of political and religious discrimination in their countries of origin. For some it is possible to return home again. They often travel back and forth for holidays and special occasions and ultimately may move back to their country of origin. Being able to maintain continuous close social ties with families of origin and other acquaintances in the native land reduces the sense of uprootedness of the family. Such close contacts also facilitate the family, especially the younger generation, to maintain their cultural heritage and identity. The cultural gap between the generations in these immigrant families may be diminished as a result. For those who know they can never go home again, the sense of isolation and the need for greater social network in this new land becomes more poignant. The social worker can encourage them to actively reach out to their ethnic communities.

In contrast to earlier immigration patterns, current immigrants come as families or parts of families (Lum, 2004). Some exceptions include undocumented immigrants from Fuzhou in Southern China (Kwong, 1997), and second generation South Asians from India and Pakistan, who frequently come as single persons. Many want to marry within their ethnic group and "mail-ordered brides" are a growing phenomenon (Loiselle-Leonard, 2001). Because immigrant brides have to adjust to new roles within their families and adapt to a different culture and geographic location, their stresses are enormous. In cases where the marriage does not work out, these women may feel trapped in this foreign land with no social supports. Some may even have to endure domestic violence since the prospect of making it outside of home in America is so dim, and the shame of going back to their home countries so unbearable (Loiselle-Leonard, 2001). Some feel trapped because their immigrant procedures have not been completed, and they fear deportation if they leave their husbands. Fortunately, recent changes in immigration laws allow some battered women without legal status to stay on (Violence Against Women's Act, 1998). This has brought relief and hope to many oppressed immigrant women.

Other families move within the United States, often from a rural to a more urban area, often due to dwindling economic opportunities. This requires establishment of new social network and adjustment in the new location as well.

Legal Status

The legal status of a family may have an effect on both individuals and the family as a whole. If a family is undocumented and fears deportation, members may become secretive and socially isolated. Latency-age children and adolescents will be discouraged from developing peer relationships because of the fears of others learning about their status. When applying family systems theory, we see that as the external boundaries of these families become more rigid; a corresponding trend toward more diffuse internal boundaries may lead to greater enmeshment within the family. The family may resist seeking necessary social and health services lest they be deported. There is even more anxiety about this post 9-11.

Some undocumented immigrants come to this country on their own, leaving behind their families and support system. An example is the recent influx of immigrants from Fuzhou, Southern China (Kwong, 1997). These single immigrants have experienced enormous hardship, handicapped by language deficiency and the enormous economic burden of having to repay the smuggling debts to come to this country (Kwong, 2002). Moreover, the lack of medical benefits makes life even harder when they have health or mental health problems (Kwong, 2002). A social worker working with this population in the Chinatown in New York City revealed that perhaps due to social isolation and enormous stress, many individuals suffering from schizophrenia, after some brief psychiatric treatment, relapse as often as four times in a year.

Length of Time in the Community

The length of time living in the community may differ for individual family members. Usually family members who have arrived earlier are more assimilated than other members. A current phenomenon involves mothers from Guatamela or South America first immigrating to the United States and then sending for their children. These circumstances can certainly impact on individual and family development. Not only does the disruption of the primary caregiver at a critical period affect the child's development, the subsequent reunion at an older age in this country could also cause some adjustment problem for the family. Sciarra (1999) suggested that the issues these families face include resentment of the child over the parent's earlier "abandonment," the conflict between loyalty towards the reunited parents and the interim caregiver from whom the child is now forced to separate, inadequate parental authority and leadership, and the different level of acculturation between the parent and the child. Sciarra found that techniques such as reframing the intergenerational conflicts as intercultural issues and stating the treatment goal as working toward biculturalism helpful.

The problems faced by other immigrant families are the exact opposite of these reunited families. These have been called the "astronaut families" (Irving, Benjamin, & Tsang, 1999). Because of the political instability in Taiwan or Hong Kong in the past decade, many Chinese families migrated to the United States and Canada. However, such moves often mean an economic loss to these families since the breadwinner, usually the father, experiences some economic downturn in his career as his professional qualifications and experiences overseas are often not recognized here. Many families opt to have the children and the mother migrate first, while the father "shuttles" back and forth to join the family periodically. Not only does it strain the marital relationship, sometimes resulting in affairs and marital breakdown, it also jeopardizes the father-children relationship. These are high prices to pay for migration.

Language

Language is the medium through which families communicate. Often families may use their own native language at home, but begin to use English in contacts with the outside community. Sometimes children may prefer English as they see knowledge of this language as most helpful for survival in their newly adopted country. This may lead to conflict within the family. A most literal communication problem may develop when parents speak no English and children speak only minimally their native tongue. Another key factor affecting family communication is that members relocate at different ages. Because of attending American schools and developing peer relationships, children often pick up the new language and culture more quickly than their parents. This may lead to shifts in the power structure of the family as the parents' limited English competence can erode their authority (Hong, 1989). In some situations, the children may assume the role of interpreter and cultural broker for the family, and sometimes even the leadership role since they have better knowledge about community resources. This may be especially difficult for cultures in which the generational hierarchy within the family is important (Tamura & Lau, 1992).

One of the challenges in work with a bilingual family is that a bilingual worker has to decide which language to adopt and when. Caution should be taken to ensure that the worker does not appear to be "siding" with either the English or native speaker. For families in which the children can understand but not speak the native language, it is important for the bilingual worker to speak mostly in the native tongue even when talking to the children to indicate that the language is respectable and to show respect to the parents (Hong, 1989). When an interpreter is needed, care must be taken if the worker decides to use a family member as interpreter to ensure that he or she does not avoid or distort sensitive messages. For example, social workers must ensure that the interpreting family member does not avoid explorations of suicidal ideations when he or she does not feel comfortable asking the questions and believes that it would not happen (Hong, 1989). Discussion with an external interpreter before meeting with the family is also helpful to ensure they understand the major thrust of the session (Caple, Salcido, & Cecco, 1995; Lee, 1982).

Health Beliefs

Families from different cultures have varying beliefs about health, disease, and treatment (Congress & Lyons, 1992). Many medical anthropologists have contended that individuals' cultural beliefs influence the way they perceive the etiology of an illness, interpret the symptoms, and act on the symptoms (Cheng, 2001; Kleinman, 1980; Tseng, 2001). Individuals' and families' health beliefs, which include their perception of their susceptibility, the seriousness of the consequence of an illness, and the benefit of medical intervention affects their readiness to use preventive health service and to seek actual help when a family member faces an ailment (Hsu & Gallinagh, 2001; Rosenstock, 1990). Families' reaction to an illness can affect the course, outcome, and level of incapacitation of an illness and the families' adjustment to it (Rolland, 1994). For example, a delay in seeking treatment for HIV/AIDS because of stigma could lead to more devastating and lasting impact on the family through transmission of the illness to other family members.

Among many Asians, mental illness is seen as the result of malingering bad thoughts, a lack of will power, and personality weakness (Narikiyo & Kameoka, 1992; Suan & Tyler, 1990; Sue & Morishima, 1982). Hence, self-control and solving one's own problems are culturally valued, and seeking help from mental health professionals is often delayed (Boey, 1999; Loo, Tong, & True, 1989; Zhang, Snowden, & Sue, 1998). Given Asian Americans' tendency to somatize emotional distress, emphasize the physical expression of one's distressed state (Kleinman, 1980; Sue & Morishima, 1982; Tseng, 2001; Zhang et al., 1998), or subscribe to the holistic mind-body-spirit conceptualization, they are likely to turn to physicians, herbalists, acupuncturists, fortune tellers, or ministers for help instead of mental health professionals (Kung, 2001; Sue, Nakamura, Chung, & Yee-Bradbury, 1994; Uba, 1994). Some Hispanics may rely on botanicas or spiritualists as the first and sometimes the only approach to dealing with health or mental health problems (Congress & Lyons, 1992). The intense stigma attached to mental illness in some cultures also poses barriers to seeking mental health service. Some of these impediments to help-seeking among Asians include the attribution of psychiatric problems to hereditary causes, interpreted as "genetic taints" and "bad seeds" (Pearson, 1993; Sue & Morishima, 1982). Because of the sociocentric nature of the Asian culture (Triandis, 1989), families are concerned about the loss of face and avoid reaching out for help beyond the immediate family, thus overburdening the family (Kung, 2001; Sue & Sue, 1999; Sue & Morishima, 1982). Hispanics may seek to avoid the label of "loco" because of the stigma connected with this designation (Congress & Lyons, 1992).

In face of physical illness, many immigrants prefer to use health care methods other than traditional Western/European medical care involving diagnosis, pharmacology, X rays, and surgery (Congress & Lyons, 1992). The social worker who wishes to understand families must study their unique health care beliefs.

Crisis Events

Families can encounter developmental crises as well as "bolts from the blue" crises (Congress, 1996). Developmental crises may occur when a family moves from one life stage to another. Stages in the life cycle for culturally diverse families may be quite different from those for traditional Caucasian middle-class families. For example, for many culturally diverse families the "launching children" stage may not occur at all, as single and even married children may continue to live in close proximity to the parents (Uba, 1994). If separation is forced, this developmental crisis might be especially traumatic.

Families also deal with "bolts from the blue" crises in different ways. During the 9-11 attack on the World Trade Center people from more than 80 countries died (Lum, 2004). There has also been concern that many victims, especially those who were undocumented, were never acknowledged and their families often were not able to secure the assistance that others received. A family's reaction to crisis events is often related to its cultural values. Chapter 2 looks at a Jamaican family and how they were able to cope with the sudden traumatic loss of their husband and father. The death or injury of the male head of household may be especially traumatic for an immigrant family that highly values the role of the father as a provider. While rape is certainly a major crisis for any family, the rape of a teenage girl may be especially traumatic for a family that highly values virginity before marriage.

Because of cultural differences, families may have varied perceptions of child-rearing practices and child abuse. Some families may be accused of child abuse and become involved with child protective agencies and the legal system. This is perceived as a crisis to many families and especially so for those that perceive court-ordered counseling upon disciplining a child as an outrageous punishment—a crisis that evokes tremendous anger and shame (Waldman, 1999). Different beliefs about behavioral problems may result in different approaches to remedy these problems. However, some approaches may result in parents being accused of abuse and neglect. For example, methods such as coining or cupping administered by parents to help reduce the child's pain may leave scars that may be misinterpreted as child abuse (Uba, 1994). Some parents may refuse to have their children take medication because of possible side effects or because of their health beliefs, and as a result, they are accused of child neglect (Fadiman, 1997). Such accusations, when experienced as uncalled for and deeply shameful, can cause a major crisis to families.

Holidays and Special Events

Each family has particular holidays and special events. Some events mark transitions from one developmental stage to another, for example, a christening, a bar mitzvah, a wedding, or a funeral. It is important for the social worker to learn the cultural significance of these events, as they are indicative of what families see as major transition points in their lives. Some ethnic families have their own high holidays, such as Lunar New Year, which is often considered as important to many Asian families than Thanksgiving to many native-born Americans, if not more so. It is worth encouraging immigrant families to celebrate their own important holidays to help them uphold their tradition and to strengthen their cultural identity.

Contact With Cultural and Religious Institutions

Contact with cultural institutions often provides support to an immigrant family. Family members may use cultural institutions differently. For example, a father may belong to a social club, the mother may attend a church where her native language is spoken, while the adolescent children may refuse to participate in either because they wish to become more Americanized. Religion may provide much support to culturally diverse families and the clinician will want to explore their contact with formal religious institutions. Some clansmen's associations are common among Asian Americans, often providing important support to immigrant families. For example, they provide significant financial support for new Chinese immigrants from Fuzhou in New York City (Kwong, 1997). The support among business owners is also found to be an important factor accounting for the successes among many Korean American businesses (Park, 1997). The social worker should be aware of these resources to be able to help families tap into them. Most Asian clansmen's groups, however, do not provide assistance or support on psychosocial issues due to the lack of knowledge of the immigrant groups.

Values About Education and Work

All families have differing values about work and education, and culture is an important influence on such values. Social workers must explore what these values are in order to understand the family. Economic and social differences between the country of origin and America can affect immigrant families. For example, employment in a low-status position may be very denigrating to the male breadwinner. It may be especially traumatic for the immigrant family when the father cannot find work or only work of a menial nature. This is often a result of the individuals' professional qualifications and experiences in their native land not being recognized in this country. Such a downward move in the socioeconomic hierarchy often induces additional stress and challenges for many immigrant families.

Sometimes a conflict in values arises due to competing desires of family members. This occurred when an adolescent son was accepted with a full scholarship to a prestigious university miles from home. While the family had always believed in the importance of education, the parents believed that the family needed to stay together and that they did not want to have their only child leave home, even to pursue education.

Another example occurs when American latency-age children often attend large schools far from their communities and begin to develop peer relationships apart from their families. For culturally diverse families that come from backgrounds in which education has been minimal and localized, and where young children were forced to work and care for younger siblings, the American school system with its focus on individual academic achievement and peer relationships may seem strange. Furthermore, immigrant children who bring a history of individual or family oppression may feel very isolated and lonely in their new academic environments.

Some cultures value education differentially for different genders. For example, many Hispanic girls drop out of school because academic attainment for girls is not highly valued compared with boys (Zambrana & Zoppi, 2002). More importantly, these girls have major responsibilities in taking care of the household and younger siblings. They often find little or no time left to attend to their academic demands after school and thus have a hard time keeping up with academic work, and eventually drop out of school.

Values About Family Structure—Power, Hierarchy, Rules, Subsystems, and Boundaries

Each family has its unique structure, its beliefs about power relationships, rules, boundaries within and outside the family, and significance of certain familial relationships. Some of these may be related to the cultural background of the family. The clinician needs to explore these family characteristics individually, but also to understand them in the context of the family's cultural background.

Culturally diverse families may have differing beliefs about male-female relationships, especially within marriage. Families that promote a male-dominant hierarchical family structure may encounter conflict in American society with its more egalitarian gender relationships. This may result in an increase in domestic violence among culturally diverse families. Traditionally gendered roles within the family also exert significant impact on the family, especially when circumstances change after migration. For example, in some cultures women are expected to take care of internal familial affairs, including household chores and child care, while men are expected to work outside and be income earners. However, changes in socioeconomic status of the family after migration may necessitate both spouses to work outside of home. If the role of domestic caretaker continues to be rigidly assigned only to women, they may become overburdened. In situations in which the woman is able to find a job while the man is unemployed, if the family lacks flexibility in their role adaptation, conflict, blame, and burden within the family may become so enormous that it may threaten the survival of the family unit.

Not only is gender hierarchy much affected by cultural norms, so is generational hierarchy. More traditional cultures tend to ascribe much higher authority and respect to the older generation, and in some the parental authority can at times be rather absolute (Tamura & Lau, 1992). Clinicians should recognize such inherent cultural differences, and sometimes mediate between the generations. They have to navigate cautiously: they should show respect to the family's culture on the one hand, but tactfully facilitate communication across the generation on the other hand, in order to ease tension and conflict. Through careful mediation, it is hoped that views from both sides can be heard and considered in final decision making. However, sometimes the worker may have to accept that some cultures do dictate that senior members have the ultimate power in decision making.

Finally, families from different cultures may place varying emphasis on family subsystems. In Western culture, the spousal subsystem is considered the bedrock of the family (Minuchin, 1974). In some cultures, though, the primary unit is the parental subsystem, emphasizing the co-parenting role between the spouses. Moreover, the parental subsystem could be much more inclusive; for example, not only are grandparents, aunts, and uncles important partners in the parental subsystem, but godparents' role could also very significant in Hispanic families (Garcia-Preto, 1996). Clinicians should be conscious of cultural values and practices so as not to leave out important system players who could be valuable resources to the family. In some cultures, like that of traditional Chinese, the parent-child subsystem (both the father-son and mother-son dyads) and even the relationship among brothers are considered more important than spousal relationships (Tamura & Lau, 1992).

Whether or not the boundary within a family or a subsystem is considered appropriate or overly diffuse is also very cultural (Olson & Gorall, 2003). For example, in some Asian cultures, since the future care of the aging mother is dependent on the son, and the mother-son bond is usually close, a mother is often seen as being intrusive in the son's marital relationship and sometimes domineering toward the daughter-in-law (Berg & Jaya, 1993). In some Asian families, for the child to sleep with the parents till the age of 8 or 10 is considered a very normal practice, and it does not necessarily indicate marital dysfunction or enmeshment between parent and child (Berg & Jaya, 1993). Social workers have to avoid judgmental attitudes toward families that have different cultural values from their own.

The following vignette (Congress, 2002) illustrates how the culturagram can be used to better understand a family with its unique cultural background and to provide treatment intervention:

Mrs. Maria Sanchez, 32 years old, contacted a family service agency in her community because she was having increasing conflicts with her 12-year-old son, José, who had begun to cut school and stay out late at night. She also reported that she had a 9-year-old daughter, Maritza, who was "an angel." Maritza was very quiet, never wanted to socialize with other children, and instead preferred to stay at home with her mother helping her with household chores. Maria indicated the source of much conflict was that José believed he did not have to respect Manuel, as the latter was not his real father. José complained that his mother and stepfather were "dumb" because they did not speak English. The past holidays had been especially difficult as José had disappeared for New Year's weekend. At 20, Maria had moved to the United States from Puerto Rico with her first husband José Sr. The two were very poor in Puerto Rico and had heard there were better job opportunities here. When José Jr. was an infant, José Sr. had made a visit back to Puerto Rico and never returned. Shortly afterward, Maria met Manuel, who had come to New York from Guatemala. After she became pregnant with Maritza, they began to live together. Manuel indicated that he was very fearful of returning to Guatemala, as several people in his village had been killed in political conflicts. Because Manuel was undocumented, he had been able to find only occasional day work. He was embarrassed that Maria had been forced to apply for food stamps. Maria received minimum wages as a home care worker. She was very close to her mother, Gladys, who had come to live with the family 9 years ago. Gladys had urged Maria to seek help from a spiritualist to help her with her family problems before she went to the neighborhood agency to ask for help. Manuel has no relatives in New York, but he has several friends at the social club in his neighborhood.

Not only does the culturagram help the social worker assess families from different cultural backgrounds, but also to begin to move toward appropriate interventions. After completing the culturagram (see Figure 1.2), the social worker was better able to understand the Sanchez family, assess their needs, and begin to plan for treatment. She noted that Manuel's undocumented status was a source of continual stress in this family. She referred Manuel to a free legal service that provided help for undocumented people in securing legal status. She also explored their religious affiliation and found that although the family subscribed to the Catholic faith, they had not attended church since they came to this country, because they could not find a church with Spanish-speaking priests. The worker helped the family find a Catholic church in the neighborhood which has a weekly mass in Spanish and a large proportion of Hispanic parishioners. The church later became a support network for the family as Maria and Maritza became involved with women's and children's groups at the church.

The social worker recognized some kind of communication problem across the generations. While José and Maritza are bilingual, they often speak English at home, which for the most part Maria and Manuel do not understand. The adults communicated with each other and the children in Spanish. Maria and Manuel sometimes wanted to practice their English with the children, but the latter, especially José, were rather impatient with their parents' broken English. In any case, communication was limited

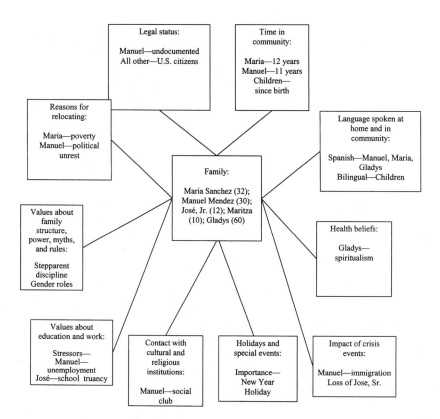

FIGURE 1.2   Culturagram applied to case example.

Note: Previous version of this case vignette appeared in Congress, E. (2002). Using the culturagram with culturally diverse families. In A. Roberts & G. Greene (Eds.), *Social work desk reference* (pp. 57–61). New York: Oxford University Press.

to basic information exchange and rule setting. The worker encouraged the couple to study English in a free adult education program in their neighborhood. The bilingual worker, however, was careful to speak in Spanish when seeing the couple and especially during family sessions so as to subtly convey her respect for the language to the children. When she had individual sessions with the children she used English since they were better able to express themselves.

Due to language barriers, José occasionally had to act as interpreter on behalf of the family, for instance when the family had to deal with the Social Security Department or with his grandmother's medical doctors during a serious illness that involved hospitalization. José was sometimes resentful toward these familial obligations as it took away time from being with his peers. He also felt that all his mother and stepfather wanted was to ask him to help out in the family and to impose rules on him, without ever caring about his needs. The worker reframed his responsibility for the family as having an honorable task as cultural broker, but recognized his need for appropriate autonomy. While the worker worked toward the therapeutic goal of empowering the parents, especially the mother, to assert control over José, she also acted as a mediator to help the parents understand José's need to gain more age appropriate independence.

Maritza's social withdrawal was also explored. It was found that Maritza wanted to stay home to do the household chores as this was expected of her as a girl. She noted that her family did not think it appropriate that men in the family (her father Manuel and her brother José) help out with household chores, She wished to spare her mother from additional chores after a hard day's work outside, and lighten her grandmother's load because of her frail health. As a result, she sacrificed her playtime with peers and stayed home to take care of the house. The worker tactfully invited Manuel to be more involved in domestic duties on days that he did not have to work and reframed it as his way of showing his love for the family through such sacrifice. Maritza was also encouraged to attend activities at the church and after-school programs so as to socialize more with her peers.

The proceeding discussion helps to clarify how the culturagram can be used not only to assess the family, but also to help plan appropriate interventions. The culturagram has been seen as an essential tool in helping social workers work more effectively with families from many different cultures. Initial evaluation of the culturagram has been positive, and there are further plans to assess its effectiveness in promoting culturally competent practice.

REFERENCES

Addams, J. (1911). *Twenty years at Hull-House*. New York: The Macmillan Company.

Berg, I. K., & Jaya, A. (1993). Different and same: Family therapy with Asian-American families. *Journal of Marital and Family Therapy, 19,* 31–38.

Boey, K. W. (1999). Help-seeking preference of college students in urban China after the implementation of the "open-door" policy. *International Journal of Social Psychiatry, 45*(2), 104–116.

Brownell, P. (1997). The application of the culturagram in cross-cultural practice with elder abuse victims. *Journal of Elder Abuse and Neglect, 9*(2), 19–33.

Brownell, P., & Congress, E. (1998). Application of the culturagram to assess and empower culturally and ethnically diverse battered women. In A. Roberts (Ed.), *Battered women and their families: Intervention and treatment strategies* (pp. 387–404). New York: Springer Publishing.

Caple, F. S., Salcido, R. M., & di Cecco, J. (1995). Engaging effectively with culturally diverse families and children. *Social Work in Education, 17*(3), 159–170.

Cheng, A. T. A. (2001). Case definition and culture: Are people all the same? *British Journal of Psychiatry, 179*, 1–3.

Congress, E. (1994). The use of culturagrams to assess and empower culturally diverse families. *Families in Society, 75*(9), 531–540.

Congress, E. (1996). Family crisis—Life cycle and bolts from the blue: Assessment and treatment. In A. Roberts (Ed.), *Crisis management in brief treatment* (pp. 142–159). Chicago: Nelson-Hall.

Congress, E. (1997). Using the *culturagram* to assess and empower cultural diverse families. In E. Congress, *Multicultural perspectives in working with families* (pp. 3–16). New York: Springer Publishing Company.

Congress, E. (2002). Using culturagrams with culturally diverse families. In A. Roberts & G. Greene (Eds.), *Social work desk reference* (pp. 57–61). New York: Oxford University Press.

Congress, E. (2004). Crisis intervention and diversity: Emphasis on a Mexican immigrant family's acculturation conflicts. In R. Dorfman, P. Meyer, & M. Morgan (Eds.), *Paradigms of clinical social work* (vol. 3, Emphasis on diversity, pp. 125–144). New York: Brunner-Routledge.

Congress, E., & Lyons, B. (1992). Cultural differences in health beliefs: Implications for social work practice in health care settings. *Journal of Social Work Practice in Health Care, 17*(3), 81–96.

Fadiman, A. (1997). *The spirit catches you and you fall down: A Hmong child, her American doctors, and the collision of two cultures.* New York: Farrar, Straus, and Giroux.

Garcia-Preton, N. (1996). Latino families: An overview. In M. McGoldrick & J. Giordano, *Ethnicity and family therapy* (2nd ed., pp. 141–154). New York: Guilford Press.

Hartman, A., & Laird, J. (1983). *Family-oriented social work practice.* New York: Free Press.

Hong, G. K. (1989). Application of cultural and environmental issues in family therapy with immigrant Chinese Americans. *Journal of Strategic and Systemic Therapies, 8*(bonus), 14–21.

Hsu, H. Y., & Gallinagh, R. (2001). The relationships between health beliefs and utilization of free health examinations in older people living in a community setting in Taiwan. *Journal of Advanced Nursing, 35*(6), 864–873.

Irving, H. H., Benjamin, M., & Tsang, A. K. T. (1999). Hong Kong satellite children in Canada: An exploratory study of their experience. *Hong Kong Journal of Social Work*, *33*(1–2), 1–21.

Kleinman, A. M. (1980). *Patients and healers in the context of culture*. Berkeley: University of California Press.

Kung, W. W. (2001). Consideration of cultural factors in working with Chinese American families with a mentally ill patient. *Families in Society: The Journal of Contemporary Human Services*, *82*(1), 97–107.

Kwong, P. (1997). Manufacturing ethnicity. *Critique of Anthropology*, *17*(4), 365–387.

Kwong, P. (2002). Forbidden workers and the U.S. labor movement: Fuzhounese in New York City. *Critical Asian Studies*, *34*(1), 69–88.

Lee, E. (1982). A social systems approach to assessment and treatment for Chinese American families. In M. McGoldrick, J. K. Pearce, & J. Giordano (Eds.), *Ethnicity and family therapy* (pp. 527–551). New York: Guilford Press.

Loiselle-Leonard, M. (2001). Arranged marriage, dowry and migration: A risky combination for Hindu women. *Canadian Social Work Review*, *18*(2), 305–319.

Loo, C., Tong, B., & True, R. (1989). A bitter bean: Mental health status and attitudes in Chinatown. *Journal of Community Psychology*, *17*, 283–296.

Lum, D. (2004). *Social work practice and people of color* (5th ed.). Belmont, CA: Brooks-Cole-Thomson.

McGoldrick, M., Gerson, J., & Schallenberg, J. (1999). *Genograms: Assessment and intervention*. New York: W. W. Norton.

Minuchin, S. (1974). *Families and family therapy*. Cambridge: Harvard University Press.

Narikiyo, T., & Kameoka, V. (1992). Attributions of mental illness and judgements about help seeking among Japanese-American and White American students. *Journal of Counseling Psychology*, *39*(3), 363–369.

National Association of Social Workers. (1999). *Code of ethics*. Washington, DC: NASW Press.

National Geographic. (September, 1998). *All the world comes to Queens*.

Olson, D. H., & Gorall, D. M. (2003). Circumplex model of marital and family systems. In F. Walsh (Ed.), *Normal family processes: Growing diversity and complexity* (3rd ed., pp. 514–548). New York: Guilford Press.

Park, K. (1997). *The Korean American dream: Immigrants and small business in New York City*. Ithaca, NY: Cornell University Press.

Pearson, V. (1993). Families in China: An undervalued resource for mental health. *Journal of Family Therapy*, *15*, 163–185.

Rolland, J. S. (1994). *Families, illness, and disability: An integrative treatment model*. New York: Basic Books.

Rosenstock, I. M. (1990). The health belief model: Explaining health behavior through expectancies. In K. Glanz & F. M. Lewis (Eds.), *Health behavior and health education: Theory, research, and practice* (pp. 39–62). San Francisco, CA: Jossey-Bass.

Sciarra, D. T. (1999). Intrafamilial separations in the immigrant family: Implications for cross-cultural counseling. *Journal of Multicultural Counseling and Development*, *27*, 31–41.

Suan, L. V., & Tyler, J. D. (1990). Mental health values and preference for mental health resources of Japanese-American and Caucasian-American students. *Professional Psychology: Research & Practice, 21*(4), 291–296.

Sue, D. W., & Sue, D. (1999). *Counseling the culturally different: Theory and practice.* New York: Wiley.

Sue, S., & Morishima, J. K. (1982). *The mental health of Asian Americans.* San Francisco, CA: Jossey-Bass Publishers.

Sue, S., Nakamura, C. Y., Chung, R. C.-Y., & Yee-Bradbury, C. (1994). Mental health research on Asian Americans. *Journal of Community Psychology, 22,* 61–67.

Tamura, T., & Lau, A. (1992). Connectedness versus separateness: Applicability of family therapy to Japanese families. *Family Process, 31*(4), 319–340.

Triandis, H. C. (1989). The self and social behavior in differing cultural contexts. *Psychological Review, 96,* 508–520.

Tseng, W.-S. (2001). *Handbook of cultural psychiatry.* San Diego, CA: Academic Press.

Uba, L. (1994). *Asian Americans: Personality patterns, identity, and mental health.* New York: Guilford Press.

U.S. Census. (2000). Retrieved from http://www.census.gov/main/www/cen 2000.html

Violence Against Women Act. (1998). Retrieved from http://4www.women.gov/ own/violence.htm

Waldman, F. (1999). Violence or discipline? Working with multicultural court-ordered clients. *Journal of Marital and Family Therapy, 25,* 503–516.

Webb, N. (1996). *Social work practice with children.* New York: Guilford Press.

Zambrana, R. E., & Zoppi, I. M. (2002). Latina students: Translating cultural wealth into social capital to improve academic success. *Journal of Ethnic and Cultural Diversity in Social Work, 11*(1–2), 33–53.

Zhang, A. Y., Snowden, L. R., & Sue, S. (1998). Differences between Asian and White Americans' help seeking and utilization patterns in the Los Angeles area. *Journal of Community Psychology, 26*(4), 317–326.

CHAPTER 2

Family and Group Approaches With Culturally Diverse Families: A Dialogue to Increase Collaboration

Elaine P. Congress
Maxine Lynn

A lthough clinicians usually study family and group work separately, it is helpful to examine how both these methods can be combined in work with culturally diverse families. This chapter focuses on comparing and contrasting assessment and intervention skills in family and group work. Each method can be used effectively with diverse families, especially if the clinician takes into account how the family's culture affects the use of family and group work.

Although there are numerous models for group work, as well as family therapy, there are few articles that integrate group work and family therapy. A review of recent literature indicated that group work has been used with family members of AIDS patients (with divorcing families) (King, 1998), and with the families of children with mood disorders (Fristad, Goldberg, & Gavazzi, 2003). Getz (2002) demonstrates how family therapy techniques can be integrated into group work. There has also been multiple family group work with families of schizophrenia (Mullen, Murray, & Happell, 2002). Earlier literature took a more theoretical look at how these two models differed and were similar (Garvin, 1986; Hines, 1988; Ritter, West, & Trotzer, 1987).

In the first edition of this book, we raised the question: How close and how disparate are family therapy and group work? A focus on the similarities emphasizes the generic nature of practice, increases understanding of differences, and helps family and group workers learn new skills to enhance their work with clients. For both family and group work clinicians must be tuned in to their own biases and prejudices and be sensitive to cultural differences between themselves and clients. In addition, clinicians must be aware of the immediate social system and environment, as well as the larger community in which the family belongs (Norton, 1978). This chapter will include a case example to illustrate how a group worker and a family therapist approach assessment and treatment for a culturally diverse family.

Important topics in the beginning stages of family and group work are composition, engagement, and assessment. Discussion about contracting, building norms, and roles lead into the middle phases of treatment, where different interventions of both family and group work are compared. Contrasting termination issues for families and groups in the final stage of treatment are discussed. Conclusion and recommendations based on this dialogue between a group worker and family therapist conclude this chapter.

CASE EXAMPLE

This family was referred for mental health services 8 months after the World Trade Center (WTC) disaster during which the husband Monty, a computer technician, was killed. The family is of West Indian background but had adopted the Hebraic Pentecostal faith and was quite attached to their church. The family includes Marliene, 35 years old, and 5 children, Helene, age 12, Samuel, age 10, Josie and Jon, 6-year-old twins, and Monty, 6 weeks old, born in February.

Marliene had previously worked as a school aide in the local public school, but she had been immobilized and unable to cope since the birth of her baby. She was diagnosed with an intense grief reaction, as well as depression. Her daughter Helene had failing grades in school, was frequently truant, and demonstrated withdrawn behavior in school. At home Helene had assumed a caretaking role. Samuel was diagnosed as having an ADHD disorder, had frequent fights with other children, and was in a special education class. The 6-year-old twins did not show any symptoms of distress, although the teachers have noticed the children attended school in mismatched clothes. After Marliene missed a "well baby" checkup a referral was made to a major agency that worked with families affected by the WTC disaster.

The family lives in public housing and there was income from pension, insurance, and other WTC supports. Marliene has a father and sister who lived near her and were very supportive. The congregation and the pastor were another support system. Her in-laws had not been supportive except for one of her husband's sisters.

Marliene came to the agency with a church sister and the baby after two cancelled appointments. She seemed very depressed but refused a psychiatric consult for medication. She talked about how her husband had managed the household, paid bills, helped the children with schoolwork, and took care of conflicts. She had to take care of the children and cook. She was attending community college and sang in the choir. She worked part-time in the school to keep an eye on her young twins. She related that her last pregnancy was difficult; she had gained a great deal of weight, had arthritic pain in her joints, and was tired all the time. She said that the children should be helping her but they are fighting all the time.

Marliene seemed interested in joining a group for WTC widows. Other services put in place included a homemaker, a group for Helene, Big Brothers for the boys, and family counseling in the home. Samuel was already in a group.

A home visit described the home as disorderly. There were several days worth of unwashed dishes, and roaches were all over the apartment. The beds were unmade. Clothes and items were strewn all over. There had also been many new things contributed by WTC relief, for instance a new computer in a box as well as other electronics and baby clothes.

Marliene, dressed in a housedress, yelled at Helene, who appeared to be taking care of her siblings. She broke up one fight and yelled at her brother to leave the twins alone. Josie was parading through the house with only underwear on. Marliene yelled at Helene for not remembering to buy diaper wipes and bread. A

TV and radio were on as well as a video game. The worker noted the need for parenting and household skills. Marliene was angry that the school had called her to say that Samuel and Helene were not doing homework. She felt the school needed to be supportive and she could not help the children with their work because she didn't know how. Her husband had taken care of this.

SYSTEMS THEORY

Although the unit of attention is different for family and group work, the most obvious similarity between these two models is that they both rely heavily on systems theory. This suggests that a change in one member affects every other member as well as the system as a whole. A family therapist interprets symptoms in one member as meaning the family is experiencing stress and is having difficulty maintaining its previous equilibrium. Each family member is seen as both affecting and being affected by external stress. Behavior is seen as circular, rather than lineal. In terms of the previous case example, a family therapist believes that not only Marliene but every member of the family has been affected by the sudden traumatic loss of the husband and father.

Both group and family therapists believe that context is important, both historical and in the here and now. A critical difference, however, is that from the very beginning the family therapist can draw on a vast family history, whereas the group worker must create a history in the group. Everyone has had an initial group experience in the family, and Yalom (1995) speaks of problems in the initial group experience as the prime motivator for clients to seek group therapy. Both group and family therapists see their respective treatment unit as providing the context for change, and both would examine and use process in the therapeutic sessions to help effect change of individual members. Cultural issues form the fabric of the context and need to be examined within the chosen intervention.

INCLUSION

A beginning issue for both family and group workers is inclusion. With families there is little choice. As a familiar proverb states,

"One can chose one's friends, but not one's family." An early family therapist believed that all family members living in the same household should participate in family therapy (Ackerman, 1966). There are difficulties of having all family members participate. In the case example, Helene and the twins may believe that their mother Marliene and brother Samuel have the problems and only they should be seen for therapy. Some family therapists include extended family living elsewhere (Boszormenyi-Nagy & Spark, 1973). With this approach, a family therapist might want to include Marliene's father and sister who lived nearby. It is interesting to note that Monty's parents have broken off contact with Marliene and their grandchildren. Often trauma like a sudden death can reawaken old conflicts and lead to divisions. One wonders about the previous nature of the relationship between Marliene and her in-laws and how positively they felt about her when their son was alive.

The family may experience further isolation and stigma because they are members of a minority group. Prejudice may aggravate the feelings of trauma and loss they have experienced. Also, since 9-11 and the subsequent passage of the Patriot Act, non-American-born families may feel especially unwelcome.

Families who have lost members to 9-11 are a special group. There have received much in the way of financial and social support. Yet the very help they received might contribute to stigmatization, as they are continually reminded about how different they are from other families. They may want to move on with their lives, but are continually reminded that they are family survivors of 9-11.

There have been numerous groups formed through the workplace and social work agencies after the World Trade Center tragedy. The uniqueness of this event, coupled with the commonality of sudden loss and the intense trauma experienced by individuals who lost significant others, colleagues, and friends all at the same time, have provided an arena for group work practice.

A most important issue for members of a group is inclusion (Northern & Kurland, 2001). WTC widows have strong affective ties from the common experience. However, they may not feel the group can meet their needs or that the worker will be there for them. All new members are cautious about being hurt (Northern &

Kurland 2001). In this situation, though, there is already significant pain and this will affect the inclusion process. The West Indian background of this family may also affect inclusion since a great deal of attention and media focused on mainstream Americans who died, and not on immigrants and persons of color.

Marliene had many offers to join groups. She was generally reluctant since she had never been a client and was unclear about what mental health services were. Since members share many commonalties, these groups formed post 9-11 quickly became cohesive leading to intense sharing of feelings and ventilation. Marliene, however, may not be ready for a group and may be cautious of being hurt yet again. Yet the group experience can help Marliene with needed advice on negotiating the numerous systems that she has to deal with, confirmation of her feelings, and opportunities to explore issues which she can not discuss with her family and friends. Another kind of group for Marliene might be a parenting skills group, especially as there is some indication of a need for this type of group.

Helene has been parentified and is taking over the maternal functions in the family. A group could allow her to become 12 years old again and not always have to feel so responsible. Samuel may be able to join a group for children with ADHD or perhaps a specific group for children who have lost a parent in that tragedy. The 6-year-old twins may benefit from a playgroup where they could deal with their understanding of what happened and the loss of their father through play. Children often heal through reenactments in play (Lynn & Nisivoccia, 2001).

All of the children who lost a parent in the WTC crisis share a powerful homogeneous bond. It may be important, however, for the children to mix with other children who did not have the same experiences. Group experiences can provide needed nurturance. Groups can further recognize and build on members' strengths (Lynn & Nisivoccia, 2001).

The power in this family has shifted substantially. Marliene's husband managed the family financially and emotionally. Marliene, overwhelmed by grief, could not assume this role. The children were left to take on parenting functions and looked for a powerful person to protect them. Group work is a modality that often deals with power and influence and increases a person's individual power.

ENGAGEMENT

Heterogeneity and homogeneity of group composition are often problematic in initial group development. Group therapists know that some heterogeneity encourages growth, but too much leads to scapegoating and early termination (Yalom, 1995). The "Noah's Ark" principle of group composition provides a means of introducing heterogeneity without encouraging scapegoats (Yalom, 1995). Yet in family therapy, there is by definition heterogeneity in terms of age, role, and power. Certainly in families there is often one parent, one child, or one male member. A possibility for this family might be to involve Helene in a girls group. This might be important as she could be a child while participating in this group.

A group experience for Samuel might help him learn to relate to male peers, and if the group leader is male, provide an opportunity for interaction with a male role model. In group, Samuel can connect with others in a different way than in his family, as there are no demands on him to assume a specific familial role because of his gender.

In group work, new members have no shared history, and an initial task for the group leader is to facilitate the development of a group culture (Shulman, 1999). Groups are based on the democratic value that each member has equal power, and therapist continually works toward ensuring that each member has an equal opportunity to participate (Brown, 1991). Groups that formed because of 9-11 do have a unique quality of a powerful shared history. This shared history, however, sometimes creates a reluctance to become a member of a group. Families of 9-11 victims have been given so many opportunities to join groups or see counselors that often they feel saturated by "helpers."

In contrast with groups, families have preexisting power differences, and the therapist may choose either to reinforce these differences or to create other power differentials within the family. In the West Indian family discussed previously, Samuel, because of his gender, may have been asked to assume responsibilities beyond his years. Many of the youth who lost parents in the World Trade Center have assumed increased responsibilities beyond their chronological age. Therefore, it might be important for children to be in more heterogeneous groups with children who have not lost a parent in the World Trade Center.

A family therapist might strive to restructure the family so that the mother makes more decisions. One might question how culturally sensitive it would be to attempt to change the structure of this family, and be concerned that this might have unfavorable consequences.

Engagement of clients is essential in both group work and family therapy. Often it is difficult to engage a family if there is an identified patient, as families often believe that therapists should only treat and cure the member who is showing symptoms. This belief may be especially strong among culturally diverse families unfamiliar with the systems perspective in family therapy or the efficacy of therapy in general. Marliene may be denying that she and the whole family are in need of family treatment. She might just interpret her symptoms as a time limited reaction to her loss on 9-11, and deny the need for ongoing treatment for herself and her family.

Another reason this family might be difficult to engage is that Marliene may deny problems with Samuel. Often families rationalize or deny symptoms in children to avoid acknowledgment of problems that could bring shame on the family. This may be an especially important issue for an immigrant family that is trying to survive and fit into a new unfamiliar country. The family may be sensitive to the issue that if a family member has a problem, this person may not be accepted. To seek treatment for Samuel's problems might signify that the family is not all right, that a family member is damaged. The family may be more receptive to Samuel's participation in an activity group than in family therapy.

ASSESSMENT

As part of the assessment process a family therapist studies the structure of the family, the hierarchical arrangement, the type and degree of connection between people, communication patterns, decision making, and prevailing values and myths. It was very difficult for this family to pursue help since many West Indian families are reluctant to seek professional help. In fact, we can speculate that if the family had not experienced such a traumatic loss they never would have come for treatment. Even now there may be a focus on "fixing" individual family members' problems, such as Marliene's depression or Samuel's ADHD, rather than focusing on family systemic issues, that all have been affected by their traumatic loss. After 9-11 this family suddenly became a single-parent family, with Samuel thrust into the role of the oldest male. There was special concern about Samuel because he was the oldest male and already had a preexisting ADHD disorder.

Families often have different reactions to trauma. Marliene's extended family was very supportive, while Monty's family became less available to Marliene and the children. The family therapist might also ask what the prior relationships with extended families were. There may have been previous conflicts between Marliene and her in-laws. Perhaps they even unconsciously blamed Marliene for the loss of their son (e.g., if she hadn't been so concerned about money and encouraged him to take that job in the World Trade Center, etc.). The family may value education highly and Samuel's ADHD diagnosis may be especially threatening now that he is the oldest male and must carry forth the father's name now that he is gone. Monty was a computer technician; there may be concern that Samuel will never be able to achieve the educational and vocational competence of his father.

CONTRACTING

Contracting takes place both in family treatment and group work. Contracting with this family for family treatment may be difficult if they do not see the need for family work or if they feel only one member has a problem. An additional concern in doing family work with 9-11 survivors is that the family therapist not allow himself/herself to become a replacement for the lost family member.

The contract for group work has to be very clear so that members do not have false expectations. Shared history, remember though, has sometimes created a reluctance to participate in a group. Affected people have been given so many opportunities to join groups or see counselors that they may feel saturated by offers of help.

BUILDING NORMS

From the beginning into the middle stage of group treatment the group worker must struggle to create group norms. The goal of groups that were created after 9-11 is to help members develop a mutual aid system. To facilitate achieving this, members must develop appropriate norms that include listening to each other, respecting differences, and helping others participate. This can be a challenging prospect when members may be extremely wounded and needy. Group members can benefit a great deal from receiving the support of other group members who have experienced loss and trauma from the 9-11 disaster. Group members may develop new norms to help them cope within the group and in their outside lives.

Families, on the other hand, already have very strong norms. In fact, the existent norms of families may make it difficult for the family therapist, as an outsider, to initially connect with the family. With Marliene's family, the family must explore existing norms, especially in terms of relating to strangers, as well as communicating past and present feelings. The family's norms and values in terms of education, work, and raising children must be explored as well. In this family Monty was a very strict disciplinarian. Now that Monty is gone, and Marliene is depressed, there may be much less structure in this family than previously.

The family therapist may have to build appropriate norms for becoming involved in therapy. The practitioner can teach clients that family therapy can help them with their problems. Families can also be encouraged to develop the norm that makes it appropriate to communicate their feelings openly and honestly in therapy.

CLINICAL ISSUES IN FAMILY THERAPY AND GROUP WORK

The worker's role, especially in terms of transference and countertransference, is particularly significant in family therapy. Often original family constellations are re-created as the therapist is drawn into the family system. If a male family therapist works with this family, he could very easy become Monty, the lost father and husband. This may become apparent when different family members begin to depend on the male family therapist to make important decisions. If the family therapist is a woman, various members may have negative feelings about the therapist having a position of power and control, especially if the family comes from a culture where women have limited education and power.

Strong countertransference feelings are often evoked in the family therapist, as all therapists have had their own unique familial experiences. Countertransference feelings can be especially strong in working with family survivors of 9-11 because we all shared this overwhelming experience. Because of the intensity of 9-11 and its traumatic effect on everyone, there is a major risk of vicarious traumatization for the family therapist. This concept has been defined as the negative effect on the therapist after prolonged work with traumatized clients (Cunningham, 2003). Vicarious traumatization may affect the ability of the therapist to work effectively with survivor victims of 9-11.

The therapist may have a negative countertransference that Marliene should pull herself together as this is her responsibility, despite her loss. Another negative counter-transference reaction might be to push the family away because the family therapist is so overwhelmed by the tragedy of losing a family member in 9-11. This response to vicarious traumatization can occur both to family and group therapists (Cunningham, 2003).

In group treatment the irrational aspects of relationships between the members and between the members and leader influences the group a great deal. Transference underlies distortions and angry feelings that may emerge in group. The widows and their children have powerful feelings toward authorities that they may feel were responsible for what happened. They have been caught up in systems that promised to provide help and did not come through. They may have fantasies that the leader can make it better or bring back the individual who was killed. They easily place superhuman powers on the leader as well as view the leader/therapist as all knowing or all caring. The rage that many widows have can be displaced onto the worker. Since many of the children have not received attention from the grieving parent the children may present more demands.

TREATMENT MODELS AND TECHNIQUES

While family and group therapists use similar techniques, including support, reframing, confrontation, and interpretation to bring about changes, clinicians should always be aware of a significant difference. Group members often do not see each other between sessions. In fact, social contact in between sessions is usually discouraged in therapy groups (Yalom, 1995), although children in groups often see other group members in class. Families who are seen for family therapy, however, continue to live with each other. Because of this continued close proximity the family therapist must be careful, especially in the use of confrontation and interpretation, or encouraging family members to use these techniques, with the risk of possible negative consequences between sessions.

Different models have been identified for family therapy and group work. Family intervention models include the psychodynamic, structural, humanistic, communication, strategic, and narrative. The structural and communication models have been noted for their usefulness in work with immigrant families (Ho, 1987). Reframing and symptom reduction are effective treatment techniques frequently used with immigrant groups. A psychodynamic family therapist would focus on making more conscious repressed feelings about severe losses. With our case example, the therapist might explore with family members ambivalent feelings they might have had about Monty and also feelings of guilt and responsibility for this death. (If only I had made him stay home that day, because he had such a bad cold, etc.) There would also be an attempt to connect this loss with previous losses the family had experienced, such as loss of grandparents and leaving their homeland to travel to the United States. A therapist who follows the structural model of family therapy would try to reorganize the family by making it clear that the mother is in charge and the children should listen to her. A therapist would be concerned that since this tragedy occurred Marliene has abrogated her role as an authority figure in the family. A family therapist from the humanist school, such as Satir, would work on building up the self-esteem of each family member, especially Marliene and Samuel, who have been scapegoated as family problems. A communications family therapist would encourage family members to speak more openly especially in terms of their feelings. He or she might identify certain family members who get stuck in certain roles and whose behavior has become rigid and solidified. A strategic family therapist might interpret Marliene's depression as an attempt to continually remind the family of the loss they have suffered. He or she might circumscribe the symptom within certain limits or reframe the issue. Using a paradoxical intervention, the family therapist might tell

Marliene that she should continue to be depressed as this holds the family together. A narrative family therapist would not come to the family with any set ideas, but rather would allow each family member to tell his or her own story and thus create their own reality. No matter which family treatment model the therapist uses, one must remember that this family is from a culture that may be very different from that of the therapist and this may have a major influence on the course of treatment.

Social group work models presume health. This model becomes useful for this family since they did not feel they had a need for mental health services. The behaviors of this family can be viewed not as symptoms, but rather as ineffective or non-helpful adaptation to the traumatizing experiences. Groups can also fill another loss that this family experienced. Through the husband's work affiliation with a union, many events occurred among families, and now this family has experienced the loss of a peer network. The social group work model helps members develop new peer networks.

The group modality using a crisis intervention framework would be helpful to the family, especially the children. Children are more vulnerable to stressful events. Groups cushion stressful events, recognize and build on members' strengths, and strengthen coping skills (Lynn & Nisivoccia, 2001). The stress of the WTC tragedy created opportunities to develop strategies for adaptation, a major focus of a crisis intervention group. The crisis created powerful bonds so that groups could become quickly cohesive and accomplish a great deal of work in a short period of time. Using a health model, groups can be done in school environments, which further normalizes the process.

Group work includes a remedial model that reflects a treatment orientation and therapeutic aspects. In the model, individual change would be expected and activities would be directed to fostering change. With group treatment, the range of interventions can be psychodynamic, supportive, or psychoeducational.

Marliene would benefit from a group treatment approach for her depression and to deal with life changing issues. She could more effectively deal with her intense grief and have her basic needs addressed. Samuel could benefit from a group experience that addresses his ADHD, as well as a treatment oriented group to help him cope better with the loss of his father. Helene could benefit from a treatment oriented group to deal with her traumatic loss and her changed role within the family.

TERMINATION

Termination in group work is very different than termination in family therapy. When a group terminates, members often never see each other again. Group workers, however, must not minimize the group experience and must carefully work through individual and group feelings about termination. This may be especially true in groups in which members have experienced severe losses, such as groups with family members of 9-11 victims.

In contrast, when a family terminates treatment, the individual family members will continue to have ongoing contact with each other. Terminating with a family, however, can awaken previous feelings of loss that the family therapist must be prepared to address in the final sessions. Feelings of loss may be especially acute for families from diverse backgrounds who have experienced other recent losses. This would be especially true for the family who endured the sudden loss of husband and father. Individual members may be referred for ongoing therapy. The family should also be advised that they can return for family treatment at any future time that they feel it would be helpful.

CONCLUSIONS AND RECOMMENDATIONS

This chapter describes the similarities and differences of group and family work in the context of practice with an immigrant family who has experienced a recent, severe loss. The knowledge of both group and family therapy theory and techniques should enhance the practice skills of group and family workers. A growing dialogue between the two models should help professionals make a decision about whether family therapy, group treatment, or a combination of both would be more effective in working with specific culturally diverse families.

Being attentive to cultural diversity cuts across all modalities. The worker must be aware of his/her own cultural background and assess how this impacts treatment. The worker must also be sensitive to cultural nuances and be aware of biases and assumptions about the client's culture. Whatever model is selected, the social worker should be able to maintain a family approach within group therapy, as well as a group perspective in working with families. To achieve this goal, the following guidelines have been developed.

1. Students in helping professions should be prepared for more integrated practice by the study of group and family models in work with culturally diverse clients and their families.
2. Practitioners should explore the possibility of their clients being helped by both family and group work.
3. In working with a group, a practitioner should always be cognizant of family dynamics that affect group functioning.
4. In working with a family, a family therapist must be mindful that the family is a group and that group processes affect family functioning.
5. The dialogue between family therapy and group work should continue.
6. Research on the interrelationship and effectiveness of a dual perspective can be conducted.
7. Understanding the culture of the client affects the intervention arena and allows for a more integrated approach to helping. Practitioners using both or ether modality should address cultural differences in an open and direct method with their clients.
8. Both family therapists and group members can benefit from an increased range of interactions by using an integrated model in work with culturally diverse clients.

REFERENCES

Ackerman, N. (1966). *Treating the troubled family*. New York: Basic Books.
Boszormenyi-Nagy, I., & Spark, G. (1973). *Invisible loyalties: Reciprocity in intergenerational family therapy*. Hagerstown, MD: Harper and Row.
Brown, L. (1991). *Groups for growth and change*. New York: Longman.
Cunningham, M. (2003). Impact of trauma work on social work clinicians: Empirical findings. *Social Work, 48*(4), 451–459.
Fristad, M., Goldberg, A., & Gavazzi, S. (2003). Multi-family psychoeducation groups in the treatment of children with mood disorders. *Journal of Marital and Family Therapy, 29*(4), 491–504.

Garvin, C. (1986). Family therapy and group work: Kissing cousins or distant relatives in social work practice. In M. Parnes (Ed.), *Innovations in social group work: Feedback from practice to theory* (pp. 1–15). New York: Haworth.

Getz, H. (2002). Family therapy in a women's group: Integrating marriage and family therapy and group therapy. *Family Journal, 10*(2), 220–224.

Hines, M. (1988). Similarities and differences in group and family therapy. *Journal for Specialists in Group Work, 13*(4), 173–179.

Ho, M. (1987). *Family therapy with ethnic minorities.* Newbury Park, CA: Sage.

King, L. (1998). A cultural challenge: Multiple family groups for post-separation and post-divorce families in Hong Kong. *Social Work With Groups, 21*(1/2), 77–87.

Lynn, M., & Nisivoccia, D. (2001). Crisis intervention activity groups in the schools. In A. Drews, L. Carey, & C. Schaefer (Eds.), *School based play therapy* (pp. 177–193). New York: John Wiley and Sons Inc.

Mullen, A., Murray, L., & Happell, B. (2002). Multiple family group interventions in first episode psychosis: Enhancing knowledge and understanding. *International Journal of Mental Health Nursing, 11*(4), 225–233.

Northern, H., & Kurland, R. (2001). *Social work with groups* (3rd ed.). New York: Columbia University Press.

Norton, D. (1978). *The dual perspective: Inclusion of ethnic minority content in the social work curriculum.* New York: Council on Social Work Education.

Ritter, K. Y., West, J. D., & Trotzer, J. P. (1987). Comparing family counseling and group counseling: An interview with George Gazda, James Hanson and Alan Hoestadt. *Journal of Counseling and Development, 65,* 295–300.

Shulman, L. (1999). *The skills of helping individuals and group* (3rd ed.). Itasca, IL: Peacock.

Yalom, I. (1995). *The theory and practice of group psychotherapy* (4th ed.). New York: Basic Books.

CHAPTER 3

Managing Agencies for Multicultural Services

Roslyn H. Chernesky

The nation's health and social agencies mirror the cultural diversity of the United States population today. Multicultural workforces and clients are no longer atypical. Demographics indicate that by the mid 21st century, about 50% of Americans will be racial and ethnic minorities. The Hispanic population is the largest growing ethnic group, while Asians have the highest rate of growth among racial groups (Clemetson, 2003). One in every four Americans is expected to be of Hispanic heritage. Immigrants and refugees are changing the demographic composition of America as foreign-born resident populations increase and individuals and families from a wide variety of cultures, ethnicities, and nationalities relocate throughout the states in search of better opportunities and conditions. What was once regarded as an urban phenomenon can now be seen across the country in towns and rural communities. Moreover, the trend toward a more diverse population and workforce is expected to continue.

Both workers and clients bring to agencies socially relevant and culturally significant group affiliations that differentiate them by behavioral norms, values, language, and priorities. The workplace now reflects diverse ways of thinking and viewing the world. As a result, increasing diversity is challenging the dominant culture that has supported a relatively homogeneous workforce.

Social service agencies continue to face two challenges in this multicultural environment: a) managing workplaces in which workforces have become increasingly heterogeneous in terms of gender, race, age, religion, sexual orientation, ethnicity, and national origin; and b) meeting the service needs of client populations who may represent a wide range of very different cultures, languages, values, religions, and pre-immigration or refugee experiences.

The first is referred to as *managing for diversity competence*, defined as "creating a climate in which the potential advantages of diversity for organizational or group performance are maximized while the potential disadvantages are minimized" (Cox & Beale, 1997, p. 2). The second is referred to as *cultural competency*. Cultural competency is defined as a system of service that "acknowledges and incorporates—at all levels—the importance of culture, the assessment of cross-cultural relations, vigilance towards the dynamics that result from cultural differences, the expansion of cultural knowledge, and the adaptation of services to meet culturally-unique needs" (Cross, Barzon, Dennis, & Isaacs, 1989, pp. iv, v).

When demographic changes in the workforce were predicted nearly 2 decades ago (Johnston & Packer, 1987), the immediate goal was to increase an organization's diversity by recruiting, hiring, and retaining workers from backgrounds considered relevant to the organization's mission and work. The second goal was to enable workers to make their maximum contribution and to succeed regardless of race, ethnicity, gender, age, or disability. Administrators and managers were expected to tap the potential of all employees, take advantage of worker differences, and capitalize on the talents of the various populations (Chernesky, 1997). A discrimination-and-fairness paradigm initially prevailed as organizations focused on equal opportunity, fair treatment, and compliance with federal and state requirements. While this legalistic approach may have opened doors to diverse workers, it did not provide a strong basis for managing diversity. An acceptance-and-celebration paradigm followed and valuing diversity became the focus of organizational efforts. Today, emphasis is placed on organizational cultures and work environments to address obstacles that prevent all workers from contributing (Gummer, 1998; Tsui & Gutek, 1999).

Many social service agencies are struggling with these earlier goals. They have not yet successfully recruited heterogeneous workforces nor systematically celebrated cultural differences.

Agencies with multicultural workforces, however, are recognizing that managing diversity has taken on new meanings and directions today. Two emerging factors have helped to recast managing diversity. On the one hand, organizations learned that they were not really making the most of having multicultural workforces. Rather than integrating their diverse workers into the mainstream, this diversity in work and work assignments was actually narrowly used. Perhaps the best example in social service agencies is when Latino workers are expected to work with Latino clients and communities, and are called upon to translate for clients. Secondly, organizations learned that the benefits typically associated with multicultural workplaces might not be apparent when workforce diversity brings tensions and conflicts that are neither recognized nor addressed.

Organizational leaders are now being called upon to create and sustain an organizational climate that insures that diversity-related dynamics enhance rather than minimize performance and productivity. In fact, leaders are being asked to take proactive steps to transform their agencies and, in this way, create truly multicultural or diversity competent organizations. If creating diversity competent workplaces is not enough, social service agencies are further challenged to provide culturally competent services and programs. Leaders must find ways to deliver culturally appropriate services and avoid offering what might be inappropriate, ineffective, or potentially damaging services to their multicultural client populations.

This chapter focuses on these two challenges facing social service agencies today: managing diversity competent agencies and providing culturally competent services. The dilemma for agencies is that the recruitment and retention of a diverse workforce does not necessarily result in culturally competent services. However, success in achieving culturally competent services and programs requires diverse workforces, thereby planting the seeds for tensions and conflicts that have the potential for creating unproductive workplaces. Although the two challenges are integrally related, they are discussed separately here. The chapter begins with managing for diversity competence, and draws upon the more recent literature that is intended to help businesses and organizations develop diversity competent organizations. Their experiences offer lessons for social service agencies.

The chapter then focuses on developing cultural competency in services and service delivery systems. This discussion draws heavily on literature from the child welfare and mental health fields, where attention to cultural competency and the need for it have received extensive attention. The overall theme that unites these two is the role of organizational leaders to effectively respond to the challenges and opportunities posed by the presence of social-cultural diversity among workers and clients in their agencies. Responsibility for achieving and maintaining diversity competent organizations and culturally competent services rests with top-level executives. An agency's commitment to diversity and cultural competence can be realized only through organizational leadership, a perspective shared by many organizational scholars.

MANAGING FOR DIVERSITY COMPETENCY

The value of well-managed multicultural organizations has been recognized for a long time. If managed well, organizations can reap the benefits of creating an environment that enables all employees to work together to achieve organizational goals. Diversity competent agencies have policies and practices that are responsive to the needs of all workers. Because the culture of these organizations recognizes and appreciates differences, respects uniqueness, and distributes rewards and resources without regard to race, sex, age, ethnicity, or national origin, there is little prejudice, discrimination, and intergroup conflict (Cox, 1991).

Workforce diversity is associated with improved performance of organizations. It can enhance problem solving and decision making, increase creativity and innovation, advance the overall quality of personnel through better recruitment and retention, and create a climate of fairness and respect that all workers find conducive to higher levels of productivity and higher quality performance (Carr-Ruffino, 1999).

If workforce diversity is managed poorly, there can be negative effects and obstacles to high performance organizations; organizations can suffer losses in productivity, morale, and even staff. There is likely to be less effective communication; lower levels of social attraction, interaction, and relations; lower levels of attachment, commitment, and satisfaction to the organization; less interest in staying; and higher actual turnover. An increase in tension and conflict among workers is not unusual (Lobel & Kossek, 1996; Tsui & Gutek, 1999). Clearly managing for diversity competence is both an opportunity and a challenge for managers.

Contributing Factors

A number of factors can contribute to problems in multicultural organizations. Individual, intergroup, and organizational factors combine to create a diversity climate in organizations. The diversity climate in turn influences individual outcomes and organizational effectiveness. A particularly potent organizational factor is *institutional bias*. These are patterns within organizations, ingrained in policies and practices, which unwittingly provoke and exacerbate what diversity brings to the workplace. They tend to be invisible, inadvertent, and subtle, favoring some and disadvantaging others (Cox, 1994). Organizations often reflect attitudes, values, and expectations that disadvantage workers who do not share the majority culture. Those who differ from the majority culture are often outsiders and because they are unable to measure up to the majority standards, they cannot reap the benefits. Thus, the bias creates barriers to full participation by organization members from different cultural backgrounds. According to Cox (1994), areas in which institutionalized bias is found include a) norms about work hours and times; b) performance evaluation; c) criteria for rewards including advancement; d) job interviewing; e) policies and benefits related to balancing work and family; f) expectations around written and oral presentations; g) stereotypes of effective leadership, collegial, and managerial behavior; and h) the physical design of the workplace. While each practice is likely to pose problems for many or even all workers, the differential impact of each depending upon workers' cultural backgrounds may be hidden. There is considerable research to support the affects of these practices on diverse workforces (Chen & DiTomaso, 1996; Lobel & Kossek, 1996).

Workers, for example, often find themselves falling short when they are unable to demonstrate or unwilling to emulate the standard of effective management that is traditionally based on attributes stereotypical of White male managers. Behaviors of Latino or Asian workers may be viewed in terms of lack of initiative or too much passivity. Women supposedly lack suitable management qualities is a major reason for the gender-based glass ceiling that limits their advancement to top management levels. The glass ceiling, a popular metaphor from the 1980s, refers to barriers that are virtually transparent, yet so strong that they prevent women and people of color from moving up in an organization's hierarchy (Chernesky, 2003; Gibelman, 2000). Women managers continue to receive lower organizational rewards including pay, promotion, and desirable work assignments and training opportunities—even when they have "the right stuff." Similarly, the expectation that managers should work evenings or travel and forfeit family responsibilities fosters the "mommy track," a channeling of women into positions with almost no opportunity for advancement.

Organizations may tolerate behaviors that discriminate or harass, thus making the workplace inhospitable and offensive to workers that are not members of the majority group (Chernesky, 1998). Harassment along racial, ethnic, and gender lines has the potential to create disrupting tensions in the workplace. Although blatant examples of discrimination or harassment may be rare in social agencies, there are examples of more subtle discrimination, either conscious or unconscious unjust actions taken against an individual based on racial or gender stereotypes. Two typical examples are the cases in which a woman who speaks up at a meeting later finds that her remarks were attributed to the man seated next to her, or the African American professional who finds she or he is mistaken for a support person. In addition, many situations exist where racial slurs, jokes, and epithets, albeit not necessarily vicious or threatening, pollute the work environment. The humor and joking that may at one time have relieved tension or frustration, reduced boredom, or once served as a socially acceptable means to express feelings, create hostile or inhospitable cultures today and are likely to be illegal especially if they are condoned (Chernesky, 1998). The Supreme Court has recently set guidelines for assessing employer liability for working conditions in which sexual harassment is so unendurable that employees choose to resign (Greenhouse, 2004).

The experience of minority women in the workplace suggest there is reason to be seriously concerned about sexual harassment, racial and sexual discrimination, and the lack of support from supervisors and coworkers. Recent studies have found that workers' gender and race affect social interactions, shape perceptions, and influence supervisors and coworkers who are ethnically different from them. African American and Latina women reported feeling more isolated and less supported. They worried about losing their jobs, and were more likely to receive disciplinary actions, and receive less mentoring (Hopkins, 2002; Mor-Barak, Cherin, & Berkman, 1998). In addition, both supervisors and workers seem to hold stereotypical attitudes toward the lifestyle and work habits of African American women. As the women react to these attitudes, their increased stress leads to poorer quality work and absenteeism, thus further reinforcing those stereotypes (Hughes & Dodge, 1997).

Many patterns stem from the old ways things have been done in organizations. Outmoded rules, policies, and practices remain intact today despite the tremendous changes taking place in the nature of the workforce. Shaped by attitudes, beliefs, and values of older generations, they are less tolerant and inclusive today. Iglehart (2000) points out that an agency's history is one characteristic that can be an obstacle to diversity competency. An agency's history may lead to particular populations holding strong negative views that deter them from using the services or inhibit the agency's capacity to recruit staff from those groups. An organization's experience, perhaps decades ago, can also be introduced at critical times as a reminder of why the organization would not want, for example, to hire women with young children or men wearing head covering. Stories are passed on, reinforcing the bias, to those who may never have been part of the organization at the time of the initial occurrence. These stories are an important part of the organization's culture, and the fact that they take on myth-like qualities makes them even more powerful as obstacles to change.

Tools and Techniques

Over the past decade, a number of tools and techniques have gained favor as ways of supporting the integration of diversity into the organization. There seems to be general agreement that special attention must be given to practices that attract and sustain a diverse workforce, build upon the strengths of workers, and foster relationships that are necessary for jobs to get done. Without this special attention, workers are likely to feel excluded, disregarded, or shut out, and time will have to be spent on communication breakdowns because of cultural misunderstandings or conflicts.

Celebrating Diversity

Bringing together workers on a regular or occasional basis to celebrate various cultures has proven valuable for increasing awareness and appreciation of diversity. These may include luncheons devoted to eating ethnic foods, sharing in traditional holiday events, and arranging opportunities to purchase crafts or items representing different cultures, perhaps for holiday gift giving. Workers can come together to plan and conduct a series of presentations for all program staff on working with different client populations. One agency devotes time each year for workers to share their own cultural experiences and, in this way, prepare their colleagues to work with Caribbean, Dominican, Ecuadorian, Puerto Rican, and African American families. Celebrating cultural heritages can be valuable for clients as well as workers. Organizing annual special events, such as Hispanic or Latino Day can involve workers and families in sharing food, music, dancing, storytelling, and a history or language lesson.

Diversity Work Groups

Organizational practices that expose people to different others have been found to be related to success in fostering diversity. Pluralism councils, core groups, or dialogue groups have been effectively used. These are generally small, focused groups or multicultural discussion sessions that bring together workers of diverse backgrounds who want to learn how to more effectively work with those from different gender, racial, and/or cultural backgrounds. The groups can be used to allow participants to air grievances as they relate to biases or discrimination, and lead to improved understanding among participants. For women or minorities who have felt it best to remain silent about sexism or racism, the group offers a safe and supportive context for raising issues. At the same time, workers may learn how to manage their tendency to see any conflict or criticism as the result of racism or sexism through these groups. Mere exposure to and experience with members of the opposite gender and other ethnicities on this somewhat intimate level can in itself decrease bias and tension.

When given organizational responsibility to plan and develop an organization's multicultural initiatives or diversity strategy, diversity groups or councils are important structures that can promote diversity. They may identify concerns, determine whether problems being experienced are associated with diversity, and propose solutions such as workshops, policy changes, or celebrations of various cultures. They serve as resources to organizational units that are following through on the diversity plan, and they monitor the progress of change. These groups can also play a role in transferring knowledge about what is learned about managing diversity from one part of the organization to another. If provided access to upper management, the work of these groups can more readily be translated into policy-related decisions.

Diverse work teams also have the potential to enhance an organization's efforts. In some situations, when teams or task forces are being formed, organizations deliberately attempt to create diversity in their membership. Teams are an example of using the natural work settings to expose people to others who have different backgrounds, which can help break down stereotypes. As part of regular work activities, encouraging cross-cultural alliances to develop can offer learning opportunities. Diverse work teams do not guarantee improved relationships, and can even thwart, further exacerbate, or intensify the problems that occur when people of diverse backgrounds are brought together (Thompson & Gooler, 1996).

Mentoring

Mentoring approaches have also been used, although with mixed results. Mentoring is generally career oriented, helping those who are getting stuck in their careers or are blocked by the glass ceiling. Mentoring may also be an organizational response to turnover when diverse workers are leaving at high rates or in disproportionate numbers. These workers may believe they will never fit or make it in the organization, or may question whether doing so is worth it. There is increasing evidence that supports the link between workers' perception of being accepted by the organization, job satisfaction and organizational commitment, and organizational turnover. Workers outside the organizational mainstream who feel excluded and perceive a large discrepancy between their desired image and their image in the organization may choose to leave (MorBarak & Cherin, 1998).

The traditional mentoring model assumes the mentor as expert is able to advise and guide the mentee, who is the learner. This assumption is less valid with workforce changes, and senior mentors may be as much learners as junior workers in today's diverse work environment. Therefore, new formal mentoring approaches are being created to legitimize and facilitate relationships between individuals who might otherwise not easily build rapport with one another. Unlike the more traditional one-on-one hierarchical mentoring models, peer mentoring around common challenges posed to particular identity groups is thought to be more effective. Although natural peer relationships may occur through day-to-day work, organizations may have to foster peer mentoring through a kind of buddy system in which newcomers are matched with workers who have a few more years of experience.

Mentoring circles bring together senior and mid-level mangers for the specific purpose of supporting the development of mid- and lower-level managers. Coaching is an alternative that is used to provide a sounding board, support, active listening, and advice to help individuals reflect on their experiences and develop a wider repertoire of responses to handling current challenges. Mentoring approaches that organizations may initiate seem to work best when participation is voluntary and is accompanied by some training on building relationships and working with people of different backgrounds. It is also important that mentoring is built into the organization's reward system to demonstrate that serving as a mentor or mentee is appreciated and that the time and effort required is recognized (Kram & Hall, 1996).

Diversity Training

The focus on training workers to be better prepared to deal with the changing realities of the workplace is considered a key component for making workforce diversity an asset rather than a liability. The immediate objectives of diversity training are to increase workers' cultural sensitivity, understanding, or skills. The diversity literature proposes three stages of training, which progressively increase the involvement required of trainees. In the first stage, training focuses on increasing employee awareness of diversity issues. Heightened awareness is considered essential to bringing about changes in attitude or behavior. The second stage focuses

on increasing understanding with the intent toward changing attitudes. Breaking down stereotypes is emphasized. In the third stage,
workers learn interpersonal and communication skills that can lead
to new behaviors in the work setting (Ford & Fisher, 1996).

The long-term expectation is that training will improve the
organization's climate and culture in relation to workforce diversity. From this perspective, training is viewed as an essential component of an organizational change agenda rather than a mechanism
reinforcing the status quo. There is little empirical evidence, however, that diversity training brings about the desired productive
multicultural workforce. Research is extremely limited and meth-
odologically problematic. Samples in the majority of studies are
small, and consist primarily of homogeneous groups of college
students who volunteer and receive much more extensive multicultural training than would ordinarily be received in workforce diversity trainings. The lack of attention in the research to trainer
variables, curricula and/or manuals, and specific goals or desired
outcomes, as well as the failure to examine comparability among
studies that use a variety of measurement scales, demonstrate a
severe limitation to the generalizability of the research to real-
world practice (Schwam-Harris, 2004).

Nevertheless, a number of factors have emerged that seem to
increase the likelihood that training will be valuable. An organization's readiness to benefit from training is critical to its effectiveness
at managing diversity. Prior to training, an organizational analysis
is important. By first addressing what diversity means in and to
the organization, what the diversity goals are, and what will be
supported in order to attain diversity, the training is likely to fit
the organization. Since training as an isolated initiative does not
seem to have much impact, other interventions are necessary to
support it. Training works when integrated with the organization's
affirmative action and equal opportunity efforts, related policy
decisions, and incentives that reward workers who demonstrate
culturally sensitive and appropriate behaviors, and when supported
by a clear and strong commitment to diversity among top management (Ford & Fisher, 1996).

Multicultural training does not always achieve its intended
goals. Some critics say it is futile to try to change attitudes through
workshops and seminars. Many participants resent the presump-
tion that they are not tolerant or sensitive and need such training.
Training can even create or contribute to additional or heightened

conflict in the workplace by highlighting biases and prejudices, making individuals feel guilty, or reinforcing stereotypes and negativity. It can also lead to greater polarization among workers, and even more complaints about behaviors deemed improper (Egan, 1993; Murray, 1993). Perhaps the harshest criticism about training comes from those who expect too much from it and do not realize that structural interventions are necessary in addition to training for success in managing diversity (Ford & Fisher, 1996).

Diversity training is more likely to be effective as a technique of organizational change when there are skilled trainers knowledgeable in group work skills, human behavior, and change processes, and who emphasize training workers in team building, problem solving, and communication skills. Approaching issues of diversity in an inclusive manner that presents similarities as well as differences, avoids confrontation and blame, and does not force employees to expose thoughts or feelings they are not yet ready to bring forth is also more likely to lead to effective outcomes (Schwam-Harris, 2004).

Policies

Organizations are recognizing that written policies can be effective in preventing racial, ethnic, and sexual harassment from taking root and creating hostile work environments. The reputation and public image of agencies can easily be tarnished, while worker morale is damaged, because of racially motivated remarks, ethnic slurs, and subtle forms of intimidation that fall within the definition of sexual harassment—lingering, intimate touches, repeated sexual innuendoes or comments about aspects of a person's physique. Increasingly, therefore, agencies are developing and distributing general policies that acknowledge the dignity of each worker and right to work in an environment free of undue personal harassment, stress, and interpersonal friction. These policies specifically forbid unnecessary forms of harassment, racial tensions, and demeaning behavior, and spell out the penalties, including dismissal or personal legal and financial liability. The policies also place on record the organization's expectation and approval for coming forth to report incidents.

Organizational Change

Despite these suggestions, it seems as though few organizations have actually succeeded in meeting the challenge posed by diverse workforces and in developing diversity competent organizations. Not surprisingly, a more recent literature has emerged that presents a number of models to organizational leaders in businesses and for-profit organizations (Carr-Ruffino, 1999; Cox, 2001; Kossek & Lobel, 1996; Tsui & Gutek, 1999). While some recommend strategies directed at individuals or groups, most propose structural interventions and point to the need for a process of deep organizational change, recognizing that organizations must reevaluate an organization's dominant culture with its underlying values and belief systems.

The proponents of organizational change call for "a systemic approach toward an ultimate goal of institutionalizing a new culture—one that welcomes diversity and allows all members to use their skills and abilities to achieve their full potential in pursuit of business and personal goals" (Cox, 2001, p. 30). Cox (2001) refers to this change as "systems alignment" (p. 14), an approach that is intended to identify and then change current practices and procedures to fit with the goal of managing workforce diversity. He suggests three areas of the work environment that are essential to systems alignment: a) time factors—the way time is scheduled; b) space factors—the way the physical environment is arranged; and, c) people processing factors—the way workers are recruited, hired, and rewarded. Only by paying attention to these, Cox claims, will organizations be able to overcome diversity-toxic cultures that make it impossible to successfully embrace diversity among members.

Similarly, Hyde (2003, 2004) sees the need for agencies to engage in comprehensive multicultural organizational development (MCOD) as a way of transforming their organization's culture and eliminating patterns of racism, sexism, or other oppressions within their organizations. The approach can serve as a guide to implement holistic multicultural change using principles of a planned, long-term, systemic, action-oriented process (Grieger, 1996). MCOD is based on an assumption that achieving a truly multicultural workplace requires a reconfiguration of power and privilege. It is a strategy that recognizes that diversity initiatives to establish and tap the potential of heterogeneous workforces, and to accept and celebrate differences are important but are only first steps. MCOD poses numerous challenges for organizational leaders, especially since it is not easily implemented.

The most important lesson derived from this literature is that the effect of demographic diversity in the workplace can be moderated, but much depends on the organization's climate and culture. As Tsui and Gutek (1999) note, "the reality is that diversity is a liability until and unless processes are in place to manage the negative dynamic and to release diversity's hidden potential" (p. 143).

PROVIDING CULTURALLY COMPETENT SERVICES

Just as the workforce is undergoing dramatic changes in its composition, the client populations in our social and health agencies are reflecting the same shifts. Agencies generally recognize the necessity to respond to the unique needs of these populations who are not from the majority culture nor viewed as mainstream American. In addition, there are many clients who have known an immigrant or refugee experience, severe economic conditions, upheavals and losses, or ongoing ethnic and civil warfare. Those who arrive and remain in the United States illegally and without documentation are a growing population. Increasing numbers are likely to be uprooted from their lives in the States as family members are deported, caught in the federal special registration net targeted today mostly toward Muslim cultures (Kinetz, 2004). Adoption, child custody, divorce, employment, public assistance, and domestic violence all reflect international and global dimensions today.

The consequences to multicultural clients of receiving services that are not culturally competent continue to be documented. Agency barriers restrict access to services and agency practices lead to incorrect assessments and treatment based on race or ethnicity. Child welfare studies indicate that children of color are overrepresented in child protection caseloads and that racial inequities exist in reporting, decision making, child removal, and permanency planning (Roberts, 2001). Disparities in access to health care and quality of care are well documented, suggesting that racial and ethnic minorities receive a lower quality of health care than Whites, even after taking into account differential access to care. Among the contributing factors are stereotypical behaviors, bias, and prejudice

(Johnson & Smith, 2002). There is also strong support to demonstrate that health outcomes of older adults have less to do with differences in biology or culture and more to do with English-language proficiency and access to quality preventive and treatment services (Capitman, 2002).

Mental health agencies have not fared much better in delivering culturally appropriate services to ethnically diverse families (Dana, 1998b; Fong & Gibbs, 1995). Studies of mental health care found high inpatient hospitalization rates for minorities, inappropriate and delayed treatment, inadequate referrals, premature stopping of treatment, and ineffective case management. These patterns have been attributed to misdiagnosis, language and communication barriers during admission and assessment, and feelings of alienation from the process (Siegel, Davis-Chambers, Haugland, Bank, Aponte, & McCombs, 2000).

The importance of the cultural context in which programs are delivered and direct service takes place must be understood. Agencies must not only be vigilant about the ways in which they might be failing to provide effective services, but also about how their services might be inappropriate, ineffective, and potentially damaging to multicultural client populations. They must continue to struggle with how to design and deliver services that meet culturally unique client needs. Healy (1996) warns that given "the relatively poor track record of social agencies in addressing the concerns of 'domestic minority groups' including African American and Latinos . . . responding sensitively and effectively to international populations will not come easily" (p. 101).

Culturally competent agencies are those whose policies, behaviors, and attitudes combine in such a way that the agency and its workers can effectively provide services in multicultural situations. Isaacs and Benjamin (1991) see culturally competent organizations as a) valuing diversity, b) having the capacity for cultural self-assessment, c) being aware of the dynamics inherent when cultures interact, d) having institutionalized cultural knowledge, and e) having developed adaptations to service delivery that reflect an understanding of cultural diversity. Most importantly, these five elements are manifested at every level of an organization—policy making, administrative, and practice levels.

Tools and Techniques

Staffing

Traditionally, efforts to design more culturally sensitive agencies and services reflect the struggle to overcome the underrepresentation of diversity in staffing. The primary strategy therefore has been to acquire multicultural and bilingual staff, which would make it possible to match clients and staff ethnically and linguistically. Four approaches are used: hiring multicultural and bilingual professional staff; hiring indigenous non- or paraprofessionals; using interpreters; and helping staff from dominant cultures acquire cross-cultural skills to work with diverse client groups. Cultural competency also requires strategies that modify program designs and service delivery, address policies, and incorporate organizational self-assessments.

Many agencies have indeed made important strides in diversifying their workforce. Nevertheless, hiring professional staff of similar ethnic and cultural backgrounds as clients has rarely yielded a significant cohort of desired workers in a dominant agency. Success in acquiring multicultural and bilingual staff continues to be problematic and is likely to remain so (Fong & Gibbs, 1995). It generally requires considerable effort and creativity to reach out to potential sources, as well as careful examination of the recruiting, interviewing, and hiring processes to identify what may be inadvertent barriers.

As difficult as it might be to obtain diverse staff, retaining them can be as difficult. Focusing only on recruitment is unlikely to be sufficient. Workers tend to leave when so few individuals are hired that they perceive themselves as "tokens," isolated, or having been channeled into particular areas because of their diversity. The proportion of minorities in a dominant cultural setting is an important context that affects workers' perceptions and the meanings given to their experience. Opportunities for promotion and advancement are of concern, particularly in agencies that have achieved diversity of staff at lower levels and have almost none at the supervisory and management levels. Job satisfaction and turnover, as well as job performance, seem to be related to how workers see themselves fitting into and being able to advance in an organization (Chernesky, 1998).

As an alternative, when it is not possible to employ professional staff who are from the same populations as clients, agencies turn to paraprofessional indigenous workers—from the population, culture, or community being served—who are expected to be better able to relate to clients as well as bridge the different cultures. As multicultural and bilingual paraprofessionals, they work alongside professionals from dominant ethnic and cultural populations as case aids, social work assistants, and interpreters. While helping families understand what agencies need from them, they also help agencies understand the needs of their diverse families and communities.

Across the country, there is a critical shortage of bilingual professional staff. The shortage results in using interpreters as a substitute. A qualified interpreter may be the only alternative when staff is neither fluent nor effective in the target language. Too often, children or even maintenance personnel serve as interpreters, raising professional and ethical issues (O'Neill, 2003). A study of Spanish-speaking patients using interpreters in a pediatric clinic found serious errors that could cause clinical problems and place patients at risk, even among official interpreters (Marcus, 2003). Guidelines for using interpreters point out that a) agencies should not use family members or friends to interpret unless the client knows of the option to have a qualified interpreter yet prefers a family or friend, b) young children or youth should not be used to interpret, c) agencies should not depend on untrained staff to interpret, d) qualified interpreters should be used, and e) telephone language lines should be used only when absolutely necessary (*Achieving Cultural Competence*, 2001). As the Latino population rapidly grow, the incapacity of social work to provide services in Spanish has prompted national concern. Pressure to ensure that Spanish-speaking persons and people with limited English proficiency receive quality services comes from the federal government, NASW, and agencies across the country, all trying innovative approaches to providing culturally competent services to clients in their native languages (O'Neill, 2003). A pending New York City law would require all city human service agencies to make all documents available in six languages and to provide translation to clients by phone or computer for all languages within a reasonable time (Kaufman, 2003).

Multicultural Training

Because workers are relatively unprepared to work with diverse cultural populations, and they need cross-cultural skills to work with different populations, staff training is emphasized to prepare effective multicultural practitioners (Rogers, 1995; Zayas, Evans, Mejia, & Rodriguez, 1997). Cultural awareness or sensitivity training is used to help individuals gain an understanding of their own personal values, whereas cross-cultural training focuses on learning about cultures of different groups. Both have a long tradition in the field. They assume that by learning about cultural differences, workers can learn to accept and respect differences between and among people, and will be able to communicate more effectively, thus developing strategies for effective intervention. Agencies have used training to increase cultural awareness, as well as to help workers become aware of their own culture and cultural values and understand how their behavior is influenced by culture. Training helps workers understand their assumptions and stereotypes about other cultures, as well as the attitudes and behaviors of minority persons toward their own culture and toward the majority culture. Training also focuses on culture commonality and cultural specificity in working with ethnically diverse populations and includes skills in cross-cultural communication.

Several excellent examples of multicultural training are presented in the professional literature. Training in cultural sensitivity of child protection workers that focuses on attitudes, knowledge, and skill building is described by Stevenson and her colleagues (Stevenson, Cheung, & Leung, 1992). Beckett and Dungee-Anderson (1996) present an eight-step training model that is grounded in multicultural communication. It is used to train social workers to communicate sensitively and competently with individuals from other ethnic and cultural groups. Zayas and colleagues (1997) describe a cultural competency training program developed for case managers and counselors delivering emergency psychiatric services to Hispanic children and families in crisis. The discussion of the content and format of the 1-day training workshop and its 6-month follow-up booster session details the way topics were approached.

Program Design

Existing programs are likely to require modifications if they are to meet the needs of clients from diverse cultural populations. Guarnaccia and Rodriguez (1996) point out that program planning, development, and implementation of culturally competent services require an understanding of culture. They stress that agencies need to determine what they mean by culture and how culture will be used in their programs. They must go beyond viewing culture as creating a physical setting and hiring staff with language proficiencies, to incorporating the much more complex dimensions of culture.

After examining 98 mental health programs serving ethnic and minority children and families, cross-cutting issues and characteristics in these programs emerged and provided valuable lessons applicable to social service and health services in designing culturally competent programs (Isaacs & Benjamin, 1991). Agencies that effectively served ethnic minority groups had promoted access, availability, and acceptance, which led to high utilization of their programs. Their physical environments were welcoming and attractive based on clients' cultures. They created a positive image of the agency and its programs in the community.

At times, agencies must work toward changing negative perceptions of their services or clients to encourage use. Programs that are community based with strong linkages to the community are more likely to have good reputations and greater credibility. Colon (1996) stresses the importance of extending an agency's boundary into the community. They maintain and use informal community resources, leaders, and networks on behalf of their clients. Even physical location, as a freestanding center or clinic in a particular ethnic minority community, is an asset. Agencies that deliver services directly in the community, in settings that are familiar and comfortable, as in the home, the school, church, or community centers, are more easily seen as community resources that increase access. Agency personnel that play active roles in the community, such as members of parent-teacher associations, school or community boards, and agencies that contribute to the community beyond their services by making their rooms or copying machines available for community groups, for instance, create a positive image that also increases access. Participation in community events like health fairs, parent education meetings, and little league games help reinforce the notion that the agency is part of the community.

A number of examples of culturally competent programs have emerged since the late 1990s. They illustrate ways in which diverse client populations can be reached and served when creative approaches and innovative methods are used (Bryant, 2002; Colon, 1998; Delgado, 1998; Delgado & Santiago, 1998; Kung, 2001; Rodriguez-Andrew, 1998).

Policy-Making Level

Cultural competence crosses many levels and must be addressed at the policy-making level, by managers and administrators. Agency policy makers can begin by building a diverse board (Rutledge, 1995). Many nonprofit boards do not reflect the demographic diversity of the community or the clients served. Rarely are diverse boards achieved by chance alone but a deliberate process with planning and leadership can lead to successful identification, selection, and appointment of new members who belong to targeted groups (Daly, 2002).

There are many steps that agency policy makers can take. They can a) examine their organization's mission statement and incorporate cultural competence into it and into its long range planning; b) establish linkages with the community and develop ways for representatives from the community's different cultural populations to make their voices heard and participate in shaping agency policy; c) set standards for multicultural services that incorporate cultural competence; d) insure that workers and managers are representative of their clients' cultures; e) commit resources to training board members and staff on cultural competence; f) require that unbiased research and data collection on minorities be undertaken to guide their decision making; g) see that services are delivered and programs are provided flexibly and creatively to fit the needs of the targeted multicultural client populations and to be truly accessible to minority communities; and, h) support efforts to design programs in collaboration with minority community groups with the intention of eventually turning them over to the community groups to operate on their own (Chernesky, 1997).

Agency Self-Assessment

Agency self-assessments are attracting greater attention as a way to examine how well an organization addresses cultural competency. In some instances, the goal of incorporating standards and measures in a review process is to eventually enable agencies to see whether improved client outcomes result from cultural competency. In the mental health field, the New York State Office of Mental Health is developing a comprehensive set of performance measures to be used as tools for monitoring adherence to principles of cultural competency. Incorporation of cultural competency in mental health systems is based on the assumption that when an individual's culture and values are understood, respected, and reflected in the treatment, the individual will be more responsive to and satisfied with the care provided, and as a result, will demonstrate better clinical outcomes (Siegel et al., 2000). Geron (2002) points out the need for sound measures of cultural competency for tracking, assessing, and evaluating to understand whether efforts to achieve cultural competency are effective. Discussing some of the limitations assessing cultural competency, he notes that the instruments have not yet been tested for validity or reliability and do not really measure whether culturally competent care is actually provided. Dana (1998b) also notes that standards and performance measures can serve as tools for agencies to assess whether they comply with principles and practices of cultural competency, but the absence of standards of adequate care for services to multicultural populations is of concern in many fields.

A number of organizational assessment tools have been developed to help agencies gauge their cultural competency. Also referred to as diversity audits, they do not claim to have been tested for validity or reliability nor to actually measure whether culturally competent care is being provided. Nevertheless, they help agencies understand how much further they may have to go to achieve cultural competency. Moreover, agencies that are engaging in self-assessment are taking an essential step in demonstrating a commitment toward becoming culturally competent.

Dana (1998a) used a checklist that was able to provide baseline information for assessing cultural competence in three agencies in the fields of aging, health, and child welfare. An assessment framework suggested for the aging field directs diversity assessments be made in regard to the agency's mission, governance and administration, personnel practices and staffing patterns, service offerings and caregiving approaches, targeting and outreach, and marketing approaches (Capitman, Hernandez-Gallegos, & Yee, 1991). A framework for assessing cultural competency in health organizations includes interpreter services, appropriate recruitment and retention, training, coordination with traditional healers, use of community health workers, and culturally competent health promotion (Brach & Fraser, 2000). Nash (1999b) offers a tool for child welfare agencies that focuses on the organization's vision, mission and core values, the governing board, leadership, programs, policies, and practices.

Assessing the extent to which workers perceive their inclusion or exclusion in an organization provides a measure of how workers from diverse backgrounds relate to the organization and to their work groups. This measure taps organizational culture, and the fit between the individual and the organization, a critical factor related to job satisfaction and organizational commitment (Mor Barak & Cherin, 1998). Another measure of organizational culture and how individuals from diverse cultural and ethnic groups, as well as women, experience their fit and comfort with their agency assesses how hostile or inhospitable organizational environments may be for workers who are not from the dominant culture (Chernesky, 1998). The Child Welfare League of America (1996) self-assessment tool (Figure 3.1), included in its membership requirements, is intended for agencies to use to determine whether their services are nondiscriminatory, sensitive and respectful of cultural and ethnic diversity, and reflective of the communities they serve.

Achieving cultural competency may require more than changes in staffing, training, and program design, and a willingness to engage in self-assessment. Just as managing for diversity competency seems to require fundamental organizational change, a similar level of change may be essential to effectively provide culturally competent services. Because progress toward cultural competency will involve issues of resources, power, and justice, there are likely to be differences about and conflict around how they are to be

Requirement Number 5

"The agency gives evidence that its services are nondiscriminatory in relation to race, ethnicity, gender, sexual orientation, handicap, and language; its staff, board and services are sensitive to and show respect for the cultural and ethnic diversity of its customers."

Interpretation

The agency reflects the community it serves, through the board, its staff, and its clients. Consideration for the unique ethnic and cultural customs and language of clients and recognition of handicapping conditions should be reflected in agency policy and service delivery in order to help assure quality practice.

5.1 The agency actively recruits, employs, and promotes qualified staff and board members broadly representative of the community it serves and administers its personnel practices without discrimination based upon age, gender race ethnicity, sexual orientation, nationality, handicap, or religion of the individual under consideration.

5.2 The agency makes its services available and accessible to the community and does so in full accord with all applicable legal and regulatory requirements.

5.3 The agency has prepared to meet the needs of clients from the community served who do not speak the primary language used by the agency.

5.4 The agency endeavors to assist hearing impaired, visually impaired, or otherwise physically challenged persons in the agency's defined community.

5.5 The agency's long-range plan and annual operating plans reflect the multicultural nature of the community.

5.6 Cultural responsiveness is an integral part of the agency's programs and is included in the evaluation of agency staff members and administrators.

5.7 Cultural differences are considered in formulating policies and procedures for intake, assessment, disposition, and case management activities.

5.8 The agency addresses cultural responsiveness as part of its inservice training activities.

5.9 The agency addresses cultural responsiveness as part of its board orientation program.

FIGURE 3.1 Child Welfare League of America 1996 Self-Assessment Tool.

Source: Child Welfare League of America (1996). *CWLA agency self-improvement checklist and membership requirements.*

allocated and redistributed. Decisions related to how to best reach and serve culturally diverse client populations will invariably affect the status quo, and those who are benefiting from existing arrangements may lose their advantaged positions (Nybell & Gray, 2004).

ORGANIZATIONAL LEADERSHIP

There is a consensus among those who study and write about managing diversity and cultural competency that the single most essential component for success is strong organizational leadership. Strong leadership communicates the belief that diversity is valued and is beneficial to the agency and everyone in it. As has been noted, "in the absence of explicit leadership, all other efforts may appear hollow" (Capitman et al., 1991, p. 76).

The challenge for organizational leaders is to take "proactive steps to create and sustain an organizational climate in which the potential for diversity-related dynamics to hinder performance is minimized and the potential for diversity to enhance performance is maximized . . . [It] is about improving organizational performance by optimally utilizing every member's abilities and by leveraging diversity as an organizational resource" (Cox & Beale, 1997, pp. 13–14). Nash (1999a) states, "the systemic, long-term valuing of cultural competence in agencies requires a top-down commitment to an ongoing review of organizational culture. This commitment, both professional and organizational, begins with the tone that is set by the leaders of the organization" (p. 4). As noted,

> This commitment must be maintained through sustained changes in many management practices, such as hiring, program design, service evaluation, policy development, and community outreach. Managers have to make a substantial investment in exercising active leadership, energy, time, and organizational resources. The potential gains for engaging in this process, however, are substantial. (Mederos & Woldeguiorguis, 2003, p. 127)

Four aspects of leadership are considered essential: a) creating and sharing a vision, b) establishing an organizational structure to launch and maintain a diversity initiative, c) demonstrating personal commitment and involvement, and d) integrating diversity work with all other agency practices, policies, procedures, and systems to achieve necessary alignment (Cox, 2001).

An essential first step is for organizational leaders to envision how they would like their agency to look if it were diversity and culturally competent. Only by seeing what one is aiming for, engaging in the visioning process with key agency members, and sharing that vision will it be possible to assess how far the agency may have to go to achieve it, and what will have to be done to move in that direction. Strategic planning, with its focus on the organization's internal strengths and weaknesses and its external opportunities and threats, provides one framework for this kind of envisioning. Diversity audits or cultural competence self-assessments are also valuable for management and board members to identify readiness for change, areas to be addressed, and progress made. Ideally, assessment should be ongoing, reflecting a continuous quality improvement approach. Mederos and Woldeguioruis (2003) recommend a number of ways diversity and cultural competency could be managed. The suggestions offered here draw upon their recommendations (Figure 3.2).

CONCLUSION

There is a consensus that managing diverse workforces and multicultural organizations, as well as attaining culturally competent programs and services, are essential. Despite the consensus and estimates about the changing workforce and client populations, there is not much evidence of achieving more inclusive organizations for people of non-dominant cultures. According to any of the key diversity indicators—minority staff, multicultural organizational leaders, women managers, board representation—agencies have a long way to go. Progress seems to be slow toward attaining diversity competent agencies and culturally competent service delivery. It has been suggested that there may be a lack of impetus to change, a denial about the risks of not paying attention to diversity, or even a sense that enough progress has already been made. Ramos (2004) attributes the slow progress to organizational leaders who believe that diversity can and should be achieved

1. Expand upon the agency's core mission to acknowledge the interests and needs of target populations.
2. Establish ongoing collaborative relationships with cultural affinity agencies and community members.
3. Bring in people from target communities as ongoing partners in redesigning services.
4. Modifying existing services to better meet the needs of target populations.
5. Undertake an ongoing personal and managerial self-inventory.
6. Cultivate a nondefensive and searching openness about personal and organizational values.
7. Create a safe and supportive environment for examining personal and institutional privilege.
8. Recognize that work styles and services are not neutral but are value-laden.
9. Redesign work teams and service delivery systems that are deliberately inclusive and diverse.
10. Acknowledge that the agency has historically had oppressive effects on certain populations and take steps to remedy them.
11. Develop systems to monitor under- or overrepresentation of populations and to measure program outcomes.
12. Make developing and maintaining staff diversity a core task and ongoing process.

FIGURE 3.2 What organizational leaders need to do.

Based on Mederos, F., & Woldeguiorguis, I. (2003). Beyond cultural competence: What child protection managers need to know and do. *Child Welfare, LXXXII*(2), 125–142. Reprinted with permission of the author. Copyright 2003 by Child Welfare.

without fundamentally changing the way their organizations function. He claims that leaders only want those with different backgrounds to do basically the same things in the same ways that they have always been done.

Given the increased heterogeneity of the workforce and client populations, organizational leaders will realize that they have to create and sustain organizational cultures and environments that support diversity and cultural competency. Because there is no set way or standard approach to succeed, agency executives have many opportunities to be creative and innovative as they respond to the challenges in managing in a multicultural environment.

REFERENCES

Achieving cultural competence: A guidebook for providers of services to older Americans and their families. (2001, January). Retrieved from http://www.aoa.gov/prof/adddiv/cultural/addiv_cult.asp

Beckett, J. O., & Dungee-Anderson, D. (1996). A framework for agency-based multicultural training and supervision. In Y. Asamoah (Ed.), *Innovations in delivering culturally sensitive social work services: Challenges for practice and education* (pp. 27–48). Binghamton, NY: Haworth Press.

Brach, C., & Fraser, I. (2000). Can cultural competency reduce racial and ethnic disparities? A review and conceptual model. *Medical Care Research and Review*, 57(1), 181–217.

Bryant, A. (2002). 'Reverse integration' at an adult day health center. *Generations*, 26(3), 59–64.

Capitman, J. (2002). Defining diversity: A primer and review. *Generations*, 26(3), 8–14.

Capitman, J. A., Hernandez-Gallegos, W., & Yee, D. L. (1991, Fall/Winter). "Diversity assessments" in aging services. *Generations*, 73–76.

Carr-Ruffino, N. (1999). *Diversity success strategies*. Boston: Butterworth Heinemann.

Chen, C. C., & DiTomaso, N. (1996). Performance appraisal and demographic diversity: Issues regarding appraisals, appraisers, and appraising. In E. E. Kossek & S. A. Lobel (Eds.), *Managing diversity: Human resource strategies for transforming the workplace* (pp. 137–163). Cambridge, MA: Publishers.

Chernesky, R. H. (1997). Managing agencies for multicultural services. In E. Congress (Ed.), *Multicultural perspectives in working with families* (pp. 17–33). New York: Springer Publishing.

Chernesky, R. H. (1998). Advancing women into the managerial ranks. In R. L. Edwards, J. A. Yankey, & M. A. Altpeter (Eds.), *Skills for effective management of nonprofit organizations* (pp. 200–218). Washington, DC: National Association of Social Workers Press.

Chernesky, R. H. (2003). Examining the glass ceiling: Gender influences on promotion decisions. *Administration in Social Work*, 27(2), 13–18.

Child Welfare League of America. (1996). *CWLA agency self-improvement checklist and membership requirements*. Washington, DC: Author.

Clemetson, L. (2003, June 19). Hispanic population is rising swiftly, Census Bureau says. *New York Times*, p. 22.

Colon, E. (1996). Program design and planning strategies in the delivery of culturally competent health and mental health prevention and treatment services to Latino communities. *Journal of Multicultural Social Work*, 4(4), 85–96.

Colon, E. (1998). Alcohol use among Latino males: Implications for the development of culturally competent prevention and treatment strategies. *Alcoholism Treatment Quarterly*, 16(1/2), 147–161.

Cox, T. (1991). The multicultural organization. *Academy of Management Executives*, 5(2), 34–47.

Cox, T. (1994). *Creating diversity in organizations*. San Francisco: Berrett-Koehler Publishers.

Cox, T. (2001). *Creating the multicultural organization.* San Francisco: Jossey-Bass.

Cox, T., & Beale, R. L. (1997). *Developing competency to manage diversity.* San Francisco: Berrett-Koehler Publishers.

Cross, T. L., Barzon, B. J., Dennis, K. W., & Isaacs, M. R. (1989). *Towards a culturally competent system of care.* Washington, DC: Georgetown University Child Development Center.

Daly, J. M. (2002). An action guide for nonprofit board diversity. *Journal of Community Practice, 10*(1), 33–54.

Dana, R. H. (1998a). Cultural competence in three human service agencies. *Psychological Reports, 83,* 107–112.

Dana, R. H. (1998b). Problems with managed mental healthcare for multicultural populations. *Psychological Reports, 83,* 283–294.

Delgado, M. (1998). Alcoholism services and community settings: Latina beauty parlors as case examples. *Alcoholism Treatment Quarterly, 16*(1/2), 71–83.

Delgado, M., & Santiago, J. (1998). HIV/AIDS in a Puerto Rican/Dominican community: A collaborative project with a botanical shop. *Social Work, 43*(2), 183–186.

Egan, T. (1993, October 8). Teaching tolerance in workplaces: A Seattle program illustrates limits. *New York Times,* p. A18.

Fong, L. G. W., & Gibbs, J. T. (1995). Facilitating services to multicultural communities in a dominant culture setting: An organizational perspective. *Administration in Social Work, 19*(2), 1–20.

Ford, J. K., & Fisher, S. (1996). The role of training in a changing workplace and workforce: New perspectives and approaches. In E. E. Kossek & S. A. Lobel (Eds.), *Managing diversity: Human resource strategies for transforming the workplace* (pp. 164–193). Cambridge, MA: Blackwell Business.

Geron, S. M. (2002, Fall). Cultural competency: How is it measured? Does it make a difference. *Generations, 26*(3), 39–45.

Gibelman, M. (2000). The nonprofit sector and gender discrimination: A preliminary investigation into the glass ceiling. *Nonprofit Management and Leadership, 110*(3), 252–269.

Greenhouse, L. (2004, June 15). Rules are set for some harassment cases. *New York Times,* p. A19.

Grieger, I. (1996). A multicultural organizational development checklist for student affairs. *Journal of College Student Development, 37*(5), 561–573.

Guarnaccia, P. J., & Rodriguez, O. (1996). Concepts of culture and their role in the development of culturally competent mental health services. *Hispanic Journal of Behavioral Sciences, 28*(4), 419–433.

Gummer, B. (1998). Current perspectives on diversity in the workforce: How diverse is diverse? *Administration in Social Work, 22*(1), 83–100.

Healy, L. M. (1996). International dimensions of diversity: Issues for the social agency workplace. *Journal of Multicultural Social Work, 4*(4), 96–116.

Hopkins, K. M. (2002). Interactions of gender and race in workers' help seeking for personal/family problems. *Journal of Applied Behavioral Science, 38*(2), 156–176.

Hughes, D., & Dodge, M. (1997). African American women in the workplace: Relationships between job conditions, racial bias at work, and perceived job quality. *American Journal of Community Psychology, 25,* 581–599.

Hyde, C. A. (2003). Multicultural organizational development in nonprofit human service agencies: Views from the field. *Journal of Community Practice, 11*(1), 39–59.

Hyde, C. A. (2004). Multicultural organizational development in human service agencies: Challenges and solutions. *Social Work, 49*(1), 7–16.

Iglehart, A. P. (2000). Managing for diversity and empowerment in social services. In R. J. Patti (Ed.), *The handbook of social welfare management* (pp. 425–443). Thousand Oaks, CA: Sage.

Isaacs, M. R., & Benjamin, M. P. (1991). *Towards a culturally competent system of care*. Washington, DC: Georgetown University.

Johnson, J. E., & Smith, N. H. (2002). Health and social issues associated with racial, ethnic, and cultural disparities. *Generations, 26*(3), 25–32.

Johnston, W. B., & Packer, A. H. (1987). *Workforce 2000: Work and workers for the 21st century*. Indianapolis, IN: Hudson Institute.

Kaufman, L. (2003, December 12). City hall plans to support translations in all tongues. *New York Times*, p. B3.

Kinetz, E. (2004, February 8). Broken promises. *New York Times*, p. 4.

Kossek, E. E., & Lobel, S. A. (Eds.). (1996). *Managing diversity: Human resource strategies for transforming the workplace*. Cambridge, MA: Blackwell Business.

Kram, K. E., & Hall, D. T. (1996). Mentoring in a context of diversity and turbulence. In E. E. Kossek & S. A. Lobel (Eds.), *Managing diversity: Human resource strategies for transforming the workplace* (pp. 108–136). Cambridge, MA: Blackwell Business.

Kung, W. W. (2001). Consideration of cultural factors in working with Chinese American families with a mentally ill patient. *Families in Society, 82*(1), 97–107.

Lobel, A. A., & Kossek, E. E. (1996). Human resource strategies to support diversity in work and personal lifestyles: Beyond the "family friendly" organization. In E. E. Kossek & S. A. Lobel (Eds.), *Managing diversity: Human resource strategies for transforming the workplace* (pp. 221–244). Cambridge, MA: Blackwell Business.

Marcus, E. N. (2003, April 8). When a patient is lost in the translation. *New York Times*, p. F7.

Mederos, F., & Woldeguiorguis, I. (2003). Beyond cultural competence: What child protection managers need to know and do. *Child Welfare, LXXXII*(2), 125–142.

Mor Barak, M. E., & Cherin, D. A. (1998). A tool to expand organizational understanding of workforce diversity: Exploring a measure of inclusion-exclusion. *Administration in Social Work, 22*(1), 47–64.

Mor Barak, M. E., Cherin, D. A., & Berkman, S. (1998). Organizational and personal dimensions in diversity climate. *Journal of Applied Behavioral Science, 34*, 82–104.

Murray, K. (1993, August 1). The unfortunate side effects of "diversity training." *New York Times*, p. 5.

Nash, K. N. (Ed.). (1999a). *Cultural competence: A guide for human service agencies*. Washington, DC: Child Welfare League of America.

Nash, K. N. (1999b). How does an agency evaluate itself? In K. N. Nash (Ed.), *Cultural competence: A guide for human service agencies* (pp. 15–25). Washington, DC: Child Welfare League of America.

Nybell, L. M., & Gray, S. S. (2004). Race, place, space: Meanings of cultural competence in three child welfare agencies. *Social Work*, *49*(1), 17–26.

O'Neill, J. V. (2003, June). Services in Spanish unavailable to many. *NASW News*, p. 4.

Ramos, H. A. J. (2004). Nonprofit diversity: An asset we can no longer afford to ignore. *Nonprofit Quarterly*, *11*(1), 34–39.

Roberts, D. (2001). *Shattered bonds: The color of child welfare*. New York: Basic Books.

Rodriguez-Andrew, S. (1998). Alcohol use and abuse among Latinos: Issues and examples of culturally competent services. *Alcoholism Treatment Quarterly*, *16* (1/2), 55–70.

Rogers, G. (1995). Educating case managers for culturally competent practice. *Journal of Case Management*, *34*(2), 60–65.

Rutledge, J. M. (1995). *Building board diversity*. Washington, DC: National Center for Nonprofit Boards.

Schwam-Harris, M. (2004). *Diversity training in organizations: A social work perspective*. Unpublished manuscript, University at Buffalo, SUNY.

Siegel, C., Davis-Chambers, E., Haugland, G., Bank, R., Aponte, C., & McCombs, H. (2000). Performance measures of cultural competency in mental health organizations. *Administration and Policy in Mental Health*, *28*(2), 91–106.

Stevenson, K. M., Cheung, K. M., & Leung, P. (1992). A new approach to training child protective services workers for ethnically sensitive practice. *Child Welfare*, *LXXI*(4), 291–305.

Thompson, D. E., & Gooler, L. E. (1996). Capitalizing on the benefits of diversity through workteams. In E. E. Kossek & S. A. Lobel (Eds.), *Managing diversity: Human resource strategies for transforming the workplace* (pp. 392–437). Cambridge, MA: Blackwell Business.

Tsui, A. S., & Gutek, B. A. (1999). *Demographic differences in organizations*. New York: Lexington Books.

Zayas, L. H., Evans, M. E., Mejia, L., & Rodriguez, O. (1997). Cultural-competency training for staff serving Hispanic families with a child in psychiatric crisis. *Families in Society*, *78*(4), 405–412.

Section Two

Culturally Diverse Families Across the Life Cycle

CHAPTER 4

The Multicultural Triangle of the Child, the Family, and the School: Culturally Competent Approaches

Carmen Ortiz Hendricks

S
ocial work in urban public schools is one arena of multicultural social work practice in which knowledge of a client group's culture and status in society is central to service delivery. With rapidly increasing racial and ethnic diversity in cities throughout the United States, there is an urgent need to increase the numbers of bilingual, bicultural, and culturally competent school social workers, and to decrease the cultural dissonance often found between mainstream school systems and the communities they serve. This chapter looks at the complex interplay of cultures present when families and children of diverse cultural backgrounds interact with public school professionals, each representing different values, beliefs, and historical experiences, a factor frequently overlooked in the process of assessing and helping children with their learning needs. Freire (1998) considers teachers to be "cultural workers" and exhorts them to think " . . . about the learners' cultural identity and about the respect that we owe it in our educational practices" (p. 71). The same can be said of school social

workers who are required to be culturally competent practitioners and "cultural mediators" (De Anda, 1984), since they are the primary school professionals who work with children while simultaneously mediating the environmental dynamics of the family and the school. The culturally competent school social worker knows her personal and professional cultural identities and values, and is in the best position to function as interpreter of the language, experiences, and beliefs of diverse families, children, and the schools they attend.

Culturally competent practitioners recognize the importance of cultural identity and beliefs in interpersonal relationships and social interactions, especially within institutional arrangements like a school system. The school setting has a major impact on the lives of children and families. Public schools have traditionally been held responsible for transmitting the dominant, mainstream U.S. cultural values and beliefs, and promoting acculturation and assimilation to that culture. Schools have the power to strongly influence children, especially when the child's cultural background is different from the mainstream culture of society or the school. These differences may be the result of recent immigration to the U.S. or bicultural/bilingual life experiences. Schools also exert enormous power over families that have limited understanding of the school system as a whole, or families that have to deal with underfunded, overcrowded inner-city schools. These families may already feel powerless and alienated within their communities. Freire's renowned *Pedagogy of the Oppressed* (1993) urges educators and schools to be a liberating and enlightening force in the lives of children, families, and communities rather than perpetuating the oppressive broader environmental conditions.

THE MULTICULTURAL TRIANGLE

A multicultural triangle (see Figure 4.1) invariably forms when the child, the family, and the school conflict over measures of a child's ability, intelligence, or educability (Compher, 1982; Constable & Walberg, 1988). Each feels the tensions of differing cultural values and objectives, and each encompasses a culture that needs to be understood and negotiated in order to promote positive learning experiences for children (Aponte, 1976). To begin with, there may

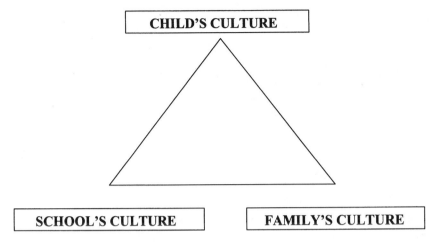

FIGURE 4.1   The child/family/school triangle.

exist radically different cultural assumptions and expectations by the family and the school regarding the following questions:

How does a particular cultural group view children?

What is it like to be a child of a particular cultural group?

How does it feel to not belong to the "dominant" mainstream cultural group?

What is it like to grow up feeling different or "less than"?

What is the particular culture of the school?

What value is placed on the parents' role in educating children?

How do different cultural groups measure intelligence?

What value do different cultural groups place on education?

How do professionals define "normalcy" or a normal range of development?

How are different behavioral norms understood and applied?

In what context are learning needs and problems defined?

How culture-bound are the labels and definitions of educability?

These questions also point to the interrelationship between a child's school performance, the family's identity, and the school's

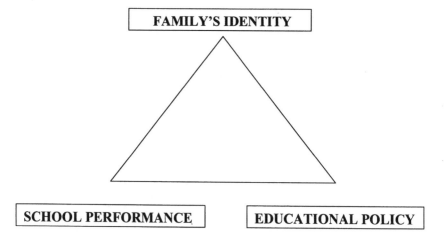

FIGURE 4.2   The identity, performance, and policy triangle.

policies and practices. Asian families value education of their children. The children's educational performance is considered to be a family matter, and it is given prominence and recognition in the Asian community (Appleby, Colon, & Hamilton, 2001, p. 139).

From a systemic point of view, what affects one part of the system has a reverberating impact on other parts of the system. Therefore, assessment of a child's school performance cannot be separate from assessment of a family's self-identity or evaluation of a school's educational policies and practices (Dowling & Osborne, 1985). The problems or positions of one by necessity affect the other. This triangle, like most triangles in family systems theory, provides many convenient issues to focus upon while avoiding the fundamental cross-cultural conflicts at hand. For example, school programs like Head Start and other early childhood intervention programs frequently expect or mandate parental participation in a child's educational plan, but these expectations are not enough to ensure parental participation. School professionals tend to focus attention on a child's educational needs while ignoring the important aspects of the parent/school relationship (Correa, 1989). Parent/professional interactions are sometimes so structured as to render parents effectively powerless as partners in their children's educational careers. Culturally competent approaches can build shared understanding and shared responsibilities between parents and school professionals. When parents are genuinely invited and properly utilized, they are an invaluable resource and highly effective collaborators in the educational process (Aponte, 1976; Chavkin & Garza-Lubeck, 1990; Correa, 1989). Parents are in the best position to assist educators and social workers in decision making while protecting and advocating for their children.

Overburdened parents may be limited in the time available to attend school conferences, or their lack of understanding may get misinterpreted as resistance or lack of interest (Delgado & Rivera, 1997; Delgado-Gaitan, 1987). Limited English proficiency combined with the lack of bilingual, bicultural, and culturally competent school personnel also limit parental participation. Language usage and professional jargon further alienate parents from participating in their child's educational plans. There are many different interpretations for such terms as *bilingual education, special education, learning disability, speech or developmental delays, attention deficit disorder, hyperactivity*, and *special needs children*. These technical terms have been socially constructed in the U.S. and are loaded with different meanings and interpretations. They also do not always translate accurately for parents (Bennett, 1988). School professionals freely use these diagnostic categories or labels that are based on mainstream, middle-class, Western standards of measurement for evaluating intelligence. In the U.S., these terms are used uniformly across a range of cultural and social class groups with little appreciation for the different life experiences that contribute to or could assist with educational difficulties.

A perfect example is the use of the term *disability*, that inevitably suggests a deficit within the individual, "a lack of adequate power, strength, or physical or mental ability; incapacity: a physical or mental handicap, esp. one that prevents a person from living a full, normal life or from holding a gainful job; and anything that disables or puts one at a disadvantage" (*Random House Webster's Unabridged Dictionary*, 2001, p. 560). Most parents will resist such categorizations of their child, and will seek to protect the child's identity from labels that appear to stigmatize the entire child rather than describe a particular difficulty in some aspect of the child's learning capacity. In *The Learning Differences Sourcebook* (1998) the authors list a range of learning difficulties including Speech and Language Disorders, Attention Deficit/Hyperactivity Disorders,

Obsessive Compulsive Disorders, Tourette Syndrome, Oppositional Defiant or Conduct Disorders, Autism, Mental Retardation and Developmental Delays, Visual or Hearing Impairments, and Environmentally Induced Impairments such as those resulting from lead poisoning or fetal alcohol syndrome. When a parent denies a diagnosis or categorization, it should not be automatically assumed that the educational assessment is correct and the parent is misguided or resistant to recognizing that the child is suffering from a mild to serious learning problem (Dowling & Osborne, 1985; Golden & Cupuzzi, 1986). Rather, parents should be asked to provide their own explanation for their child's learning difficulties. School personnel may learn some valuable information to assist them and the parents in addressing the child's needs (Bennett, 1988; Harry, 1992b; Kalyanpur & Rao, 1991). The parent's point of view may be a more accurate representation of the child's needs as well as the parent's experience of the world. For example, parents of color can see with their own eyes the disproportionate placement of children of color in special education classes. This supports the parental perception of the arbitrary nature of such designations as learning disabled, and promotes the view that special education programs are discriminatory or oppressive (Dao, 1991; Delgado-Gaitan, 1987; Kalyanpur & Rao, 1991).

Culturally competent school social workers are aware that placement in special education programs may reflect the school's culture or social values more than objective reality, especially when it relates to the underachievement of children of color from inner-city neighborhoods (Kurtz & Barth, 1989). Problems in school performance have a range of meanings to parents, children, and teachers alike. A few examples can help underscore these issues:

> Eight-year-old Maria came home sobbing that her teacher does not like her anymore and is sending her to another classroom. The mother, with her 15-year-old son as interpreter went to the school to explain to the teacher that Maria is a good girl, she works hard at her homework, and she can read and speak both English and Spanish quite well. The teacher tried to explain the learning disability that had been diagnosed in Maria, but to this Dominican mother a disability is some kind of severe incapacity like being blind or paralyzed. Her daughter is not incapacitated like that, so she continued to resist the change to a special classroom.

Elementary school teachers were frustrated with an Asian mother whose child was severely delayed in speech and language development, but she steadfastly refused all efforts to move her child to a remedial educational placement outside the immediate neighborhood. The school social worker learned that this mother had lost four children in a devastating flood that destroyed her village in Bangladesh a few years earlier. Losing a child, even to a nearby school, was too stressful for this mother, and other arrangements had to be made to meet the child's needs.

A mother, raised and educated in Jamaica, was finally able to bring her 8-year-old son to live with her in the U.S. Before leaving Jamaica, she consulted the village wise man who told her that her son would experience many difficulties during his first year in the U.S. She was convinced that when the year ended, her son's health problems and learning difficulties would cease as well.

These examples demonstrate the kinds of multicultural misunderstandings that can arise when there are different definitions of the problem at hand (Lynch & Stein, 1987). Parents may be interpreting or naming the child's difficulties in their own way, and are trying to help their child by reframing the issues in words that are more compatible with their cultural values and beliefs, and less harmful to the child's self-image (Greene, Jenson, & Jones, 1996; Harry, 1992a; McAdoo & McAdoo, 1985). These redefinitions and clarifications need to be respected no matter how strange they may seem to school officials. Parents use any number of phrases or personal narratives to explain to school professionals how they view a child's learning difficulties:

"He's just the way my brother was at this age."

"She'll grow out of it, the way I did."

"His father was just like him."

"She is much smarter than she lets on to the teachers."

"My child knows to not boast about his abilities."

"She just needs time to catch on."

These perceptions should be utilized in the child's individual educational assessment and plan and included when discussing such things as genetic predisposition, developmental or maturational factors, different historical evolutions, medical and psychological progress, and individual or family strengths. The focus is on strengths of parents' perceptions rather than on the pathology or deficits perspectives of school professionals.

Bicultural and bilingual children who hear conflicting comments about their cognitive-behavioral abilities from their parents and teachers are frequently torn between the demands of two cultures—the culture of home and the culture of school (Freeman & Pennekamp, 1988). As bicultural/bilingual children, they struggle daily to live up to teacher expectations, to learn new ways of solving problems and relating to others (Bennett, 1988; Lynch & Stein, 1987), to deal with peer demands for mainstream behavioral responses, and to remain true to family admonitions to put their culture of origin first regardless of what they experience around them. These children need "culture brokers" (Ortiz Hendricks, Haffey, & Asamoah, 1988), persons who can teach them how to negotiate conflicts and facilitate resolution of multicultural dilemmas and opportunities. When the child is biracial, they are forced to deal with the additional task of choosing one racial identity over another, an enormously stressful and difficult experience for children and youth faced with multiple developmental tasks.

When school professionals and parents use different culturally based and culturally biased criteria for describing a child's behavior, it is the child who gets caught between their respective interpretations (Ryan & Smith, 1989). "For the most part, school curricula are designed to have each student achieve certain academic milestones along a predetermined timetable . . . The problem? Not every child is on this developmental schedule" (Boyles & Contadino, 1998, p. 1). The same authors describe a number of biases in instruments that are used to assess intelligence such as "value bias," which involves designing tests so that answers reflect the responses acceptable to the dominant culture, and "linguistic bias," which means assessment of a child's knowledge of a particular language like English rather than assessment of their general language development. Before resorting to biased criteria to evaluate a child's difficulties in school, school professionals would do well to pay careful attention to the parents' criteria for normalcy and intellectual ability which holds special meaning for the families they serve. There are different cultural meanings to what school professionals may believe are uniform and universally accepted definitions of intelligence, competence, and disability (Dao, 1991; Kalyanpur & Rao, 1991). Many parents are incredulous when they are first told that their child is learning disabled or suffers from a more severe neurological impairment (Bennett, 1988). They see a healthy body, a child that can use common sense, a child who has achieved elementary academic skills in two languages, a child who has already exceeded a parent's educational attainments (Ryan & Smith, 1989). These accomplishments clearly deny a diagnosis that is designed for someone whose competence is impaired or who is mentally deficient. Parents cannot view their child as anything but intellectually superior when a 7-year-old's homework is harder than anything the parents have experienced in their own education (Spener, 1988). From a strengths perspective, by working with the definitions offered by parents, school professionals can reinforce the fact that the child is not severely incapacitated. This positions the school to motivate children and parents to address learning needs in a more empowering manner.

When examining a child's difficulties in school, educational experts point to several important themes that emerge as children and parents struggle to understand why a child is having trouble. Family identity, school performance, and educational policies are culturally bound and culturally interwoven aspects of school social work services (Harry, 1992a, 1992b). Together, these factors contribute to narrow definitions of a child's difficulties and rigid triangulations of communication among all parties concerned.

FAMILY IDENTITY

Family identity is very important when interpreting a child's developmental patterns or learning needs. The Coleman Report of 1966, a national study, reported that family background influenced an individual's school achievement more than any other factor (Andersen & Collins, 1998). Wherever there is a strong cultural value placed on the family as a whole, there is an equally strong value placed on the family's identity as a group rather than as a collection of individuals. Problems are viewed as family problems rather than issues solely of the individual. The family feels a collective shame when school professionals inadvertently or intentionally give the impression that the child's learning difficulties result from some deficit in the home or other family problem. Parents may associate the child's difficulties as tied to some family trait or characteristic or even to some past wrongdoing by a relative. On the other hand, a strong family identity diffuses stigma on a child who is having school problems. While a strong family identity engenders vulnerability in the whole family, it also serves to protect the child's identity. The child is not different because he or she is just like everyone else in the family. Lynch and Stein (1987) found that Latino and African American children were described in terms of family traits and were often not considered to be outside the family's normal range of behavior. Culturally competent practitioners recognize that family group identity has to be taken into consideration when addressing a child's learning needs. For example, a child who is withdrawn or hyperactive may be demonstrating behavior that is viewed as culturally syntonic to the family. The family may see the quiet or overactive child as exhibiting some inherited aspect of family behavior, or a part of the family's preferred mode of behavior. In other words, the child has always been this way, and it is an inherited characteristic from her grandfather or aunt. The family has always accommodated the child, and will continue to help the child deal with this behavior. They do not view the behavior as a problem or symptomatic of any other condition. Culturally competent practitioners need to build on the strength of family identity while securing remedial services for the child.

SCHOOL PERFORMANCE

When looking at the school performance of diverse children, especially immigrant and refugee children, an appreciation of the advantages and disadvantages of second language acquisition in a child's education are essential. Children can experience problems simply from the confusion associated with changing from one language at home to another language in school (Cummins, 1984; Spener, 1988). It is the school that generally assesses whether a child enters into regular English-speaking classes with a bilingual aide or if they need English as a second language (ESL) classes, or a comprehensive bilingual education program. The point of immigration in the child's life cycle has a great deal to do with how a child adjusts to English and American schools. Parents may feel that their children were doing well academically in their country of origin schools, and see their children's problems now as emerging from the high demands or tough expectations of teachers. They may even feel like their children are being singled out because of their limited English proficiency (LEP) and not other learning difficulties. Some parents are so proud of their children's ability to speak and read English that they see American teachers as overly critical of accents or mispronunciations, or expecting their children to speak English perfectly (Correa, 1989).

Parents are further confused by such terms as ESL, LEP, and IEP (Individualized Educational Plan), and special programs like bilingual education, special education, and resource rooms, and they have many misconceptions about these terms or programs. The battles fought over bilingual education had parents believing that these programs held children back rather than helped them learn better. In truth, bilingual education is ill-defined in practice and inconsistently implemented. "Critics complain that it [bilingual education] produces low-scoring students with poor English language skills. Supporters counter that . . . ultimately language minority children who learn to read and write in their native tongue will be more cognitively developed than language minority children who learn to read and write in English" (Ravitch & Viteritti, 2000, p. 187). There is limited research to support either point of view. Historically, bilingual education has focused on Hispanic children whereas Asian students have been allowed to learn primarily in English. These distinctions need to be thoroughly researched in a culturally sensitive way in order to determine what is in the best interest of bilingual/bicultural students. Many immigrant parents are adamant that their children learn English even if the parents themselves are resistant to learning the new language (Dao, 1991; Spener, 1988). These same parents are concerned that their children maintain their language of origin and not forget it. To lose the ability to speak the language of origin or native tongue frequently means losing the ability to speak to relatives and friends back home. These factors put enormous pressure on children to be bilingual at all costs. At the same time, the broader social environment in the U.S. today, with growing support for English-only laws and anti-immigrant sentiment, communicates a less than welcome environment for immigrants, migrants, and refugees.

Young children often have to struggle alone with the demands of their parents and families, the school, and the broader society. Cultural sensitivity is necessary to helping children succeed in their school performance and to navigate their bilingual and bicultural identities.

EDUCATIONAL POLICIES AND PRACTICES

The school's culture extends to things like how curricula are delivered, how reading and math are taught, and how children are evaluated. Parents frequently complain about how unstimulating curricula can be, how inflexible teaching methods can be, and how frequently a child's classrooms, programs, teachers, and even schools are changed due to some new evaluation of a child's learning needs (Sarason, 1982). Mainstream as well as immigrant parents are not always able to assert their parental authority, and they are reluctant to refuse to go along with educational practices recommended by school professionals. Parents and children get confused and frustrated when educational changes occur without their approval or understanding or without any credence given to their position or interpretation. Some parents fight back, but they are not always successful. A perfect example of this was discussed in a *New York Times* article entitled, "City Retools Special Education, But Pupils Are Slipping Through Cracks":

> Under special education law, when children do not get services, parents can request a hearing . . . Siow Wei Chu and her husband, Harry Sze, Chinese immigrants, asked that their daughter Jane be given a bilingual aide in her second-grade class at P.S. 203 in Queens, along with daily academic support. The City agreed that Jane should have a bilingual aide, but wanted to move her to another school: one that used a teaching model with a mix of 25 special ed and general ed students, and two teachers . . . At one point, the parents' lawyer asked a teacher if the family's request to keep Jane in P.S. 203, where she had been since kindergarten, was a better plan than the city proposal to more her. "Of course," said the teacher . . . Immediately before the [second] hearing, the city agreed to give the parents exactly what they had requested. Their victory was bittersweet. Instead of getting the bilingual aide at the I.E.P.

meeting on October 7, 2003, Jane would get one in September—one school year later. (*New York Times*, July 4, 2004, p. 26)

This example demonstrates that even when parents are able to advocate for their children, inefficient and ineffective school policies and overburdened and underfunded schools are a barrier to achieving educational goals. Some parents who have struggled with public schooling in the U.S. are determined that the only way to secure adequate education for their children is to avoid school policies that hinder and obstruct this objective. They try to outsmart the educational system by falsifying or losing their child's records from the country of origin in their eagerness to have their child seen as possessing normal intelligence and placed in regular, age-appropriate grades. When parents and schools are caught up in family identity issues and school policies, the child's school performance suffers.

CULTURALLY COMPETENT SCHOOL SOCIAL WORKERS

Achieving cultural competence is an ongoing, lifelong process for all social workers, and no one is born culturally competent. "Cultural competence does not come naturally to any social worker and requires a high level of professionalism and sophistication, yet how culturally competent practitioners are trained is not clear in professional education or practice" (Ortiz Hendricks, 2003, p. 75). More bilingual, bicultural, and culturally competent professionals are needed to meet the needs of fast growing, diverse client populations, and to help ensure unbiased and culturally sensitive assessments for educational, familial, and social services. Cultural competence is a fundamental necessity for school social workers, who must mediate between the client's culture and the agency's culture while increasing their sensitivity and knowledge of the values, practices, customs, and beliefs of each culture and simultaneously appreciating their own personal and professional values and beliefs.

Culturally competent school social workers need to be culturally aware, culturally sensitive, and culturally knowledgeable practitioners who are open to new ways of defining and evaluating

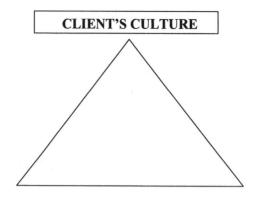

FIGURE 4.3   The cultural triangle of client/school/worker.

children and their learning needs. They do this over time and in several ways. First, they can begin by recognizing that there are many important ways in which the meanings of terms such as *learning* and *learning disabled* differ among cultural groups, and they need to examine these meanings and their significance to the parents and communities they serve. Second, they should examine the parameters of what is *normal* in child development and integrate much broader explanations of normalcy than those utilized by educational institutions. Third, they can best help parents by listening carefully to their theories about their children's difficulties, and from a constructivist approach work with parents to bridge the fine distinctions between learning difficulties and measurements of emotional and mental stability. Lastly, culturally competent school social workers have a role in advocating for alternative school policies and practices that welcome parents' participation in the educational plans for their children, and that are culturally sensitive and friendly to diverse populations. Cummins (1984) would support this holistic approach that incorporates the cultural, linguistic, and community needs of populations served, and calls for a collaborative versus an exclusionary approach to working with parents. "Children's seeming unpreparedness for mainstream schooling is only a measure of the rigidity and ignorance of our school system which creates handicap out of social and cultural difference" (p. 70).

A major contribution by school social workers involves sharing their assessment of the social and cultural needs of children and families with other school professionals. These assessments include comprehensive data and evaluation about

(1) family structures and functions,
(2) generations and length of stay in the U.S.,
(3) trauma experienced in the country of origin and in the process of immigration itself,
(4) socioeconomic conditions of the family in the country of origin and in the U.S.,
(5) educational history of all family members,
(6) racial identity, and
(7) language proficiency among all family members.

In addition, social workers should pay attention to parents' attitudes toward education. They initially may be filled with great hope and faith in the educational system in the U.S., and gradually become disillusioned, with a negative attitude developing toward education in general. Understanding these patterns can help school professionals intervene to prevent or explain the frustration parents encounter in meeting the educational needs of their children.

Lynch and Hanson (1992) propose a specific methodology for competent cross-cultural practice that includes appreciating the impact of cultural assumptions on the intervention process, enhancing cultural self-awareness, understanding the factors that contribute to cultural identification and acculturation, gathering information on other cultures, and guidelines for using interpreters or translators. It is equally important to understand how a particular culture views the helping relationship, how cultural traditions affect problem solving, and "what specific intervention skills and ways of thinking work more effectively with particular groups than those based primarily on the Euro-American frame of reference" (Dungee-Anderson & Beckett, 1995, p. 460).

Furthermore, social workers need to engage in an ongoing self-evaluation of their own cultural backgrounds and values (Lum, 1999; Pinderhughes, 1989; Aponte, 1991). This ensures their ability to listen to and hear different cultural perspectives and not just the prerogatives of their own cultural heritage or of the social work profession that is in and of itself a cultural point of view. A broad definition of cultural self-awareness includes an appreciation of the following factors:

- Personal values, beliefs, attitudes, biases, prejudices, knowledge paradigms, and how these may differ from other worldviews or values orientations.

- Differences within broad categories of diversity and differences between these groups; for example, Hispanic/Latino encompasses 19 or more different nationalities, social classes, histories, immigration experiences, and geographic locations.

- Definitions of diversity that include race, skin color, ethnicity, gender, gender expression, sexual orientation, religious and spiritual beliefs, social class and status, age, abilities, language, national origin, political beliefs, and geographic and regional locations which interact and combine in complex and significant ways. The challenge for social workers is to be cognizant of individual features of diversity while understanding the multifaceted and intersecting nature of these factors.

- Power, privilege, and oppression and how these impact on people, and define who they are, especially as members of oppressed or dominant groups.

- The impact of trauma, colonialism, dominance, and exploitation on human development and mental health.

- Identity development issues, including stages of racial identity formation (Helms, 1990), and stages of "coming out" and the formation of sexual orientation identity and gender expression.

- Multiple status integration and intersecting identity issues (e.g., a biracial adolescent struggling to solidify their identity).

- Cultural competence in all aspects of practice including work with individuals, families, groups, and communities; clinical work, research, administration, program development, policy analysis and advocacy, and community organizing.

- Culture as part of personality development and mental health and not just an economic, social, or political variable.

- The impact of bias and discrimination, especially racism, ethnocentrism, sexism, ableism, and heterosexism on the beneficiaries and survivors of these unequal power relationships.

The development of culturally competent knowledge, skills, and values is critical for social workers particularly given certain social, political, economic, and professional realities operating today. Among these realities are changing population demographics, and data on the continuing underutilization of mental health services by clients of color. The social work profession has also advanced cultural competence through its recent accreditation and ethical standards on diversity (National Association of Social Workers [NASW], 1999). NASW has developed *Standards for Cultural Competence in Social Work Practice* (2000) that was endorsed by the Council on Social Work Education in 2003. The ten standards discuss cultural competence from the following perspectives: Standard 1 refers to social workers' ethical obligation to be culturally competent practitioners as stated in the NASW Code of Ethics (Standard 1.05); Standard 2 refers to the well documented belief that self-awareness is the hallmark of culturally competent social work practice; Standard 3 speaks to the specialized knowledge that all social workers need to have and continue to develop in order to understand the history, traditions, values, family systems, and artistic expressions of major client groups served; Standard 4 addresses the need to use appropriate methodological approaches, skills, and techniques with clients that reflect an understanding of the role of culture in the helping process; Standard 5 encourages social workers to be knowledgeable about and skillful in the use of services available in the community and broader society in order to make appropriate referrals for diverse client populations; Standard 6 charges social workers with the responsibility to advocate for and empower clients, and to be knowledgeable about the effects of social policies and programs on different client populations; Standard 7 requires social workers to recruit and hire diverse workers in programs and agencies to insure diversity within the profession; Standard 8 holds undergraduate, graduate, and doctoral social work programs responsible for the education and training of culturally competent practitioners; Standard 9 speaks to the importance of possessing language diversity in work with monolingual or multilingual client populations; and Standard 10 promotes the social worker's leadership role in promoting cultural competence both within and outside the profession.

Defining cultural competence in social work practice is an enormously complex task, especially when the definitions proposed reinforce a broader and more inclusive attitude about diversity in the U.S. Diversity is creating many new tensions in North American societies where it is often experienced as a threat rather than as an opportunity to open up dialogue on intergroup conflicts, and enhance intergroup relationships. Greene (1994) speaks of *cross-cultural* and *culturally diverse* as "umbrella terms for the diversity of human experience that is rooted in ethnic, national, or religious identity, race, gender, and social class membership" (p. xii). Along similar lines, the author proposes the following definition of culturally competent social work practice for consideration:

> Culturally competent social work practice (CCSWP) encompasses a range of professional knowledge, skills and values that address the complex cultures emerging in a society from the interplay of power, privilege and oppression associated with race and ethnicity, gender and sexual orientation, religious and spiritual beliefs, social class and status, and age and abilities.

This definition recognizes that all people have a cultural group identity, and that many types and forms of group membership in society take on varying significance depending on the societal context. A societal context in which difference is not merely "different from" but is associated with "better or less than," is a society in which differences are not viewed as the norm for human behavior but rather differences are viewed as deviant or deficit. Power and privilege are then used to minimize these differences or oppress characteristics that are simply a part of human diversity. Whoever has power or is in a dominant position contributes to the oppression of those not considered within the mainstream of society (e.g., immigrant women), or those that are part of the mainstream society (e.g., White women), or those who are relegated to inferior status (e.g., lesbian women).

Culturally competent social work practice involves a dynamic, interactive assessment of a client's particular lifestyle which moves from universal categories of cultures (Latino, African American, Asian, Jewish American, Irish-Catholic, etc.) to more specific, individualized, and complex categories of cultures within cultures (Fong & Furuto, 2001; Lum, 1999). Gould (1995) proposes that a multicultural framework refutes the basic assumption that cultural identity has to be unidimensional or that becoming more of something automatically means becoming less of the original. "A multicultural framework goes beyond encouraging intercultural learning and multicultural competency to building a multicultural identity for all groups" (Gould, 1995, pp. 202–203). A specific situation can help to clarify exactly what is entailed in such a multicultural framework.

> A Puerto Rican social worker is assigned to work with a family from the Dominican Republic. Each can be viewed from very broad class, racial, ethnic, or gender categorizations, but these distinctions do not do justice to the multifaceted cultures each uniquely encompasses. The social worker is a 42-year-old Latina social worker who was born in Puerto Rico and raised in New York City. She considers herself a White, middle class, Hispanic American professional. The Velasquez family is composed of a 27-year-old woman who is a laboratory technician and a 28-year-old man who works in his cousin's food market. They are married and have two children, ages 7 and 5. The family has recently re-migrated for the third time to New York City from the Dominican Republic for a variety of family reasons. A referral is made because of suspected incidents of family violence, excessive school absences, and a recently diagnosed learning disability for the 7-year-old child. The case is automatically referred to the only Latina social worker in the school because of ethnic and linguistic commonalities.

A multicultural framework can help this social worker appreciate the similarities and differences between her and the Velasquez family. As Hispanics, they share experiences of oppression both within and outside their countries of origin. Yet each has distinct experiences as Dominicans and Puerto Ricans in the U.S., including different historical and social evolutions, English and Spanish language proficiencies, skin colors, immigration patterns, and citizenship status. The social worker can best help this Dominican family and others like them by recognizing the oppression experienced by immigrant Latinos who deal with the stress of immigration, resettlement, and family reorganization in addition to economic hardships and discrimination in the U.S. Together, the social worker and clients will engage in a multicultural encounter in which understanding each other's unique experiences will be integral to the work they do confronting an inner-city public school system (Falicov, 1995).

CONCLUSIONS

As cultural diversity increases in the U.S., school social workers are on the frontlines of empowering children and families to deal effectively with a public school system that has the power to influence the lives of children and families in positive and negative ways. The development of bilingual, bicultural, and culturally competent social workers is critical to a positive interaction and healthy relationship between the child, family, and school systems, especially when a child demonstrates some form of learning difficulty. Culturally competent social workers play a central role in appreciating and dealing with the power, powerlessness, and unequal power relationships that are inherent in these systems. All school professionals need to recognize that enhancing the parents' power to understand and attend to their children's educational needs is in the best interests of children served. "True empowerment benefits both the client system and the practitioner in that client and worker experience a sense of each other's freedom and individuality which includes a real appreciation of each other's differences and similarities" (Pinderhughes, 1989, p. 240). Empowering diverse families will result in vast numbers of children experiencing more satisfying and productive relationships with the educational system, and will help them reconcile the various cultural challenges presented by the home, the community, and the school. This is difficult work but extremely rewarding as school professionals, children, and families help each other to live in a multiculturally diverse society.

REFERENCES

Andersen, M. L., & Collins, P. H. (Eds.). (1998). *Race, class, and gender: An anthology.* Boston, MA: Wadsworth.

Aponte, H. J. (1991). Training on the person of the therapist for work with the poor and minorities. *Journal of Independent Social Work, 5*(3/4), 23–39.

Aponte, H. J. (1976). The family-school interview: An ecostructural approach. *Family Process, 15*(3), 303–312.

Appleby, G. A., Colon, E., & Hamilton, J. (2001). *Diversity, oppression, and social functioning: Person-in-environment assessment and intervention.* Boston: Allyn & Bacon.

Bennett, A. T. (1988). Gateways to powerlessness: Incorporating Hispanic deaf children and families into formal schooling. *Disability, Handicap and Society, 32,* 119–151.

Boyles, N. S., & Contadino, D. (1998). *The learning differences sourcebook*. Los Angeles, CA: Lowell House.

Chavkin, N. F., & Garza-Lubeck, M. (1990). Multicultural approaches to parent involvement: Research and practice. *Social Work in Education, 13*(1), 22–23.

Compher, J. V. (1982). Parent-school-child systems: Triadic assessment and intervention. *Social Casework, 63*(7), 415–433.

Constable, R., & Walberg, H. (1988). School social work: Facilitating home, school, and community partnerships. *Urban Education, 22*(4), 429–443.

Correa, V. I. (1989). Involving culturally different families in the education process. In S. H. Fradd & M. J. Weismantel (Eds.), *Meeting the needs of culturally and linguistically different students* (pp. 130–144). Boston, MA: College-Hill.

Cummins, J. (1984). *Bilingualism and special education: Issues in assessment and pedagogy*. San Diego, CA: College-Hill.

Dao, M. (1991). Designing assessment procedures for educationally at-risk Southeast Asian-American students. *Journal of Learning Disabilities, 24*(10), 594–601.

De Anda, D. (1984). Bicultural socialization: Factors affecting the minority experience. *Social Work, 29*(2), 101–107.

Delgado, M., & Rivera, H. (1997). Puerto Rican natural support systems: Impact on families, communities, and schools. *Urban Education, 3*(1), 81–97.

Delgado-Gaitan, C. (1987). Parent perceptions of schools: Supportive environments for children. In H. T. Trueba (Ed.), *Success or failure? Learning and the language minority student* (pp. 131–155). New York: Newbury House.

Dowling, E., & Osborne, E. (1985). *The family and the school: A joint systems approach to problems with children*. London: Routledge & Kegan Paul.

Dungee-Anderson, D., & Beckett, J. (1995). A process model for multicultural social work practice. *Families in Society: The Journal of Contemporary Human Services, 76*, 459–466.

Falicov, C. J. (1995). Training to think culturally: A multidimensional comparative framework. *Family Process, 34*, 373–388.

Fong, R., & Furuto, S. (Eds.). (2001). *Culturally competent practice: Skills, interventions, and evaluations*. Boston, MA: Allyn & Bacon.

Freeman, E. M., & Pennekamp, M. (1988). *Social work practice: Toward a child, family, school, community perspective*. Springfield, IL: Charles Thomas.

Freire, P. (1993). *Pedagogy of the oppressed*. New York: Seabury Press.

Freire, P. (1998). *Teachers as cultural workers: Letters to those who dare to teach*. New York: Westview Press.

Golden, L., & Cupuzzi, D. (1986). *Helping families help children: Family interventions with school related problems*. Springfield, IL: Charles Thomas.

Gould, K. H. (1995). The misconstruing of multiculturalism: The Stanford debate and social work. *Social Work, 40*(2), 198–205.

Greene, G. J., Jensen, C., & Jones, D. H. (1996). A constructivist perspective on clinical social work practice with ethnically diverse clients. *Social Work, 41*(2), 172–180.

Greene, R. R. (1994). *Human behavior theory: A diversity framework*. New York: Aldine de Gruyter.

Harry, B. (1992a). *Culturally diverse families and the special education system*. New York: Teachers College Press.

Harry, B. (1992b). Making sense of disability: Low-income, Puerto Rican parents' theories of the problem. *Exceptional Children, 59*(1), 27–40.

Helms, J. E. (Ed.). (1990). *Black and white racial identity: Theory, research, and practice.* Westport, CT: Greenwood Press.

Kalyanpur, M., & Rao, S. S. (1991). Empowering low-income black families of handicapped children. *American Journal of Orthopsychiatry, 61*(4), 523–532.

Kurtz, P. D., & Barth, R. P. (1989). Parent involvement: Cornerstone of school social work practice. *Social Work, 34*, 407–413.

Lum, D. (1999). *Culturally competent practice: A framework for growth and action.* Pacific Grove, CA: Brooks/Cole.

Lynch, E. W., & Hanson, M. J. (Eds.). (1992). *Developing cross-cultural competence: A guide for working with young children and their families.* Baltimore, MD: Paul H. Brookes.

Lynch, E. W., & Stein, R. C. (1987). Parent participation by ethnicity: A comparison of Hispanic, black and Anglo families. *Exceptional Children, 54*, 105–111.

McAdoo, H., & McAdoo, J. L. (1985). *Black children: Social educational and parental environments.* Beverly Hills, CA: Sage.

National Association of Social Workers. (1999). *Code of ethics.* Washington, DC: NASW Press.

National Association of Social Workers. (2000). *Standards for cultural competence in social work practice.* Washington, DC: NASW Press.

Ortiz Hendricks, C. (2003). Learning and teaching culturally competent social work practice. *Journal of Teaching in Social Work, 23*(1/2), 73–86.

Ortiz Hendricks, C., Haffey, M., & Asamoah, Y. (1988). *The roles of culture bearer and culture broker in social work practice with culturally diverse families.* Unpublished paper presented at the Annual Program Meeting of the Council on Social Work Education, Atlanta, GA.

Pinderhughes, E. B. (1989). *Understanding race, ethnicity, and power: The key to efficacy in clinical practice.* New York: Free Press.

Random House Webster's Unabridged Dictionary (2nd ed.). (2001). New York: Random House.

Ravitch, D., & Viteritti, J. P. (Eds.). (2000). *Lessons from New York: City schools.* Baltimore, MD: The Johns Hopkins University Press.

Ryan, A. S., & Smith, M. J. (1989). Parental reactions to developmental disabilities in Chinese American families. *Child and Adolescent Social Work Journal, 6*(4), 283–299.

Sarason, S. B. (1982). *The culture of the school and the problem of change.* Boston, MA: Allyn & Bacon.

Spener, D. (1988). Transitional bilingual education and the socialization of immigrants. *Harvard Educational Review, 58*, 133–152.

Winerip, M. (2004, July 4). City retools special education, but pupils are slipping through cracks. *New York Times*, pp. 1, 26.

CHAPTER 5

Social Work Practice With African American Adolescent Girls: A Process-Person-Context Model

Portia Adams

> I think when I was younger; I was very shy and kind of
> quiet, which I know is hard to believe since I'm pretty
> loud now. But then when I turned maybe fourteen, I
> just knew that I had to feel good about myself that I
> couldn't feel bad about myself and survive. Plus, I can
> feel in my singing that I have always had a voice inside
> of me that wants to keep coming. (Alaza, cited in Car-
> roll, 1997, p. 102)

Social work education encourages practitioners to meet the client
where they are, to work in collaboration, to honor self-determination, and to seek to fill the felt needs of the client. This is true for
all clients but especially relevant for clients who are marginalized in
American society. This chapter focuses on social work practice
with African American[1] adolescent girls. Necessarily, the discussion
will cover the relationship and position of social work with Black

---

[1]The terms African American and Black will be used interchangeably in this chapter.

communities. Using a strengths perspective and an ecological systems frame it presents socio-historical conditions; attitudes and ideologies of the culture; and racial oppression in the areas of health, mass media, social welfare, employment, legal institutions, and education. It also describes helpful treatment strategies when working with Black adolescent girls.

SOCIO-HISTORICAL CONDITIONS

Currently, social work education has sought to balance clinical and ecological models by encouraging a person-in-environment perspective. This approach allows the social worker to recognize the interaction between the individual and his or her family, peers, community, culture, history, and societal systems. Often macro- and micro-systems are dealt with separately. This writing seeks to mend this divide. The big picture has a critical impact on Black communities and practitioners. Social workers, whether White, Asian, Latina, or Black, bring into the budding therapeutic alliance perceptions of the profession, and present and past social welfare policies, along with their specific racial, class, and gender statuses. Acknowledging this baggage is one step toward lessening its disparaging aspects. Social work, like many institutions and as a product of its environment, has served to maintain the status quo. A brief history of social work practice, policy, and research with African American communities makes available an understanding of how clients of color view the profession.

While recognizing its benevolent intent, the social work profession has colluded with the dominant society's need for assimilation and reinforcement of racial hierarchies. Settlement house leaders such as Jane Addams supported segregated services and the purposeful exclusion of Black Americans (Gordon, 1994; Miller & Berman-Rossi, 1994). From the aid to widows (1910) to the New Deal and Social Security (1935) programs, Blacks felt the brunt of industrialization and the Great Depression, yet were shut out of governmental aid and employment opportunities (Gordon, 1994). *Brown v. the Board of Education* (1954), though supported by liberal social scientists, did not present parity in educational funding as a basic human right, but as if integration on its own would remedy the "fundamentally damaged psyches" of Black children (Scott,

1997). The strategy enlisted White pity and also implied that all Black institutions were inherently inferior to White institutions (Scott, 1997). A full discussion of the unintentional costs of integration for Black communities is too lengthy to pursue in this writing; however, this brief exchange is illustrative of the prominence and pervasiveness of dialogues about Black psychological inferiority, low self-esteem and self-hatred. Black communities have recognized the various manifestations of attention or neglect by conventional social work institutions. The policy changes began with the neglect of the social welfare of Black people under slavery, through Reconstruction and the beginning of the twentieth century. Social work policies and practices worked within segregationist institutions. For oppressed communities history has a special importance. This brief outline is presented to explain why many Black communities are suspicious of social work services and research.

Social science research has focused on the psychological ills of Black communities. Social science research documented its perception of a low self-esteem bordering on self-hatred in Black Americans dating from 1914 until the 1960s (Clark & Clark, 1939, 1950; Horowitz, 1939; Lind, 1914; Lewin, 1941). This was consistent with a majority view that Black families and communities were essentially overrun with pathology. Cross (1991) reviewed personal and group identity studies of Blacks from 1939–1960, using only studies that employed standardized instruments. He found one personal identity study, and near consensus in 17 group identity studies that Blacks had low self-esteem. The *Moynihan Report* (Moynihan, 1965) confirmed the belief that the Black family was a "tangle of pathology." It described Black women as matriarchs who have undermined the status of Black men.

The negative focus on African American women and girls has not gone unrecognized by these groups. In the 1970s, there were substantial increases in foster care placement, portrayals of Black women as deficient mothers, and of young Black women as welfare queens. "While African-Americans make up 29% of the nation's poor, they constitute 62% of the images of the poor in the leading news magazines and 65% of the images of the poor on the leading network television news programs" (Gilens, 1996, p. 520). Entman and Rojecki (2001) provided a statistical review of media depictions of Black females and White females in the top movies of 1996:

Black female movie characters shown using vulgar profanity: 89%.

White female movie characters shown using vulgar profanity: 17%.

Black female movie characters shown being physically violent: 56%.

White female movie characters shown being physically violent: 11%.

Black female movie characters shown being restrained: 55%.

White female movie characters shown being restrained: 6%.

Blacks are aware of dominant perceptions of Black females as deficient, harsh, and threatening. The authors hypothesized that "Ethnic images seem to be related to the social distance that people wish to maintain between themselves and other groups" (Entman & Rojecki, 2001).

Currently there has been a diminution of governmental services and an increase of personal responsibility discourses. The urban areas continue to deteriorate, the economy has turned away from higher paying manufacturing jobs to low paying service sector jobs, and young adults from impoverished areas are finding life difficult in the new global economy. Social services as a mediator of often punitive social welfare policies are viewed as hostile, withholding, and irrelevant, and are the target of blame when things go wrong.

DEMOGRAPHICS

This section presents the health, education, legal, and economic experience of African American adolescents in the U.S. There are about 36 million African Americans in the United States, representing 12.9% of the population (U.S. Census Bureau, 2003a). In 2000, the population of Black adolescents (between 13–17) numbered nearly 3 million children. Among children under the age of 18: 46% lived with a single parent, 34% lived in two-parent households, and 13% lived in a grandparent's home (Annie E. Casey Foundation [AECF], 2003, p. 4). "In 1999, 42% of all Black children in female head-of-household families were living in poverty, compared with

9.4% of adolescents in two-parent families" (AECF, 2003, p. 6). African American children are more likely than White children to live in neighborhoods where the following characteristics exist: 35% of families are female-headed, there are a high number of high school dropouts and high levels of unemployment, and up to 19% of the population is poor (AECF, p. 9).

Race-based disparities in the area of health persist: "In 2001, the age-adjusted death rates for the Black population exceeded those for the White population by 40 percent for stroke, 29 percent for heart disease, 25 percent for cancer, and almost 800 percent for HIV infection" (the impact of HIV will be discussed later) (National Center for Health Statistics [NCHS], 2003, p. 7). Though the birth rate for Hispanic and Black Americans continues to be higher than White Americans, Black fertility and birth rates have been in a steady decline during the past decade (NCHS, 2003, p. 3; AmeriStat, 2003). "The birth rate for teenagers declined for the 10th consecutive year in 2001. The birth rate for unmarried Black women declined steadily over the past decade to 70 per 1,000 in 2000, [in comparison] the birth rate for unmarried Hispanic women increased for the third year in a row to 98 per 1,000" (NCHS, 2003, p. 3).

As mentioned earlier, the economic situation of African Americans at the beginning of the 21st century continued to deteriorate. In 2000, 34% of African Americans between the ages of 16–19 were unemployed, compared with only 15% of White American adolescents (AECF, 2003, p. 8). Manufacturing jobs disappeared. Many entry-level jobs moved to the suburbs.

> Entry-level jobs available in central cities tend to pay less than similar jobs in the suburbs . . . Minorities tend to earn less than whites—even when they have similar educational levels—and they possess far fewer material and financial assets than whites. (O'Hare & Pollard, 1999, p. 1)

In 2001, the annual median household income was lowest among Blacks (about $29,470) and highest among Asians ($53,600) and Whites ($46,300), followed by Hispanics ($33,000) (U.S. Census Bureau, 2003c, p. 1). In 2000, the household median net worth was $79,400 for White householders, $7,500 for Black householders, and $9,750 for Hispanic householders (U.S. Census Bureau, 2003b, p. 1).

"Minorities still lag far behind whites in terms of net savings and accumulated or inherited assets" (O'Hare & Pollard, 1999, p. 3). The future outlook for economic parity with Whites is doubtful because of the continued lopsided inheritance of wealth. "Between 1987 and 2011 the baby boom generation stands to inherit approximately $7 trillion . . . the average black family headed by a person over the age of sixty-five has no net financial assets to pass down to its children" (Oliver & Shapiro, 1997, p. 6; Wise, 2003). As Wise points out,

> To place this in the proper perspective we should note that this amount of money is more than all the outstanding mortgage debt, all the credit card debt, all the savings account assets, all the money in IRAs and 401k retirement plans, all the annual profits for U.S. manufacturers, and our entire merchandise trade deficit combined. (Wise, 2003, p. 2)

From 1997 to 2003, in the area of education, the number of Black American high school graduates has fluctuated around 80% (Stoops, 2004). Though there has been an increase in high school graduates and a decrease in dropouts, the percentage of Blacks who have dropped out of school is 12% compared with 7% of White adolescents (AECF, 2003, p. 7). Unfortunately, "In the first, national data across 37 states found racial disproportionality across all states in incarceration, out-of-school suspension, and expulsion" (Skiba et al., 2003).

As for drug use: "Contrary to popular assumption, at all three grade levels (8th, 10th, and 11th grades) African American youngsters have substantially lower rates of use of most licit [cigarettes and alcohol] and illicit drugs [marijuana, cocaine, crack, heroin, inhalants, hallucinogens, LSD, amphetamines, etc.] than do Whites" (Johnston, O'Malley, & Bachman, 2002, p. 39).

Violent crime rates have declined since 1994, reaching the lowest level ever recorded in 2002 (U.S. Department of Justice, 2003). "From 1999 to 2000 violent crime rates fell for almost every demographic group considered: males, females, whites, blacks, non-Hispanics, and 12-to-24-year-olds" (U.S. Department of Justice, 2003). Yet, penalties for crime and drug abuse have increased and are disproportionately allotted. "For drug offenses, African-Americans are 48 times more likely than Whites to be sentenced to juvenile prison . . . For youths charged with violent offenses, the average length of incarceration is 193 days for Whites, 254 for African-Americans, and 305 for Latino youth" (Building Blocks for Youth, 2000).

This brief statistical examination of Black youth presents a mixed picture: Decreases in teen pregnancy, crime, crime victimization, drug use, and in the dropout rate, yet increases in disproportionate imprisonment and sentencing, school suspensions and expulsions; poor health outcomes especially in the area of HIV, and in unemployment; and a lopsided inheritance system that threatens the possibility of upward mobility by African Americans in the U.S.

PERSON-PROCESS-CONTEXT

The preceding sections outlined the socio-historical, macro-system and exo-system framework for many African American adolescent girls. This section seeks to describe the micro-system and the role of ecologically aware clinical social work practice. In the case of people of color in the United States who are negotiating an often neglectful, biased, and sometimes hostile environment, social factors have critical significance. The following discussion of the *person-process-context* model is based on the work of Joyce West Stevens (2002) (see Figure 5.1). Stevens's model is complex, dynamic, and nuanced. This writing will not do justice to it but an understanding of some of its components is relevant and instructive.

There is another actor to acknowledge in the person-in-environment model especially when dealing with Black adolescent girls; it is the *intersubjectivity*. Intersubjectivity represents "the domain by which the individual self is linked to others and to the self-related elements (empathy, assertion, and recognition) of contextual experiences" (Stevens, 2002, p. 187). Empathy, assertion, and recognition are responses the self expresses in interaction with others. These qualities can be adaptive or maladaptive. Adaptively, intersubjective responses can be critical thinking, analyzing power relationships, awareness of multicultural viewpoints, and a focus on the view of valued and respected people in their community. Maladaptively, the intersubjective reaction channels self-hatred, contempt, disrespect, and alienation (Stevens, 2002). Social work

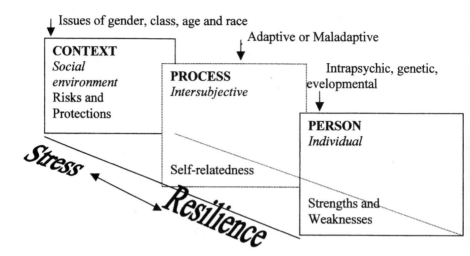

FIGURE 5.1   Based on the person-process-context model of intersubjectivity processes by Stevens (2002).

From *Smart and sassy: The strength of inner-city Black girls* by J. W. Stevens. New York: Oxford. Copyright 2002 by Oxford University Press, Inc. Reprinted with permission of the author.

practice is well positioned to facilitate adaptive intersubjective responses. Between context and the person, intersubjectivity mediates, and interprets for the individual the environmental context. This model challenges the deterministic view that hostile environments produce damaged people.

> The interactive model has special significance for adolescents of color precisely because the model incorporates the person-in-situation transactional construct and an ecological perspective. Consequently, it is best suited to clarify how social stigma is negotiated in a hostile environment whether in a healthy or maladaptive way. (Stevens, 2002, p. 9)

With this model, racial and sexual oppression and its spin-offs need not produce damaged people. A positive by-product of negative majority discourses and institutions is *subjugated knowledge*. Subjugated knowledge lies outside the dominant dialogue; it is based in actual lived experiences of oppressed people, thus, it is valid and personal. "As an oppressed minority, subjugated knowledge provides the means by which Black females resist negative definitions of self rendered by the dominant group" (Stevens, 2002, p. 19). While mainstream culture has described Black girls as marginal, threatening, needing to be restrained, and as an economic burden, Black girls and their communities have questioned the mainstream as a valid source of information.

ADOLESCENCE

Traditional perspectives of adolescence portray the young person as a lion in a cage. Pacing angrily it dreams of breaking out and running free in the wilderness, on its own, alone. The chief tasks of adolescence, as defined by Western cultures, are to develop one's own identity versus one's family, and to complete separation-individuation processes that started in early childhood. Brown and Gilligan (1992) expanded this picture of adaptive maturity by documenting the importance of relationships for girls. In contrast to the traditional view of the lion running free alone, this perspective depicts a free lioness linked to her community. In this scenario, the lioness has its family and peers; thereby, maintaining its freedom and attachments.

SPECIAL ISSUES FOR BLACK GIRLS

There is some evidence that African American girls do not experience adolescence the same way White American girls do (Adams, 2003). Black girls tend to experience puberty earlier than White girls (Brown et al., 1998, p. 18). Adolescence may start earlier and end earlier for Black girls in comparison with White girls (Stevens, 2002). In addition to receiving gendered role messages, Black girls are often learning how to critically interpret what is said and what is left unsaid about their racial group. African American girls do not experience a decrease in self-esteem during adolescence as White American girls do (more discussion to follow). They are not as affected by media images (Milkie, 1999) or by body size as White girls are (Brown et al., 1998; Crocker & Lawrence, 1999). In response to confusing and impossible ideals, Gilligan and Brown (1992) stated that girls often opt for silence and withdrawal; thus, the decrease in their self-esteem during adolescence is a result of this self-erasure. Though a useful formulation, Gilligan's work on adolescent girls was limited in its generalizability. The girls she interviewed were mainly White, middle-class and upper-middle-class girls, with a small number of privileged girls of color. Pastor, McCormick, and Fine (1996) stated " . . . urban girls of color do not have the option to 'go underground' within white-dominated, class-based institutions as Gilligan (1993) has so aptly demonstrated white middle-class girls can do" (p.16).

One of the chief differences in the experience of adolescence for these groups is that Black girls do not experience a crisis in self-esteem. Since the 1970s Black girls have consistently rated fair to high self-esteem, as well as higher self-esteem than girls from other racial groups (Adams, 2003; Gray-Little & Hafdahl, 2000; Twenge & Crocker, 2002). This high self-esteem is highly associated with social supports, and adaptive development in stressful situations. Adolescence, with its concomitant cognitive and racial identity development, is a time for critical thinking and meaning making. For Black girls, individuality is important, but so is *knowing who your people are* (Stevens, 2002). Identity is, in this case, a combination of a Black girl's unique character and what they hold in common with their extended family and kin.

HIV/AIDS

Positive racial identity development, critical thinking, subjugated knowledge, and a stable and high sense of self-esteem are vital assets when oppressed communities are faced with intense and multiple environmental stressors. This is especially true now due to the presence of HIV/AIDS in Black communities. "In 2001, the AIDS case rate among African American adults/adolescents was almost 10 times higher than among Whites (76.3 per 100,000 compared to 7.9) (Kaiser Family Foundation [KFF], 2003, p. 1). Nearly 70% of infected Black women were most likely infected through heterosexual contact (KFF, 2003, p. 2). And most alarmingly:

> Although, African American teens (ages 13–19) represent only 15% of U.S. teenagers, they accounted for almost two thirds (61%) of new AIDS cases reported among teens in 2001. A

similar impact can be seen among African American children
under the age of 13. (KFF, 2003, p. 2)

Hence, when working with Black girls, creating and maintaining
adaptive intersubjective responses (to confront stigma), assisting
racial identity development (to provide positive models and successful strategies), addressing sexual and reproductive self-care and
protection, building critical thinking, and improving relational
skills are fundamental tasks (Stevens, 2002).

SEVEN DOMAINS AND TASKS OF ADOLESCENCE

Stevens (2002) delineated seven domains in adolescence that Black
adolescent girls need to address:

Racial, ethnic, sex, and gender role commitment concerns issues of
sexual expression, body image and reproduction.

Care protective sensibility refers to having empathy, a developed
sense of self-care, and protection of the self and others.

Role model formulation speaks to the importance of proximal and
distal role models.

The *decision making* practiced in interpersonal realms can develop a sense of self-efficacy.

Dating/mate selection integrates sexuality with intimacy.

Opportunity mobility addresses educational or vocational pursuits.

Finally, *adulthood preparation* is taking on self-responsibility for
financial and reproductive choices, as well as developing a sense
of respect for self and others (p. 28).

Social workers can use a subset of these domains or all of them
in practice with Black teens.

IMPLICATIONS FOR SOCIAL WORK PRACTICE

Tools for engagement and the creation of a therapeutic alliance
include the following: Self-awareness, knowing one's own culture,
and understanding White privilege, institutional racism, and inter-

nalized racial oppression. Pinderhughes (1989) stated, "Feelings aroused in clinicians who work with patients whose culture differs from their own are more frequently than not negative and driven by anxiety, they can interfere with successful therapeutic outcome" (p. 21). As mentioned earlier, simple pejorative mass media images may reinforce desires for social distance from African American teenagers, and racial difference in the therapeutic relationship may also trigger unconscious distancing and other defense mechanisms by both client and practitioner. Methods for confronting prejudices include acknowledging and challenging negative associations with Black urban cultures and making a commitment to confront these issues. Don't believe the hype: Approach cross-cultural work armed with socio-historical and political knowledge of Black American communities, keeping in mind that there is no one way to be Black. Using cultural naiveté, a respectful curiosity (Dyche & Zayas, 1995), and allowing clients to matter will deepen relationships. Transparency and an explicit contract will facilitate self-empowerment. Exploring intersubjectivity, in this case how a Black girl interprets the world, and noting its benefits, will facilitate discussion and the development of a therapeutic alliance.

GROUP WORK WITH AFRICAN AMERICAN ADOLESCENT GIRLS

There is no one way to treat Black adolescent girls; as when targeting any oppressed community and/or problem, social workers use theory and practice techniques that are responsive to the client, the situation, and the practitioner's abilities. Nevertheless, group treatment has many characteristics that are especially helpful in treating Black adolescent girls.

Group treatment employs different theories (psychodynamic, psychoeducational, mutual aid, cognitive-behavioral, etc.) and can be used conjointly with individual, family, and psychopharmacological treatments. In the group modality, teenagers feel more empowered than in the therapeutic dyad. Groups lessen adolescent narcissism, and offer a space for practicing new social skills. Relationships with an authority figure (via the group leader) can be safely dismissed, embraced, and renegotiated. Groups also facilitate ego building by providing interactions that strengthen judgment, reality testing, the regulation of impulses, the development of mastery and competence, empathy, and critical thinking. Groups provide space to discuss what's right or wrong, space for diversity of dress and relationships, space for caring and mutuality, and can be safety valves for familial relationships (thereby preserving those relationships).

Often in groups, Black adolescent girls share knowledge, feelings, and care through stories. Their narratives are not ancient fables but real life occurrences that they have experienced or witnessed. In group, three important self psychological practices can be employed: *Mirroring*, finding one self reflected in others; *idealizing*, identifying with valued people and attributes; and *belonging*, finding one's pack or posse (Stevens, 2002). Using group to address these aspects of identity development and focusing on any of the seven domains categorized by Stevens presents a useful group treatment strategy for Black girls. The following is a case study of a Black teen girls group this author led. It demonstrates the use of intersubjectivity (adaptive and maladaptive), subjugated knowledge, mirroring, and belonging.

CASE VIGNETTE

Five out of six group members have arrived on time. This is a program designed to prevent the out-of-home placement of children, and the teen girls group's purpose is to support their experience of adolescence. Each member has a brother who has been referred for court mandated services, but the girls come voluntarily. Taking a family systems perspective and noting that girls tend not to present externalizing behaviors like their brothers, but instead tend to express internalizing behaviors such as depression and risky sexual activities, the girls were invited for treatment. The group has lasted 1^1/2 years; it will be ending in 5 weeks, due to the group leader's departure.

The girls are between 15 and 17 years of age. Tanya, the youngest—15 years, has a 2-year-old son and lives with her family; Jessica has a 1-year-old and stays with the father's mother, who is very supportive; and Pam is 16 years old but acts considerably younger and lives with her chronically depressed mother. Gloria is 16 years old with an over-controlling mother who is always telling her not to hang around "those bad girls." Gloria is an A student, and resents her mother's mistrust. Shaniqua is 16 years old, just making it through school, she and her brother had been sexually abused as small children, and her brother has refused to return to school. The teens have journeyed through the beginning phases, beyond the "nuthin wrong with me" stage, have identified their individual goals, survived the power and control and intimacy phases, and are struggling with termination. Tanya starts by announcing she will be attending an alternative school next week. She has been working on this for months. She had been out of school for the 2 years since her pregnancy, and maneuvering the school systems, and getting the records transferred (even with her social worker's help) had been a lot of work. The other members congratulate her. Jessica is also thinking about returning to school and speaks with Tanya about how to do it.

Pam told the group that a teacher had said that he didn't have to do a thing and he would still get paid. Shaniqua and Tanya said that their school had the worst teachers. Shaniqua spoke about a flirtatious and sinister school janitor and how she told him that she would get the security guard if he continued speaking to her disrespectfully. Members discussed happenings at school and the flirtatious and sinister school janitor. Then the girls related similar lecherous experiences with older men, and their feelings of fear, embarrassment, and anger. (Prior to this meeting, the members had several discussions about sexual abuse and feeling betrayed.) Their exchange ranged from tears to rage, they saw their own anguish and disappointment in each other's eyes. They continued to discuss ways to protect oneself in that situation.

Shaniqua speaks of how her mother continues to drink and smoke too much, and how an aunt had died due to high blood pressure, yet her mother does not seem to care. Pam speaks of how her mother doesn't leave her bedroom. Gloria joins in on how her mother is quick to criticize her, anticipating her failure. Jessica speaks of her boyfriend cheating on her. The group leader noted the theme of being failed by the adults around you, and asked, "How have I failed you?" First Shaniqua and Gloria denied feeling that the group leader had failed them. Tanya and Pam offered that I had not fixed their families yet I was leaving and that they felt betrayed. Other members agreed, and further elaborated their disappointment. Shaniqua announced that she bet that after I leave the agency I would go to Jamaica for a vacation. The members drew an elaborate picture of how I would be living the high life. When they were satisfied with the picture of my contentment, I asked what they would be doing. Members spoke of being in limbo; their families were not as chaotic yet they have resisted improvement, and some may even be in worse shape. The members discussed how important these family members and friends are. Later they spoke of their own fears of failure.

The members used their own language and stories to communicate the importance of self-care, boundaries, protection, responsibility for one's actions, and hopes for a lush life. The group leader did not question their viewpoints; they confronted each other from a point of care. While their familial relationships may be complicated, they offered empathy, support, critical thinking, and a sense of belonging to each other.

Robinson and Ward (1991) and Ward (1996) distinguished between bad and good methods of struggles taken by African American teenage girls, which they categorized as *resistance for survival* and *resistance for liberation*. Resistance for survival involves "self-denigration due to the internalization of negative self images, excessive autonomy and individualism at the expense of connectedness to the collective, and . . . 'quick fixes' such as early and unplanned pregnancies, substance abuse, school failure and food addictions" (p. 89). Resistance for liberation " . . . involves a process of confronting and rejecting oppressive negative evaluations of blackness and femaleness, adopting instead a sense of self that is self-affirming and self-valuing" (p. 91).

CONCLUSION

These are difficult times, especially for African American teenage girls. HIV threatens Black communities and HIV/AIDS has attacked Black communities; thus, necessitating a sustained, multilevel defense. The person-process-context model illustrates how adaptive intersubjective responses may lead to greater self-care and protection, and how maladaptive intersubjective responses may lead to self-blame and disastrous inaction. Knowing the sociohistorical experience, the origins of pathological definitions of Black families in social science research, and mass media misrepresentations may help practitioners understand the adaptive nature of subjugated knowledge. The demographics reflect centuries of oppression and resistance. These numbers document efforts within Black communities to care for its children: decreases in teen pregnancies, drug abuse, dropping out, and crime. The statistics also show the likelihood that Black children will live from paycheck to paycheck and this may persist for generations.

High self-esteem and resilience are strengths to be employed in ecologically based social work practice with African American adolescent girls. Alaza asserted: "I can feel in my singing that I have always had a voice inside of me that wants to keep coming" (Carroll, 1997, p. 102). And as announced 20 years earlier by an African American woman poet:

> You may write me down in history
> With your bitter, twisted lies,
> You may trod me in the very dirt
> But still, like dust, I'll rise. (Maya Angelou, 1978)

REFERENCES

Adams, P. E. (2003). Understanding the high self-esteem of Black adolescent girls (Doctoral dissertation, Washington University in St. Louis, 2003). *Dissertation Abstracts International, 64*(06), (UMI No. 3095496).

AmeriStat. (2003). *U.S. fertility rates higher among minorities.* Washington, DC: Population Reference Bureau.

Angelou, M. (1978). *And still I rise.* New York: Random House, Inc.

Annie E. Casey Foundation. (2003). *Kids count pocket guide. Population Reference Bureau.* Retrieved from http://www.aecf.org/kidscount/african_american_pocketguide.pdf

Brown, K., McMahon, R., Biro, R., Crawford, P., Schreiber, G., Similo, S., Waclawiw, M., & Striegel-Moore, R. (1998). Changes in self-esteem in Black and White girls between the ages of 9 and 14 years. *Journal of Adolescent Health, 23,* 7–19.

Brown, L. M., & Gilligan, C. (1992). *Meeting at the crossroads: Women's psychology and girls' development.* New York: Ballantine Books.

Building blocks for youth. Resources for disproportionate minority confinement/ Overrepresentation of Youth of Color. Retrieved from http://www.building blocksforyouth.org

Carroll, R. (1997). *Sugar in the raw.* New York: Three Rivers Press.

Clark, K. B., & Clark, M. P. (1939). The development of consciousness of self and the emergence of racial identification in Negro preschool children. *Journal of Social Psychology, 10,* 591–599.

Clark, K. B., & Clark, M. P. (1950). Emotional factors in racial identification and preference in Negro children. *Journal of Negro Education, 19*, 341–350.

Crocker, J., & Lawrence, J. S. (1999). Social stigma and self-esteem: The role of contingencies of worth. In D. A. Prentice & D. T. Miller (Eds.), *Cultural divides: Understanding and overcoming group conflict* (pp. 364–392). New York: Russell Sage.

Cross, W. E. (1991). *Shades of black: Diversity in African-American identity.* Philadelphia: Temple University Press.

Dyche, L., & Zayas, L. H. (1995). The value of curiosity and naivete for the cross-cultural psychotherapist. *Family Process, 34*, 389–399.

Entman, R. M., & Rojecki, A. (2001). *The black image in the white mind: Media and race in America.* Chicago: University of Chicago Press.

Gilens, M. (1996). Poverty and race in America: Public misperceptions and the American news media. *Public Opinion Quarterly, 60*, 515–541.

Gilligan, C. (1993). *In a different voice: Psychological theory and women's development.* Cambridge, MA: Harvard University Press.

Gordon, L. (1994). *Pitied but not entitled: Single mothers and the history of welfare, 1890–1935.* New York: The Free Press.

Gray-Little, B., & Hafdahl, A. (2000). Factors influencing racial comparisons of self-esteem: A quantitative review. *Psychological Bulletin, 126*, 26–54.

Horowitz, R. E. (1939). Racial aspects of self-identification in nursery school children. *Journal of Psychology, 7*, 91–99.

Johnston, L. D., O'Malley, P. M., & Bachman, J. G. (2002). *Monitoring the future national results on adolescent drug use: Overview of key findings, 2001* (NIH Publication No. 02-5105). Bethesda, MD: National Institute on Drug Abuse.

Kaiser Family Foundation. (2003, September). *Fact sheet: African Americans and HIV/AIDS* (#6089). Washington, DC: Sonia Ruiz, Jennifer Kates, & Claire Oseran Pontius.

Lewin, K. (1941). Self hatred among Jews. *Contemporary Jewish Record, 4*, 219–232.

Lind, J. E. (1914). The color complex in the Negro. *The Psychoanalytic Review, 2*, 404–414.

Milkie, M. A. (1999). Social comparisons, reflected appraisals, and mass media: The impact of pervasive beauty images on Black and White girls' self-concepts. *Social Psychology Quarterly, 62*, 190–210.

Miller, I., & Berman-Rossi, T. (1994). African-Americans and the settlements during the late nineteenth and early twentieth centuries. *Social Works With Groups, 17*, 77–95.

Moynihan, D. P. (1965). The Negro family: The case for national action. United States Department of Labor, Office of Policy Planning and Research, Washington, D.C. Full text in L. Rainwater & W. L. Yancey, *The Moynihan report and the politics of controversy* (pp. 39–124). Cambridge: M.I.T. Press.

National Center for Health Statistics. (2003). *Teen birth rate continues to decline: African-American teens show sharpest drop.* Hyattsville, MD: Centers for Disease Control and Prevention.

O'Hare, W. P., & Pollard, K. M. (1999). America's racial and ethnic minorities. *Population Bulletin, 54*(3). Washington, DC: Population Reference Bureau, Inc. Retrieved from www.prb.org/pubs/population_bulletin/bu54-3/part4.htm

Oliver, M. L., & Shapiro, T. M. (1997). *Black wealth/White wealth*. New York: Routledge.

Pastor, J., McCormick, J., & Fine, M. (1996). Makin' homes: An urban girl thing. In B. J. Leadbeater & N. Way (Eds.), *Urban girls: Resisting stereotypes, creating identities* (pp. 15–34). New York: New York University Press.

Pinderhughes, E. (1989). *Understanding race, ethnicity, and power: The key to efficacy in clinical practice*. New York: The Free Press.

Robinson, T., & Ward, J. V. (1991). "A belief in self far greater than anyone's disbelief:" Cultivating resistance among Black female adolescents. In E. D. Rothblum & E. Cole (Eds.), *Professional training for feminist therapists: personal memoirs* (pp. 87–103). New York: Haworth Press.

Scott, D. M. (1997). *Contempt and pity*. Chapel Hill: The University of North Carolina Press.

Skiba, R., Simmons, A., Staudinger, L., Rausch, M., Dow, G., & Feggins, R. (2003). *Consistent removal: Contributions of high school discipline to the school-prison pipeline*. Paper presented at the 2003 Harvard Civil Rights School to Prison Pipeline Conference, February 2003. Retrieved from http://www.civilrights project.harvard.edu/research/pipeline03/SkibaEXECv4.pdf

Stevens, J. W. (2002). *Smart and sassy: The strengths of inner-city Black girls*. New York: Oxford University Press.

Stoops, A. (2004). *Educational attainment in the United States: 2003*. Washington, DC: U.S. Census Bureau. Retrieved from http://www.census.gov/prod/ 2004pubs/p20-550.pdf

Twenge, J. M., & Crocker, J. (2002). Race and self-esteem: Meta-analyses comparing Whites, Blacks, Hispanics, Asians, and American Indians and comment on Gray-Little and Hafdahl. *Psychological Bulletin, 128*, 371–408.

United States Census Bureau. (2000a). *Profile of the country's Black population*. Retrieved December 22, 2001, from http://www.census.gov/Press-Release/ www/2000/cb00-27.html

United States Census Bureau. (2000b). *Rankins, comparisons and summaries of census 2000*. Retrieved December 17, 2001, from http://www.census.gov/population/ www/cen2000/phc-t9.html

United States Census Bureau. (2003a). *Census Bureau facts for features*. Retrieved December 27, 2003, from http://www.census.gov/Press-Release/www/2003/ cb03ff01.html

United States Census Bureau. (2003b). *Asset ownership of households: 2000*. Retrieved December 28, 2003, from http://www.census.gov/hhes/www/wealth/ 1998_2000/wlth00-1.html

United States Census Bureau. (2003c). *Asset ownership of households: 1998 and 2000 highlights*. Retrieved December 28, 2003, from http://www.census.gov/hhes/ www/wealth/1998_2000/highlights.html

United States Census Bureau. (2000d). *Profile of the country's Black population*. Retrieved December 22, 2001, from http://www.census.gov/Press-Release/ www/2000/cb00-27.html

Wise, T. (2003, May 24). *The mother of all racial preferences*. Znet Daily Commentaries. Retrieved December 28, 2003, from http://www.zmag.org/sustainers/ content/2003-05/24wise.cfm

CHAPTER 6

Working With Culturally Diverse Older Adults

Irene A. Gutheil
Janna C. Heyman

U nderstanding cultural diversity and practicing in a culturally competent way are key components of social work.
The term cultural diversity is broad, and includes a range
of perspectives. While recognizing that there are many ways to
approach a discussion of cultural diversity, this chapter is limited
to examining ethnic diversity among the older population and the
implications for social work practice.

It is widely recognized that the older population of the United
States is growing. Less attention, however, has been directed to
the growing ethnic diversity of tomorrow's older adults. The increasing diversity within this country's older population is changing
the face of aging. Yeo (2003) refers to the "ethnographic imperative" of the growing numbers of ethnic older adults and the diversity
within ethnic groups.

According to the 2000 census, persons 65 and older numbered
almost 35 million, 12.4% of the total population (U.S. Census
Bureau, 2001a). This represented an increase of 3.7 million persons
since 1990. By the year 2030, the older population is expected to
increase twofold, and by 2030, persons age 65 and older are ex-

The authors wish to thank Debra Greenberg, PhD, for contributing case materials for this
chapter.

111

pected to represent 20% of the total U.S. population (U.S. Department of Health and Human Services, 2002).

This older population is growing increasingly diverse. Whites represent the majority of older persons (87.8%); Blacks/African Americans represent 8.1%, and Asians represents 2.3% (U.S. Census Bureau, 2001a). The U.S. Census grouped Hispanics of any race in one category. Almost 5% of the older persons designated themselves as Hispanic or of Hispanic descent. While still primarily a younger group, the median age of Hispanics is estimated to increase from 25.8 years in 2000 to 26.7 years in 2003 (U.S. Census Bureau, 2004).

According to a U.S. Department of Health and Human Services (2002) report,

> Minority populations are projected to represent 25.4% of the elderly population in 2030, up from 16.4% in 2000. Between 1999 and 2030, the white population 65+ is projected to increase by 81% compared with 219% for older minorities, including Hispanics (328%), African Americans (131%), American Indians, Eskimos, and Aleuts (147%) and Asians and Pacific Islanders (258%). (p. 3)

The challenges in addressing the needs and concerns of a diverse older population are complex. In addition, differences within ethnic groups must be acknowledged and understood. For example, while Hispanic elders may share a common language, they come from many countries of origin. Mexican Americans represent 53% of the older population, Cubans 16%, Central and South Americans 13%, Puerto Ricans 10%, and other Hispanics 8% (U.S. Census Bureau, 2001b). Asian Americans do not share a common language, and come from over 30 different nations (Yeo, 2003). Understanding of the growing diversity among older adults must also take into account differences within the non-Hispanic White population (Yeo, 2003). Immigrants from Europe, the former Soviet Union, and the Middle East bring rich and vastly different cultural heritages.

HEALTH CONCERNS

Health, one of the issues most commonly associated with aging, may be experienced differently by different ethnic groups. According to data from the 2000 Census, 27% of persons over age 65 rated their health as fair or poor, compared with 9% for all persons. The self-reported rating of health differed between ethnic groups. Older African Americans (40.9%) and Hispanics (36.9%) were more likely to rate their health as fair or poor, compared to 24.2% of older persons who were White (Barnes, Adams, & Schiller, 2003). Objective data also indicate health disparities between groups. Chronic illnesses are more likely to occur among African American and Hispanic populations than among Whites (Hooyman & Kiyak, 2005).

A strong body of research illustrates the vulnerability of older Hispanics to health concerns. In a national study, Mui, Choi, and Monk (1998) found that Hispanic older adults, when compared with their African American and White counterparts, were most severely impaired, both functionally and cognitively, and had the highest mean number of depressive symptoms. Espino, Parra, and Kriehbiel (1994) found that the mortality rates of older Mexican Americans in Texas were higher than non-Hispanic Whites for deaths caused by diabetes, renal failure, congestive heart failure, and multiple systemic diseases. Sacco and colleagues (1998) found that Hispanics had a "twofold increase in stroke incidence compared with whites" (p. 259).

The older African American population also faces increased health risks. Hooyman and Kiyak (2005) report on data from the National Center for Health Statistics indicating that African American older adults have higher rates of hypertension, cerebrovascular disease, and disability compared with non-Hispanic Whites. The incidence of stroke for African Americans is higher than that of Whites (Sacco et al., 1998). As Beckett and Dungee-Anderson (2000) state, "Regardless of the criteria used, older African Americans have poorer health than elderly Caucasians" (p. 277). These authors also point out that older African Americans are more likely to have mental health concerns than Whites, but are less likely to use mental health services (Beckett & Dungee-Anderson, 2000).

The total Asian American population reached 10.2 million in 2000, with the elderly accounting for approximately 800,000 (U.S. Census Bureau, 2001a). This group represents the third largest minority population. Although this population is growing, there is limited data available on health indicators of older Asians. However, a recent study of Asian American older persons in New York City (Asian American Federation of New York, 2003) found that over one half rated their health as excellent or very good. This study further found that, compared with national norms, older Asian Americans reported higher rates of high blood pressure, cataracts, and diabetes, but a lower rate of arthritis. However, the National Center for Health Statistics (2003) has documented lower age-adjusted death rates for the Asian American population than for the White population.

Cultural differences may impact on health concerns in subtle ways. Dhooper (2003) identified a salient cultural value of Asians Americans: family centeredness. The family is often viewed as more important than the individual (Wong, 2001). This may lead to misdiagnosis of mental disorders when the older adult is viewed through a Western lens that values autonomy and independence (Beckett & Dungee-Anderson, 2000).

ECONOMIC CONCERNS

Although there has been significant improvement in the economic status of older persons since the advent of Social Security, about 10% of older adults are poor (U.S. Department of Health and Human Services, 2002). Factors associated with poverty include being a woman, being 75 years of age or older, and living alone. Being a person of color is a powerful risk factor for older women and men alike. African American and Hispanic older adults have lower incomes than their White counterparts, regardless of gender (Hooyman & Kiyak, 2005).

Cantor and Brennan (2000) found that 60% of the older Hispanics in New York City had incomes under $8,500 per year. Looking past generalizations to examine in-group diversity, Cantor and Brennan found that income differed by national origin, with Puerto Rican and Cuban older adults having the highest income and Dominicans and other older Latinos among those with the lowest. Turning to African American older persons in New York City, the researchers found that two thirds of this population had incomes near or below the poverty line. This was substantially more than the 43% of White older adults in or near poverty, but substantially less than the 85% of Hispanics facing economic hardship. Nationally, older African Americans and Hispanics have poverty rates 2.5 times higher than Whites (Hudson, 2002).

There is an inverse relationship between socioeconomic status and health problems. Poverty, low education, and low income have been associated with major diseases, such as cardiovascular disease, cancer, diabetes, and hypertension (Feinstein, 1993). The course of these conditions can be altered by early intervention. However, problems with access to heath care make early intervention unlikely for many older persons.

For older adults, one of the primary barriers to access to health care is financial. Although Medicare is the primary source of coverage for older persons, a significant amount of health care costs is not covered under Medicare. Older persons often pay out-of-pocket for personal health care. Caplan (2002) states that almost one fifth of Medicare beneficiaries' health care is paid out-of-pocket. For Medicare low-income beneficiaries without Medicaid, the average out-of-pocket cost represents 39% of their income (Lamphere, Bee, & Brangan, 1998). Access to health care coverage is generally related to income; those with higher income often have private insurance to supplement Medicare.

The challenges of economic need may vary for different ethnic groups. For example, McPherson (1995) notes that 75% of all Native Americans over age 65 live on reservations, often in substandard housing. Polacca (2001) studied Native Americans and Alaska Natives, and found differences in access to care between those that live on a reservation and those that do not. Those on reservations are eligible for a variety of government programs and benefits compared with those who do not reside on the reservation. According to Polacco, for most older Native Americans and Alaska Natives, education has been poor both on and off reservations, resulting in low incomes.

ASSESSMENT

Assessment of the older adult combines an understanding of biological, psychological, and social factors. Special attention must be paid to environmental factors because, in the face of changing or declining abilities, older persons are often profoundly impacted by their physical environments. The key components in assessment of any older adult are: physical health, psychological functioning, emotional well-being, social functioning, functioning regarding activities of daily living, financial well-being, and environmental issues (McInnis-Dittrich, 2002). Cultural issues, too, are a critical, but often overlooked, component of the assessment.

To arrive at an accurate assessment, older persons must be understood in the context of their families. A growing awareness of the importance of families in the lives of older adults has come with the increasing appreciation of the role of family caregivers as a bulwark of this country's long-term care system. Whereas it was once common to discuss older adults in popular and even professional literature as individuals with little connections with families, there is growing appreciation of the depth of the relationships between older persons and their families. Moreover, the reciprocity of these relationships is recognized and celebrated. For the most part, it is impossible to understand older adults outside of the family context. This may be particularly true with ethnic older persons, where there is a strong family orientation and family is seen as the primary source of care (Damon-Rodriguez, 1998; Gelfand, 2003).

There may be differences within ethnic groupings regarding who is expected to provide this care. For example, not all Asian Americans have the same expectations. In Vietnamese families, all children are expected to care for their parents, often on a rotating basis (Tran, Ngo, & Sung, 2001). For Korean families, this responsibility is likely to fall to the eldest son (Kim & Kim, 2001).

While there is limited information on Arab American older persons, one of the largest studies of Arab Americans (Fakhouri, 2001) found them at the center of the extended family. The majority lived with their spouse or children. Over two thirds of those that do not live with their children saw them at least twice a week, indicating the importance of close contact among family members. Interestingly, almost two thirds of the 230 Arab Americans in Fakhouri's study were born outside the United States.

The family's immigration history may be a critical factor in assessment. Because of their ineligibility for many programs, undocumented immigrants may be particularly vulnerable (Gelfand, 2003). Reasons for immigration and whether immigration was a result of traumatic events in the country of origin need to be considered. It is also critical to understand the degree of the older person's acculturation and ethnic identity (Harris, 1998). As Damon-Rodriguez (1998) writes, "Many ethnic elders have a life style created both from their country of origin . . . and their country of residence" (p. 61). It is important to assess the degree of acculturation and identification of other family members as well. Disparities between older persons and others in their families can lead to misunderstandings, disappointments, and at times, conflicts.

Language is another key component of the assessment. It is not possible to assume that an older adult who has lived in the United States for many years is proficient in English. Some settle in neighborhoods or communities with others who speak their language, and they have little need to learn English.

It is critical that the social worker understand that many ethnic older adults "seek intervention only as a last resort and with limited understanding of the traditional helping process" (Beckett & Dungee-Anderson, 2000, p. 284). Accurate assessment must take into account the client's cultural values. For example, older persons from traditional Asian cultures may not be comfortable with professional intervention because of a wish to protect family honor (Harris, 1998). Cultural values may also determine how health concerns are understood and how symptoms are interpreted. Berkman and her colleagues (2002) note that culturally sensitive assessment protocols are needed to adequately assess factors such as health care beliefs and patterns of family relationships.

While families are understood to be the primary source of care to older adults, it is important to recognize that caregiving and support are not one directional. Often, it is the older adult who is providing for younger family members. The most striking example of this phenomenon is grandparents raising grandchildren. While this caregiving crosses ethnic groups, African American and Hispanic grandparents are more likely to assume this role than are White grandparents (Hooyman & Kiyak, 2005). Historically, the role of African American grandparents has always been important in the family (Gelfand, 2003).

Becker and his associates (2003) examined intergenerational reciprocity among African Americans, Hispanics, Filipino Americans, and Cambodian Americans. They found mutual assistance to be an integral part of family life for all four groups. The pattern of mutual assistance did differ between the groups, reflecting broader cultural values. "These portraits of mutual assistance illustrate how family continuity is perpetuated in culturally specific ways" (p. S157).

Assessment of older adults and their family caregivers must always include an understanding of the strengths that can be drawn upon. Older adults, dealing with the numerous challenges and losses of later life, are continuing lifelong patterns of coping and adaptation (Gutheil & Congress, 2000). Family strengths, such as the strong family orientation of many ethnic groups (Gelfand, 2003), should also be identified. At the same time, it is important not to assume that strong family orientation means that service providers do not have to plan for or reach out to ethnic older persons. When needs increase, older persons may have to turn to formal services, even when they prefer assistance from family members (Gelfand, 2003). Family caregivers, too, may need help from the formal service system. Even in cultures with a strong commitment to the importance of family over the individual, caregivers may be burdened, isolated, and in need of support (John & McMillian, 1998).

SERVICE UTILIZATION

Access to services is a primary issue for ethnic older persons. Higher service needs do not translate into greater service use. Although there are mixed findings regarding utilization of services by older persons of color, there is general concern that the service needs of these individuals are not being adequately met. In addition, there is evidence that family caregivers of ethnic older adults make less use of formal services than do their White counterparts (Dilworth-Anderson, Williams, & Gibson, 2002).

In their study of New York City's older population, Cantor and Brennan (2000) describe utilization of formal services by older Hispanics as "relatively minimal" (p. 181). They further note that over 40% of older African American needed more services than they received. Even when they access services, older persons of color may not receive the best care. For example, a recent study found that African Americans are four times more likely than Whites to be in nursing homes with fewer resources (Mor, Zinn, Angelelli, Teno, & Miller, 2004).

Hooyman and Kiyak (2005) enumerate a range of barriers to service utilization. They divide these barriers into a) cultural and economic barriers, and b) structural barriers in the service system. Among the cultural barriers are language differences, perceived stigma associated with service use, fear or lack of trust in care providers, and lack of knowledge. Structural barriers include lack of services oriented to and provided by specific ethnic groups, lack of transportation to services (which may be some distance from the ethnic neighborhood), and staff who are not conversant in the language or culture of ethnic older persons (p. 478).

Other system considerations may also play a role in service utilization. For example, if older persons are given information about diabetes when they are hospitalized for their illness, there is no assurance they will fully understand what diabetes is or how it can be managed. The institution may have distributed the information in a manner the older person is unfamiliar or uncomfortable with. Recommendations, such as dietary changes, may feel foreign. In addition, the older person may feel he or she can get better help from the informal support system. If the institution has not reached out to family members, the opportunity to form a partnership in providing care may be lost. Finally, some older persons may have more confidence in traditional healers than in Western medicine.

One of the most widely recognized barriers to service is lack of proficiency in English, and limited services provided in other languages. For example, among New York City's Asian American older adults, speaking English well was associated with use of formal services (Asian American Federation of New York, 2003). When older persons do not speak English and service providers do not have people available to translate, family members may be asked to serve in this capacity. While it may be comforting for an older person to have a family member present during an interview, using family to translate may create serious obstacles. The older adult may be uncomfortable talking openly about certain health conditions or situations with the family member present. This may be particularly problematic when the family member is young or not the same gender, or when the situation involves abuse by a family member. The family member serving as translator may alter the communication during translation. There may be various reasons for this, including wanting to make the statements by the service provider more culturally appropriate, and protecting family privacy when speaking for the older adult. At times, the service provider has no way of knowing that the meaning of the communication has been altered.

CROSS-CULTURAL PRACTICE

As Yeo writes: "Cross cultural interactions are going to be the norm" (2003, p. 38). With the increasing diversity of the older population and service providers alike, there will be many challenges. Cross-cultural communication requires an understanding of both worldviews as well as attention to addressing miscommunications (Damon-Rodriguez, 1998). The social worker needs to be as informed as possible about the client's culture and be sensitive to the impact of difference (Beckett & Dungee-Anderson, 2000).

Equally important, social workers must examine their own values, cultural background, and life experiences, and assess the impact of these factors on their worldview. A high level of self-awareness is critical to culturally competent practice. Social workers must consider their experiences with persons from other cultures and aim to understand how this will impact their work (Harris, 1998). In addition, social workers "must recognize that they may never be totally free of prejudices and biases, which can emerge from hiding in insidious ways if their existence is denied" (Rogers, 1995, p. 63).

The social worker who anticipates working with a different ethnic group can prepare by learning as much as possible about the history, values, and beliefs of this group. Using the necessary caution to avoid making assumptions that all persons from an ethnic group experience the world in the same way or hold the same values, the social worker nonetheless enters into the relationship with information that may help him or her better understand the older person.

However, it is unlikely that social workers can be prepared for every ethnic group they may encounter, or that being prepared necessarily will help them accurately understand that unique individual. Consequently, the cultural literacy model, while helpful, is not sufficient. Dyche and Zayas (1995) advocate a process oriented approach that they define as operating from two attitudes: cultural naïveté and respectful curiosity.

> We define naïveté as a state of openness and receptivity. Curiosity is defined as an activity that flows from the naïveté and is composed of both the impulse to look beyond assumptions, and the love of surprise. . . . We have consistently observed that when an immigrant or minority client first meets a medical or mental health care provider, the strongest impressions are left not by the professional's skill or knowledge of the client's culture, but by an attitude that reassures the client that he or she will be treated respectfully. (pp. 390, 394)

Respect is a critical component of a therapeutic relationship. In many cultures, older persons are shown more respect and deference than in this country (Yeo, 2003). Consequently, the way a social worker greets and treats an ethnic older adult may strongly influence the development of the relationship with both the older person and the family.

When working with any older person, it is important to demonstrate respect by slowing the process to accommodate to his or her pace if necessary, or adapting to individual sensory or cognitive limitations. However, with ethnic older adults, other factors may need to be taken into consideration. It may be necessary to anticipate how to greet the individual. Maintaining eye contact or shaking hands may not be considered respectful. Yeo (2003) underscores the importance of gestures and advises that some gestures may be considered offensive by different cultures, such as showing the bottom of one's shoe to a traditional Middle Eastern older person.

END-OF-LIFE ISSUES

For older persons, at a stage when death is a more immediate reality than at any other phase of the life cycle, end-of-life planning can become a compelling issue. The health care system in the United States is based on a model that values individual autonomy (Braun, Pietsch, & Blanchette, 2000). This is reflected in the use of advance directives to enable individuals to express their preferences for end-of-life care or name someone to represent them as a decision maker should they become incapacitated.

The supremacy of individual autonomy, however, is not embraced by all ethnic groups. For example, Hispanics may be more comfortable with collective rather than individual decision making, with the family playing a central role (Talamantes, Gomez, & Braun, 2000). Naming a family member as a health care agent may be difficult when the wish is for the family to act as a collective (Morrsion, Zayas, Mulvihill, Baskin, & Meyer, 1998).

Asian Americans also have strong traditions of family responsibility. Family members may feel that protecting the older relative is a duty, and may not want the elder to be given information about a terminal illness. Older persons may not wish to control their own health care decision making, raising issues about completion of an advance directive that may make health care providers uncomfortable (Yeo & Hikoyeda, 2000). Providers need help understanding and respecting the role of family and culture when working with ethnic older adults.

At the same time, it is important to find culturally appropriate ways to approach a discussion of advance care planning. Ethnic older persons and their families often lack a clear understanding about advance directives. For example, researchers have found that Hispanics were less knowledgeable about living wills than African Americans and non-Hispanic whites (Caralis, Davis, Wright, & Marcial, 1993; Romero, Lindeman, Koehler, & Allen, 1997). Romero and colleagues (1997) note that "knowledge and education potentially can be modified by interventions and proactive measures" (p. 298). They stress that cultural values, beliefs, and experiences play a vital role in decisions at the end of life.

TREATMENT APPROACHES

The choice of treatment approach is based on the needs, capacity, and values of the older person and his or her family. Understanding of and respect for the role of the older adult in the family and the expectations the family has about care of its older members are paramount. In addition, the broader cultural context of the family must be considered. The social worker must be prepared to accept that not every intervention, no matter how well thought out, will be well received or turn out as anticipated.

Mrs. R., a 77-year-old woman, moved at age 40 from Barbados to the U.S., where she met her husband, also from Barbados.

Her husband, age 92, had children from his first marriage, but Mrs. R. has little contact with them. There were no children in the present marriage. Mrs. R. worked until age 75, and remains active in her church. Her husband is moderately demented and his wife provides the care he needs in the home. Mrs. R. missed several appointments at the clinic where she receives medical care. When she finally did come to the clinic, it was noted that she had lost weight and described some stress in providing care for her husband. In addition, there were bruises on her arms and leg. The social worker, Ms. Stone, was called in and met with Mrs. R. It took several sessions for Mrs. R. to share that her husband hit her. Mrs. R. did not see this as unacceptable, but was forthcoming about the abuse only because she became frightened when her husband picked up a chair and smashed it against the wall. Mrs. R. felt it was her responsibility to be loyal to her husband even if this put her at risk. She was so protective of him that it was not possible to obtain an accurate history that would have helped determine if the abuse was related to the dementia.

Ms. Stone wanted to help Mrs. R. find a safe place to live as it appeared that Mr. R.'s violent behavior had escalated. (This was in a state where there is no mandatory reporting of elder abuse.) Initially Mrs. R. agreed, and Ms. Stone began work on finding an alternative living situation and putting a service plan together for Mr. R. Shortly thereafter, Mrs. R. announced that she intended to remain in the home so she could be there to care for her husband.

Mrs. R. made it clear that her first responsibility was to care for her husband, and she would not leave him. She did agree to join a support group for older women who had been abused. While she continues to insist that she will not fail in her responsibility to her husband, she does attend the group once a month. Ms. Stone, while frustrated in her efforts to help Mrs. R. insure her personal safety and consider putting her own needs before her husband's, has helped Mrs. R. connect with a resource that keeps her connected to others and may serve as a lifeline if the situation becomes more dangerous.

Social workers should bear in mind that today's generation of older adults is not, in general, accustomed to seeking mental health services. For some ethnic older persons, seeking mental health services would stigmatize the family. There may be issues involved in accepting other kinds of services as well. Older persons and adult children alike may view asking for help from the formal system to be an indication of the family's failure to provide the care that is expected of them (Gelfand, 2003). Therefore, even when reaching the point of seeking services, families may struggle with accepting the help that is offered.

Social workers must take these considerations into account when making treatment and service recommendations. While the social worker may quickly be able to identify the "best" treatment and service package for an older client, the older person and his or her family may have very different ideas of what they are able to accept. Consequently, social workers need to be flexible in their approach to serving ethnic older adults and their families. They must listen to direct and indirect communications about what is viewed as acceptable by the individuals involved.

CONCLUSION

Social work will be challenged in the coming years to serve an increasingly diverse older population. To effectively serve ethnic older adults, social workers need to bear in mind that older persons are generally integral parts of their families. Social workers must recognize that the ways older adults and their families understand, experience, and cope with age-related changes may be strongly influenced by their cultural heritage. This cultural heritage may influence the ways help is given, whether help is sought outside the family, and how offers of help will be received. In addition, depending on the generation and degree of acculturation, family members may view age-related concerns in different ways or may have very different views about the best ways to manage them (Gutheil & Tepper, 1997).

In a diverse society, practice with older adults and their families is built on knowledge and skills from three general areas: generalist social work practice, gerontological social work practice, and cross-cultural practice. Social workers need to be able to draw on all three areas to practice effectively. They also need to be clear about the influence of their own values and cultural heritage on their work, so they do not impose their own worldview on others.

REFERENCES

Asian American Federation of New York. (2003). *Asian American elders in New York City: A study of health, social needs, quality of life and quality of care.* New York: Author.

Barnes, P. M., Adams, P. F., & Schiller, J. S. (2003). Summary health statistics for the U.S. Population, National Health Interview Survey, 2001. National Center for Health Statistics. *Vital Health Statistics, 10*(217), 1–14.

Becker, G., Beyene, Y., Newsom, E., & Mayen, N. (2003). Creating continuity through mutual assistance: Intergenerational reciprocity in four ethnic groups. *Journal of Gerontology: Social Sciences, 58B*(3), S151–S159.

Beckett, J. O., & Dungee-Anderson, D. (2000). Older persons of color: Asian/Pacific Islander Americans, African Americans, Hispanic Americans, and American Indians. In R. L. Schneider, N. P. Kropf, & A. J. Kisor (Eds.), *Gerontological social work* (pp. 257–301). Belmont, CA: Brooks/Cole.

Berkman, B., Maramaldi, P., Breon, E. A., & Howe, J. L. (2002). Social work gerontological assessment revisited. *Journal of Gerontological Social Work, 40* (1/2), 1–14.

Braun, K. L., Pietsch, J. H., & Blanchette, P. L. (2000). An introduction to culture and its influence on end-of-life decision making. In K. L. Braun, J. H. Pietsch, & P. L. Blanchette (Eds.), *Cultural issues in end-of-life decision making* (1–9). Thousand Oaks, CA: Sage.

Cantor, M. H., & Brennan, M. (2000). *Social care of the elderly.* New York: Springer Publishing.

Caplan, C. (2002). *What share of beneficiaries' total health care costs does Medicare pay?* Washington, DC: American Association of Retired Persons.

Caralis, P. V., Davis, B., Wright, K., & Marcial, E. (1993). The influence of ethnicity and race on attitudes toward advance directives, life-prolonging treatments, and euthanasia. *Journal of Clinical Ethics, 4*(2), 155–165.

Damon-Rodriguez, J. A. (1998). Respecting ethnic elders: A perspective for care providers. *Journal of Gerontological Social Work, 29*(2/3), 53–72.

Dhooper, S. (2003). Health care needs of foreign-born Asian Americans. *Health & Social Work, 28*(1), 63–73.

Dilworth-Anderson, P., Williams, I. C., & Gibson, B. E. (2002). Issues of race, ethnicity, and culture in caregiving research: A 20-year review (1980–2000). *Gerontologist, 42*(2), 237–272.

Dyche, L., & Zayas, H. H. (1995). The value of curiosity and naivete for the cross-cultural psychotherapist. *Family Process, 34*(4), 389–399.

Espino, D., Parra, E., & Kriehbiel, R. (1994). Mortality differences between elderly Mexican American and non-Hispanic Whites in San Antonio, Texas. *Journal of the American Geriatric Society, 42*(6), 604–608.

Fakhouri, H. (2001). Growing old in an Arab American family. In L. K. Olson (Ed.), *Age through ethnic lenses* (pp. 160–170). New York: Rowman & Littlefield.

Feinstein, J. S. (1993). The relationship between socioeconomic status and health. *Milbank Quarterly, 71,* 279–322.

Gelfand, D. E. (2003). *Aging and ethnicity.* New York: Springer Publishing.

Gutheil, I. A., & Congress, E. (2000). Resiliency in older people: A paradigm for practice. In E. Norman (Ed.), *Resiliency enhancement* (pp. 40–52). New York: Columbia University.

Gutheil, I. A., & Tepper, L. M. (1997). The aging family: Ethnic and cultural considerations. In E. P. Congress (Ed.), *Multicultural perspectives in working with families* (pp. 89–105). New York: Springer Publishing.

Harris, H. L. (1998). Ethnic minority elders: Issues and interventions. *Educational Gerontology, 24*(4), 309–323.

Hooyman, N. A., & Kiyak, H. A. (2005). *Social gerontology: A multidisciplinary perspective* (7th ed.). Boston, MA: Pearson Education.

Hudson, R. B. (2002). Getting ready and getting credit: Populations of color and retirement security. *Public Policy and Aging Report, 12*(3), 1–2.

John, R., & McMillian, B. (1998). Exploring caregiver burden among Mexican Americans: Cultural prescriptions, family dilemmas. *Journal of Aging and Ethnicity, 1*(2), 93–111.

Kim, S., & Kim, K. C. (2001). Intimacy at a distance, Korean American style: Invited Korean elderly and their married children. In L. K. Olson (Ed.), *Age through ethnic lenses* (pp. 45–58). New York: Rowman & Littlefield.

Lamphere, J. A., Bee, S., & Brangan, N. (1998). *Low-income older Americans and their health coverage needs.* Washington, DC: American Association of Retired Persons.

McInnis-Dittrich, K. (2002). *Social work with elders.* Boston: Allyn & Bacon.

McPherson, B. D. (1995). Aging from a historical and comparative perspective: Cultural and subcultural diversity. In R. Neugebauer-Visano (Ed.), *Aging and inequalities* (pp. 31–77). Toronto: Canadian Scholar Press.

Mor, V., Zinn, J., Angelelli, J., Teno, J., & Miller, S. (2004). Driven to tiers: Socioeconomic and racial disparities in the quality of nursing home care. *Milbank Quarterly, 82*(2), 227–256.

Morrison, R. S., Zayas, L. H., Mulvihill, M., Baskin, S. A., & Meyer, D. E. (1998). Barriers to completion of healthcare proxy forms: A qualitative analysis of ethnic differences. *Journal of Clinical Ethics, 9*(2), 118–126.

Mui, A. C., Choi, N. G., & Monk, A. (1998). *Long term care and ethnicity.* Westport, CT: Auburn House.

National Center for Health Statistics. (2003). Early release of selected estimates based on data from January–March, 2003 National Health Interview Survey. Retrieved from www.cdc.gov/nchs

Polacca, M. (2001). American Indian and Alaska Native elderly. In L. K. Olson (Ed.), *Age through ethnic lenses* (pp. 113–122). New York: Rowman & Littlefield.

Randall, V. R. (2003). *Demographics and the Latino population.* Retrieved from http://academic.udayton.edu/health/01status/elderly01a.htm

Rogers, G. (1995). Educating case managers for culturally competent practice. *Journal of Case Management, 4*(2), 60–65.

Romero, L. J., Lindeman, R. D., Koehler, K. M., & Allen, A. (1997). Influence of ethnicity on advance directives and end-of-life decisions. *Journal of the American Medical Association, 277*(4), 298–299.

Sacco, R. L., Boden-Albala, B., Gan, R., Chen, X., Kargman, D. E., Shes, S., et al. (1998). Stroke incidence among white, black, and Hispanic residents of an urban community: The Northern Manhattan Stroke Study. *American Journal of Epidemiology, 147*(3), 239–268.

Talamantes, M. A., Gomez, C., & Braun, K. L. (2000). Advance directives and end-of-life care: The Hispanic perspective. In K. L.Braun, J. H. Pietsch, & P. L. Blanchette (Eds.), *Cultural issues in end-of-life decision making* (pp. 83–100). Thousand Oaks, CA: Sage.

Tran, T. V., Ngo, D., & Sung, T. H. (2001). Caring for elderly Vietnamese Americans. In L. K. Olson (Ed.), *Age through ethnic lenses* (pp. 59–70). New York: Rowman & Littlefield.

U.S. Census Bureau. (2001a). *U.S. Census 2000 population reports.* Washington, DC: Author.

U.S. Census Bureau. (2001b). *Current population survey March 2000, ethnic and Hispanic statistics branch, population division.* Retrieved June 28, 2004, from http://www.census.gov/population/socdemo/hispanic/p20-535/tab01-1.txt

U.S. Census Bureau. (2004, June 14). *Annual estimates of the population by sex and age of Hispanic or Latino origin for the United States: April 1, 2000 to July 1, 2003 (NC-EST2003-04-12).* Retrieved June 28, 2004, from http://www.census.gov/Press-Release/www/releases/archives/race/001840.html

U.S. Department of Health and Human Services. (2002). *A profile of older Americans: 2002.* Washington, DC: Author.

Wong, M. G. (2001). The Chinese elderly: Values and issues in receiving adequate care. In L. K. Olson (Ed.), *Age through ethnic lenses* (pp. 17–32). Oxford: Rowman & Littlefield.

Yeo, G. (2003). The ethnogeriatric imperative. *Case Management Journals: The Journal of Long Term Home Health Care, 21*(1), 37–45.

Yeo, G., & Hikoyeda, N. (2000). Cultural issues in end-of-life decision making among Asian and Pacific Islanders in the United States. In K. L. Braun, J. H. Pietsch, & P. L. Blanchette (Eds.), *Cultural issues in end-of-life decision making* (pp. 101–125). Thousand Oaks, CA: Sage.

CHAPTER 7

Grandparents Raising Grandchildren From A Multicultural Perspective

Carole B. Cox

G randparents have always played major roles in the lives of their grandchildren, but in recent years this role has magnified in intensity, as more and more grandparents have become the primary caregivers of grandchildren. According to data from the 2000 U.S. Census, the numbers of grandparent caregivers continue to increase with 1 in 20 children under the age of 18, approximately 4.5 million children, being raised by a grandparent without the biological parent present (Simmons & Dye, 2003).

Moreover, although the increase in these families is occurring throughout the population, it has been most noticeable among ethnic minority groups. The proportion of these grandparent-headed families varies with race and ethnicity. Fewer than 5% of Caucasian non-Hispanic children are raised by grandparents, compared with 13.2% of African American children, 7.8% of Hispanic children, and 10.6% of American Indian and Pacific Islander children (Simmons & Dye, 2003).

Many reasons have been given for the rapid growth of these families. Among these are substance abuse by parents (Kelly, 1993), HIV/AIDS (Joslin & Brouard, 1995), incarceration (Dressel & Barnhill, 1994), homicide (Kelly & Danato, 1995), and mental illness (Dowdell, 1995). Child welfare policy also contributes to grandparent-headed families, as it mandates that children removed from a biological parent be placed as a priority with a relative (Gleeson, 1999). In most cases, this relative is the grandparent.

At the same time, it is important to note that most grandparents provide care outside of the formal child welfare system through private and informal family arrangements. It is estimated that for every child being raised by a relative in the formal system, six are being raised informally (Harden, Clark, & Maguire, 1997). Grandparents are often reluctant to become involved with agencies, as bureaucratic processes could threaten their roles as primary caregiver to the child, and a formal relationship could also aggravate conflict with the biological parents. They may also be reticent about submitting their homes and families to investigations and agreeing to agency demands. However, this reticence also means that they are less likely to receive financial assistance and benefits (Ehrle, Green, & Clark, 2001).

CHARACTERISTICS OF GRANDPARENT CAREGIVERS

The majority of grandparent caregivers are between 55 and 64 years with approximately one quarter over the age of 65 (American Association of Retired Persons [AARP], 2004). Poverty is pervasive among these families with 27% living below the poverty line. Custodial grandparents have also been found to have high rates of depression, poor self-rated health, multiple chronic health problems, and limitations in functioning that can affect their daily activities (Emick & Hayslip, 1999; Roe et al., 1996).

Social isolation is a major problem confronting grandparents, as many have had to give up their activities as they began caring for their grandchildren. Such feelings of isolation and alienation have been found to be very prevalent among African American and Hispanic grandparents who are providing care due to AIDS or the substance abuse of the parents (Minkler & Roe, 1993; Joslin & Harrison, 1998).

Given the many needs of custodial grandparents and the growth of grandparent-headed families among ethnic groups, it is important to consider the ways in which ethnicity and culture influence the experiences of these families. This chapter discusses the ways culture impacts on grandparent roles and behaviors and the ways in which ethnicity may affect the appropriateness of interventions. The chapter also describes the use of a model of empowerment training that has been effective in working with culturally diverse custodial grandparents.

ETHNICITY AND CULTURE

Ethnic groups are bound by a shared culture that dictates values, beliefs, traditions, and norms for behavior. Culture acts as a set of shared symbols, beliefs, and customs that shape individual or group behavior (Ogbu, 1993). It influences the ways in which people interact and interpret actions, and thus can be a major determinant of the way that grandparents experience their roles.

Ethnicity, as distinct from culture, refers to a group's shared sense of peoplehood, based on a distinctive social and cultural heritage passed on from generation to generation (Gordon, 1964). In the United States, this sense of peoplehood is primarily associated with race, religion, or national origin as people identify themselves as belonging to a specific ethnic group based on one of those characteristics.

It is important to also note that although others may recognize persons as being members of a distinct ethnic group, individuals differ on the extent to which they themselves actually maintain this identification. In addition, ethnicity is not a constant. Its importance in a person's life varies with the length of time since immigration as well as with the ease with which groups can assimilate into the greater society. Consequently, any assumptions regarding the ease with which grandparents have accepted the parenting role must be made with caution.

The grandparent role itself is influenced by culture and traditions. Whether grandparents play active pivotal roles in the family, providing direct care for the grandchildren, or play more distant roles is often culturally determined. In some societies, grandparents are relied upon to care for the children while the parents work. In other societies, grandparents are not expected to be involved in the daily lives of the grandchildren. Accordingly, their roles may be more that of storyteller, family historian, and occasional baby-sitter. Whatever the traditional role, however, most grandparents raising their grandchildren had never anticipated being the primary and sole caregiver and are doing so out of necessity rather than choice.

Assimilation can be a particular source of stress, as those most assimilated may resent having to forego other roles and activities that had been sources of enjoyment in order to parent their grandchildren. Conversely, those who are less assimilated may find themselves in constant struggles with grandchildren who do not adhere to the traditional culture or its expected behaviors. In particular, adolescents may resent limitations on their autonomy or other cultural expectations regarding behavior. Such conflicts, as they cause further dissention in the relationship, further undermine the well-being of the grandparents.

Variations in assimilation underscore the importance of understanding the role that culture can play in grandparent-headed households. Stereotyping, which overlooks and ignores the individual and uses assumptions that may not be valid, ignores the reality of the individual grandparent's situation. Without recognition of this reality, it is difficult to design or offer interventions that can effectively assist the family.

Culture and Interventions

The issues encountered by these families often require individual and family counseling. Feelings of loss and grief over the absence of a child's parents frequently permeate the relationship and make parenting even more difficult. These problems are magnified by the fact that many of the children come to the grandparents after years of neglect or abuse and are thus prone to behavioral problems and difficulties in school. Even with high rates of need, however, grandparent caregivers are unlikely to access services, particularly if they are not in a formal relationship with the grandchild (Shore & Hayslip, 1994; Ehrle & Green, 2002).

Many factors may underlie this reluctance to use the formal system. For many, raising the grandchild is shameful and connotes failure on the part of the family. The associated stigma can be a barrier to seeking help (Heywood, 1999). For those who are less assimilated and adhere more closely to cultural traditions, accepting the role of custodial grandparent may be perceived as a normative duty, and using assistance, regardless of needs, may be viewed as conflicting with traditional expectations and norms.

Systems designed to assist families and protect children can also be offensive to grandparents. Workers may reflect attitudes that blame grandparents for the failures of their children and thus question their ability to parent their grandchildren. Inexperienced child welfare workers can cause grandparents to feel that they are dealing with an adversarial bureaucracy rather than a supportive program (Pinson-Milburn & Fabian, 1996).

A multicultural perspective on interventions recognizes that the oppression and discrimination that many ethnic minority grandparents have suffered from the formal service system can act as a barrier to service use. Histories of inadequate services, long waits, and insensitive staff can be powerful deterrents to using needed programs. In addition, those who have come from countries where officials, including social workers and social agencies, cannot be trusted, may identify them with historical hurt and injustice and thus have difficulty perceiving them as potential helpers (Cox & Ephross, 1998). In offering interventions to grandparents, these many potential barriers must be considered so that the lack of utilization is not perceived as a lack of real need.

Understanding the ways in which culture and ethnicity may affect the perception of help-seeking and assistance is a prerequisite for service utilization. It is important to know not only why help is being sought but also what help-seeking means to the grandparent. This implies the worker's understanding of varying ethno-cultural perspectives of needs for assistance, possible stigmas associated with receiving help, who else in the family should be involved in the process, and a person's receptivity to receive assistance from another ethnic group.

For many groups, interventions that emphasize growth, enhancement, and learning may be more attractive than those that focus on counseling and problem solving. Programs that emphasize services for the children, be they recreational, educational, or therapeutic, may also be more appealing than those focusing on the needs of grandparents.

Trust is a prerequisite for the development of relationships with ethnically diverse grandparent caregivers. Grandparents need to feel that the worker understands and empathizes without being judgmental and without stereotyping. Consequently, it is important that practitioners are aware of their own beliefs and values and the ways in which they influence their responses and actions. This necessitates recognizing their own attitudes regarding the grandparents' situations and their assumptions regarding the grandparent's ability to raise the grandchildren after their own children have failed.

As in all social work relationships, the goals that are developed should be realistic and meaningful to the individual grandparent. This means being in accordance with their own sense of ethnic identity and its adherence to traditional values and norms. In some instances, goals may be more radical than would be dictated by tradition—such as those focusing on self-advocacy and leadership. Consequently, in setting goals it is important to know about cultural traditions, but not to be limited by these traditions, since any individual grandparent may not share equal adherence to them. For example, assuming that a grandmother seeks to maintain a traditional role of remaining in the home can negate her interest in expanding and developing her abilities to assume a leadership role in her community.

Support Group

Support groups can play important roles in combating the isolation that is frequently experienced by grandparent caregivers. Support groups for grandparents have developed across the country and have become import sources of assistance as they combat a sense of isolation, offer a means of socialization, and can also help in educating and teaching.

However, the importance of support groups in serving ethnic and minority grandparents remains uncertain. A national survey conducted by the American Association of Retired Persons (AARP, 2004) found that only a minority of participants in support groups were either African American (34%) or Hispanic (8%). Given that these two groups are the most likely to be raising their grandchildren, their low rate of participation is an issue of concern. The findings suggest that outreach is either ineffective in reaching these populations or that the support groups are not addressing the needs of these populations.

Ethnicity and culture are important factors to consider in the design of support groups. Indeed, for some persons the idea of sharing with others in a group setting may be completely contradictory with established norms of behavior. One does not share problems or family difficulties outside of the immediate kinship circle, to do so may be to risk contempt, shame, or exclusion. Thus, many may be resistant to participating in a group publicized as a setting in which persons can discuss their problems and issues. Increasing participation may depend on redefining the group as one focusing on parenting skills or education.

Concomitantly, as discussed above, it is imperative not to assume that because a person belongs to a specific group that they strongly adhere to particular cultural values and behaviors. Any one individual may be quite willing to join a support group and openly discuss problems and concerns. In addition, ethnic differences fade in importance compared with the common problems shared by the grandparents. Moreover, if a group is developed in accordance with traditional beliefs with the worker sensitive to and knowledgeable about ethnic values and norms, even those strongly adhering to cultural norms and values may find participation rewarding.

African American Culture and Grandparents

A history filled with discrimination and oppression has had a major impact on the roles of the African American grandparent in this country. In fact, it is impossible to ignore the role of slavery as an influential factor in the position of women in African American culture. As slaves forced to work in the fields and in households, women found themselves assuming roles that conflicted with the primary traditional ones associated with child rearing. At the same time, they were often the pivotal figures in the slave household, holding the family together. With emancipation, many families moved north, where women frequently had an easier time than men finding work. Consequently, many were thrust into the role as primary provider for the family.

During this period, grandmothers were frequently called upon to raise the grandchildren as the adult children searched for work (Jackson, 1986) or migrated to urban areas in the North and West (Burton & Dilworth-Anderson, 1991). From the early 19th century until the mid-1960s, it was common for the Black grandmother to accept and raise her own grandchildren as well as more extended kin and orphans.

The legacy of slavery, coupled with years of discrimination and oppression, has encouraged self-sufficiency as a common trait among Black women (Tate, 1983). Black women have tended to internalize the black community's perceptions of them as strong, independent, and resourceful (Watson, 1974). In fact, when such feelings of competency are threatened, African American women acting as caregivers are particularly vulnerable to stress and depression (Cox, 1995).

Given this tradition of caring for grandchildren, however, it is important to recognize that most African American grandparents today did not anticipate raising their grandchildren. They do so out of a sense of family responsibility and obligation to keep the children out of the child welfare system. At the same time, research indicates that as custodial grandparents they struggle financially, feel stressed over the responsibility, and worry over their ability to continue to raise the child (Brown & Mars, 2000).

Hispanic Culture and Grandparents

The value of familism, which places the needs of the family above those of the individual, with a sense of duty to offer emotional and material support to family members, is often used to characterize Hispanic culture (Sabogal, Marin, & Otero-Sabogal, 1987). This value places strong emphasis on the importance of children and the elderly, and the strong obligation to help each as needed. Moreover, to the extent that adult children are perceived as not meeting these obligations and roles are not being adequately enacted; there is an increased likelihood of intergenerational dissatisfaction (Cox & Gelfand, 1987).

Gender roles tend to remain strong among first generation Hispanic immigrants, particularly among older persons. These norms expect that men will be controlling, authoritarian, possessive, and good providers to the family, demonstrating characteristics associated with machismo. Women are expected to be protected, submissive in relation to the male, and protective of their children.

In her study of elderly Puerto Rican women, Sanchez-Ayendez (1994) found that child rearing was viewed as the primary responsibility and one that persists through adulthood. At the same time, although motherhood is a central role for women, other roles such as breadwinner and wife may also be enacted. Moreover, with suitable mentors and encouragement, younger Hispanic women have assumed effective leadership positions in the community (Lazzari, Ford, & Haughey, 1996).

It is a common practice for older Hispanics to assist their children with child care. When Hispanic families immigrate to the United States, their role as child care providers often becomes even more critical as it contributes to the family's ability to succeed. However, such involvement does not assure that conflicts will not ensue according to value differences between the generations (Gelfand, 1993). Grandparents assuming the parental role due to the absence or incapacity of their adult children may find themselves experiencing considerable role conflict and strain as they struggle to adjust their traditional role perceptions to the reality of the new society (Burnette, 1999).

Empowerment Groups With African American and Hispanic Grandparents

Empowerment training is a specific intervention, usually offered in groups that can assist grandparents in coping with their new roles. Empowerment entails developing feelings of self-reliance and self-esteem including innate strengths and abilities, so that an individual feels in control of herself and her environment. Consequently, empowerment training is particularly appropriate for parenting grandparents struggling to cope with their grandchildren and their environments.

The author has developed a program in empowerment training that has been effectively offered to African American and Hispanic grandparents (Cox, 2000). The training, which involves 14 classes, was developed in consultation with custodial grandparents, support group leaders, and others working with grandparents in the community. These discussions highlighted concerns that were the most stressful for grandparents and the most appropriate for empowerment training. The course teaches new patterns of responses and behaviors as well as preparing grandparents to become advocates in the community. Among the topics offered are the importance of self-esteem, communication, dealing with behavioral issues, loss and grief, substance abuse, advocacy, navigating the service system, and legal issues. The complete curriculum has been published and is being used with many different grandparent groups (Cox, 2000).

Both African American and Hispanic grandparents shared a common interest in each of the subjects, with these interests overcoming cultural separateness. In fact, upon completion of the course, African American grandparents gave presentations to Hispanic groups through use of a translator on grandparent issues. These presentations were so successful that they were invited back several times. This is a further indicator of how common problems outweigh any cultural separateness.

There are differences between the groups, however, that can affect their roles as parenting grandparents. The African Americans are better educated, having generally completed at least the 8th grade. In comparison, the majority of Hispanic grandparents completed only primary school with several having no formal schooling. None of the Hispanics were educated in the United States and the majority had only limited proficiency in English.

The grandparents had varied relationships with their grandchildren. The majority of Hispanic grandparents were in an informal relationship without legal custody or guardianship. Often, the parents were involved, with the grandparents providing care during the day and sometimes overnight while the parent worked. In contrast, the majority of African American grandparents did have legal custody of the grandchildren and there was little, if any, contact with the parents. Consequently, the African Americans were responsible for making decisions regarding the grandchildren while the Hispanics had only limited authority. Several felt that they were given the responsibility of child rearing but did not have the ability assure the welfare of the grandchildren.

The two groups also differed with regard to their involvement in the community and their use of services. The African Americans, in contrast to the Hispanics, were accustomed to assuming active community roles with many involved as volunteers in Head Start or in local political organizations. Both groups were knowledgeable about services and programs, but the Hispanics were much less assertive about demanding benefits or services. Limited English and a lack of translators further hindered their activism.

The two groups were distinct in their approaches to the empowerment training. The African American grandparents were more likely to discuss, question, and challenge the material, each

other, and the group leaders. They were also very open in discussing family issues and problems, including their disappointment
with their own children.

In comparison, the Hispanic grandparents, even in a group
led by a facilitator from the same ethnic background, required
more encouragement to share their concerns. They were eager to
learn and absorb the material but reluctant to discuss any negative
interactions with their family. In particular, they were reticent
about discussing issues such as substance abuse and AIDS, or difficulties with their own children.

Both groups were eager to learn how to communicate with
their grandchildren, to understand them, and to deal with a perceived lack of respect. They all felt that adolescents were more
difficult to raise than younger children. Both sets of grandparents
were equally worried about protecting their grandchildren and
assuring their safety in regard to both the environment and their
peers. However, the African American grandparents were more
anxious about the emotional health of their grandchildren, many
of whom were in counseling. With the loss of the parent, they
were also more interested in learning how to deal with grief and
assisting their grandchildren to cope.

At the conclusion of the training, both African American
and Hispanic grandparents felt they benefited from the group
experience. Both felt more comfortable in discussing problems
with their families, making their own needs known, and in asserting
themselves in the home and with agencies. Several of the Hispanic
grandparents reported that they had begun reinforcing their roles
within the family, including making their own needs known and
their concerns about the grandchildren. In addition, they also
became more involved in local politics with some accompanying
a group to the state capital to lobby for more after-school programs
for children. Indicative of the impact of the empowerment was
the logo that the Hispanic grandparents developed for their own
support group—a tree with large branches and strong roots, sym-
bolizing the important role of grandparents in the family.

SUMMARY

Given the large proportion of grandparents among ethnic minority
populations, effective social work with these groups demands a

multicultural perspective. These grandparents bring values to their new roles. They come with traditions and histories that can continue to influence their interactions with their grandchildren and the systems with which they must interact. At the same time, it is important to recognize that such interactions may in fact be influenced by the systems themselves. Indifference and discrimination have also affected the willingness of many of these grandparents to seek assistance.

Social workers are in key positions to ease the burdens and challenges faced by these families. But, in order to be most effective they must themselves be sensitive and knowledgeable about specific cultures and the ways in which they may affect both the roles of the grandparents as well as their perception of needs. With this background, and an awareness of their own values and possible biases and attitudes, relationships can be developed that can strengthen grandparents and their families.

The empowerment training model offers an intervention that helps to develop skills and coping abilities of grandparents. The model is proven to be applicable to two ethnically diverse populations with varying backgrounds and experiences but with shared concerns. The success of the model indicates that by recognizing and being sensitive to cultural influences, grandparents, regardless of ethnicity, can learn and grow through the program as they further develop their own self-efficacy.

Above all, it is imperative to recognize that culture and ethnicity are important facets of identity and social interactions, but that they are impermeable. Indeed, grandparents who are able to integrate their own rich cultural heritage with the norms and expectations of American society are in the strongest positions to be powerful influences on the lives of their grandchildren.

REFERENCES

American Association of Retired Persons. (2004). *Grandparent support groups and minority outreach to grandparents raising grandchildren.* Paper presented at the 2004 ASA/NCOA Joint National Conference, San Francisco, CA.

Brown, D., & Mars, J. (2000). Profile of contemporary grandparenting in African-American families. In C. Cox (Ed.), *To grandmother's house we go and stay: Perspectives on custodial grandparenting.* New York: Springer Publishing.

Burnette, D. (1999). Social relationships of Latino grandparent caregivers: A role theory perspective. *Gerontologist, 39,* 49–58.

Burton, L., & Dilworth-Anderson, P. (1991). The intergenerational family roles of aged Black Americans. *Marriage and Family Review, 1*(1), 311–330.

Cox, C. (1995). Comparing the experiences of black and white caregivers of dementia patients. *Social Work, 40,* 343–349.

Cox, C. (2000). Empowerment practice: Implications for interventions with African American and Latina custodial grandmothers. *Journal of Mental Health and Aging, 6,* 385–397.

Cox, C. (2000). *Empowering grandparents raising grandchildren: A training manual for group readers.* New York: Springer.

Cox, C., & Ephoss, P. (1998). *Ethnicity and social work practice.* New York: Oxford.

Cox, C., & Gelfand, D. (1987). Familial assistance, exchange and satisfaction among Hispanic, Portuguese, and Vietnamese elderly. *Journal of Cross-Cultural Gerontology, 2,* 241–255.

Dowdell, E. (1995). Caregiver burden: Grandparents raising their high risk children. *Journal of Psychosocial Nursing, 33,* 27–30.

Dressel, P., & Barnhill, S. (1994). Reframing gerontological thought and practice: The case of grandmothers with daughters in prison. *Gerontologist, 34,* 685–691.

Ehrle, J., & Green, R. (2002). *Children cared for by relatives: What services do they need?* (Number B-46, Series in New Federalism). Washington, DC: The Urban Institute.

Ehrle, J., Green, R., & Clark, R. (2001). *Children cared for by relatives: Who are they and how are they faring?* (Number B-28, Series in New Federalism). Washington, DC: The Urban Institute.

Emick, M., & Hayslip, B. (1999). Custodial grandparenting: Stresses, coping skills, and relationships with grandchildren. *International Journal of Aging and Human Development, 48,* 35–61.

Fuller-Thompson, E., & Minkler, M. (2000). The mental and physical health of grandmothers who are raising their grandchildren. *Journal of Mental Health and Aging, 6,* 311–323.

Gelfand, D. (1993). Immigration and the older Latino. In M. Sotomayor & A. Garcia (Eds.), *Elderly Latinos: Issues and solutions for the 21st century* (pp. 79–92). Washington, DC: National Hispanic Council on Aging.

Gleeson, J. (1999). Kinship care as child welfare service: Emerging policy issues and trends. In R. Hegar & M. Scannapieco (Eds.), *Kinship foster care: Policy, practice, and research* (pp. 136–154). New York: Oxford University Press.

Gordon, M. (1964). *Assimilation in American life.* New York: Oxford University Press.

Harden, A., Clark, R., & Maguire, K. (1997). *Informal and formal kinship care.* Washington, DC: Department of Health and Human Services.

Heywood, E. (1999). Custodial grandparents and their grandchildren. *The Family Journal: Counseling & Therapy for Couples & Families, 7,* 367–372.

Joslin, D., & Brouard, A. (1995). The prevalence of grandmothers as primary caregivers in a pediatric population. *Journal of Community Health, 20,* 383–401.

Joslin, D., & Harrison, R. (1998). The hidden patient: Older relatives raising children orphaned by AIDS. *Journal of the American Medical Women's Association, 53,* 65–71.

Kelly, S. J. (1993). Caregiver stress in grandparents raising grandchildren. *Journal of Nursing Scholarship, 25*(4), 331–337.

Kelly, S. J., & Danato, E. G. (1995). Grandparents as primary caregivers. *Maternal and Child Nursing, 20,* 326–332.

Lazzari, M., Ford, H., & Haughey, K. (1996). Making a difference: Women of action in the community. *Social Work, 41,* 197–205.

Minkler, M., & Roe, K. (1993). *Grandmothers as caregivers: Raising children of the crack cocaine epidemic.* Newbury Park: Sage.

Ogbu, J. (1993). Differences in cultural frame of reference. *International Journal of Behavioral Development, 16,* 483–506.

Pinson-Milburn, N., & Fabian, E. (1996). Grandparents raising grandchildren. *Journal of Counseling & Development, 74,* 548–555.

Roe, K., Minkler, M.. Thompson, G., & Saunders, F. (1996). Health of grandparents raising children of the crack cocaine epidemic. *Medical Care, 34,* 1072–1089.

Sabogal, F., Marin, G., & Otero-Sabogal, R. (1987). Hispanic familism and acculturation: What changes and what doesn't? *Hispanic Journal of Behavioral Sciences, 9,* 397–412.

Sanchez-Ayendez, M. (1994). Elderly Puerto Rican women. In M. Sotomaya (Ed.), *Triple jeopardy: Aged Hispanic women—insights and experience.* Washington, DC: National Hispanic Council on Aging.

Shore, R., & Hayslip, B. (1994). Custodial grandparenting: Implications for children's development. In A. E. Gottfried & A. W. Gottfried (Eds.), *Redefining families: Implications for children's development* (pp. 171–218). New York: Plenum Press.

Simmons, T., & Dye, J. (2003). *Grandparents living with grandchildren 2000, Census 2000 brief.* Washington, DC: United States Census Bureau.

Watson, V. (1974). Self-concept formation and the African-American woman. *Journal of African-American Issues, 2,* 226–236.

Section Three

Selected Culturally Diverse Populations

CHAPTER 8

Clinical Practice With Immigrants and Refugees: An Ethnographic Multicultural Approach

Jessica Rosenberg
Manny J. González
Samuel Rosenberg

Throughout history, the reasons that lead people to leave all that is familiar to them, their homes and loved ones, and travel thousands of miles away to the unknown have remained remarkably similar: immigrants and refugees are seeking better lives, economic security, and political and religious freedom. In some cases, they are fleeing from the terrible horrors of torture and war. And in most cases, despite the harsh circumstances surrounding their lives in their country of origin, the immigrant and refugee experience is one colored by loss and uncertainty.

Newcomers to the United States can be divided into three categories: legal immigrants, refugees, and undocumented immigrants. This population has similarities and some important differences. All contend with the stressors of being strangers in a strange land and with the difficulties associated with adjustment to a new culture. However, the majority of legal immigrants come to the United States by choice, having engaged in planning and often joining family and friends in their new country. They may, in varying degrees, feel prepared, financially and emotionally, for the transition. Refugees, in contrast, are typically fleeing from their country of origin. They have no other option but to leave. They may be desperate, afraid, and alone, and most likely have been victims of or witness to traumatic violence. It is likely that they will never return to their country of origin. In sum, the circumstances surrounding refugee migration are likely to be of pronounced distress. Section 601 of the Illegal Immigration Reform and Individual Responsibility Act of 1996, enacted September 30, 1996, stipulates that "a person qualifies as a refugee prosecuted for political reasons if forced to undergo, has a well founded fear of being compelled to undergo, or resists a coercive population-control procedure. Also the Act set a combined annual ceiling of 1,000 persons who may be granted refugee or asylee status under this provision" (U.S. Department of Justice, 1999, p. 109). Finally, there are an unspecified number of persons who enter the United States annually without documentation. These individuals are generally trying to escape poverty and squalor in their countries of origin. Many undocumented immigrants suffer greatly in their travels to the United States. Rape, acts of violence, and physical hardship are not uncommon. Furthermore, undocumented immigrants are often in a state of constant worry that they will be discovered by the U.S. authorities and deported. They are suspicious of any government or official institution and are wary of seeking legal or health services. Undocumented immigrants are barred from many endeavors U.S. citizens take for granted, such as the legal right to work, to hold a driver's license, and to collect social security, despite their contribution to the tax base. The millions of undocumented immigrants in the United States, many of whom work under harsh conditions and for substandard wages, constitute an invisible, shadow subculture, which has become essential to the functioning of the U.S. economy.

Life transitions, environmental problems and needs, the effects of acculturation stress, and interpersonal conflict may often compel immigrants and refugees to seek out mental health services. Mental health practitioners (e.g., clinical social workers, psychologists, psychiatric nurses) then, provide services to those recognized as conventional immigrants, refugees from a variety of cultural and regional origins and an unspecified number of undocumented immigrants with a host of legal, economic, and public health concerns. The varying needs of this diverse group constitute a challenge to the social work profession and its historical commitment to ease the process of adjustment to a new society. The scope of this chapter, restricted by length, is directed toward a discussion of the needs of the more vulnerable among this population; as the more vulnerable are most likely to be recipients of social services.

TARGET POPULATION

Due to the strict quotas established by current immigration policy, a significant number of immigrants are highly educated, affluent members of their countries of origin. For this group, the vicissitudes of unemployment, and/or low wages are likely to be less severe compared with the majority of newcomers. Nonetheless, cultural, language, and adjustment issues remain serious concerns during the adjustment period. During 2002 there were 108,647 persons admitted to the United States who reported occupations in executive and management, professional, and technical areas. During the same year, 450,231 persons were admitted reporting to be operators, fabricators, laborers, and the overwhelming majority with no occupation working outside home (U.S. Department of Labor, Bureau of Labor Statistics, 2004). The latter group of immigrants (those with no occupation working outside the home) and refugees to the United States struggle with a host of socioeconomic problems that include low employment, language and cultural barriers, low education and occupation status, and discrimination. Poverty is pervasive among this population, who often come from rural or developing countries and typically lack employment skills.

This chapter examines contemporary immigration to the United States and highlights the major psychosocial conditions shaping the experience. The focus is on recent immigrants, referred to as "first generation." The chapter also explores the mental health needs, access to services, and implications for clinical practice applicable to this population. Research shows that although immigrants and refugees are at increased risk for a host of psychological problems such as depression and traumatic stress, they are less likely to access treatment, due to lack of availability of culturally competent services, their own cultural prohibitions against participating in mental health care, limited insurance, and a general mistrust of government agencies (Padilla, 1997).

Immigrants settling in the United States come from all over the world. The Immigration Act of 1965 and subsequent immigration policy initiatives enacted in 1986 and 1996 resulted in a large influx of immigrants from Latin America and Asia. Since 1980, the Asian population in the United States has increased from 3.5 million to more than 10 million. The Hispanic population is estimated to have grown to over 30 million, approximately 13% of the total population (U.S. Bureau of the Census, 2000). At least 70% of this growth in population is attributed to immigration (Taylor, 1998). Data on the refugee population reveals that they are disproportionately young. Of the 6.1 million refugees worldwide for whom demographic data are available, 45.6% are aged less than 18 years, although the proportion of children and adolescents varies considerably by region (e.g., 56% of refugees in Africa, 23% of refugees in Europe) (U.S. Department of Homeland Security, 2004).

In sum, immigrants and refugees constitute a diverse ethnic, cultural, and socioeconomic group that is at high risk for psychosocial problems, with different styles of help-seeking behavior. The Department of Health and Human Services (see U.S. Department of Homeland Security, 2004) reports that the percentage of legal immigrants in the caseload of the Aid to Families with Dependent Children (AFDC) program fell from 6.0% to 5.3%. This decline mirrored the overall decline of the total Temporary Assistance for Needy Families. In 1998 5.1% of the Food Stamp caseload was foreign-born persons (U.S. Department of Homeland Security, 2004). It should be noted that the level of social services utilized by this group is proportionately lower than their absolute population numbers would suggest.

It is well-known that culture strongly influences the way people experience the world. In the multicultural ethnographic framework proposed in this chapter, clients' unique personal narratives are elicited. This perspective suggests that services to clients and client systems must be based on a comprehensive understanding of their life in their country of origin, their journey to the United States, and their experience of immigration in the United States.

PSYCHOSOCIAL RISKS/NEEDS

Immigrants and refugees to the United States face formidable challenges in the areas of cultural adjustment, language acquisition, and economic subsistence. Many, if not most, recent immigrants and refugees arrive in the United States with limited English language proficiency. Immigrants and refugees may often feel confused and marginalized in this country where they do not fully speak nor understand the dominant language. In describing his experience as a high school student in California, a recent immigrant from Argentina said, "I felt the other students didn't like me because I spoke strangely and often didn't understand those who spoke to me. I didn't know how to maneuver in the culture—how to get around and get things done" (Rosenberg, 2000). Consequently, he became withdrawn, his educational performance lowered, and he eventually engaged in antisocial behavior.

In addition to causing social marginalization, language limitations are a critical factor contributing to unemployment and low wage occupations. Immigrants who do not speak English and have a low level of educational attainment have difficulty finding gainful employment and are generally trapped in low paying, unskilled jobs. The U.S. Department of Labor, Bureau of Labor Statistics (2004) reports that for the period of 1996 to 2002, only approximately 7% of 25–34-year-old workers born in the U.S. had not completed high school. In contrast, about 26% of recent immigrants in the age group had not obtained a high school diploma.

Access to Systems of Care

Difficulties in accessing services among the immigrant and refugee population stem from three primary areas: First, for those from countries of origin in which mental health problems and mental health care are perceived very negatively, seeking treatment is not culturally acceptable, and accordingly, some immigrants and refugees will choose not to seek services. Second, because many of these individuals lack adequate health insurance and have limited funds, many lack the means to access mental health care. Third, services themselves are not often designed with a multicultural awareness, including employing staff with appropriate linguistic skills. As such, existing services may not appeal to or seem relevant to many immigrants and refugees.

The Undocumented Immigrant

Because they typically do not have health insurance, many undocumented immigrants will not seek services on a consistent basis. Current systems of care are rarely designed to meet the needs of undocumented immigrants. For example, in the wake of 9-11, a large number of undocumented persons were adversely affected because they were either present during the attack and/or because they and their families depended on the downtown financial district area for their livelihood. It is well known that a large number of undocumented immigrants, primarily of Latino origin, provided a source of available and inexpensive labor to businesses in and around the disaster area (e.g., janitorial workers and restaurant workers). Nonetheless, despite their representation among the victims of 9-11, undocumented immigrants, due to their illegal status, may not be eligible for some services. Given the convergence of the social, economic, and legal obstacles experienced by this population, they are at high risk for falling through the cracks and being exposed to the more pernicious consequences of mental illness.

The Post 9-11 Climate: Heightened Tensions and Obstacles

The post 9-11 world ushered in a climate characterized by stricter policies for immigrants, as well as increased fear and suspicion among the public toward foreigners. The backlash against immigrants of Middle Eastern descent is well documented (Bernstein, 2004), with numerous accounts of being targets of hostile actions, including unlawful detainment and deportation. In addition, many immigrants, regardless of their country of origin, are subject to longer waits for immigration applications and work permits, and experience more frequent denials of driver's licenses. The net effect of this chilled climate is a tendency among many immigrants to be apprehensive of seeking help from social institutions including the legal system, health care services, and social service organizations.

Cultural Norms

Mental illness, perhaps more than any other psychosocial condition, elicits powerful cultural responses. Mental illness has been understood to acquire religious significance, endowing the ill person with special gifts or devilish powers. In many cultures, mental illness is a taboo subject, a cause for shame among families with a mentally ill member.

For example, Vietnamese culture considers a mentally ill person to be born under an unlucky star and ill fated. Mental illness brings shame upon the family, affecting the fortunes and future of the whole family. As such, families are likely to try to care for the ill member within the confines of the family rather than seek outside help (Ganesan, Fine, & Lin, 1989).

Attitudes toward mental illness can vary considerably even among groups with many shared cultural traditions. In particular, class, level of education, and whether one comes from a rural or urban background, mediates perceptions toward mental health. For example, attitudes of urban, well-educated Mexicans from the capital city will differ considerably from those residing in rural Guatemala, and their attitudes in turn will be different from those of Colombians.

In working with immigrants and refugees, it is essential to understand how their culture views mental illness. Working within cultural frameworks can greatly enhance services. For example, one mental health center partnered with the local *curanderos* or *santeros* who, operating within a belief system that spirits inhabit the material world, utilize their healing arts with the Latin American immigrant community. The mental health center invited these local healers to help their clients. They found that the participation of the santeros was symbolically important as an acknowledgment of their cultural place within the community, and as a result, they gained increased participation and credibility among the Latin American immigrant community (Rosenberg, 2000).

Linguistic Barriers

Among the greatest challenges facing the provision of clinical services is the shortage of bicultural, bilingual mental health practitioners. Demographic trends indicate that the number of non-English speaking clients is expected to continue to rise, but there are few bilingual social service providers. The demand for bilingual/bicultural social workers far exceeds the supply, and as the non-English speaking population continues to grow at a rapid pace, it is expected that their need for social services will grow as well (Ortiz-Hendricks, 2004).

Communication problems prevent many immigrants and refugees from accessing services, and reports of staff insensitivity to clients who are not proficient in English are not uncommon. Many service programs routinely rely on clients to provide translators, typically family or friends. This practice is strongly discouraged due to the proximity of the person translating to the client; the information gathered will be censored and generally incomplete. In addition, it is often the younger members of families who acquire language skills at a faster pace. As such, it may be culturally distonic for an adult family member to disclose personal information to a son, daughter, niece, or nephew. As has been stated already in this book, it is important to advocate for the development of professional translators who can enhance comfort levels, particularly during the initial stages of counseling.

For many immigrants and refugees, language represents the primary means for retaining a sense of heritage, safeguarding cultural identity and expressing emotionality. Because language has such a central place in the treatment of immigrants, mental health practitioners who wish to communicate effectively with monolingual or bilingual clients must first find out what language the client communicates best in, and then must demonstrate sensitivity to the fact that people who are in a state of crisis or who are experiencing significant psychological distress may struggle to communicate in a second language, and may also regress to the use of their native language as the primary means of expression. Researchers (see González, 2002) have suggested a relationship between linguistic inaccessibility and underutilization of clinical services by immigrants. Human service organizations engaged in community outreach initiatives to immigrant and refugee populations, therefore, must ensure that immigrants have access to competent bilingual and/or bicultural clinicians.

CLINICAL FACTORS

Psychosocial Assessment

Conducting a careful psychosocial assessment is a crucial element in developing an appropriate diagnostic plan for treating immigrants and refugees. In his work with Indochinese refugee clients, Kinzie (1981) identifies five central areas of inquiry that form the assessment stage of treatment: a) life in the country of origin, b) the escape process, c) refugee camp problems, d) attitudes and concerns about life in the United States, and e) future outlook.

The following case vignette illustrates the importance of sound diagnostic psychosocial assessment.

L., a young Latino woman of about 34 or 35, was hospitalized on a psychiatric unit for about 3 years. The police, who had found her in the street, homeless, very poorly groomed, and very depressed, had brought her in. She presented as catatonic, with flat affect, no eye contact and was verbally nonresponsive. A male psychiatrist who didn't speak Spanish initially interviewed her. The woman just sat with her head down, didn't make eye contact, and didn't answer any questions, probably because she didn't understand. But even if the interview had been in Spanish, she might not have answered. The psychiatrist noted her poor eye contact, flat affect, and nonresponsive state and diagnosed her as schizophrenic and she was put on antipsychotic medication. In the case of this woman, the medication sedated her more. She became more isolated, more depressed, and for 2 years she sat, doing absolutely nothing.

At this point, a Puerto Rican nurse took an interest in the woman and started to talk to her, as much as possible, with the goal of establishing a personal relationship with L. Finally L. began to respond, very little, but she was talking.

The treatment team working with L. had failed to conduct a sound psychosocial assessment. Her chart noted "Place of origin: El Salvador" but the implications of this were never explored. The nurse learned that the woman was in El Salvador in the 1980s and that she had seen her whole family—her husband and children—killed by the Salvadorian military in front of her. She was the only survivor. Somehow she was smuggled out of the country, brought to New York, was with somebody for just 3 months, and then got lost. L. was extremely depressed and suffering from posttraumatic stress disorder, yet she was misdiagnosed as schizophrenic and placed on the wrong medication.

In a sound diagnostic psychosocial assessment, the significance of L.'s country of origin, that is, the fact that El Salvador was torn by civil war in the 1980s, would have been explored and perhaps L. might not have languished for years in the back wards of a psychiatric inpatient unit (Rosenberg, 2000).

Consequently, it is clinically indicated when providing services to immigrants to pay particular attention to the following areas:

1) Client's country of origin has experienced violence due to war, civil war, invasion, paramilitary violence. Has client experienced directly any aspects of organized violence? Has client's family been affected by violence? Has client witnessed violent acts?

2) Determine whether client's life experience is primarily rural or urban. Despite globalization, most rural areas in the underdeveloped world lack basic services generally taken for granted by practitioners: running water, electricity, telephones, medical care and, most importantly, mental health care. Lack of exposure to these amenities affects the receptiveness and willingness of immigrants to engage in a therapeutic process.

3) Assess the relative power assigned to gender and try to evaluate the character of gender relations in the client's culture of origin. It is particularly important when working with families to respect the power protocols established by the client's background at the initial stages of engagement. This in no way constitutes an acceptance of unequal power relations in the family. It is however, a culturally competent approach to gather information and engage the client system in the therapeutic process.

4) Evaluate the levels of loss experienced by the client and get an approximation of its impact given the client's life experience. Adults and adolescents will experience family separation or loss of friends in emotionally distinct ways. Try to elicit from the client a picture (genogram of sorts) of all the different parts of the family and their current location.

The high rate of violent life events as well as high stress associated with the immigration experience can place immigrants and refugees at increased risk for a number of the following clinical conditions, as detailed in the *Diagnostic and Statistical Manual of Mental Disorders—Text Revised* ([*DSM IV-TR*]; American Psychiatric Association, 2000): Posttraumatic Stress Disorder, Acute Stress Disorder, Adjustment Disorders, and Major Mood Disorders.

Traumatic Stress Disorders

Posttraumatic stress disorder (PTSD), is a disabling psychiatric disorder that develops subsequent to experience of a life threatening or traumatic event such as war combat, terrorism, and violent attacks such as rape and assault (Herman, 1992). Posttraumatic stress disorder can severely interfere with daily functioning. Symptoms include flashbacks, sleep problems and nightmares, feelings of isolation, guilt, paranoia, and panic attacks. Persons suffering from PTSD typically repeatedly relive the traumatic event through painful memories and are prone to intense feelings of fear, helplessness, and horror. Often such feelings are accompanied by anxiety or panic attacks.

Studies of psychotherapy with South East Asian refugees provide numerous accounts of severe hardship, including torture and other war-related horrific experiences (Ganesan, Fine, & Lin, 1989). It is estimated that the vast majority of the Indochinese refugees that entered the United States following the 1975 collapse of the South Vietnam government were exposed to severe brutality and cruelty and debilitating living conditions in their home country. Such clients may struggle with depressed and irritable moods, pervasive feelings of being unsafe, and feelings of intense guilt, especially if they survived when others did not.

It is important to note that immigrant and refugee children are also vulnerable to traumatic stress disorders. When immigrant parents dream of bringing their children to the United States, they usually do so with the belief that their quality of life will improve. They flee political persecution, extreme economic desperation, and look to the "land of opportunity," with the expectation that living in a democratic society will result in educational and employment opportunities. On arrival to the United States, however, the reality of sheer survival often becomes paramount. Finding housing and some type of employment become primary goals. Igoa (1995) has observed that, "In low-income immigrant families, it may be difficult for parents to nurture their children because the uprooting experience itself saps the parents' energy" (p. 40). Children in the family are often left to cope on their own, with the hope that they both (parent and child) learn English and acculturate as quickly as possible. The multiple losses the children and their families have gone through, the fears, confusion, sadness, and alienation they may feel are often left unattended. Urrabazo (2000), for example, has noted the multiple traumas that undocumented Hispanic families have been exposed to in their attempt to cross the border into the United States: robbery, sexual assault, and physical and psychological torture. Yet it is these losses and "unspoken" traumas that immigrant children carry with them into their new schools and that teachers, educational administrators, and school mental health personnel (e.g., guidance counselors, school social workers, school psychologists) are confronted with.

Adjustment Disorders and Depression

Immigrants and refugees are frequently diagnosed with adjustment disorders and depression (Yu, 1997). While such disorders are typically less severe in intensity and duration than traumatic stress disorders, they can be disabling and cause significant distress. According to the *DSM IV-TR* (American Psychiatric Association, 2000), the central feature of adjustment disorder is distress that markedly exceeds what is normally expected by a stressor and impairment in job, academic, or social functioning.

Major depression or dysthymic disorders are characterized by two or more of the following symptoms: appetite decrease or increase, sleep decrease or increase, fatigue or low energy, poor self-image, reduced concentration or indecisiveness, and feelings of hopelessness. These symptoms cause clinically important distress or impair work, social, or personal functioning. These psychological disturbances are viewed as prevalent among immigrants and refugees because of the combination of past harrowing experiences in their country of origin and ongoing psychosocial stressors in the United States. In a study of 147 adult Vietnamese Americans, depression was correlated to acculturation problems (Tran, 1993).

For instance, in looking specifically at what is known about the incidence of mental health among Hispanic immigrant children and adolescents, studies consistently show that Hispanic youth seem to be particularly vulnerable. Psychiatric epidemiological studies of children and adolescents appear to suggest that Hispanic youth experience a significant number of mental health problems, and in most cases, more problems than Caucasian youth (U.S. Department of Health and Human Services [USDHHS], 2001). Glover and colleagues (1999), for example, found that Hispanic youth of Mexican descent in the southwest reported more anxiety-related problem behaviors than White students. Lequerica and Hermosa (1995) also found that 13% of Hispanic children screened for emotional-behavioral problems in pediatric outpatient settings scored in the clinical range on the Childhood Behavior Checklist (CBCL). Similarly, other studies (e.g., Achenbach, Bird, Canino, & Phares, 1990; Chavez et al., 1994; Vazsonyi & Flannery, 1997) appear to indicate a greater frequency of delinquency behaviors among Hispanic youth in middle schools as compared with Caucasian youth.

In addition to anxiety and behavioral problems, depression is a serious mental health predicament affecting the psychosocial functioning and adjustment of Hispanic youth. Studies of depressive symptoms and disorders have revealed more psychosocial distress among Hispanic youth than Caucasian adolescents (USDHHS, 2001). This finding may be related to the fact that about 40% of African American and Hispanic youth live in poverty, often in chaotic urban settings that disrupt family life and add considerable stress to their already fragile psychological condition (Allen-Mears & Fraser, 2004). Nationally, for example, Roberts and colleagues (1995) and Roberts and Sobhan (1992) have empirically noted that Hispanic children and adolescents of immigrant descent report more depressive symptomatology than do Caucasian youth. In a later study that relied on a self-report measure of major depression, Roberts and colleagues (1997) found that Hispanic youth of Mexican descent attending middle school were found to have a significantly higher rate of depression than Caucasian youth, at 12% versus 6%, respectively. These findings held constant even when level of psychosocial impairment and socio-demographic variables were taken into account.

Family Disruption

The impact of war and migration on children and families is profound. Family violence, marital problems, and acting out among children and adolescents are some of the manifestations of family disruption. Intergenerational tensions between parents who adhere to cultural traditions and their children who often acculturate at a faster pace are common. A significant number of refugee applications since 1997 have been granted for family reunification, typically when a spouse and children join a refugee already in the United States. Many of the recent refugees who arrived from Eastern Europe, Afghanistan, and Ethiopia did so for family reunification. The stressors impacting these families are severe, with such families likely to struggle with family dysfunction (González, Lopez, & Ko, 2005).

Individual, Family, and Group Treatment Considerations

While group and family treatment can be quite beneficial, it is a treatment decision that is best made with client consensus. Group and family modalities may not necessarily be culturally indicated, particularly with clients for whom sharing personal information is culturally distonic. Some cultural groups have a prohibition against sharing personal material with outsiders or even among family members. With such clients, a referral to group or family treatment can be disruptive to the healing process. For example, in one instance of a social worker working with a Muslim woman, the social worker assumed that the client would feel a sense of a community from participating in a support group for Muslim women and referred her. The client, citing her discomfort at discussing taboo topics such as marital satisfaction with members of her own cultural group, quickly dropped out of treatment.

In the treatment of some of Hispanic immigrants and refugees—like Cuban Marielitos and balseros—individual, family, and environmental interventions, however, may be quite appropriate (see González et al., 2005). The "Mariel boatlifts" of the "Marielitos" represents the third migration wave of Cuban immigrants. This third migration wave ushered into the United States more than 125,000 Cubans. The exodus of this group has at times been depicted as chaotic because of the many overcrowded boats that in a brief span of time arrived in the state of Florida (Miami), bringing thousands of individuals and families in need of political asylum and freedom. Cuba's persistent economic crisis and its political deterioration set the stage for the fourth wave of migration: Cuban "balseros." Balsero is the Spanish term that describes an individual who has left Cuba on a raft or small boat. From 1989 to 1994, over 37,000 Cuban balseros have successfully reached Miami, Florida by dangerously traveling on small boats and rafts. González (2002), for example, has noted that from an ecological-systems perspective, the mental health problems of Hispanic immigrant patients will be significantly reduced if they are assisted in mediating complex social systems, in obtaining community resources, in attaining vocational/job skills, and in learning English as a second language. Likewise, the family reunification issues of Cuban Marielitos and balseros must be addressed via an ecologically based family treatment approach. Therefore, ecological structural family therapy, bicultural effectiveness training, and the social/environmental change agent role model are recommended as viable treatment approaches that may ameliorate the family reunification dynamics and conflicts presented by Cuban immigrant/refugee patients.

Research evidence (Szapocznik et al., 1978; Szapocznik et al., 1991; Szapocznik et al., 1997) appears to suggest that ecological structural family therapy is an effective treatment approach in addressing intergenerational conflict and acculturation differences in Hispanic families primarily of Cuban descent. Because the locus of the patient's dysfunction is not only internal but also external in nature, ecological structural family therapy stresses the interaction between the organism and its environment. Based on the theoretical and clinical work of Aponte (1974) and Minuchin (1974), this family treatment approach highlights the stress of acculturation and its disruptive impact within the structure of the Hispanic family. This treatment model pays careful attention to how normal family processes may interact with acculturation processes to create intergenerational differences and exacerbate intrafamilial conflict.

Altarriba and Bauer (1998) suggest that when applying ecological structural family therapy to Cuban immigrants an assessment of the interaction between the individual patient and his/her environment should be conducted early on, during the initial phase of treatment. The diagnostic assessment process should include an appraisal of the boundaries between and among family members, the strength of the relationships between and among family members, an understanding of the hierarchal and authority structure of the family, and an examination of any inherent contradictions in the request for service.

Szapocznik and associates (1997) have empirically studied the value of ecological structural family therapy in assisting Hispanic Cuban families address their interactional problems from both a content and process level. At the content level, the cultural and intergenerational conflicts can be the focus of clinical attention, making this model of family therapy particularly specific to the Cuban family. At the process level, this treatment model aims to modify the breakdown in communication processes resulting from intensified cultural and intergenerational conflicts. The content and process distinction is crucial in treating maladaptive family reunification issues often found in Cuban patients who have entered the United States via the Marielitos or balsero migration wave.

Bicultural Effectiveness Training (BET), developed at the Spanish Family Guidance Center at the University of Miami by Szapocznik and colleagues (1984, 1986), is predicated on structural family theory and is delivered as a 12-session psychoeducation treatment approach. Empirically tested with Cuban American families experiencing conflict with their adolescent children, bicultural effectiveness training is specifically designed to decrease accultura-tion-related stresses of two-generation immigrant families. For Cuban balsero patients who may be integrating into U.S.-based, established family systems, this intervention model may be useful in treating family reunification dynamics.

Given the fact that many recently arrived Cuban refugees often lack instrumental support from their U.S.-based extended families, many attempt to negotiate complex environmental conditions (e.g., employment, housing, health care, learning English as a second language) with minimal appropriate guidance. Atkinson and colleagues (1993b) developed a dimensional intervention approach (social/environmental change agent role model) for the mental health treatment of ethnic/racial minority patients that recognizes the impact of the social environment in promoting or handicapping psychological growth and development. Within this treatment model, the mental health clinician treating Cuban patients can function as an agent for change, or as a consultant or advisor to an identified individual patient acting to strengthen the patient's support systems.

Atkinson and associates (1993a) recommend that the following three factors be diagnostically assessed when treating an ethnic (immigrant or refugee) patient: a) the patient's level of acculturation, b) the perceived cause and development of the presenting problem (internally caused versus externally/environmentally caused), and c) the specific goals to be attained in the treatment process. In implementing this treatment model with Cuban refugee patients, however, mental health care providers must be prepared to extend their professional role beyond that of psychotherapist to that of advocate, mediator, educator, and broker (González, 2002).

An essential feature of the engagement stage of the treatment process in the ethnographic multicultural approach entails learning about client's cultural norms with respect to sharing personal material, the client's values and belief system, and their linguistic styles of communicating within family and group systems. The ethnographic multicultural approach is illustrated in the following case vignette:

A., a South American woman in her mid thirties, entered therapy, presenting with depressed mood and eating binges. She is undocumented, and employed off the books as a full-time nanny, where she often binge eats. A. recounts a horrific journey to the United States in which she and others from Latin America were smuggled in a filthy, hot, oil tanker. A. relates that while she was not physically harmed, she witnessed her companion being raped.

In the initial phase of treatment, A. educated her American-born, Spanish-speaking therapist about the political and economic upheaval in her country of origin, her traumatic journey to the United States, and her fears about being deported. The process of therapy became a shared voyage. The social worker's posture was open and curious about learning about A.'s culture, and the patient, in turn, became increasingly enthusiastic about treatment via this "guided journey." This approach greatly helped A. to establish a trusting bond with her therapist, enabling her to fully express her range of feelings about premigration traumas. Her compulsive eating diminished and her mood improved.

AN ETHNOGRAPHIC
MULTICULTURAL APPROACH

Mental health professionals need to develop a service approach that is culturally competent. Unfortunately, the concept of cultural competence is an idea that has suffered from the lack of fit between the theoretical conception of competence and the execution of competence as practiced by social workers, psychologists, psychiatrists, and sociologists (Leigh, 1998; Rosenberg, 2000; Vega & Murphy, 1990). Practitioners need to reframe the idea of competence into something that utilizes concepts from anthropology, adopting some of the methodologies and the approaches of the discipline, and searching with both a clinical lens and an ethnographic lens to begin to imagine what it must be like to be in the position of a person of another racial/ethnic category or cultural group.

Valle (1986) has described the elements necessary for the development of what he terms "cross-cultural competence." These include

1. A working knowledge of the symbolic and linguistic "communicational" patterns of the target ethnic minority group(s);
2. Knowledge and skill in relating to the naturalistic/interactional processes of the target population; and
3. A grasp of the underlying attitudes, values, and belief systems of the target population.

An ethnographic multicultural approach to working with immigrants and refugees is based on a comprehensive understanding of their life in their country of origin, their pre-migration stressors, their journey to the United States, and their initial experience of immigration in the United States. During this process, practitioners must adopt a clinical curiosity analogous to what a person experiences when traveling in unknown territories. Thus, the client becomes the cultural guide who leads the way into areas and experiences that heretofore were unknown to the practitioner (Green, 1998; Leigh, 1997). As this process evolves, the practitioner becomes an educated traveler by becoming acquainted through study and reflection with the cultural and social aspects of the client's premigration culture. In effect, a parallel process of mutual trust evolves, where the practitioner openly acknowledges a desire to learn from the client and at the same time, demonstrates to the client an interest in her/his experiences by becoming acquainted with the client's cultural background. An informed traveler has an a priori appreciation of unknown places and is capable of formulating incisive questions. Concomitantly, the client feels empowered by being able to teach the practitioner about the nuances of her/his culture and develops a feeling of acceptance of difference generally lacking in the immigrant experience.

Clinically, this process results in the construction by the client of a narrative, containing genuine and intimate information. In this manner, the client does not feel intruded upon and establishes her/his own pace of disclosure. Again, it is important to reiterate that this is an interactive process where the client guides the journey, and the practitioner actively demonstrates interest and concern.

CONCLUSION

The psychosocial needs of immigrants and refugees vary considerably. The extent to which an individual is prepared for the transition to life in the United States, particularly with regard to educational and employment readiness, can impact on how well he or she adjusts. Clinical syndromes often seen in this population include traumatic stress and adjustment disorders and depression. Such symptoms may, in part, derive from experiences surrounding the individual's life in his or her country of origin and their presentation will be shaped by cultural norms. Clinical practice with the population must begin with a comprehensive assessment process that includes developing an understanding the premigration experience. Psychotherapy with this population should be undertaken with an open and inquisitive attitude and a willingness to learn about the client's culture. Mental health practitioners, who become attuned to listening to their clients with a "cultural ear," can utilize an ethnographic multicultural approach, as described in this chapter, to help and empower clients and to promote trust and healing in the treatment encounter.

REFERENCES

Achenbach, T. M., Bird, H. R., Canino, G., & Phares, V. (1990). Epidemiological comparisons of Puerto Rican and U.S. mainland children: Parent, teacher, and self-reports. *Journal of the American Academy of Child and Adolescent Psychiatry, 29*(1), 84–93.

Allen-Meares, P., & Fraser, M. W. (2004). *Intervention with children and adolescents: An interdisciplinary perspective.* New York: Allyn and Bacon.

Altarriba, J., & Bauer, L. M. (1998). Counseling Cuban Americans. In D. Atkinson et al. (Eds.), *Counseling American minorities* (5th ed., pp. 280–296). New York: McGraw-Hill.

Aponte, H. (1974). Psychotherapy for the poor: An ecostructural approach to treatment. *Delaware Medical Journal, 46*(3), 1–7.

Atkinson, D. R., Morten, G., & Sue, D. W. (1993a). *Counseling American minorities: A cross-cultural perspective* (4th ed.). Madison, WI: Brown and Benchmark.

Atkinson, D., Thompson, C. E., & Grant, S. K. (1993b). A three dimensional model for counseling racial/ethnic minorities. *The Counseling Psychologist, 21*, 257–277.

American Psychiatric Association. (2000). *Diagnostic and statistical manual of mental disorders.* Washington, DC: American Psychiatric Press.

Bernstein, N. (2004, July 20). For immigrants, stories of scrutiny and struggle. *New York Times*, p. B3.

Chavez, E. L., Oetting, E. R., & Swaim, R. C. (1994). Dropout and delinquency: Mexican-American and Caucasian non-Hispanic youth. *Journal of Clinical Child Psychology, 23*(1), 47–55.

Ganesan, S., Fine, S., & Lin, T. Y. (1989). Psychiatric symptoms in refugee families from South East Asia: Therapeutic challenges. *American Journal of Psychotherapy, 43*(2), 218–228.

Glover, S. H., Pumariega, A. J., Holzer, C. E., Wise, B. K., & Rodriguez, M. (1999). Anxiety symptomatology in Mexican-American adolescents. *Journal of Family Studies, 8*(1), 47–57.

González, M. J. (2002). Mental health intervention with Hispanic immigrants: Understanding the influence of the client's worldview, language, and religion. *Journal of Immigrant and Refugee Services, 1*(1), 81–92.

González, M. J., Lopez, J., & Ko, E. (2005). The Mariel and balsero Cuban immigrant experience: Family reunification issues and treatment recommendations. *Journal of Immigrant and Refugee Services, 3*(1/2), 141–153.

Green, J. W. (1998). *Cultural awareness in the human services: A multiethnic approach* (3rd ed.). Boston: Allyn and Bacon.

Herman, J. (1992). *Trauma and recovery.* New York: Basic Books.

Igoa, C. (1995). *The inner world of the immigrant child.* Mahwah, NJ: Lawrence Erlbaum Associates.

Kinzie, J. D. (1981). Evaluation and psychotherapy of Indochinese Refugee patients. *American Journal of Psychotherapy, 35*, 251–261.

Leigh, J. W. (1997). *Communicating for cultural competence.* Boston: Allyn and Bacon.

Lequerica, M., & Hermosa, B. (1995). Maternal reports of behavior problems in preschool Hispanic children: An exploratory study in preventive pediatrics. *Journal of the National Medical Association, 87*(12), 861–868.

Minuchin, S. (1974). *Families and family therapy.* Cambridge, MA: Harvard University Press.

Ortiz-Hendricks, C. (2004). A strategic plan for the development of the Latino social work workforce. *The Latino Social Work Task Force* (Available from NASW NYC, 50 Broadway, NYC, NY 10014).

Padilla, Y. (1997). Immigrant policy: Issues for social work practice. *Social Work, 42,* 595–606.

Roberts, R. E., Chen, Y. W., & Solovitz, B. L. (1995). Symptoms of DSM-III-R major depression Among Anglo, African, and Mexican American adolescents. *Journal of Affective Disorders, 36*(1–2), 1–9.

Roberts, R. E., Roberts, C. R., & Chen, R. (1997). Ethnic differences in levels of depression among adolescents. *American Journal of Community Psychology, 25*(1), 95–110.

Roberts, R. E., & Sobhan, M. (1992). Symptoms of depression in adolescence: A comparison of Anglo, African, and Hispanic Americans. *Journal of Youth and Adolescence, 216*(6), 639–651.

Rosenberg, S. (2000). Providing mental health services in a culture other than one's own. *Reflections: Narratives of Professional Helping, 6,* 32–41.

Szapocznik, J., Scopetta, M. A., & King, O. E. (1978). Theory and practice in matching treatment to the special characteristics and problems of Cuban immigrants. *Journal of Community Psychology, 6*(2), 112–122.

Szapocznik, J. (1984). Bicultural effectiveness training (BET): A treatment intervention for enhancing intercultural adjustment in Cuban American families. *Hispanic Journal of Behavioral Science, 6*(4), 317–344.

Szapocznik, J., Rio, A., & Perez-Vidal, A. (1986). Bicultural effective training (BET): An experimental test of an intervention modality for families experiencing intergenerational/intercultural conflict. *Hispanic Journal of Behavioral Science, 8*(4), 303–330.

Szapocznik, J., Herns, O., & Rio, A. T. (1991). Assessing change in family functioning as a result of treatment: The structural family systems rating scale (SFSR). *Journal of Marital and Family Therapy, 17*(3), 295–310.

Szapocznik, J., Kurtines, W., & Santisteban, D. A. (1997). The evolution of structural ecosystemic theory for working with Latino families. In J. Garcia & M. C. Zea (Eds.), *Psychological interventions and research with Latino populations* (pp. 166–190). Boston: Allyn and Bacon.

Taylor, R. L. (1998). Minority families in America: An introduction. In R. L. Taylor (Ed.), *Minority families in the United States* (pp. 1–17). Englewood Cliffs, NJ: Prentice Hall.

Tran, T. V. (1993). Psychological traumas and depression in a sample of Vietnamese people in the United States. *Social Work, 18,* 184–194.

Urrabazo, R. (2000). Therapeutic sensitivity to the Latino spiritual soul. In M. T. Flores & G. Carey (Eds.), *Family therapy with Hispanics: Toward appreciating diversity* (pp. 205–227). Boston: Allyn and Bacon.

U.S. Bureau of the Census. (2000). Mapping Census 2000: The geography of U.S. diversity. Retrieved July 17, 2004, from http://www.census.gov/ftp/pub/hhes/saipe/90data/tab/51_89.html

U.S. Department of Health and Human Services. (2001). *Mental health: Culture, race, and Ethnicity—A supplement to mental health: A report of the Surgeon General.* Rockville, MD: Author.

U.S. Department of Homeland Security. (2004). *The triennial comprehensive report on immigration.* Retrieved July 24, 2004, from http://uscis.gov/graphics/index.htm

U.S. Department of Justice, Immigration and Naturalization Service. (1999, July). *Annual report: Refugees fiscal year 1997.* Washington, DC: U.S. Government Printing Office.

U.S. Department of Labor, Bureau of Labor Statistics. (2004). *Working in the 21st century.* Retrieved July 24, 2004, from http://stats.bls.gov./opub/working/pages5b/htm

Valle, R. (1986). Cross-cultural competence in minority communities: A curriculum implementation strategy. In M. Miranda & H. H. Kitano (Eds.), *Mental health research and practice in minority communities* (pp. 29–50). Rockville, MD: National Institute of Mental Health.

Vazsonyi, A. I., & Flannery, D. J. (1997). Early adolescent delinquent behaviors: Associations with family and school domains. *Journal of Early Adolescence, 17*(3), 271–293.

Vega, W. A., & Murphy, J. W. (1990). *Culture and the restructuring of community mental health.* Westport, CT: Greenwood Press.

Yu, M. (1997). Mental health services to immigrants and refugees. In T. D. Watkins & J. W. Callicutt (Eds.), *Mental health policy and practice today* (pp. 164–181). Thousand Oaks, CA: Sage.

CHAPTER 9

Working With Russian-Speaking Jewish Immigrants

Robert Chazin
Tatyana Ushakova

T he past several decades have witnessed a sharp increase in the number of émigrés into the United States from countries around the world. One particularly large immigrant group has been the Jewish immigrants from the former Soviet Union (FSU). Since 1965, when the United States liberalized its immigration laws, hundreds of thousands of Jews have immigrated to the United States from different parts of the FSU. Using different data, various agencies have reported different numbers of émigrés to the United States. Most sources exclude Russian Jews who came to the United States by direct invitation of U.S. citizens, or as illegal immigrants or nonimmigrant visitors (such as U.S. college students) who obtain permission for permanent residence after arrival. Kliger's analysis (2004) estimates the number of Jewish immigrants who came to the United States from the FSU since 1970 at 780,000, about 15% of the total Jewish population in the U.S.

In the former Soviet Union, Jews were identified by passport stamps. The space marked "nationality," noted "Jewish," which indicated their ethnicity, rather than religion, since practicing any religion at that time was strongly discouraged. Although many

Russian-speaking Jews were Russian in many respects, including their language, cultural rituals and holidays, music, and literature, they were not viewed as Russians in their homeland. In contrast, Americans viewed the Jewish immigrants' language and culture as indicators of their Soviet/Russian, rather than Jewish, background. Some Jewish immigrants note with bitterness, "We became Russians when we left Russia." Contemporary literature compounds the status confusion of this group through the use of many names for this population such as "Soviet Jews" and "Russian Jews." In this chapter, this population will be referred to as Russian-speaking Jewish immigrants, which reflects their primary language of communication and their cultural diversity.

Social work has always stressed that in cross-cultural service, workers and the agencies in which they work must understand the special needs and cultures of the various ethnic groups they serve (Chazin, Hanson, Cohen, & Grishayeva, 2002; Congress, 1994; Drachman & Halberstadt, 1992; Hanson, Phillips, Chazin, & Grishayeva, 2003). Translating this tenet into practice is difficult, but is especially challenging when working with the Russian-speaking Jewish immigrants from the former Soviet Union.

Viewed according to origin, culture, hopes, and expectations of their new life in the United States, they are a heterogeneous rather than homogeneous group. According to ethnic origin, Jewish immigrants comprise three groups: Ashkenazim, Sephardim, and Marathi Jews. Ashkenazim are descendants of Jews from Germany, Poland, Austria, and Eastern Europe. Most come from Russia (the central part of the FSU), and from Ukraine, Belarus, and the Baltic region (the western part). They usually speak Yiddish or Slavic languages such as Russian, Ukrainian, and Polish. Sephardim originated in Spain and Portugal. Their ancestors were among the Jews expelled from Spain and Portugal during the Spanish Inquisition. Marathi or Oriental Jews ("Arab Jews") are of Middle Eastern origin, from various countries of the Near East or Central Asia. While colloquially they are called Sephardic Jews, they have no ancestral ties to Spain. Marathi Jews, such as the Bukharian Jews, came from Central Asia, especially from towns such as Bukhara and Samarkand.

Regardless of differences in origin and culture, Russian-speaking immigrants share some common characteristics. Family structure is one. Typically, the Soviet family was a close-knit, emotionally connected, interdependent, three-generation unit. Grandparents often resided with and were fully involved in the family. They cared for their grandchildren, performed various household chores, and contributed to the family financially. Gender roles of husband and wife were clearly defined and differentiated. Although both husband and wife worked, the wife carried additional responsibility for the household and the children. Recognition of the wife's contribution is seen in the use of two family names, the husband's and the wife's. Regarding children, parents were responsible for their care and protection, and the school was responsible for their socialization. Older parents significantly contributed to the family and remained the responsibility of their adult children. Young couples often remained dependent on their parents, further strengthening family ties and interdependence (E. Bentsianov, personal communication, May, 1995; Drachman & Halberstadt, 1992). Such particularly close family ties, while a premigration strength, can create post-migration difficulties.

In considering the Soviet Jewish immigrant experience, a framework that views migration as a process of stages provides a fuller understanding (Drachman & Halberstadt, 1992). This framework underscores the necessity of understanding more than the resettlement experience. The émigrés' life in their native lands, the culture they carry with them, and their experience in traveling from their homeland to the United States must also be understood. This view considers immigration as comprising three phases: premigration, transit, and resettlement. All three phases are discussed here, as well as some case examples of immigration difficulties and implications for social work practice with these immigrants.

PREMIGRATION

The premigration experiences of Russian-speaking Jews are similar in some respects and different in others. Important factors to be considered include the time of immigration, the nature of the decision to emigrate, and the regions of origin.

Time of Immigration

A major difference among Russian-speaking immigrants is related to the time of immigration. Russian-speaking émigrés can be divided into four groups according to the time of immigration. The earliest group, the "refusniks," was followed by those emigrating between 1980 and 1990; a third wave followed, emigrating until the late 1990s; and a fourth wave came over the past several years.

In the post-Stalin era, information about the life in the new Jewish state of Israel became more available in the Soviet Union. Israeli activities in the FSU stimulated the Soviet Jews' interest in Israel, encouraging many, especially the young, to learn Jewish history, the Hebrew language, and Jewish rituals. These activities served to restore a sense of Jewishness among Soviet Jews (Wiesel, 1987). Because of this movement and the fact that the government restricted emigration to those who intended to reunite with their relatives in Israel, most chose Israel as their destination (Ro'I, 1991, p. 327, cited in Orleck, 2001, p. 530). By the late 1960s, however, only a few hundred received permission to leave; numerous applications were denied permission. Forced to wait for permission for several years, this group, called the refusniks, suffered great hardship. During their wait the government punished them for their attempt to emigrate by denying them state benefits such as employment and housing and subjecting them to KGB investigation. In addition, their fellow citizens would frequently harass and humiliate them.

These early refusniks were followed by a second group who emigrated between the years 1980 and 1990. The majority of this second wave of émigrés chose the United States and were Ashkenazi. This group was less religious and more educated, with fewer ties to Israel than the Sephardim and Marathi. In need of educated professionals and technicians, the Israeli government pressured U.S.-based charitable groups and immigration agencies to refuse to help the Russian-speaking Jews immigrate to the United States. The American groups rejected Israel's request (Weinstein, 1988). In the late 1980s, the Soviet government increased Jewish emigration quotas. At about the same time, the United States again changed its immigration policy.

Generally, those who emigrated since 1980 (and particularly since 1990) benefited from more humane Soviet governmental policies. Although their leaving was easier, the reasons for migrating remained painful. Motivations included the fear of Chernobyl radiation, political turmoil, increased economic hardship, and growing anti-Semitism and threats of pogroms by an anti-Semitic grassroots movement. Despite this stress, many émigrés were less motivated than the earlier refusniks; they left the Soviet Union reluctantly, fearful of changing their homeland (Chazin, 1995; Drachman & Halberstadt, 1992).

Complicated political relationships between the Soviet Union, Israel, the United States, and the Arab countries in the 1970s and 1980s directly affected the number of émigrés and their choice of destinations. Until the mid 1970s, Jewish émigrés mostly went to Israel. In the 1980s, under pressure from the United States government, the Soviet government increased their quotas for Soviet Jews to emigrate. Simultaneously, the United States granted this group refugee status,[1] further easing their immigration by creating the Federal Refugee Resettlement Program to facilitate effective resettlement of refugees and to assist them in achieving economic self-sufficiency. The Program granted them various entitlements such as eligibility for citizenship in 5 years after entering the U.S., Medicaid, English as a second language training, case management services, and the "dollar-for-dollar matching" to those national voluntary agencies serving refugees (The Refugee Act of 1980, reauthorized through the year 2002; H.R. 3061).

A third group arrived from late 1980s until the late 1990s. After 1990, under pressure from the United States, the Soviet government further dramatically eased its emigration policies. These shifts in governmental policies regarding emigration led to different experiences for émigrés depending on their time of departure. These differences will be discussed in the "Transit" section.

In addition to seeking asylum, the fourth and newest wave of immigrants whose arrival began in the late 1990s and continues to the present, many of whom were entrepreneurs in their homeland, sought greater business opportunities in the capitalist Western world. At their arrival, most spoke better English than the earlier groups, had occupational skills enabling quicker employment, were better informed about life in the United States, and held more realistic expectations about their future.

The Decision to Emigrate

Motivation to Emigrate

The most common reason for immigration among Jews was fear of anti-Semitism. This fear originated from the history of the

Jewish experience in the Russian Empire and later in the Soviet Union. From generation to generation, Russian-speaking Jews experienced or heard about the Pale of Settlement, the Holocaust, pogroms, Stalin's "Doctors Plot,"[2] and other terrible acts of anti-Semitism. They felt oppressed and unfairly targeted. In the post-Stalin era up to the mid 1980s, the incidents of real anti-Semitism were often nonviolent. It was historical memory and the perception of discrimination that kept Russian-speaking Jews alarmed and guarded. The Jewish preimmigration experience was one of hyper-vigilance; one of constant fear and anticipation of discriminative actions—"it is not happening yet, but may happen at any time in the future."

Despite this widespread fear, the presence of Soviet Jews in higher education, professional, and business positions, suggests a more complex picture of anti-Semitism. The evidence of official persecution in the post-Stalin era to the mid 1970s is mixed. While there were instances of college administrators or local party leaders limiting the entry of Jews into higher education, many Jews were still admitted. Thus, when immigration increased after 1970, mostly to Israel, the Soviet government, recognizing the existence of an educated Jewish population, was concerned about their loss to a perceived enemy. Further evidence of the Jewish ability to gain higher education is seen in the Soviet immigrants of the 1980s and later, who were highly educated—with more than 55% registered as scientists, professionals, and technicians (Tress, 1996). Further, some of these immigrants had held positions as directors of plants, college professors, medical doctors, and scientists with access to the top state secrets.

In addition to anti-Semitism, another reason to immigrate was the desire to reunite with extended family. Until the late 1980s, foreign travel restrictions limited visitation with family members or friends in other countries. Further contributing to immigration were poor economic conditions, ideological disagreement with the government, and a wish to perform unpermitted religious rituals. For some, there was the wish to travel beyond the borders of the FSU (less valid in the post-Soviet period when travel restrictions eased).

Factors Discouraging Emigration

Despite these motivations to emigrate, a number of factors discouraged emigration. The difficult decision to emigrate was exacerbated by increased anti-Semitism as a backlash to the Jewish emigration. Angered by the loss of significant human resources, the Soviet government increased its anti-Semitism. The general public, jealous at the Jewish population's ability to escape hardship and their own inability to escape their poor economic environment, joined by venting their anger on the Jews for the opportunity they themselves were denied. Further, there were the frequent, confusing, and sometimes harsh changes in immigration rules by the Soviet government, and the governments of Israel, the United States, and Canada. For example, some rules required that Russian Jewish émigrés surrender their jobs, sometimes apartments, while waiting for the Soviet government's decision on their immigration request. Later this rule would be repealed by the Soviets. Under another rule, immigrants couldn't go directly to their destination (if different than Israel) and had to wait for a U.S. government decision on their case for months, perhaps years, in migration centers in Europe; later the U.S. government changed that rule. Some confusing rules still exist, for example, Jewish émigrés from Ukraine must obtain their immigrants' visas not at the Ukraine's U.S. consulate, but in Poland.

The third and fourth waves of Russian-speaking Jewish immigrants enjoyed advantages their predecessors did not. First, many were able to choose their host countries, often having the choice of the U.S., Israel, Germany, and, less often, Canada and Australia. It is noteworthy, however, that many chose the United States, expecting greater economic opportunity, better national security, noncompulsory military service, and a comfortable secular and pluralistic society (Gold, 1994). Second, they had access to more information about possible host countries through their pre-immigration visits to relatives or friends already settled in host countries. Even when visiting was not possible, these newer immigrants had access to information about prospective host countries made widely available by those who had immigrated earlier.

Family Factors Influencing Emigration

It also is important for social workers to understand other aspects of the decision-making process regarding whether or not to surrender a known lifestyle for one that is unknown in a foreign land. This is stressful for most families, particularly for those consisting of three generations with close emotional and functional ties. The presence of three generations increases the possibility for disagreement about emigrating. Sometimes large, extended families separate, some members remaining behind while others emigrate. In this scenario, both those left behind and those who depart feel the pain of the family breakup. Even if differences are resolved and the family emigrates as a complete unit, initial dissension may later haunt the family. Or, different members of a family may immigrate to different countries. Such family disintegration may lead some family members to struggle to reunite the whole family. Other families may suffer a complete breakup as separated family members assimilate to different cultures. Even if the differences are resolved and the family reunites or emigrates as one complete unit, the initial dissension may later torment the family. Adjustment difficulties may evoke the earlier reluctance and disagreements of some family members, resulting in bitter recriminations and blame for their emigration and present predicament.

The Case of Mr. and Mrs. P.

The following case illustrates the painful family separation and accompanying losses which are often the case for Russian-speaking Jewish immigrants. Mr. and Mrs. P. lived and worked in a major Russian city, enjoying successful careers. Their oldest son, his wife, and their child lived with them. They maintained their Jewish identity by following Jewish rituals clandestinely, speaking Yiddish, and learning Hebrew. They hid their Torah behind volumes of Leo Tolstoy and lit their ritual candles on Shabbat. All family members wished to leave Russia, but they strongly disagreed about where to emigrate. Finally, their older son with his wife and son left for Israel, and Mr. and Mrs. P. with their younger son emigrated to the United States, where Mr. P. had relatives. Although Mr. P. was unhappy about the separation of the family, he rationalized that his grandson would gain the Jewish education in Israel which he had dreamt of for himself and his sons.

Although disappointed at his younger son's rejection of a Jewish education in a Yeshiva, Mr. P. found a Judaic community for himself and his wife, comfortable with the family's religious involvement. Over time, however, his grandchild grew distant from them not only territorially, but emotionally, too. First, their contacts were limited by weekly phone calls, then, by holiday cards. On one occasion, his favorite grandson traveled from Israel to the United States and surprisingly called from New York City to say "Happy Passover" to Mr. and Mrs. P. The grandparents were very happy about this contact, but when they invited this grandson for dinner, he simply said: "I can't. You're not kosher enough for me." For Mr. and Mrs. P., this call evoked a sense of alienation from their loved ones, a sense of their own inadequacy, helplessness, and depression for which they sought help from a mental health professional.

After the initial assessment, Mr. and Mrs. P. were referred to an ADHC program support group for Russian-speaking elderly immigrants who shared a similar experience of family separation and generational gap, as well as their new Jewish identity. The loss of the grandparent role, which carried respect and authority in their former culture, made many elderly Russian-speaking Jewish immigrants question the meaning of their lives. Through sharing their personal experience of loss, their loss of family roles could be mourned and reframed, newly emerging family status gradually accepted, and their pride in their contributions to their children's and grandchildren's freedom restored. Mr. and Mrs. P. report that their coping skills were enhanced after they heard that they were not alone in their grief.

Regions of Origin and Cultural Differences

Considering the vast expanse of the former Soviet Union and the fact that émigrés came from some 15 different republics, it is not surprising to find significant regional differences in social class, occupation, and education. These influence their relationships with one another and their adaptation. These émigrés are sensitive to such differences. To understand a particular client family, the worker must be similarly sensitive. A worker must know of the client's cultural, historical, and geographical origins.

Urban Centers and the Intelligentsia

Many of the Russian-speaking Jewish immigrants originate from the urban centers of Moscow and Leningrad, which had the largest concentration of educational and cultural institutions. Although Jews found these institutions difficult to enter, many successfully pursued higher education. The urban centers generated a large number of the elite intelligentsia, including professionals, scientists, artists, and musicians, as well as many craftsmen and dissidents. These émigrés shared a rich involvement in the cultural life of their cities—the concerts, operas, theaters, and museums—a cultural life offered primarily in big cities. As metropolitan residents they are flexible, accustomed to the complex lifestyle characteristic of city life, and more verbal and articulate.

Provincial Towns in Ukraine and Belarus

Émigrés from the towns of Ukraine and Belarus differ sharply from the urban centers' cultured intelligentsia. They are more like blue collar workers or tradesmen in culture, lifestyle, and expectations. Their communities of origin offered limited social and cultural opportunities. Russian-speaking residents of these smaller communities typically knew many of their brethren. Their cultural life centered on the "palace of culture," which included movie theaters, a sports stadium, and some musical offerings but nothing comparable to the cultural life of the urban centers (Bentsianov, 1995).

It is noteworthy that many Jewish provincial immigrants speak the universal language of Yiddish and are more likely to be familiar with Jewish traditions than the intelligentsia. However, because of their small town origins they are less prepared for the demands of big-city life and for the loss of their extended families.

Odessa

In addition to the urban center and small-community subcultures discussed, a third group of Russian-speaking émigrés are those from Odessa. Odessa was one of the largest cities within the former Soviet Union, and contained the largest Jewish population in the region. Although located within Ukraine, its inhabitants considered themselves Odessans. These Jewish émigrés created a special bond, with their own unique folk language, songs, and especially their own brand of humor. They developed a separate society with its own class structure (E. Bentsianov, personal communication, May 1995).

The Baltic Republics: Latvia, Estonia, and Lithuania

Still another subculture within the Russian-speaking immigrant population is that of the Baltic émigré. The Baltic republics were annexed by the Soviets in 1940, then occupied by the Germans in World War II, and only incorporated into the Soviet system in 1945. Consequently, these émigrés lived in the Soviet system for a relatively short time, with ample opportunity to develop and preserve their own culture. The small number of Baltic Jews who had survived the Holocaust or Gulag enjoyed an active Jewish cultural life—religious centers, political parties, and youth organizations. At the time of mass migration, however, there were more Jews who migrated to this region since 1945 from the other parts of the Soviet Union, than there were natives. Some Russians and "new" Jews from Russia, Belarus, and Ukraine did not speak the Baltic nations' languages fluently. With their different cultures, they represented an occupant power. Anti-Sovietism was very strong and anti-Semitism, masked by anti-Sovietism, was directed more against all Russian-speaking newcomers than against Jews in particular.

Although the émigrés from the Baltic republics come from agricultural rather than industrialized societies, they more comfortably identify with the citizens of the industrialized Central European countries such as Germany and Poland. Consequently, the Baltic Russian-speaking immigrant brings a mix of European and Soviet cultures. For Russian-speaking Jewish immigrants there is an additional Jewish cultural element.

Other Cultures

Finally, Russian-speaking immigrants from the Caucasian and Asian areas, such as from Bukharan, Uzbekistan, and Georgia, Armenia, and Azerbaijan, must also be acknowledged. These republics differ in culture, so émigrés from these lands also differ from each other as well as from those already noted. The Bukharans, the largest immigrant group from this general population, have a history of some 2,000 years of acceptance within a Muslim society. Their culture includes both Jewish and Muslim elements and is steeped in a rich history of Jewish values that differ from contemporary Judaism. Because this group was accepted by their Muslim neighbors, they did not assimilate but preserved their own Jewish identity and culture. Culturally, they dress like their ancestors and have large families and close ties with extended family. Young couples often live with their in-laws. Values include a positive Jewish identity and financial rather than educational achievement.

Status is dependent on one's age and the number of children one has. There is a double standard in sexual relationships and an acceptance of extramarital affairs for men.

TRANSIT

Effects of the Former Soviet Union's Emigration Policy

More recent Russian-speaking émigrés have had an easier transit experience in some ways and a more difficult one in others. The relaxed Soviet emigration policies and the granting of refugee status in the United States eased Soviet Jews' relocation after 1980. However, the resultant rise in the number of Russian-speaking immigrants created new problems. In 1988, Soviet immigrants reached the refugee quota limit and stretched the resettlement funds available for refugees. Consequently, the United States limited the number of Soviet Jews applying for refugee status. Many now faced a difficult decision while waiting in American resettlement facilities located in Austria and Italy. Those not offered refugee status were given the option of entering the United States as "parolees,"[1] without the entitlements accompanying refugee status. This shift in immigration policy was particularly traumatic for those families in which some members were offered refugee status and others entrance only as parolees. Many rejected parolee status, recognizing that without benefits survival would be difficult. Families split in this way—some granted refugee status, others either having parolee status or being forced to wait—often suffered increased intergenerational, marital, and intra-familial conflict. The separation of members was particularly painful for Soviet families, because of their usual pattern of close family ties and three-generational interdependence (Bentsianov, 1995; Drachman & Halberstadt, 1992).

In 1989 another change in American immigration policy further affected the transit experience of Soviet immigrants. The United States closed its resettlement facilities in Austria and Italy and transferred its headquarters to its Moscow embassy. Émigrés still waiting in the resettlement facilities were both positively and negatively affected by this change. A positive consequence was that they had more time to learn about their new homeland and to heal the wounds caused by their losses. Also, many of them had family and friends who had emigrated earlier and were now settled in the United States, willing and able to provide support and assistance. Negatively, they were now forced to wait in the discomfort of the resettlement facilities, with little to do.

At the present time the number of Russian-speaking Jewish immigrants to the United States has significantly decreased. Since the Welfare Reform Reconciliation Act of 1996 was passed, immigrants became eligible for public assistance on the basis of citizenship status rather than legal status. Thus, regardless of one's legal documentation, lacking citizenship meant ineligibility for public welfare. All noncitizens were restricted from participation in most of the major federal benefit programs for which eligibility is based on need, such as food stamps, Supplemental Security Income (SSI), and Medicaid. These unprecedented restrictions affected not only many immigrants who were already in the country, but severely limited the ability to immigrate to the United States of many Russian-speaking Jewish families. For them, this new law means a return to the "parolees" era of immigration. In 1997, the U.S. Congress recognized the controversial aspects of the Act and restored SSI to most immigrants who were already in the United States when the welfare law was enacted. In 1998 Congress restored food stamps to immigrant children, elderly, and disabled persons. However, immigrants who entered the U.S. after the 1996 were made ineligible for any assistance using federal funding for their first 5 years of residence. New immigration security measures, which have been in effect after the World Trade Center tragedy of September 11, 2001, also have affected the Russian-speaking immigrant flow.

Expectations

Whatever else they have in common, it is likely that all immigrants carry their own special baggage of motivation, aspirations, and expectations about achievement in the new world. Soviet émigrés who held unrealistic and idealized expectations of this new society (e.g., that all of its citizens are wealthy and that its high level of technological development would assure them well-paying jobs) were abruptly and painfully disillusioned. Many of the early émigrés settled in urban centers, where their expectations of high quality of life were often dashed by the reality of unemployment, crime, and a high cost of living. Exacerbating their adjustment to their new home was the sense of special entitlement that many had. Although the Soviet government had for many years prevented their emigration, American Jewry's active support conveyed the promise of special status once in the United States. Instead, they were faced with the same adjustment difficulties that all immigrants face; learning a new language, finding suitable employment and housing, and adjusting to a new culture and environment.

Beginning in the 1980s, most Russian-speaking immigrants fared better than their predecessors. They were highly educated urban dwellers—more than 55% registered as scientists, professionals, and technicians (Tress, 1996). Russian-speaking Jewish immigrants were the only foreign-born group that tended to live in the advantaged neighborhoods. As compared with American-born Whites with similar household life cycle and socioeconomic status, the Russian-speaking Jews chose neighborhoods with lower violent crimes and safer buildings than did the American-born White households (Rosenbaum, Friedman, Schill, & Buddelmeyer, 1999). More importantly, they were able to pay for such living conditions.

Despite their economic success, even this group experienced some dissatisfaction as they confronted the same difficulties all immigrants experience. Namely, they confronted the language barrier, and the loss of prior status and identity. These immigrants carried particularly high expectations of their new country. They were often less than satisfied with the housing, job placement, and Jewish education services that the local American Jewish agencies provided. Those services were designed for the expected majority of Jewish immigrants as small-town craftsmen or farmers.

RESETTLEMENT

Having discussed the Russian-speaking émigrés' pre-immigration and transit experience, we now consider their resettlement. All immigrants confront the loss of home and lifestyle and the necessity of coping with acculturation demands in their new home, and Russian-speaking Jewish immigrants faced the same challenges. This section discusses common resettlement circumstances and the resolution of issues. Several case vignettes are included to illustrate various adjustment difficulties, acculturation paths, and useful social work services.

Choice of Community

One resettlement issue is the choice of where to relocate. The Soviet Jewish émigrés chose to reside in communities inhabited by family, friends, and those from their cities and regions of origin. The most recent wave of immigrants, post-Soviet era, could generally be expected to have the easiest resettlement experience. They arrived to find numerous local Russian-speaking communities, especially in major cities like New York. Their choice of neighborhood was influenced by their comfort with the neighborhood's character, climate, and job opportunities. They selected neighborhoods that replicated their original communities, geographically and socially. Entering a familiar Soviet culture with its Russian-speaking inhabitants, and its traditional food, music, songs, movies, and television certainly served to ease the resettlement experience.

Of course, despite their similarities, Russian-speaking communities differed one from another in some respects. This clustering by origins is especially visible in areas with large concentrations of FSU émigrés. Understandably, a city's neighborhoods of immigrants often have their own distinct populations and culture. New York City is one example of this phenomenon. One neighborhood is populated primarily by the intelligentsia of Moscow and Leningrad. Another, consisting largely of Odessans, is known as "Little Odessa." Yet a third neighborhood is composed of Bukharans with their own unique religion, language, and culture (Barber, 1987; Gold, 1994).

Economic Decisions

The Soviet and U.S. governments both provide a safety net for their citizenry. Neither system provides fully for the basic needs of its citizenry in employment, housing, and medical services. In the Soviet society, it was often difficult to obtain a well-paying job, although low status and low-paying jobs were readily available. The government forced all able-bodied adults to work, even those famous for their cultural contributions, like poets and composers.

Regarding housing, even government subsidized housing was not free since all residents were required to pay for utilities and maintenance. Medical services were mostly provided without charge, but were limited. Medicine, while inexpensive, had to be paid for except when one was hospitalized, at which time it was government subsidized. All education was provided free of charge until the late 1980s but limited to those who passed admission exams.

Russian-speaking immigrants discovered that while the U.S. government, like the Soviet government, provided assistance, U.S. aid differed markedly. In the U.S. they were able to obtain welfare money, food stamps, and other assistance without the necessity of work. The discovery and utilization of American welfare allowed these immigrants to choose different paths. The first and second waves of immigrants of the 1970s through the 1980s used welfare to learn English or gain new, marketable occupational skills. This behavior can also be explained by the immigrants' age—higher status in the FSU was typically achieved at the age of 40s or 50s, which was close to retirement age (55 for women, and 60 for men). Some immigrants considered welfare more than what they had in their country of origin and enough to live on in the U.S. Some, particularly those with higher educational and occupational status, chose welfare rather than start at the bottom of the economic ladder and work their way up (Belozersky, 1990). Still others employed the government's support for the education of their children. Some availed themselves of the government's special housing assistance to gain apartments in desired neighborhoods. And some, like many Americans, felt welfare carried a stigma that they sought to avoid at all costs.

The third and fourth immigrant waves, arriving after 1990, were different in several respects. These immigrants had experienced "perestroika," "glasnost," and the first legal private businesses in the post-Soviet Union. They spoke better English, and were better prepared for the American way of life and for aggressive business activities. A recent survey conducted for the American Jewish Committee in 2000 by the Research Institute for New Americans, found that 82% of Russian-speaking Jewish immigrants below age 65 who have lived in the United States for less than 9 years are employed. Most of the employed Russian-speaking Jews who were in the United States for more than 6 years have similar characteristics as the Americans Jewish middle class: 45% of Russian Jewish immigrants in New York City, who were in the United States for more than 6 years, have the same range of income as 48% of American Jews: $30,000 to $75,000 (American Jewish Committee, 2000).

AN ACCULTURATION MODEL

All immigrants confront the acculturation challenge of transitioning from a premigration culture to a new one. In one acculturation model, Berry (1997) proposes four acculturation scenarios. According to this model, every immigrant balances between maintaining his/her own identity and assuming characteristics of the host culture.

Berry has named four acculturation scenarios, representing different adjustment paths. *Integration* involves the ability to maintain one's own cultural identity while building a relationship with the host culture. *Assimilation* entails adoption of the host culture while rejecting major components of an immigrant's own cultural identity. *Separation* means maintaining one's own cultural identity without accepting the host culture. Lastly, *marginalization* leads to losing one's own identity without establishing a relationship with the host society. Any of those scenario can cause severe psychosocial problems for immigrant clients, and need to be assessed by a social worker. Although this model emphasizes adaptation to a host culture, Berry notes that acculturation is a reciprocal process and occurs when two groups come into contact and both groups change. Berry emphasized that the goal for immigrants is to integrate into society, and to avoid marginalization (Lecture in Hamilton College on 4/14/2004, as cited in Ripley, 2004). To apply Berry's model to the acculturation of Soviet Jewish immigrants, one must understand the preimmigrant identity of this group and the post-migration conflicts they encountered in the U.S.

Loss of Occupational and Social Status

The close-knit, interdependent, three-generational Soviet Jewish family that had been functional in the USSR is often problematic in the United States. All immigrant family members—the children, their adult parents, the parents' older adult parents—face difficult adjustment problems. Middle-aged couples with children often have a difficult time in two areas: their loss of status in the family and in the outside world. In the Soviet system these adults generally had achieved some level of social status accompanied by feelings of competency and value. They were at the peak of their earnings in their occupations and had authority within the home. In their new land they experienced limited skills in language, technology, and knowledge of their occupational fields. Unemployed émigrés have lost a major source of identity and a symbol of successful acculturation. They have also lost entry into economic work that facilitates continued success. Further, their children often mastered the English language more readily than they did and adjusted more quickly. Their simultaneous loss of status in both the community and the home was painful.

The following case illustrates the dilemma of middle-aged adults from a large city. Immigrants frequently do not qualify for the same high-level career positions they achieved in the Soviet system. They often find themselves rejected for entry-level positions in their fields of expertise because they are judged as overqualified. At the same time, their age and financial considerations often block them from beginning the education needed to gain American credentials comparable to those achieved in the Soviet system. Many thus face only the choice of unemployment or beginning in a new or related but lower status career at entry level. This drop in status is particularly painful for those who achieved higher degrees in the USSR and belonged to the intelligentsia. The decline in occupational status is often exacerbated by loss of the cultured life once treasured.

The Case of Mrs. Y.

Mrs. Y.'s experience illustrates the dilemma of many large-city Soviet émigrés. A woman in her mid 50s, Mrs. Y. sought help from a mental health clinic. In Leningrad, she was a PhD and a medical doctor, a significant achievement. Her ancestors had lived in Leningrad for many generations and had enjoyed the cultural life of the intelligentsia, with its rare books, art, antiques, opera, and the like. While atypical of the Soviet émigré, it was typical of this elite. In the United States her husband, who also had held a Soviet PhD and had a high status occupation, was unemployed. Her married son was a medical student; her married daughter studying computer programming. All three families were now on welfare.

Lost was the culturally rich, high status life she had led back in the USSR. Her professional status as a high ranking professor in a medical school had further enhanced her status. Because of this status and her social connections she had enjoyed access to literature not readily accessible to the general public and to the best of cultural life available. Despite Soviet anti-Semitism and social pressures, she had created her own insulated society. In a sense, her world was like the Ivy League world in our own society: in the Soviet system, the intelligentsia constituted a social and cultural elite, lacking only economic status.

At the mental health clinic, Mrs. Y. presented as a depressed client with some psychosomatic symptoms. The worker was sensitive to the enormity of her loss—her cultural life, social support system, and occupational status and power. The client's belief that her middle age, the normal Russian retirement age, and the lower value placed on her credentials, precluded any opportunity to begin her career again. In subsequent sessions the worker learned that Mrs. Y.'s emigration was motivated by the virulent anti-Semitism of the time and her fear for the safety of her children and grandchildren. Having lived in a close-knit family unit and not wanting to be separated from her family, she had decided to sacrifice her life in Russia for the safety of her family.

At first, Mrs. Y. was comforted by the physical closeness of the three families and her active and influential role as homemaker. However, her grandchildren, adjusting quickly, with their greater language facility and school contacts, lost respect for her. Her children, involved in their own adjustment, had less time for her. Her initial comfort changed to an acute awareness of her loss and a sense of futility, depression, and betrayal. She obsessed about having sacrificed everything, with no family appreciation or substitute gratification.

In their work the social worker focused on Mrs. Y.'s loss and her unrealistic expectations. The loss of her social system, cultural life, and occupational status were explored, as well as her expectations of recreating them. Her expectations that her children would remain a part of the same emotionally connected family she once had and would serve as a substitute for whatever loss she had to endure also were dashed by the reality of adjustment.

The social worker's understanding of the unique experience of this client both guided and facilitated the therapy. The worker understood the client's loss as well as her special resources. Because of her cultural and educational background, Mrs. Y. was more verbal, articulate, and comfortable in using her intellect in problem solving. Consequently, she was able and eager to use a cognitive, analytical therapy. Having resided in a large city, she also was more flexible and accustomed to the lifestyle characteristic of a big city (e.g., how to negotiate a complicated transportation system).

The worker's understanding of this client's cultural background and her special resources enabled her to see that Mrs. Y. could experience therapy as a means of regaining a piece of her lost intellectual life. The worker used her understanding to assist this client to work through her depression and to regain some of what she had lost. She helped Mrs. Y. recognize that, as a major city, New York had a rich cultural life of its own. The client was encouraged and aided in becoming active in the cultural life of her new home in the United States.

Marital Conflict

Various intra-familial problems arise because of the Russian-speaking émigrés' loss of their family lifestyle. One area of conflict is the husband-wife relationship. Because the husband has so much invested in his role as breadwinner, his job loss is especially painful for him. His pain then affects the marital relationship and all family relationships. Although the Soviet wife is also a worker, her lack of a job in the United States is often less painful. She is not only a breadwinner but, as parent and homemaker, retains other significant sources of gratification. The case of Mrs. T., a 42-year-old, married, Russian-speaking woman illustrates the marital tension that develops when a husband is unable to find employment while his wife succeeds. In this case the wife not only succeeds in becoming the breadwinner but maintains all three roles—wage earner, parent, and homemaker.

There are two additional pressures on adjustment in this case. One is the initial conflict about emigrating. The husband carried his reluctance and resentment about emigrating to his new home. It then became a weapon of blame as he attacked his wife for his adjustment difficulties. A second obstacle is the husband's definition of mental health service as appropriate only for those who are "crazy." This view, common in the former Soviet Union, contributes to resistance to use of mental health services, allowing problems to unnecessarily exacerbate.

The Case of Mrs. T.

Mrs. T. requested consultation for emotional disturbances with which she was unable to cope. She complained of sadness, nervousness, increased irritability, poor sleep, frequent headaches, and other physical symptoms. Two years earlier, Mrs. T. had arrived in the United States from Kiev, accompanied by her husband, son, and daughter, and her husband's parents. She reported no history of psychiatric disorders and presented a consistently good physical health record. She first experienced her symptoms about 4 months before entering therapy. After failing to resolve her problems she realized that she needed professional help. She described herself as having been a "normal" woman with a "normal" family. She now felt her family was splitting apart, and she was deeply concerned about her husband and their relationship.

In Ukraine, Mrs. T. had been an accountant at a large factory where her husband had been chief of the engineering department. Their income was above average, and their lives were satisfactory. They enjoyed longtime friends and regularly attended social events, parties, concerts, and the theater. Their two children were good students, and they had little difficulty as parents. The marital relationship had been warm, supportive, and friendly. Mrs. T. reported that their problems began when they first considered emigration.

She had initiated the idea because she feared for the family's safety in the social and economic instability of the time. She particularly feared anti-Semitism, always present in Ukraine but particularly virulent during unstable times. Her children had been very enthusiastic about relocating in the United States, but her husband and his parents had agreed only reluctantly. He maintained that they both had stable work and income and were in no immediate danger. He feared that because of his age he would be unable to begin a new life and reach the occupational level he had attained in their homeland. His parents also were against relocation, fearing its numerous demands. Despite these concerns, Mrs. T. prevailed, and they emigrated.

In the United States, Mrs. T. and her children successfully overcame major adjustment challenges. The children continued their education in public school, performing satisfactorily. After a few months of learning English, Mrs. T. completed training in a business school and received a certificate in office management and bookkeeping. She soon found a job as assistant manager at a trade company, with a salary and medical insurance sufficient to cover her family's needs.

Mrs. T.'s husband fared poorly. He gained the support of an organization that helped former Soviet scientists and engineers start their new careers. He attended an English class and classes to prepare for searching for employment. He prepared and mailed his resumes. Despite a number of interviews, however, he failed to secure a position. Gradually, his enthusiasm, motivation, self-confidence, and hope dwindled. By the time his wife found a job, he was depressed, spending most of his time lethargically at home; he was bad tempered and jealous of other family members' successes. His relationships with his wife and children deteriorated. He was irritated and angry with his wife, blaming her for the family's emigration and his current failure. His subsequent loss of all sexual interest in his wife was particularly painful for Mrs. T. because this had always been a source of mutual pleasure. Mrs. T.'s success in the work world afforded her some small solace for her painful marital situation. Aware of her male coworkers' attention and compliments, she paid more attention to her grooming, acknowledging in sessions that she now felt even more "female power" than in her youth. Her acceptance of some coworkers' dinner invitations further lifted her spirits. Her husband, however, noticing the change, became even more jealous and angry. Their marital tension increased until, frustrated and frightened by her loss of interest in her husband, she considered divorce. Aware of their long, pleasurable marriage, and blaming herself for having forced the family to emigrate, she remained unable to resolve their predicament, developing her presenting symptoms.

After a few individual sessions with Mrs. T., the social worker invited Mr. T. in to discuss the family's situation. Although initially resistant, insisting he was not "crazy" and had no need of professional help, Mr. T. reluctantly agreed to marital therapy. The work with this couple lasted several months and included both individual and joint sessions. The worker helped each spouse explore their respective psychological difficulties and the origins of their problems. Therapy afforded each partner a better understanding of the other and the dynamics of their relationship. In joint sessions the couple learned to communicate effectively, share their feelings, identify common problems, and search for optimal solutions.

By treatment's end both Mr. and Mrs. T. expressed willingness to remain together and to continue joint work on their problems. Mr. T. regained his motivation to begin a new professional
career. Through cognitive restructuring and behavioral modifica-
tion he developed the skills he needed for success in job interviews. His self-esteem and self-confidence significantly improved
so that by treatment's termination he had completed three job
interviews and was awaiting decisions. Mr. T. was more comfortable with his wife's success at work and encouraged her to pursue further professional advancement. Their relationship
improved further with the resumption of a satisfying sexual relationship. Treatment terminated with marital and family relationships greatly improved and both partners better able to identify
their issues and work together on their resolution.

Middle-aged adults are not the only family members at risk
for marital conflict. Young married couples also may experience
difficult relationship problems. On the one hand, emigration helps
some young couples to separate from the family enmeshment typical in Soviet families. Often these young couples possess occupational knowledge and skills and greater language facility than their
elders have, affording them quicker social and occupational adjustment. Other young couples, however, separated from their families
by emigration, have difficulty with resettlement. Having relied on
their parents for assistance in decision making and child rearing,
they may lack skills in both areas. This situation may be particularly
true in the intelligentsia families discussed above. Such young
couples may fight, blame each other, voice regrets about marriage
and emigration, and even talk of separation and divorce. Their
lack of awareness of the impact of their acrimony on their children
only exacerbates family difficulties (Hall & Halberstadt, 1994).

Adults and Their Parents

Another area of conflict is the relationship between adults and
their parents. In the Soviet system older adults often played a
valued role in the family, contributing to its welfare by providing
child care for grandchildren and contributing to family income.
In the United States, however, although these older adults may
continue to provide some relief from parenting responsibilities,
they may create an entirely new set of problems for their adult

children. Older adults living with their adult children may interfere in their offspring's problems, making matters worse. The older generation also suffers from its own adjustment problems. Difficulty in finding gainful employment weakens their position and status in the family in this new world, adding to the family's stress. Older adults experience a much harder time mastering English than do the younger family members. Because their grandchildren speak English better and know more about this new culture through their contact with peers and their school experience, older adults lose their authority to the younger generations, and their status in the family diminishes further. This new family structure, with the oldest generation given little respect and value, more closely resembles the American family system.

Parent-Adolescent Problems

Émigrés also struggle with relationship difficulties between parents and their adolescent children. Although generational conflict exists among all immigrant families, the adult Soviet émigrés' protectiveness adds to the problem. This parental protectiveness derives from a desire to protect children from the Soviet Union's anti-Semitism. Their protectiveness, however, conflicts with the adolescent's typical struggle for independence and use of the peer group as guide and mentor. Parental unemployment, difficulty with English, and inability to understand their children's struggle with acculturation in their peer group and school create a deeper chasm between parent and child. One consequence is an erosion of the parents' authority over their adolescent children.

The case of B. illustrates some of the difficulties Soviet immigrants confront with their adolescent children. The parents' limited ability to assist B. is partly due to their lack of understanding of his acculturation experience. As an aside, it is interesting to note that B. reported no academic difficulty at school. Soviet education does not parallel ours, and some youths find themselves academically ahead of their grade, experiencing boredom at school.

The Case of B.

A 14-year-old Russian-speaking boy, B. is the only son of a family who emigrated from Moscow 1 year ago. His parents took him to a mental health clinic, complaining of his increased irritability and poor communication with them, as well as misbehavior, withdrawal, and failing school grades. A good student in Russia, B. was initially motivated and enthusiastic in public school. Because he had attended a specialized English school in Russia, he was accepted into a regular 8th grade class in the United States. His early work produced good grades and positive teacher evaluations. After several months, however, B.'s attitude and behavior changed, his grades dropped, and he withdrew at home. In their effort to help, his parents used habitual methods of suggestion and criticism, prohibiting activities and limiting relationships. Finally, accepting their failure, they sought therapy.

After working through B.'s resistance and establishing a therapeutic alliance, the social worker elicited his concerns about his physical changes, his growing interest in sexual issues, and his difficulties in adjusting at school. He was ashamed to discuss his sexual concerns with his parents because sex was never discussed in the home. He was interested in girls, but they liked "cool" guys. In his effort to become one of them, B. copied their appearance, attitude, and behavior, losing interest in his studies. He finally found himself an outsider at school, with neither a reputation as a good student nor as "cool." He did not discuss his frustration and disappointment with his parents, believing they could not possibly understand and help. He insisted he still loved them but could not respect them because they remained Russian, whereas he desperately wanted to become "American" as soon as possible.

The social worker's treatment plan included two main elements: one focused on B., the other on his parents. With B., the worker sought to help him understand the physical and psychological changes he was undergoing and their effects, to clarify his strengths and support his efforts to use these to cope, to support his self-esteem and self-confidence by developing skills of positive self-evaluation and self-acceptance, and to help him better understand his parents' difficulties and reestablish communications with them. With his parents the worker sought to reframe their son's experience as a normal part of the adolescent's struggle for independence and to educate them as to more effective means of communicating with their son, using more approval and understanding and less criticism.

Treatment was successfully completed in about 5 months. Family relationships and B.'s school grades improved. He developed new interests in tennis and computers. At school, although

not fully accepted by the class leaders, he was less of an outsider and formed his own circle of friends. His relationship with
girls remained difficult, but it was now in the range of normal adolescent difficulty, and he was better able to cope with the
stress of social relationships.

IMPLICATIONS FOR SOCIAL WORK PRACTICE

Social work has a long history of serving many different groups of
immigrants. To assess and intervene effectively with resettlement
problems, the worker must be sensitive to the experience of each
particular immigrant group and individual. As Chazin has noted
elsewhere, cultural sensitivity in cross-cultural mental health work
is a crucial factor (Chazin, Colarossi, Hanson, Grishayeva, & Contis, 2004; Chazin et al., 2002; Hanson et al., 2003). This sensitivity
necessitates individualizing each client and having a sound understanding of the émigré's resettlement difficulties. The worker must
also be sensitive to the émigré's homeland culture and lifestyle as
well as his or her transit experience. Efforts to move too quickly
into work adjustment issues without first understanding the client's
culture and transit experience may well prove self-defeating. Because émigrés are a heterogeneous population with considerable
diversity, individualizing them is crucial to understanding each
immigrant's unique experience. Sensitivity to this issue is also
necessary to help Soviet émigrés overcome their learned distrust
of social service workers. We now consider these elements and
others and their practice implications.

Russian-Speaking Immigrant and
American Cultural Differences

In practice with Russian-speaking immigrants, the social worker
must be aware of cultural differences between Russian-speaking
immigrants and Americans. As is true of all immigrants, cultural
differences cross all facets of life, including mental health as well
as family and social relationships. The relationship of former Soviet
Union governments to their citizens is one particularly significant
factor to consider. These governments often provided citizens with
a socioeconomic safety net different than that of the U.S. The
U.S. welfare system provides the immigrant with various subsidies

that allow for choices unavailable in the F.S.U. Without fully understanding the Russian-speaking émigré's perception of welfare, the worker may find it difficult to understand and accept the émigré's use of welfare in the United States.

The Russian-speaking émigré may also have difficulty with social service personnel because of cultural differences in service delivery. In the former Soviet Union system the government and its bureaucrats provide service. Often, bureaucrats must be manipulated in order to gain benefits. In the United States, voluntary agencies play a significant role in the delivery of social services, and manipulation of the social worker is not a normal part of the transaction. The émigré who treats the social worker as a bureaucrat who must be manipulated in order to obtain service may initiate an unwanted interaction. The worker, ignorant of customary FSU transactions in securing services, risks misperceiving the émigré as psychologically disturbed, inappropriately demanding, and manipulative. The émigré then sees the worker as not understanding and, worse, uncaring.

Furthermore, social workers must be attuned to the émigré's mistrust of strangers and sense of entitlement. The Soviet system, through its persecution of Jews, fostered in them a distrust not only of governmental bureaucrats but of strangers in general. Soviet émigrés have learned to speak intimately only with family and a select group of trusted friends. Their mistrust of strangers impedes the social worker's efforts to establish rapport and a therapeutic alliance. Compounding the problem of establishing a therapeutic relationship is the émigrés' sense of entitlement. Their identification as victims, combined with American Jewry's promise of a better life in the United States, for many contributed to a sense of entitlement and unrealistic expectations of assistance and benefits.

Another general cultural difference worthy of special note is the émigrés' view of mental illness. The Russian-speaking émigré is likely to view mental illness as biologically caused and best treated with medication. The talking cure at the heart of much of American therapy is understandably viewed as peculiar. Their difficulty in seeing the connection between talking and solving concrete problems adds to their confusion. The social worker's use of communication as a healing tool evokes in these clients a lack of confidence and trust in the worker who seeks to help (Drachman & Halberstadt, 1992).

To overcome the Russian-speaking émigré's difficulty in using social services requires sensitivity to all facets of the émigré's experience and personality. The social worker must devote time to empathic listening and understanding. What was this émigré's unique native land circumstances? When and how did he or she travel from the FSU to the United States, and did he or she enter as a refugee or a parolee? What has he or she experienced in resettling? The worker's effort to understand empathically each émigré's full experience aids in healing the wounds of loss and in resolving resettlement problems. The social worker's most helpful role is as surrogate parent, providing the client with genuine interest, empathic caring, and some advice, direction, and counseling.

The émigrés' difficulty in using American mental health services, with their emphasis on communication, has other practice implications. It is more than coincidence that, although the case vignettes presented above cover a range of problems, they all involved short-term approaches. Time-limited, highly focused counseling seems most appropriate, given FSU émigrés' views and experience.

The Immigrant as Service Provider

One aid in overcoming these cultural differences is the use of bilingual fellow FSU immigrants. Social work has a history of involving indigenous people in helping their fellow compatriots to acculturate. Despite the limitations of immigrant practitioners evaluating clients in their shared native languages (Perez Foster, 2001), their own experience as émigrés uniquely qualifies indigenous people to assist professionals in bridging the cultural gap between social worker and émigré. Bilingual Russian-speaking émigrés trained as social workers in the United States are especially qualified to work with this population. Their personal experience and professional training make them ideally equipped to overcome the cultural obstacles discussed above. They possess the empathic understanding and language skill that facilitates the development of trust and understanding. One way of serving these émigrés, then, is to provide social work training and assistance to professional colleagues serving FSU émigrés.

Soviet Émigré Communities

Trained in a systems perspective, social workers are uniquely prepared to take a comprehensive view of clients and their problems. They are well aware of the need to consider their clients' history and culture. They are also committed to understanding the broader social systems within which clients function. This applies particularly to Russian-speaking émigrés, who often settle in communities with family, friends, and those of similar origins. Social workers must be aware of clients' relationships with existing neighborhood networks that can provide needed information and practical assistance. Some community networks may be informal, including family, friends, and neighbors. Others may take the form of business or professional associations and social and cultural organizations. To intervene effectively, the social worker must be aware of these resources in the client's own community.

CONCLUSION

Several themes emerge in considering the Russian-speaking Jewish immigrant presence in the United States. One theme is that there are areas that are common to all the groups. One significant common element is their close-knit, emotionally connected, multigenerational family structure. Another is their anticipation, or actual experience, of anti-Semitism in the form of restricted social, educational, and occupational opportunities.

A second theme is their exceptional heterogeneity. They are diverse in origin and culture. They come from some 15 different FSU republics, with very different cultures and lifestyles. They also differ significantly in the circumstances of their transit from the USSR to the United States. On arrival in the United States, they formed distinctly separate communities, replicating the social and geographic character of their original communities. They are aware of their differences and cluster with family, friends, and those from their homeland towns, cities, and regions.

A third theme is that despite their differences in origin, the émigrés share the experience of dealing with the challenge of relocating in a foreign land. Coming from socialist systems, they encounter one that respects independence and self-sufficiency. The loss of occupational and social status poses other hardships. The breakup of the traditional family unit constitutes further stress, particularly for the elderly.

Finally, there is the theme of a cultural mentality that presents special problems for the social worker seeking to serve Russian-speaking émigrés, namely, their distrust of social service delivery systems. Though this population may pose a considerable amount of difficulty for the social worker, it is important to remember social work's long and honorable history in assisting other immigrant groups to acculturate. The profession has developed generic knowledge and skills that can be as useful in serving these immigrants as it was with so many preceding groups. To be effective with this immigrant group, social workers must call on their skills of empathy, sensitive understanding of the client's problem and needs, and appreciation of the uniqueness of the émigré's cultural background.

NOTES

[1]The Immigration and Nationality Act (INA) defines a "refugee" as a person who is unable or unwilling to live in the country of origin "because of persecution or a well-founded fear of persecution on account or face, religion, nationality, membership in a particular social group, or political opinion." This definition excludes "economic migrants," that is, those who emigrate to seek a more prosperous life. Individuals ineligible for refugee status may be "paroled" into the United States by the U.S. Attorney General. This status may be revoked at any time and is used sparingly for emergency, humanitarian, and public interest reasons.

[2]The "Doctors Plot" was an alleged conspiracy of Jewish medical doctors to eliminate the leadership of the Soviet Union. In early 1953, shortly before Stalin's death, nine doctors, seven of them Jews, were accused of espionage and terrorist activities. Arrests were accompanied by show trials and anti-Semitic propaganda in an attempt to abort Soviet Jews' growing self-awareness and ties with world Jewry. Only the rapid de-Stalinization that followed the dictator's death in 1953 likely saved the lives of hundreds of Jews (Rapoport, 1990).

REFERENCES

American Jewish Committee. (2000). *Russian Jews in America: Status, identity and integration.* New York: American Jewish Committee.

Barber, J. (1987). The Soviet Jews of Washington Heights. *New York Affairs, 10,* 34–44.

Belozersky, I. (1990). New beginnings, old problems. *Journal of Jewish Communal Service, 67,* 124–131.

Berry, J. W. (1997). Immigration, acculturation, and adaptation. *Applied Psychology: An International Review, 46,* 5–68.

Chazin, R. (1995). *Chernobyl and its aftermath.* Unpublished manuscript.

Chazin, R., Colarossi, L., Hanson, M., Grishayeva, I., & Contis, G. (2004). Teaching brief intervention for adolescent depression: An evaluation of a cross-national approach. *Journal of Social Work Research and Evaluation, 5*(1), 19–31.

Chazin, R., Hanson, M., Cohen, C., & Grishayeva, I. (2002). Sharing knowledge and skills: Learning from school-based practitioners in Ukraine. *Journal of Teaching in Social Work, 22*(3/4), 89–101.

Congress, E. (1994). The use of culturagrams to assess and empower culturally diverse families. *Families in Society, 75,* 531–540.

Drachman, D., & Halberstadt, A. (1992). A stage of migration framework as applied to recent Soviet émigrés. In A. S. Ryan (Ed.), *Social work with immigrants and refugees* (pp. 63–78). New York: Haworth Press.

Gold, S. J. (1994). Soviet Jews in the United States. *American Jewish Year Book, 94,* 1–57.

Hall, J., & Halberstadt, A. (1994). "Subordination" and sensitivity to nonverbal cues: A study of married working women. *Sex Roles, 31*(3–4), 149–165.

Hanson, M., Phillips, M., Chazin, R., & Grishayeva, I. (in press). *Cross-national teaching and learning: Implications for social work.* Social Work Education.

H.R. 3061. House of Representatives, list entry 3061. Refugee Act of 1980 (Reauthorized through 2002).

Kliger, S. (2004, June 14–16). *Russian Jews in America: Status, identity and integration.* Paper presented at the International Conference "Russian-speaking Jewry in Global Perspective: Assimilation, Integration, and Community-building," Bar Ilan University, Israel. Retrieved July 25, 2004, from http://www.ajc.org/Russian/docs/Russian_Jews_in_America.pdf

Orleck, A. (2001). *The Soviet Jewish Americans.* Hanover, NH: University Press of New England.

Perez Foster, R. (2001). When immigration is trauma: Guidelines for the individual and family clinician. *American Journal of Orthopsychiatry, 71*(2), 153–170.

Rapoport, L. (1990). *Stalin's war against the Jews: The doctors' plot and the Soviet solution.* New York: Free Press.

Rippley, S. (2004). Acculturation and adaptation among immigrants and refugees. Retrieved July 2004, from http://onthehill.hamilton.edu/news/more_news/display.cfm?ID=7821

Rosenbaum, E., Friedman, S., Schill, M. H., & Buddelmeyer, H. (1999). Nativity differences in neighborhood quality among New York City households. *Housing Police Debate, 10*(3), 625.

Tress, M. (1996). Refugees as immigrants: Revelations of labor market performance. *Journal of Jewish Communal Services. Special issues: New Americans, 72*(4), 263–279.

Weinstein, L. (1988). Soviet Jewry and the American Jewish community. *American Jewish History, 6,* 610.

Wiesel, E. (1987). *The Jews of silence: A personal report of Soviet Jewry.* New York: Schocken Books.

CHAPTER 10

Practice With Families Where Sexual Orientation Is An Issue: Lesbian and Gay Individuals and Their Families

Gerald P. Mallon

"Are you out to your family?"

"How did your family deal with your being a lesbian?"

"Do your children know that you are gay?"

All of the above are questions that almost inevitably arise in the process of getting to know a lesbian or gay person. Families supply physical and emotional sustenance, connect us with our pasts, and provide a context within which we learn about the world, including attitudes and mores of our society (Berzon, 2001). A lesbian or gay person's family is very important. Although some radical right ideologues erroneously promote the belief that homosexuality is a threat to the family, as if it were intrinsically antithetic to the idea of family life, nothing could be further from the truth. Lesbian and gay persons need to be part of their families as much as any other individual. Given the stigmatizing status that lesbian and gay identity continues to hold for many in Western society, the family is one place where a lesbian or gay person most needs to feel accepted. Most lesbian and gay people hope that their family will continue to love and care for them after they disclose their lesbian or gay identity. For many, this is the case; sadly, for others, acceptance by one's family is not forthcoming.

Utilizing an ecological perspective of social work practice to work with lesbian and gay young people and families offers a broad conceptual lens for viewing family functioning and needs. Germain (1985) who led the development of this perspective in social work, noted that "practice is directed toward improving the transactions between people and their environments in order to enhance adaptive capacities and improve environments for all who function within them" (Germain, 1985, p. 31). As such, practitioners need to seek to influence the direction of change in both the person and the environment. With respect to a lesbian or gay young person within a family context, changing the environment means educating families and assisting them in dealing with homophobic attitudes.

Consider the following example:

> Damond is a 16-year-old, Trinidadian youngster who has been sent to the United States to live with an aunt after his mother has been psychiatrically hospitalized. His aunt, a single mother, has lupus, works full-time, and has three other children to support in her home. Damond is depressed because of his mother's illness. He is feeling isolated by his separation from his mother and the difficult acclimation to a new country and culture. In addition, Damond is dealing, in silence, with his own emerging gay identity.
>
> While cleaning Damond's room one afternoon, his aunt finds a letter that he wrote to a boy in school. Enraged, confused, and armed only with religious and culturally pejorative notions about homosexuality, even worrying that Damond's homosexuality might be contagious and put her own children at risk, she tells him that he is sick and needs help.

From this brief sketch, one can begin to see how and why this family is in crisis. There are numerous stresses in this environment. The economy requires that the aunt works to support her family despite her chronic illness; the young man is grieving over his mother's illness and his own relocation to a new environment, and dealing in silence with his own emerging gay identity. Add to this case the cultural factor, that is, that some cultures have particularly negative views of individuals (even family members) who are homosexually oriented. In addition, the fact that the young man was "found out" and did not choose to disclose his orientation, makes it is easy to see how this young person may become the target of his family's anger. As this example suggests, many personal, family, and environmental factors converge and interact with each other to influence the family. In other words, as Germain (1985, p. 43) so eloquently said it over 2 decades ago, "human behavior is not solely a function of the person or the environment, but of the complex interaction between them."

All too often, despite the increasing emphasis on family-centered social work practice (Hartman & Laird, 1983), there is a tendency for social work practitioners to see lesbian and gay persons primarily, if not solely, as individuals who are "gay" or "lesbian" rather than as members of a family of origin and as possible creators of their own family systems, families of choice (Weston, 1997), or biological families. By not acknowledging that "human beings can be understood and helped only in the context of the intimate and powerful human systems of which they are a part," of which the family is one of the most important (Hartman & Laird, 1983, p. 4), practitioners miss out on many important opportunities for fostering more positive relationships between lesbian and gay persons and their families.

This chapter, based on the author's analysis of the existing literature, qualitative data analysis from interviews conducted with lesbian and gay adolescents and their families, and 29 years of clinical practice with individuals and their families, examines the experience of lesbian and gay persons and their families through an ecological lens. Such a perspective creates a framework where individuals and environments are understood as a unit, in the context of their relationship to one another (Germain, 1985, p. 33). As such, this chapter examines the primary reciprocal exchanges and transactions that lesbian and gay persons and their families face as they confront the unique person: environmental tasks involved in a society that assumes all of its members are heterosexual. The focus of this chapter is limited to an analysis of the lesbian and gay persons within the context of their family system. The author has intentionally not explored bisexual (See Hutchins and Kaahumanu, 1991 and www.bisexual.org) or transgender identity (See Mallon, 2000 and Lev, 2004 and www.ntac.org) issues as these important identities are seen by this author as discreet areas of practice which are deserving of more comprehensive analysis and discussion. As such, the author explores the following areas: demographic issues; psychosocial risks and psychosocial needs of lesbian and gay persons; the clinical assessment issues of working with an individual where sexual orientation is the presenting issue; and recommendations for intervening with this population. Recommendations for social work practice with lesbian and gay persons and their families are presented in the conclusion of the chapter.

DEMOGRAPHIC PROFILE

The stereotype of the effeminate, White, meticulously groomed and dressed, middle- to upper-class, urban man living in a fabulously decorated house or apartment; or the butch, short-haired, husky, wearing no jewelry or makeup, motorcycle riding woman who carries her wallet in her back pocket, are the images that the popular media perpetuates about lesbians and gay men. The reality is that lesbians and gay men are part of every race, culture, ethnic group, religious, and socioeconomic affiliation and family in the United States, and most likely all other countries as well.

Since lesbian and gay persons are socialized to hide their sexual orientation, most are a part of an invisible population. In addition, in many areas of the United States (mostly outside of urban areas), it is still unsafe for most lesbian or gay people to live openly and acknowledge their sexual orientation. Therefore, there are not Census data that support or deny the existence of this population. Individuals who are socialized to hide or who have real or perceived reasons to fear for their safety do not come forward to be counted. In fact, although there is an increasing awareness about lesbian and gay persons, mainly from media representations of the population, it is safe to assume that most lesbian or gay persons in the United States remain closeted and do not live as "out" or openly lesbian or gay persons.

PSYCHOSOCIAL RISKS/PSYCHOSOCIAL NEEDS OF LESBIAN AND GAY PERSONS

Lesbian and gay persons experience environmental and psychological stresses that are more elevated than most of their heterosexual counterparts, not necessarily because of their sexual orientation, but due in large part to the negative societal response to it. Such conditions are unique to their membership in what remains in American society a stigmatized population.

As such, many lesbian and gay persons experience difficulties in the following areas:

Accessing systems of care (health, mental health, social services) (Appleby, 1998; Hunter & Mallon, 1998) that are affirming of and sensitive to the needs of lesbian and gay clients.

Mental health illness that is unique to their situation—especially anxiety related disorders, and mood disorders (Jones & Hill, 2003). Lesbian and gay youth, according to some studies (Garofalo et al., 1999; Remafedi, 1999; Rofes, 1983) are up to three times more likely to attempt suicide, than their heterosexual counterparts.

Substance abuse is generally thought to be elevated in the lesbian and gay community, since much of the initial coming out process may center on the "gay bar" scene (Finnegan & McNally, 1996).

The effect of trauma, psychological, political, and vicarious, are often reported by lesbian and gay persons as issues of concern since living within the context of a "false sense of self" and hiding or monitoring one's behaviors, mannerisms, speech, and life can be very debilitating and lead to maladaptive responses. Politically, lesbian and gay persons are frequently the subjects of "moral" debates by politicians—the issue of lesbian and gay marriage is one recent politicized issue that causes trauma for many lesbians and gay men who are tired of politicians who attempt to make their lives illegal or immoral. The issue of coming out alone—since this is a process and not a one time event, is exhausting and can lead to trauma. Lesbians and gay men who are parents and have children may experience vicarious traumatization in watching their children struggle with homophobic comments or reactions from peers or their community.

Environmental risks/needs: Although it is a common myth that all lesbian and gay persons are economically advantaged, many lesbians and gay men experience economic poverty (*Lesbian and gay poverty*, 2004), inadequate housing or threat of losing housing, and unemployment (see www.aclu.org). The literature is replete with evidence that lesbian and gay persons experience high levels of oppression and exploitation (Pharr, 1988), incidences of community violence, and discrimination on multiple levels (Herek, 1991). Racism is also an issue for lesbian and gay persons to contend with, both from inside the lesbian and gay communities, and from outside the lesbian and gay communities (Walters, 1998).

CLINICAL ASSESSMENT FOR FAMILIES WHERE SEXUAL ORIENTATION IS AN ISSUE

Although not all lesbian and gay persons need counseling because someone in the family has been identified as gay, lesbian, or bisexual, some families will come to the attention of a social services agency for a variety of reasons and services. These reasons might not at initial assessment seem to be pertaining to issues of sexual orientation.

The following actual case example illustrates the relevance of these dimensions.

A young couple, Betsy and Clark, sought help from a family service agency. Initially they identified concerns with the behavior of their 9-year-old son Todd, who was attending an after-school program. The after-school center staff reported that he was hitting other children, unable to relax during quiet time, and had frequent temper tantrums. Betsy and Clark were concerned that the center might refuse continued service, affecting their ability to maintain their employment. The social worker engaged with Betsy and Clark to assess Todd's behaviors, the tensions within the marital relationship, and both parents' satisfaction with their lives. Clark was struggling with a worsening depression that he attributed to a growing remoteness between himself and Betsy, a detachment he couldn't explain. Several times Betsy mentioned being unable to be herself in the relationship and alluded to a secret that she couldn't share. Through a skillful series of individual and joint discussions, the social worker was able to help Betsy acknowledge the reality of her lesbian sexual orientation and share this with Clark. With the secret out, the social worker, Betsy, and Clark began to identify and work together on the many decisions that each faced individually and as parents to

Todd. In reflecting upon their initial call to this particular family service agency, Betsy noted having seen a brochure in Todd's pediatrician's office describing the agency's service, including a group on parenting issues for lesbian and gay parents. Once connected to the agency, Betsy had experienced the social worker as open in her ongoing assessment of the range of possible sources of Betsy's expressed ability to "be herself" in her relationship with Clark.

The following case example explores issues of sexual orientation from a different family-centered perspective.

Shamir, a 15-year-old Pakistani male, is sitting in his bedroom in the apartment which he shares with his mother, father, and three younger brothers, reading a very personal letter that a boy in school wrote to him. He has already read this letter several times, but like many adolescents venturing into the world of relationships, he is re-reading it because it is a special letter to him. When his mother yells to him from the kitchen that he has a phone call he puts the letter down on his bed and leaves his room to get the phone. During the time that he is on the phone his 9-year-old brother enters his room and begins to read the letter that Shamir has left on the bed. The younger sibling, realizing that its contents are questionable, shows the letter to his mother.

When Shamir returns from his phone call, finding his letter missing, he begins to panic. Shamir knows that it will be obvious to anyone who reads the letter that he is gay. Up to this point, Shamir has been successful at keeping his identity a secret. But now his secret is out in the open—he is angry that he didn't have an opportunity to come out on his own terms—he has been found out—and there is a big difference! When he sees his mother's face, he knows that she has read the letter, but she says nothing to him. When he approaches her, she backs away and says, "We'll talk about this when your father gets home and when all of your brothers are asleep."

The next few hours are filled with dread and isolation for Shamir. What's going to happen? What is his father going to do? He's not prepared for this, he's terrified of the repercussions. What Shamir doesn't know is that his mother and father feel the same way—this is not the way things are supposed to be—they are not prepared for this. No one ever told them about the prospect of having a son who was gay. Should they send him for therapy? Should they send him away to protect the other boys? Should they even tell anybody about this?

For the social worker experienced in working with family systems, the situation in the above vignette presents the ideal opportunity for an intervention. A crisis has occurred, the family is in turmoil, and everyone is poised for something to happen. Family members are confused, frightened, filled with shame, unprepared, and angry. They can act in a reckless manner, lashing out at the individual who has disclosed, or they might fall into a conspiracy of silence and become completely paralyzed and numbed by the circumstances. Professionals who have spent years with families, or even those who have recently entered the field, know that what happens next is not always predictable. When the situation involves an issue of sexual orientation in the family, one can almost guarantee that there will be a great deal of ambivalence in this process. Coming out in the context of a family system can yield unpredictable outcomes.

THE COMING OUT PROCESS WITHIN A FAMILY

Coming out, a distinctively homosexual phenomenon (see Cass 1979, 1983/1984, 1984; Coleman, 1981, 1987; Troiden, 1979, 1988, 1989), is defined as a developmental process through which lesbian and gay people recognize their sexual orientation and integrate this knowledge into their personal and social lives (De Monteflores & Schultz, 1978). Although several theorists have written about coming out as a uniquely adolescent experience (Hetrick & Martin, 1987; Mallon, 1998, 1998b, 1998c; Malyon, 1981), developmentally, the coming out process can eventuate at any stage of an individual's life. Therefore, it is important to consider the consequences of a person coming out in the context of his or her family, as a child, as an adolescent, as an unmarried young adult, as a married adult, as a parent, or as a grandparent.

The events that mark coming out and the pace of this process vary from person to person. Consequently, some people move through the process smoothly, accepting their sexuality, making social contacts, and finding a good fit within their environments. Others are unnerved by their sexuality, vacillating in their conviction, hiding in their uneasiness, and struggling to find the right fit.

Although the experience of an adolescent coming out is qualitatively different from that of a parent or an adult who comes out, there are several conditions, broadly conceived, that all family members share. Earlier literature (Silverstein, 1977) focused primarily on the negative consequences of disclosure, and indeed there can be many, but a range of responses to a family member's disclosure is perhaps a more appropriate characterization. The following description by Rothberg and Weinstein (1996), captures many of the salient aspects of this experience:

> When a family member comes out there are a multitude of responses. At one end of the spectrum is acceptance . . . but rarely, if ever, is this announcement celebrated. Take for example, the announcement a heterosexual person makes to his or her family of origin of an engagement to marry. This is usually met with a joyous response, a ritual party and many gifts. The lesbian and gay man do not receive this response. Instead, the coming out announcement is often met with negative responses which can range from mild disapproval to complete non-acceptance and disassociation. These responses, though usually accepted, cause considerable stress and pain for the lesbian and gay person seeking approval. (p. 81)

Religious Factors

Some families, particularly families with strong religious convictions, may openly condemn homosexuality, unaware that one of their own family members is lesbian or gay (Helminiak, 1997; Herman, 1997).

Blumenfeld and Raymond (1993) note that families with strong religious convictions often support their views of their religion even against a family member. Personal biases, particularly cultural or religious biases that view a lesbian or gay identity negatively, can make "coming out" to one's family a painful experience. This distress is manifest by this young person's narrative:

> Everybody in the family knew that I was gay. The only person that couldn't deal with me being gay was my mother. Everyone else that I thought was going to have a hard time, didn't. My mother is a devout Jehovah Witness and she has a very hard time with my being gay. She has said that she hated me and to this very day she tells me that it is against God's will and

it's against His proposition and when the day comes for Him to take over the world again I'm going to suffer. She always says that she doesn't want me to suffer because I am her son, but she doesn't realize that she is making me suffer because of the ways that she acts toward me.

Social workers must be aware of the strong anti-lesbian and gay sentiment held by many religious groups and the impact that this has on family members for whom sexual orientation is an issue. The Bible has historically been erroneously used as a weapon against lesbian and gay persons, causing a great deal of distress in many families of faith. Several excellent resources (Cooper, 1994; Metropolitan Community Church, 1990; Parents & Friends of Lesbians and Gays, 1997) exist that provide practitioners with an alternative lesbian and gay affirming perspective.

Cultural Factors

Race and cultural ethnicity can also play important roles in the disclosure process. Persons of color, many of whom have experienced significant stress related to oppression and racism based on skin color or ethnicity, may experience even greater difficulty coming out within the family context, as some may view a lesbian or gay sexual orientation as one more oppressed status to add to one's plate (Greene, 1994; Savin-Williams & Rodriguez, 1993; Walters, 1998).

People of color who are lesbian/gay/bisexual confront a tricultural experience. They experience membership in their ethnic or racial community and in the larger society. In addition, they are not born into the lesbian/gay community. Many become aware of their difference in adolescence and not only must deal with the stigma within their own cultural/racial community but must also find a supportive lesbian/gay community to which they can relate. The lesbian/gay community is often a microcosm of the larger society, and many may confront racism there, as in the larger society. To sustain oneself in three distinct communities requires an enormous effort and can also produce stress for the adolescent (Chan, 1989; Hunter & Schaecher, 1987; Morales, 1989). The reality is that lesbian and gay persons are part of every race, culture, ethnic grouping, class, and extended family.

Emotional Factors

If the lesbian or gay identified individual chooses to come out voluntarily, then he or she has had time to prepare for the event. Some individuals may have role-played their coming out process with a supportive friend or therapist, others may have written a letter or planned the event after experiencing positive disclosure events with several other trusted confidants. The truth, however, is that in most cases, even if the individual has had time to prepare for this event, the actual moment of disclosure catches most families off guard. Families have frequently not had this period of time to prepare and are often shocked by the disclosure. Jean Baker (1998), psychologist and mother of two gay sons, expresses these feelings perfectly when she writes:

> I still recall the night so vividly. Gary was helping me with dinner, which he occasionally did. He had just gotten a new haircut and immediately I hated it. I still don't know why, because it had never occurred to me that Gary might be gay, but for some reason I said to him, "With that haircut people will think you're gay." He hesitated for a moment and then, looking directly at me he said, "I think maybe I am."
>
> I stared at my son, totally speechless, stunned, momentarily unable to react. Then I started crying and found myself talking incoherently about the tragedy of being gay . . . I rambled on senselessly about homosexuality as an adolescent phase, something people can grow out of, something that may be just a rebellion . . . Knowing what I know about homosexuality and having examined my own feelings and attitudes, I think my reactions that night were deplorable. My son deserved to hear immediately that I respected him for his honesty and his courage. What he heard instead was that his mother thought being homosexual was a tragedy.
>
> As I think about my reactions that first night and during subsequent days and nights, I am still ashamed of what I learned about myself as a mother dealing with a son's homosexuality. Instead of thinking first about how I could help my son cope with what he might have to face in a society so condemning of homosexuals, I focused on how I felt. Though I didn't want to admit it, I was concerned about the prejudice and stigma I myself might have to face. (pp. 41–43)

Feelings surrounding the initial disclosure can range from shame, to guilt, to embarrassment, or even complete disassociation. Acceptance is also a possible reaction, but one that is seldom experienced by most lesbian and gay persons.

Managing Disclosure to Others

Deciding how to manage the disclosure of a lesbian or gay sexual orientation to the family is an important consideration at this point. The family that reacts extremely negatively to the disclosure, for instance, a child being thrown out of the home by parents or a spouse being told to leave their home by their partner, may require outside intervention to assist them in dealing with the disclosure, which should be viewed as a crisis situation. Who to tell and who not to tell, and how to address the disclosure within the context of the family are other issues that families must eventually discuss. Getting through the initial crisis of disclosure, however should be the primary focus of the intervention.

Being "found out," as illustrated in Shamir's case presented earlier in this chapter, precipitates a somewhat different type of crisis that may also require immediate intervention. In the sections that follow, we will explore the possibilities of a child or adolescent's coming out in his or her family system.

WHEN A CHILD COMES OUT WITHIN THE FAMILY SYSTEM

Although disclosure can occur at any point in the developmental process, for the purposes of this section, the issues as they pertain to a child or adolescent who comes out or is found out by their family will be specifically addressed.

Although one of the primary tasks of adolescents is to move away from one's family toward independence, families are still extremely important economic and emotional systems for them. Lack of accurate information about lesbian and gay identity and fears about individuals who identify as lesbian or gay lead many families to panic about how to manage the disclosure of a family member.

The following two case examples illustrate several points with respect to the coming out process for adolescents.

Yuan Is Found Out

Yuan Fong is a Chinese American, 18-year-old senior in a public high school in a large West coast city. He resides with his parents, who are Chinese born, in an apartment with an older brother, age 20, and two younger siblings, ages 12 and 10. Yuan is the captain of the football team, well liked by his peers and by teachers. He is a very handsome young man. Yuan has dated a few girls, but is so into his football career that it leaves little time for anything else. Yuan has been aware of his feelings for guys for some time and has been trying to repress these feelings. Recently, however, he met a guy named Tommy who he really likes, and Yuan's feelings have become more difficult to repress. Tommy and Yuan begin to see each other, first as friends, and then their friendship blossoms into a romance.

One evening, while talking to Tommy on the phone, Mrs. Fong overhears their conversation. It seems to her that Yuan is speaking to Tommy like she would expect him to speak to a girl that he was dating. When Yuan hangs up the phone his mother confronts him about what she heard. Yuan blows it off and laughs, blaming her interpretation on her imperfect English, but he knows that this is not the case. He is in a panic because he knows that his mother will not let this go.

Mrs. Fong becomes hypervigilant about Yuan and begins to search his room while he is at school. She finds letters that Tommy has written to Yuan and then when she finds a small card from a lesbian and gay youth group she takes it as confirmation that her son Yuan is gay. Mrs. Fong shares this information with her husband, who chastises her for snooping in their son's room. But they are both upset and unprepared for how they should deal with this new information that changes their notion of their family.

When Yuan arrives home from football practice, both Mr. and Mrs. Fong ask to speak with him. They tell him what they have found and ask him if he is gay. Yuan, fearful and caught off guard, is unsure of how to respond, but it seems like there is no way out. Even though he is pretty sure that he is gay, Yuan tells them, "I think I am bisexual," rationalizing that being half gay is easier that being totally gay. Mr. and Mrs. Fong ask if he has ever been sexually abused by someone, they ask if he is just going through a phase, and insist that he is going to see their family doctor. Although they do not say it out loud, Mr. and Mrs. Fong are also concerned about how this will affect their two younger children. Yuan has on occasion baby-sat when they went out, they wonder if Yuan might molest the younger children. This family is obviously in a crisis state.

Robin Comes Out

Robin is a 17-year-old Caucasian who lives with her mother, father, and two younger sisters on a small family-run farm in the Midwest. Robin is an average student, in the 11 grade in a public high school. Robin has a very close friend named Patsy who is a year older and attends the same school. After an initial period of confusion, Robin and Patsy realize that they have strong feelings for one another—that are "more than just a phase." Although neither of them identify as lesbian at first, in time they first come to label their identity as gay, and then later are comfortable calling themselves lesbian.

Robin has always been close to her family and has always been helpful around the farm. Not wanting to lie to her parents, Robin decides that she should tell her parents how she feels about Patsy. She plans the event, making sure that it is an evening when her sisters are already in bed and asks her parents to sit with her in her bedroom. She starts by telling her family that what she needs to tell them is not an easy thing to tell, but that she loves them and wants them to know her for who she really is. They seem puzzled thinking that they already know their daughter quite well. She explains that since she was little, about 6 or 7, she has always liked other girls, not boys. She tells that at first she thought the feelings would go away, but they didn't. At this point, her mother and father are completely aghast about what she is trying to tell them. Robin makes it clear and says, "Mom, Dad, I still like girls and I have come to understand lately that I am a lesbian."

Robin's parents are without words. They are completely unprepared for having a lesbian daughter. They suggest therapy, they ask if she is sure and suggest that it still might be a phase, they ask if it is her way of rebelling against them. She answers no to all of their queries. Robin's parents are in shock, confused, embarrassed, and unsure of what to do. Robin's disclosure has created an imbroglio for the family that all are unprepared to deal with.

Like many families, these families had little accurate information about lesbian and gay persons and as a consequence relied mostly on myths as their primary source of information. At first both families believed that their family member's differentness might be an adolescent phase. Both families suggested that their young person should attempt to change their sexual orientation via therapy. Additionally, although it was almost too frightening to mention, the families expressed fears about the possible molestation of younger siblings by their lesbian or gay child. These families, like most families who have had to deal with an unexpected disclosure, are clearly in a state of shock. Consequently, they are unprepared for their teens growing up lesbian or gay in a heterosexual world. Most parents never allow themselves to think that they might have a child who is lesbian or gay. Parents are also aware of the shame and secrecy surrounding homosexuality, and as such are unsure of what their child's disclosure will mean for them and for the other family members.

In some cases, though not in Yuan or Robin's case, the disclosure of a gay identity can lead to an array of abusive responses from family members. In other instances, a lesbian or gay disclosure can lead to a youth's expulsion from their home, and to out-of-home placement. In many families the crisis of disclosure is resolved after the initial reaction of shock and the family moves forward. When a parent comes out in a family context, however, the issues are quite different.

WHEN A PARENT COMES OUT WITHIN THE FAMILY SYSTEM

When a parent or a spouse comes out, or is found out by family members, there are unique repercussions. As observed in the above case examples, lack of accurate information about lesbian and gay identity and fears about individuals who identify as lesbian or gay lead many families to panic about how to manage the disclosure of a family member. The issues of shame and stigma serve to further complicate these issues. The following two case examples illustrate several points with respect to the coming out process for family members. A father discloses his gay identity to his son in the first case example; a husband is unexpectedly "found out" by his wife in the second scenario.

A Gay Dad's Disclosure

Wade, an African American 5th grader, attending Catholic elementary school, resides in a large urban environment in a mid-income housing apartment with his dad, Brandon, aged 35, and Joe, his "uncle." Wade was 10 when his dad decided to tell him that Uncle Joe, who had lived with the family for 8 of Wade's 10 years, was really his life partner.

Brandon decided to disclose his gay orientation to Wade because he felt that he was getting older and he wanted him to know the truth about his dad. He didn't want anyone to make fun of Wade or for him to find out that he was gay before he had the opportunity to tell him. Brandon planned the disclosure and sat with Wade privately in their kitchen to tell him. Joe, although not initially involved in the disclosure, joined them after Brandon and told Wade.

At first Wade was shocked and denied that his dad or Uncle Joe, with whom he had an excellent relationship, were gay. Wade said he didn't want to talk about it. Although he didn't say it at the time, he was embarrassed that his friends and teachers in school would find out about his dad and that he would be treated differently. After the initial disclosure Wade began to distance himself from his dad and Uncle Joe. When Brandon checked in to see how things were going with him, Wade simply replied that things were "fine."

But things were not fine. Wade began to have problems in school (prior to the disclosure Wade was an A student) and on two occasions, Wade's Dad received notices from school notifying him that Wade had gotten into trouble in the classroom. Noting this marked change in behavior, the social worker at the school phoned Wade's dad and asked him to come into school for a conference.

Marcellino and Marta

Marcellino, a 35-year-old Latino, has been married to Marta, a 31-year-old Latina for 8 years. They have two children, Pedro, age 6, and Isabel, age 4. They live in a small house in a suburb of a large southern city, which is comprised primarily of working class Latinos like themselves. Although they have been married for 8 years, Marcellino has known since he was a teenager that he is "different." When he married, he thought that his feelings for men would change, but they did not. He never discussed these feelings with Marta, but some part of him always thought that she knew. Although Marcellino never engaged in dating relationships with men, he frequented gay bars and sometimes a local bathhouse in the urban area near his home.

One evening, while Marcellino was exiting a well known gay bar in the city near where they lived, he ran into Marta's sister, Sonia. Sonia immediately confronted him about being in the gay bar and he denied being gay, saying that he just met a friend from work who was gay. His sense of panic however was evident. Sonia went to her sister's home, asked to speak with her privately, and told her about seeing Marcellino coming out of the gay bar. Marta was devastated by this information and asked Sonia if she could watch her children so that she could talk to Marcellino privately.

When Marcellino arrived home, Marta met him at the door and asked for an explanation. Marcellino initially denied that he had been in the bar, but after a few minutes acknowledged that he had indeed been there and further noted that it was not his first time. Marta told Marcellino that he had to leave their home immediately. She screamed that he had exposed her and her children to all kinds of things and that he had lied to all of them. Marcellino did not know where to turn. His family lived in Peru and he did not have a close family support system other than Marta and his children. Marcellino pleaded with Marta to go with him to see someone—a marriage or family therapist. Marta refused and told him to leave their home immediately.

Marcellino was confused, now estranged from his partner and his children, and feeling completely dejected. Marcellino went to the home of a coworker to ask if he could stay the night. In the morning he went to visit his parish priest to ask for counseling. The priest referred him to a family center in the community. Marta was devastated, ashamed, and told no one about her separation from Marcellino, except her sister.

Although the issues of disclosure for a parent coming out to his child are far different than for a wife who finds out that her husband is gay, both case examples reflect the level of denial, shock, and confusion that some family members experience in this process. In the first case, Brandon has clearly thought out his disclosure, and it seems that he will work with his son to process this new information. In the second case, though, Marta and Marcellino have definitely not planned the disclosure and the consequences of his being found out seem to be, at this juncture, quite weighty for him and his family. Most families bring themselves out of a crisis without professional help; others will need support during the disclosure of a lesbian or gay identity, so that the family may remain intact and its members may grow through the experience (Fraser, Pecora, & Haapala, 1991; Kaplan, 1986; Tracy, Haapala, Kinney, & Pecora, 1991). Others will need assistance. The benefits of a family support and family counseling have particular relevance in each of these four cases.

TREATMENT CONSIDERATIONS WITH FAMILIES WHERE SEXUAL ORIENTATION IS THE ISSUE

Family-centered services often call for crisis intervention services, at least in the initial phases of the disclosure process. Families experiencing high stress, such as the disclosure of a lesbian or gay sexual orientation may find that their regular coping mechanisms have broken down, leaving them open to change in either a positive or negative direction. The family member's increased vulnerability under these conditions can serve as a catalyst to seeking help to resolve their immediate issues (Tracy, 1991; Weissbourd & Kagan, 1989). If professionals trained in family preservation techniques can be available and gently encouraging, the pressure families feel can motivate them to change and to share their concerns. The immediate goal of this intervention is clearly to move the family out of crisis and to restore the family to at least the level of functioning that existed before the crisis (Kinney, Haapala, & Booth, 1991). Many Family Preservation professionals go well beyond that goal, increasing families' skill levels and resources so that they function better after the crisis than they did before.

　　Utilizing a family-centered approach (Brown & Weil, 1992; Hartman & Laird, 1983) for working with families, the following sections suggests some intervention guidelines for practitioners.

Intervention

Addressing issues of sexual orientation disclosure requires professionals to first explore their own personal, cultural, and religious biases about persons who are homosexually oriented. Although many professionals might believe that they are unbiased in their approach to lesbian and gay persons, all professionals must first examine their own bias and be comfortable dealing with issues that are seen by most in Western society as "sensitive." Although most professionals receive little, if any, formal training on dealing with issues of sexual orientation in child welfare, there are several recent books (Anastas & Appleby, 1998; Mallon, 1998a) that can be helpful for professional development.

Initial Preparations

Keeping people safe is one of the primary goals of this intervention. Workers should be aware that issues of sexual orientation can frequently lead to violence within the family system. Being able to predict the potential for violence is an essential skill for workers to possess.

Preparing for the initial meeting by gathering information (for example talking to the referring worker—if the case has been referred—or by gathering information directly from the family members by calling them to schedule an interview) can assist in forming a positive relationship that might make things easier when the worker arrives at the home. In some situations, as in Marcellino and Marta's case, it might be a good idea to schedule the initial meeting outside the family's home in a public, structured environment such as a restaurant or a community center. When situations are potentially volatile, meeting in a public place can make it easier for family members to retain control.

The Initial Meeting

Whenever possible, the initial meeting should take place in the home of the family. In three of the four cases presented above, this would be advisable. Meeting clients on their own turf is an integral part of the philosophy of family preservation. Professionals should be conscious of being considerate and careful with all family members. In cases when a disclosure of sexual orientation is involved, family members might view the person who has come out or been found out as the only person who needs to be spoken with.

In some cases family members should be met with one at a time. This is particularly true for the family members who are most upset, pessimistic, or uncooperative. In most cases, they should also be talked with first. This individual needs to feel important and understood. Deescalating this family member and gaining his or her confidence can be helpful in supporting the process and encouraging other family members to participate. Engaging in active listening techniques—using "I" statements (Kinney et al., 1991, chapter 4); permitting the professional to share their own feelings about the situation; notifying family members of the consequences of their actions; calling for a time out; seeking the assistance of a supervisor, if necessary; reconvening at a neutral location or actually leaving the home if the situation escalates to a point where police intervention is necessary, are all options that professionals may need to consider and act upon during their initial visit.

Subsequent Contacts

The first session is usually the most fragile one. The family who has had a member disclose their sexual orientation is, as noted, in a crisis mode. Family members in crisis feel vulnerable and anxious. Some may be angry, and others mistrustful. Many families feel secretive about disclosing family business to a stranger, especially when it pertains to a sensitive issue like one's sexual orientation. The goal in the first session is usually to calm everyone down. Establishing trust and forming a partnership between family members and the professional are the next steps.

Assessing Strengths and Problems and Formulating Goals

In subsequent sessions, the professional will need to assist the family in organizing information about their crisis. Workers should work with family members to minimize blame and labeling and instead focus on generating options for change. This may be facilitated by working with the family to reach consensus about the fact that their family member is in one way not as they thought he or she was, but at the same time, still the same person that they have always been. Assisting family members with shaping less negative interpretations about a lesbian or gay identity is an important place to begin. Helping families to define problems in terms of their own skill deficits by settings goals, making small steps, prioritizing issues of concern for the family, and being realistic with family members can lead families back toward homeostasis. In the context of an emerging managed care environment, and as a means toward addressing issues of accountability, utilizing standardized outcome measures to test the veracity of clinical interventions with clients has increasingly become a significant aspect of practice (Bloom, Fischer, & Orme, 1995; Blythe, Tripodi, & Briar, 1994).

Helping Families Learn

One of the most dominant elements that is apparent in each of the case vignettes is the lack of accurate and relevant information about lesbian and gay individuals. The myths and misconceptions that guide families are graphically present in their initial concerns about molestation, about the need for therapy, and about the possibility of changing one's sexual orientation. Changing families notions about lesbian and gay family members is not always a smooth or easy process. A great deal of the worry that families have about lesbian and gay persons is based on irrational fear and shame. The disclosure of a lesbian or gay sexual orientation within a family context spreads the societal stigmatization of homosexuality to all family members. Goffman called this phenomenon "courtesy stigma" (Goffman, 1963).

Although they caution about developing realistic expectations for all families, Kinney and associates (1991) posit that there are several ways to facilitate learning with clients: a) direct instruction; b) modeling; and c) learning from one another. These strategies can be useful in helping families affected by issues of sexual orientation as highlighted below.

Direct Instruction

The social work professional who engages a family with issues of sexual orientation must be prepared to present and provide a great deal of direct instruction with family members. Providing families with accurate and relevant information about their child or their family members' orientation is an essential part of this process. Bibliotherapy, providing families with reading material, is an integral component of this strategy. Although finding this information is not the problem that it once was (as there is a plethora of information available), workers may have to access this information by visiting a local lesbian or gay bookstore or via the Internet, as the books are frequently not carried in mainstream bookstores. Increasing the family's knowledge about homosexual orientation (Baker, 1998; Borhek, 1983, 1988; Dew, 1994; Fairchild & Hayward, 1989; Griffin, Wirth, & Wirth, 1986; Strommen, 1989; Switzer, 1996; Tuerk, 1995) and knowing about resources that support families, like Parents and Friends of Lesbians and Gays (Parents and Friends of Lesbians and Gays, 1990, 1997; www. pflag.org; www.glpci.org) are important ways to strengthen and support the families of lesbian and gay persons. Furnishing young people with literature, especially work written by lesbian and gay young people for lesbian and gay young people, is one of the most beneficial techniques that can be employed (see Alyson, 1991; Due, 1995; Heron, 1994; Kay, Estepa, & Desetta, 1996; Miranda, 1996; Monette, 1992; Reid, 1973; Savin-Williams, 1998; Valenzuela, 1996; Wadley, 1996a, 1996b). Videos and guest speakers can and should also be utilized in this process. Such information is useful in assisting the lesbian or gay oriented youngster in abolishing myths and stereotypes and correcting misconceptions about their identity. This information can also help educate non-gay teens about their lesbian and gay peers (Berkley, 1996; Greene, 1996).

During the past decade, many high schools and colleges have housed lesbian, gay and straight alliances (see www.glsen.org) and many cities have LGBT Community Centers (see www.lgbt centers.org). These and other community-based organizations that might house lesbian and gay friendly programs in mainstreamed community centers are important referral sources for social work practitioners and as such practitioners should know how to locate these organizations and be prepared to visit them.

The Internet and the world wide web have liberated lesbian and gay persons from their extreme isolation, supplying them limitless opportunities to communicate with other gays and lesbians in chatrooms and on bulletin boards. Most lesbian, gay and bisexual adolescents have little access to information about their emerging identity and few adult role models from whom to learn. In recent years the Internet has grown exponentially. Its growth has permitted thousands of lesbian and gay persons who may not be able to openly visit libraries or bookstores, or who may live in geographically isolated areas, to gain information and connect with others.

Although there is a very limited body of literature that focuses on the impact of disclosure on the non-gay spouses of lesbian and gay persons (Buxton, 1994; Gochros, 1989, 1992), there is an excellent website, known as the Straight Spouses Network, located at www.ssnetwk.org, that offers valuable support to the partners of lesbian or gay spouses. Ali (1996), MacPike (1989), and Saffron (1997) have all addressed issues of parental disclosure to their children. An excellent website that addresses the concerns of the children of lesbian and gay parents (Children of Lesbian and Gay Parents Everywhere—COLAGE) is located at www.colage.org.

Although published sources can be purchased at lesbian and gay bookstores in metropolitan areas, these sources and many others not mentioned here can also be ordered via the Internet at the following addresses: www.Amazon.com or www.Barnesand Noble.com.

Modeling

The social worker modeling behaviors to show clients how to do them is a very useful strategy for working with families who are dealing with issues of sexual orientation. The lesbian or gay adolescent who comes out or the family who is affected by a disclosure might benefit from attending a support group with other individuals or family members who share their experience. Individuals and family members, anxious about attending a support group for the first time, might very much benefit from a professional who agrees to accompany the client to the session. Accompanying the client to purchase books about lesbian and gay topics at the bookstore, or attending a lesbian or gay run function with clients can be other ways for workers to model acceptance for the client. Linking clients to religious leaders in their communities and of their faith, who have an affirming stance about lesbian and gay individuals can also be a useful modeling experience for family members.

Learning From Others

Families can also learn from one another by connecting with other families where sexual orientation is an issue. If connections with other families cannot be made in person because of geographic distance, the Internet can be a useful substitute. There are many sites that include opportunities for lesbian and gay individuals and families affected by issues of sexual orientation to communicate with one another. It is the responsibility of the professional working with the family to identify and access resources for support within the community where families live. Workers need to be aware of these resources and visit them prior to making referrals to clients.

Social workers must also be prepared to assist families in overcoming barriers that will inevitably occur while assisting them in the learning process. Acknowledging, validating, and rewarding small signs that family members are considering new options and beginning to try them is also an important task for workers.

Solving Problems

Social work practitioners trained in problem resolution strategies must incorporate issues of sexual orientation into such designs. Professionals must focus on listening to and helping families to clarify what is causing them the most discomfort. Intervening with clients to assist them in intrapersonal problems can occur via direct interventions, cognitive strategies, values clarifications, and behavioral strategies. These are all methods suggested by Kinney and colleagues (1991, pp. 121–124).

Most families dealing with issues of sexual orientation need help controlling and clarifying their own emotions. Assisting families to develop effective communication skills and problem solving strategies is a major focus of the family preservation model that can be effective with lesbian and gay children, youth, and families.

CONCLUSION

All family-centered services, notwithstanding issues of sexual orientation, from family support to family preservation, maintain the position that children and adolescents are best reared by their own families. Viewed ecologically, both assessment and intervention with families must focus primarily on the goodness of fit (Germain & Gitterman, 1996) between the lesbian or gay individual and those other systems with which he or she is in transaction, the most central in this case would be the family. Many of the issues that surface when a family member discloses or is dealing with aspects of sexual orientation, can be best dealt with by a competent social worker trained in family systems. Such issues must be viewed as deficits within the environment, dysfunctional transactions among environmental systems, or as a lack of individual or family coping skills or strategies (Loppnow, 1985). Providing education and intensive training effort for family-centered practitioners (Faria, 1994; Laird, 1996) that would help them feel competent about broadly addressing issues of sexual orientation could provide support for families in crisis and prevent unnecessary family disruption. Family-centered practitioners must also be prepared to serve as advocates for their clients, including a lesbian and gay child or adolescent; a parent who identifies as lesbian or gay; or for a couple where one of the partners identifies as other than heterosexually oriented.

Family-centered social practitioners, working with the primary goal of keeping families together, can deliver these services within the context of the client's natural environment—their community. Programs like the Homebuilders model (Kinney, Haapala, & Booth, 1991) have opportunities to help families grappling with issues of sexual orientation. Community-based family and children's services centers also provide many opportunities for addressing issues of sexual orientation within the family system. These approaches also have relevance for other situations where spouses or parents come out as lesbian or gay. Working with family systems in their communities makes social workers in family-centered programs ideally situated to see what is really going on in a family's natural environment. By being located in the home or in the community, the worker is able to make an accurate assessment and design an intervention that will support and preserve the family system. With a greater awareness of issues of sexual orientation, family-centered practitioners can educate parents, ease the distress experienced by couples where one partner is lesbian or gay and the other is heterosexual, as well as model and shape new behaviors that can transform lives for young lesbian and gay persons.

REFERENCES

Ali, T. (1996). *We are family: Testimonies of lesbian and gay parents*. London: Cassell.
Alyson, S. (1991). *Young, gay and proud*. Boston: Alyson Publications.

Anastas, J., & Appleby, G. (Eds.). (1998). *Not just a passing phase.* New York: Columbia University Press.

Appleby, G. A. (1998). Social work practice with gay men and lesbians within organizations. In G. P. Mallon (Ed.), *Foundations of social work practice with lesbian and gay persons* (pp. 249–270). New York: Haworth Press.

Baker, J. M. (1998). *Family secrets, gay sons: A mother's story.* New York: Haworth Press.

Berzon, B. (2001). *Positively gay: New approaches to gay and lesbian life* (3rd ed.). Berkeley, CA: Celestial Arts.

Bloom, M., Fischer, J., & Orme, J. G. (1995). *Evaluating practice: Guidelines for the accountable professional* (2nd ed.). Needham Heights, MA: Allyn & Bacon.

Blumenfeld, W., & Raymond, D. (Eds.). (1993). *Looking at lesbian and gay life.* Boston, MA: Beacon Press.

Blythe, B., Tripodi, T., & Briar, S. (1994). *Direct practice research in human service agencies.* New York: Columbia University Press.

Borhek, M. V. (1983). *Coming out to parents.* New York: Pilgrim Press.

Borhek, M. V. (1988). Helping gay and lesbian adolescents and their families: A mother's perspective. *Journal of Adolescent Health Care, 9*(2), 123–128.

Brown, J., & Weil, M. (Eds.). (1992). *Family practice.* Washington, DC: Child Welfare League of America.

Buxton, A. P. (1994). *The other side of the closet.* New York: Wiley.

Cass, V. C. (1979). Homosexual identity formation: A theoretical model. *Journal of Homosexuality, 4,* 219–235.

Cass, V. C. (1983/1984). Homosexual identity: A concept in need of a definition. *Journal of Homosexuality, 9*(2/3), 105–126.

Cass, V. C. (1984). Homosexual identity formation: Testing a theoretical model. *Journal of Sex Research, 20,* 143–167.

Chan, C. (1989). Issues of identity development among Asian American lesbians and gay men. *Journal of Counseling and Development, 68*(1), 16–20.

Coleman, E. (1981). Developmental stages of the coming out process. *Journal of Homosexuality, 7*(2/3), 31–43.

Coleman, E. (1987). Assessment of sexual orientation. *Journal of Homosexuality, 13*(4), 9–23.

Cooper, D. (1994). *From darkness into light: What the Bible really says about homosexuality* (3rd ed.). Tucson, AZ: Cornerstone Fellowship.

Dew, R. F. (1994). *The family heart: A memoir of when our son came out.* Reading, MA: Addison-Wesley.

De Monteflores, C., & Schultz, S. J. (1978). Coming out: Similarities and differences for lesbians and gay men. *Journal of Social Issues, 34*(3), 59–72.

Due, L. (1995). *Joining the tribe: Growing up gay and in the 90's.* New York: Anchor Books.

Fairchild, B., & Hayward, N. (1989). *Now that you know: What every parent should know about homosexuality.* New York: Harcourt Brace Jovanovich, Publishers.

Faria, G. (1994). Training for family preservation practice with lesbian families. *Families in Society,* 416–422.

Finnegan, D. G., & McNally, E. B. (1996). Chemical dependency and depression in lesbians and gay men: What helps? In M. Shernoff (Ed.), *Human services for gay people: Clinical and community practice* (pp. 115–130). New York: Harrington Park.

Fraser, M., Pecora, P., & Haapala, D. (1991). *Families in crisis.* New York: Aldine de Gruyter.

Garofalo, R., Wolf, C., Wissow, L. S., Woods, W. R., & Goodman, E. (1999). Sexual orientation and the risk of suicide attempts among a representative sample of youth. *Archives of Pediatric Adolescent Medicine, 153,* 487–493.

Germain, C. B. (1985). The place of community work within an ecological approach to social work practice. In S. H. Taylor & R. W. Roberts (Eds.), *Theory and practice of community social work* (pp. 30–55). New York: Columbia University Press.

Germain, C. B., & Gitterman, A. (1996). *The life model of social work practice* (2nd ed.). New York: Columbia University Press.

Gochros, J. (1989). *When husbands come out of the closet.* New York: Haworth Press.

Gochros, J. (1992). Homophobia, homosexuality, and heterosexual marriage. In W. Blumenfeld (Ed.), *Homophobia: How we all pay the price* (pp. 131–153). Boston, MA: Beacon Press.

Goffman, E. (1963). *Stigma: Notes of the management of a spoiled identity.* Englewood Cliffs, NJ: Prentice-Hall.

Greene, B. (1994). Lesbian and gay sexual orientations: Implications for clinical training, practice and research. In B. Greene & G. M. Herek (Eds.), *Lesbian and gay psychology: Theory, research, and clinical applications* (pp. 1–24). Thousand Oaks, CA: Sage.

Greene, Z. (1996). Straight, but not narrow-minded. In P. Kay, A. Estepa, & A. Desetta (Eds.), *Out with it: Gay and straight teens write about homosexuality* (pp. 12–14). New York: Youth Communications.

Griffin, C., Wirth, M. J., & Wirth, A. G. (1986). *Beyond acceptance.* Englewood Cliffs, NJ: Prentice-Hall.

Hartman, A., & Laird, J. (1983). *Family-centered social work practice.* New York: Free Press.

Hartman, A., & Laird, J. (Eds.). (1985). *Child welfare handbook: Context, knowledge, and practice.* New York: Free Press.

Helminiak, D. A. (1997). *What the Bible really says about homosexuality.* San Francisco: Alamo Square Press.

Herek, G. M. (1991). Stigma, prejudice and violence against lesbians and gay men. In J. C. Gonsiorek & J. D. Weinrich (Eds.), *Homosexuality: Research implications for public policy* (pp. 60–80). Newbury Park: Sage.

Herman, D. (1997). *The anti-gay agenda—Orthodox vision and the Christian right.* Chicago: University of Chicago Press.

Heron, A. (Ed.). (1994). *Two in twenty.* Boston: Alyson Publications.

Hetrick, E., & Martin, A. D. (1987). Developmental issues and their resolution for gay and lesbian adolescents. *Journal of Homosexuality, 13*(4), 25–43.

Hunter, J., & Mallon, G. P. (1998). Social work practice with lesbian and gay persons within communities. In G. P. Mallon (Ed.). *Foundations of social work practice with lesbian and gay persons* (pp. 229–248). New York: Haworth Press.

Hunter, J., & Schaecher, R. (1987). Stresses on lesbian and gay adolescents in schools. *Social Work in Education, 9*(3), 180–188.

Jones, B. E., & Hill, M. (Eds.). (2003). *Mental health issues in lesbian, gay, bisexual, and transgender communities*. Washington, DC: APA.

Kaplan, L. (1986). *Working with multi-problem families*. Lexington, MA: Lexington Books.

Kay, P., Estepa, A., & Desetta, A. (Eds.). (1996). *Out with it: Gay and straight teens write about homosexuality*. New York: Youth Communications.

Kinney, J., Haapala, D., & Booth, C. (1991). *Keeping families together: The homebuilders model*. Hawthorne, NY: Aldine de Gruyter.

Laird, J. (1996). Family-centered practice with lesbian and gay families. *Families in Society, 22,* 559–572.

Lesbian and gay poverty. Retrieved on January 28, 2004, from www.tased.edu.au/tasonline/tasqueer/nat_issu/poverty

Lev, A. I. (2004). *Transgender emergence: Therapeutic guidelines for working with gender variant people and their families*. New York: Haworth Press.

Loppnow, D. M. (1985). Adolescents on their own. In J. Laird & A. Hartman (Eds.), *A handbook of child welfare: Context, knowledge, and practice* (pp. 514–532). New York: Free Press.

MacPike, L. (Ed.). (1989). *There's something I've been meaning to tell you*. Tallahassee, FL: Naiad Press.

Mallon, G. P. (Ed.). (1998a). *Foundations of social work practice with lesbian and gay persons*. New York: Haworth Press.

Mallon, G. P. (1998b). *We don't exactly get the welcome wagon: The experiences of lesbian and gay adolescents in child welfare systems*. New York: Columbia University Press.

Mallon, G. P. (1998c). Social work practice with lesbian and gay persons within families. In G. P. Mallon (Ed.), *Foundations of social work practice with lesbian and gay persons* (pp. 145–181). New York: Haworth Press.

Malyon, A. K. (1981). The homosexual adolescent: Developmental issues and social bias. *Child Welfare League of America, 60*(5), 321–330.

Metropolitan Community Church. (1990). *Homosexuality not a sin, not a sickness: What the Bible does and does not say*. Los Angeles: Author.

Miranda, D. (1996). I hated myself. In P. Kay, A. Estepa, & A. Desetta (Eds.), *Out with it: Gay and straight teens write about homosexuality* (pp. 34–39). New York: Youth Communications.

Monette, P. (1992). *Becoming a man: Half a life story*. New York: Harcourt Brace Jovanovich.

Morales, E. S. (1989). Ethnic minority families and minority gays and lesbians. *Marriage and Family Review, 14,* 217–239.

Parents & Friends of Lesbians and Gays. (1990). *Why is my child gay?* Washington, DC: Parents and Friends of Lesbians and Gays.

Parents & Friends of Lesbians and Gays. (1997). *Beyond the Bible: Parents, families and friends talk about religion and homosexuality*. Washington, DC: Author.

Pharr, S. (1988). *Homophobia: A weapon of sexism*. Inverness, CA: Chardon Press.

Reid, J. (1973). *The best little boy in the world*. New York: Ballantine Books.

Remafedi, G. (1999). Sexual orientation and youth suicide. *Journal of the American Medical Association, 282,* 1291–1292.

Rofes, E. R. (1983). *I thought people like that killed themselves*. San Francisco: Grey Fox Press.

Rothberg, B., & Weinstein, D. L. (1996). A primer on lesbian and gay families. In M. Shernoff (Ed.), *Human services for gay people: Clinical and community practice* (pp. 55–68). New York: Harrington Park.

Saffron, L. (1997). *What about the children? Sons and daughters of lesbian and gay parents talk about their lives.* London: Cassell.

Savin-Williams, R. C. (1998). *And then I became gay.* New York: Routledge Press.

Savin-Williams, R. C., & Rodriguez, R. G. (1993). A developmental clinical perspective on lesbian, gay male and bisexual youth. In T. P. Gullotta, G. R. Adams, & R. Montemayor (Eds.), *Adolescent sexual: Advances in adolescent development* (Vol. 5, pp. 77–101). Newbury Park, CA: Sage.

Silverstein, C. (1977). *A family matter: A parent's guide to homosexuality.* New York: McGraw Hill.

Strommen, E. F. (1989). "You're a what?" Family member reactions to the disclosure of homosexuality. *Journal of Homosexuality, 18*(1/2), 37–58.

Switzer, D. K. (1996). *Coming out as parents.* Louisville, KY: Westminister John Knox Press.

Tracy, E. M. (1991). Defining the target population for family preservation services: Some conceptual issues. In K. Wells & D. Biegal (Eds.), *Family preservation services: Research and evaluation* (pp. 138–158). Newbury Park, CA: Sage.

Tracy, E. M., Haapala, D. A., Kinney, J., & Pecora, P. (1991). Intensive family preservation services: A strategic response to families in crisis. In E. M. Tracy, D. A. Haapala, J. Kinney, & P. Pecora (Eds.), *Intensive family preservation services: An instructional sourcebook* (pp. 1–14). Cleveland, OH: Mandel School of Applied Social Sciences.

Troiden, R. R. (1979). Becoming homosexual: A model of gay identity acquisition. *Psychiatry, 42*, 362–373.

Troiden, R. R. (1988). *Lesbian and gay identity: A sociological analysis.* Dix Hills: General Hall, Inc.

Troiden, R. R. (1989). The formation of homosexual identities. In G. Herdt (Ed.), *Lesbian and gay youth* (pp. 43–74). New York: Harrington Park Press.

Tuerk, C. (1995, October). A son with gentle ways: A therapist-mother's journey. *In the family: A magazine for lesbians, gays, bisexuals and their relations, 1*(1), 18–22.

Valenzuela, W. (1996). A school where I can be myself. In P. Kay, A. Estepa, & A. Desetta (Eds.), *Out with it: Gay and straight teens write about homosexuality* (pp. 45–46). New York: Youth Communications.

Wadley, C. (1996a). Shunned, insulted, threatened. In P. Kay, A. Estepa, & A. Desetta (Eds.), *Out with it: Gay and straight teens write about homosexuality* (pp. 57–60). New York: Youth Communications.

Wadley, C. (1996b). Kicked out because she was a lesbian. In P. Kay, A. Estepa, & A. Desetta (Eds.), *Out with it: Gay and straight teens write about homosexuality* (pp. 58–60). New York: Youth Communications.

Walters, K. L. (1998). Negotiating conflicts in allegiances among lesbian and gays of color: Reconciling divided selves and communities. In G. P. Mallon (Ed.), *Foundations of social work practice with lesbian and gay persons* (pp. 47–76). New York: Haworth Press.

Weissbourd, B., & Kagan, S. L. (1989). Family support programs: Catalysts for change. *American Journal of Orthopsychiatry, 59*(1), 20–30.

Weston, K. (1997). *Families we choose: Lesbian and gay kinship.* New York: Columbia University Press.

CHAPTER 11

Arab American Families: Assessment and Treatment

Nuha Abudabbeh

One hundred and fifty million Arabs live in 22 countries located in the Middle East (Palestine, Jordan, Syria, Lebanon, and Iraq), the Gulf region (Saudi Arabia, Kuwait, Oman, United Arab Emirates, and Yemen), and Africa (Egypt, Libya, Sudan, Tunisia, Algeria, and Morocco). Arabs are defined as those who speak the Arabic language and claim a link with the nomadic tribes of Arabia (Hourani, 1970). All Arab countries have in common their written language. The spoken Arabic differs from one country to the other, at times significantly enough not to be understood by one another. In addition to the common written language, different Arabs share similar cultural values about family, marriage, and children. Despite some basic commonalities, however, there are differences between Arab countries as impacted by their geography, histories, religious affiliation, and ethnic composition. One important consideration for a practitioner is whether the country is conservative or liberal. The more liberal the country (e.g., Lebanon) the more similarities with Western attitudes and norms. The more conservative the country (e.g., Saudi Arabia) the more likely families will be different in customs and expectations.

Several historical events have impacted on the Arab world as it has had to deal with significant upheavals following the end of an era of grandeur and power brought about with the birth and growth of Islam (7th to 10th century). After the domination of the Arab world by one force or another, occupation by the West and the creation of Israel in its midst, millions of Arab immigrants have endured a variety of political, economic, and social events before and after their arrival in the United States.

Arab Americans can be described as a multicultural, multi-racial, and multiethnic mosaic population (Abudabbeh & Nydell, 1993). There have been three major waves of immigration to the United States. The first wave began in the 1930s until WWII, the second after the creation of the State of Israel (1948), and the third after 1967. The three different waves of immigrants traveled for different reasons and their immigration challenges were also different. Nevertheless, the Arab Israeli war of 1967 was a trigger for a convergence of these three groups, forging a cultural group with its own unique values and norms.

Approximately 3.5 million Americans are of Arab descent (U.S. Census Bureau, 2000). Two thirds of this population resides in 10 states; one third of the total live in California, New York, and Michigan. About 94% live in metropolitan areas. Lebanese Americans constitute the greater part of the population, with the exceptions of New Jersey where Egyptians are the majority, Syrians in Rhode Island, Palestinians in Illinois, and the Iraqi/Chaldeans in Illinois, Michigan, and California.

At least 85% of Arab Americans have a high school diploma, and more than 4 out of 10 have a Bachelor's degree or higher, compared with 24% of Americans. Seventeen percent of Arab Americans have a post graduate education, a figure twice that of Americans. Of the school age children, 58% are in elementary school, 22% in college, and 7% in graduate school. Occupationally 64% of Arab Americans are in the labor force, 73% in managerial, professional technical, sales, or administrative fields. Compared with the 27% of overall Americans employed in service industries, only 12% of Arab Americans are employed in service. Most Arab Americans work in the private sector (88%) and 12% hold government jobs. Median income for Arab Americans reported in 1999 was $47,000.00, compared with the average American income of $42,000.00. Close to 30% of Arab Americans have an income of more than $75,000.00, in contrast to 22% of non-Arab Americans having that level of income (Arab American Institute, 2003).

The majority of Arab Americans are Christian (U.S. Census bureau, 2000). Of the 77% of Arab Americans who are Christian, the majority are Catholic, 23% Orthodox, and 12% Protestant.

According to survey results from a sample of Arab Americans, conducted in June of 2003 (500 families), the percentage of Muslims remained 24% (Zoghby, 2003).

Among the Muslim Arab American population, a disproportionate number are Shiite Muslims. The Shi'a and Sunni Muslims, while essentially adhering to the same tenets of Islamic principles, differ with respect to the relationship between the leader (the cleric) and the *umma* (the people). Prophet Mohammed taught Islam as transmitted through the Quran. The Quran is believed to be the literal word of God. The Quran provides guidance as to what pleases God and does not contain explicit doctrines except by implication. In contrast the Hadith and Sunna do contain specific instructions and commands for everyday life. Such social issues as division of property, marital laws, requirements and custody issues were derived from the sayings of the prophet Mohammed (hadith) and from his practices (sunna). The basic five pillars of Islam, regardless of origin or interpretation are as follows:

1. Oral testimony that there is one God and that Mohammed is his prophet.
2. Ritual prayers five times a day with certain words and postures of the body.
3. Giving of alms to the poor.
4. Keeping a strict fast of no liquid or food from sunrise to sundown during the month of Ramadan.
5. Holy pilgrimage to Mecca once in a lifetime at a specific time of the year.

A general injunction was added, *jihad*, that carries the universal meaning that every Muslim must exercise strenuous intellectual, physical, and spiritual efforts for the good of all (Shabbas & Al-Qazzaz, 1989).

PSYCHOSOCIAL NEEDS

There is a scarcity of information available on the psychosocial needs of the Arab American community. This is a relatively young community in its emergence as a visible group entity. In contrast to the early immigrants' assimilation into the American life, the last 30 years have made the Arab American community more visible. These changes were triggered by several historical events, such as the discovery of oil in Arab countries, the creation of the State of Israel and the creation of a disenfranchised Palestinian refugee population, and the beginnings of the Islamization of the Arab world. These events made the average American more aware of Arab Americans, and unfortunately this awareness was often associated with negative stereotyping of Arab American. After an initial negative stereotyping of Arab Americans, who were seen as one indivisible group (which included the highly assimilated early immigrants such as Casey Kasem the entertainer, cabinet member Donna Shallah, and comedian Danny Thomas), the image of Arab Americans seemed to begin to change to a less negative one. Early immigrates such as Danny Thomas, etc., assimilated with a great deal of ease because of their religious affiliation (Christian). They were instrumental in enabling more recent immigrants in improving common negative stereotype of the Arab in the United States. The events of 9-11, however, seemed to have arrested that change and replaced this improved image of the Arab American with a more sinister one.

In 1967 the community began coming together as a cohesive group, unified initially by outside political events (the October Arab Israeli war). The defeat of Arabs in that war triggered the establishment of a wave of Arab American organizations to address political issues and issues of discrimination. Only one organization was created to provide for economic and social needs: ACCESS in Detroit. Subsequent to the creation of ACCESS, two other organizations, namely Naim Foundation in Washington, DC, and the Brooklyn Clinic in Brooklyn, New York, were created. ACCESS and the Brooklyn Clinic remain the two major centers providing social and economic needs for the Arab American population. Of the three centers, only NAIM Foundation was established with a primary focus on providing mental health services. To date, mental health services remain of secondary importance to the Arab American community. This is not because of the diminished incidence of mental health concerns, but rather because other issues are perceived by community leaders as being of higher priority. Based on the experience at the NAIM Foundation during its years of service (1987–1999), as well as the number of calls that were received during a radio mental health call in program in

Arabic (1990–2001), there were clear indications of a high incidence of psychosocial problems within this community.

Calls were documented at the NAIM Foundation, where a counselor provided crisis intervention 2 days out of the week for a period of 2 years. The following was the nature of the calls received:

1. 37% of the calls were to complain and/or receive guidance in dealing with domestic issues.
2. 17% of the calls were to talk to a counselor because the person felt lonely.
3. 15% of the calls were made to seek guidance in parenting.
4. 15% of the calls were made to inquire about professionals in different fields that spoke the Arabic language. (Abudabbeh, 1995)

In contrast to the calls received by a counselor at NAIM Foundation, the calls received by the author, the producer as well as the host, covered a larger range of topics. During the 11 years of the call-in Arabic radio program, which was of 1-hour duration, a brief description of different mental health problems was presented. The presentation covered every diagnosis in the *DSMIV-Revised* and also different social issues. During its early creation, the radio program was heard in almost all parts of the United States. In the latter period however, it was heard only in Detroit, which has one of the highest concentration of Arab Americans in the country, and in the Washington, D.C. metropolitan area. The program in fact made its debut during the Gulf War, when the community was in dire need of social and psychological services. During that period it was a venue to express Arab Americans' frustrations, as well as their pain about the impact of that war on their extended families in the Middle East. The program was also a vehicle to learn about the role of the mental health provider. It is interesting to note that the radio psychologist becoming a well known person to the community at large facilitated and encouraged the community to seek professional help for psychological problems. In fact, people seeking help came to mental health professionals at NAIM Foundation from other states because they had built a trusting relationship with the "doctor" on the radio. The issues most discussed on the radio included marital issues and parenting issues.

Serious mental illness was the least broached subject. However, a description of the different diagnostic categories did trigger seeking of professional help to either rule out the presence of a serious mental illness, to find a second opinion on a person in treatment with someone else, or to discuss the case of a relative with a mental illness in the country of origin. In other words, the radio program was an instrument that facilitated the seeking of advice on serious mental illness. These calls occurred, not on the radio itself (where it may be something to be ashamed of), but privately.

Mental health remains a new focus of attention for young Arab Americans. For example, as recently as 1999, in his book on Arabs in America, Suleiman (1999), a sociology professor, covered a variety of topics on Arab Americans, without a chapter on mental health. There was, however, a whole section dedicated to the Arab American identity. This young community continues to prioritize such issues as political status, social problems related to discrimination, and more recently legal problems after 9-11. Because of 9-11, exposure to wars prior to arrival to the United States, and the stress of acculturation to a radically different host country, however, Arab Americans remain at high risk for emotional disorders.

Suleiman's book (1999) did include a chapter on general health. Hassoun's (1999) research on the health problems of Arab American focused attention on the Dearborn population. Her study concluded that this particular population, which has a disproportionate percentage of a lower socioeconomic class of Arabs, suffered from a high incidence of diabetes, hypertension, and high cholesterol. She also observed that they had a tendency to either minimize or cover up their health problems. Some families denied and/or concealed having such serious illnesses as beta-thalassemia (similar to sickle cell anemia), for fear that it would impact on their daughters' eligibility for marriage.

Barkouki and Winter (1991) and Meleis (1991) in their research have addressed the psychological risk factors faced by Arab Americans. Meleis focuses on the gender issue by pointing out that the Arab female is at a higher risk because of the multiple roles required of her. Barkouki and Winter (1991), on the other hand, point to the significant differences between Arabs and the host country (USA) as a major contributor to acculturation stress, describing it as a "cultural exhaustion."

The incidence of mental illness among Arabs at large has been reported as higher in some Arab countries (United Arab Emirates and Saudi Arabia) in comparison to Western countries and other developing countries (Dwairy, 1998). Dwairy attributes this high incidence of psychiatric morbidity to the sudden changes that oil producing countries had to cope with. The family transformation was another contributing factor. Studies comparing the incidence of mental illness among Arab families have concluded that families that maintained a traditional lifestyle, in contrast to those who led a more Western, individualistic lifestyle, were less vulnerable to mental disorders. Women and children were also found to be at higher risk For example, 31% of women, in contrast to 20% of men in the United Arab Emirates were diagnosed with mental illness (Dwairy, 1998). Sixty-five percent of outpatient visits in Saudi Arabia were made by children. In Arab countries where the population was exposed to conflict and war (Palestine, Lebanon, Iraq, and Sudan), a high prevalence of psychological disorders has been recorded, especially among children (Dwairy, 1998). Referrals to the Naim Foundation (1991–1999) consisted mostly of patients from Saudi Arabia. This may have been due to several reasons, including those provided by Dwairy (1998). Other reasons for the higher utilization of mental health services among Saudi Arabian and other oil rich countries may be attributed to persons' financial ability to seek the needed services. This was certainly the case in the Washington, D.C. metropolitan area, where the majority of those who sought treatment where either those from wealthier countries or the wealthier classes of Arab countries. Another reason for seeking professional help was to seek advice on a situation that needed to be kept secret from others and may not necessarily have been due to the presence of a mental illness.

The case of a young Saudi student exemplifies some of the issues that are impacted by cultural values, the stress of accultura- tion to a radically different culture, and the complexity of ap- proaching the problem within the specific cultural context. The Saudis are a more conservative group than other Arabs such as the Lebanese. Ahmad in fact was typical of a conservative Saudi in that he observed all of the tenants of Islamic obligations, includ- ing that of not engaging in intimacy prior to marriage. He sought individual therapy having been diagnosed in Saudi Arabia as suffer- ing from an anxiety disorder. He also wanted to seek further treatment because he wanted to verify his diagnosis and to consult whether he may need medication. Ahmad had been placed on medications in Saudi Arabia, but had not been in therapy. After an interview and subsequent testing, it became clear that Ahmad might have had a learning disorder that had never been diagnosed, nor attended to prior to his consult. His situation was further complicated by not being able to discuss his issues with his family because the family relationships were extremely formalized and intra-family communications were never personal. In other words, Ahmad had no one to confide in, neither to discuss his fears and his anxieties with, nor to seek advice from. One solution he considered was the option of getting married, as he found himself without any companion or any family members to rely on. As he was tempted to date, he immediately made plans to marry.

In contrast to the dilemmas facing Ahmad, two young Arabs, one male and the other female sought treatment for depression related to having been diagnosed with attention deficit disorder (Syrian, male) and posttraumatic stress disorder (Iraqi, female). The woman had been incarcerated for 9 years for political reasons. Both were from Western and educated backgrounds, one was Christian and the other Muslim. Their siblings referred them and both were from close-knit families. Both also had a secret that they could not share even with their closest siblings. The male was gay but wished he could find a way to change, knowing that his family could never accept his sexual preference. The female engaged in lesbian liaisons and was in fear of these relationships ever being discovered by her family.

Another client, Salma, sought help to deal with the lingering traumatic effects of rape. Because of the sexual taboos in her culture (despite the extent of the westernization of her family), she was unable to share this with her family. Her inability to share this crisis event with her mother was more traumatizing to Salma than the event itself.

There is a clear difference between the four Arab clients discussed above and the majority of Western clients, who seek help primarily to resolve individual problems and to acquire insight and skills to enhance their independence and other personal goals. The four Arab young men and women in contrast, were depressed and anxious, and in addition to wanting to feel better this had to be accomplished within the family context. The family was a significant part of the resolution of the problem. Unlike the individualistic Western model of achieving an inner resolution, Arabs strive to change in harmony with others, as the self remains elastic and includes significant family members or partners.

CULTURAL FACTORS IMPACTING ON PERSONALITY DYNAMICS AND ATTITUDES TOWARD MENTAL ILLNESS AND TREATMENT

The main differences between Arabic and Western psychodynamics are in the following areas:

Individuation: Unlike the Western and even more so the American emphasis on individuation, Arabs are almost opposed to individuation. For example, an Arab American family may seek help because a son or daughter expresses an interest in enrolling in a school away from home.

Coping mechanisms: Arabs cope with stressors by reaching out to others, or by denying the importance of these stressors. Because Arabs focus less on intrapsychic mechanisms. they are less likely to be self-examining and self-reflective. This often leads to placing the blame on outside forces or on others. Often God or a higher force is to blame or thank for certain events in life. The family's role in preparing their children for a successful place in society consists of teaching them appropriate social and cultural roles. Learning these skills enables individuals to achieve successful jobs, friendships, and assume their roles as partners and parents.

Personality dynamics: Independence is not emphasized as a positive attribute, as the culture is geared toward a collective paradigm. Within the collective mindset, an Arab strives to please others, unlike the Westerner, who is conditioned to meet his or her own needs (self-actualization). Whereas a Westerner may experience depression because they have failed in their goals, the Arab will feel depressed because he failed others or was viewed unfavorably by those around him. An Arab person's behavior and values are more directly impacted by what the family and his immediate community expect of him than by his own conscience.

Collective cultural norms coupled with lack of the intrapsychic element impact attitudes toward both the mentally ill and toward the treatment of mental illness. Some of the attitudes toward mental illness are similar to those that existed in the Western culture prior to the dissemination of information on mental illness. It is interesting to note that there is a difference in attitude depending on socioeconomic class. If the Arab family is middle class, the more concerned they are about making the right societal impression, and the more likely they are to attach shame to the presence of any mental health problems. Less educated and poorer families, although more accepting of the situation or the person with the mental illness, are more likely to be misinformed about the etiology of that illness.

With the lack of emphasis on intrapsychic factors in the development and understanding of personality, the role of psychotherapy remains at best a mystery. In some ways this is not peculiar to Arabs. With the more recent emphasis on short-term treatment and the proliferation of psychopharmacological treatment, psychotherapy has been given a secondary role in treatment. It is interesting, however, that among a certain number of Arabs, there is a rejection of medication and an emphasis on psychotherapy. Most of those who seek therapy are more educated and have been more influenced by Western values.

TREATMENT

There are significant differences between Arab American families, depending on country of origin, socioeconomic background, and level of acculturation. When educated about mental illness and psychological problems, and given a vehicle for seeking confidential help, Arab families welcome the possibility (Abudabbeh, 1996). Given the newness of focusing on mental health needs, they respond well when the therapeutic intervention approximates a social visit without compromising the therapeutic alliance. As Arabs are a highly socialized society, any activity that fosters extreme formality would be likely to slow down the building of trust and thus delay treatment outcome. Although this may not necessarily be true in all situations, decisions have to be made based on the particular individual being seen. The following example illustrates how an appropriate, socially acceptable intervention can be added to the treatment protocol to enhance outcome.

Recently a young Arab female was referred to the author for individual therapy. An uncle accompanied her to therapy as an escort, because she as a single woman would not have been allowed to travel without a guardian. The family was almost illiterate and from a rural part of an Arab country. Making visits to the office approximates a social event and to make it as similar as possible to an event that was familiar to the girl and the uncle, the uncle was allowed into the sessions and different food or drinks were served on each visit.

Should this approach be used with every Arab client? The answer is no. In this case an initial assessment of the situation indicated the need for this approach. It was clear that excluding the uncle would have led to a possible sabotage of treatment. Including him was actually useful, as he learned how to better interact with the girl and was also able to inform other members of the family so that certain approaches could be used after the termination of therapy. Building a good relationship with the uncle also increased the possibility of enlisting him as a person who will look out for his niece in his own country. Making therapy similar to social visits enhances the development of trust and reinforces the whole concept of therapy. Thus therapy becomes associated with a familiar, useful, and positive experience.

Other strategies used by this author have included making home visits and accepting invitations to cultural events. Whether it is a visit to a medical doctor or a therapist, this is a culture that is very sensitive to social markers related to how one is treated. Often a "doctor" is trusted because he or she is someone who is "nice" to clients. That person has to be liked, akin to whether the therapist has good bedside manners or not.

Based on this group's secrecy, it is clear that group therapy is not usually a therapeutic option. Psychodynamic psychotherapy is another treatment approach that is not advisable because of the lack of psychic introspection. The most successful approaches are interpersonal, cognitive-behavioral, and ego supportive. The cognitive-behavioral approach is most applicable when dealing with an educated Arab American. What seems to have worked for the less educated is interpersonal—with a heavy emphasis on didactic—approach. In other words, there is no one therapeutic approach to be applied to Arab Americans, and there must be flexibility in choosing the approach depending on the background and the presenting personality dynamic. As described above there are significant differences among Arabs depending on the country of origin, socioeconomic class and/or level of education, and level of acculturation.

Cognitive-behavioral therapy (CBT) was the treatment approach that worked very well for an Arab female from a Middle Eastern background. She was born and raised in the United States—thus acculturation was not an issue, she was a college graduate, and the family was middle class. Despite having all the characteristics making her a good candidate for CBT, her appearance (head covered), and traditional lifestyle seemed initially to give a different impression. In contrast to this case, a young Arab man was referred for therapy by his psychiatrist after an unsuccessful trial at medicating him for posttraumatic stress disorder. Initial attempts at using CBT did not lead to any improvement in his condition. He had also refused to be medicated. Since neither a pharmacological nor therapeutic intervention seem to be working and it became clear that medication was a necessity, the approach was shifted to an educational one. Subsequently the sessions were geared toward convincing him about the necessity of accepting medication. The nature of posttraumatic stress disorder and the role of medication in treating this disorder was explained to him.

One approach that seems to be of great value to this population, as evidenced by the number of people seeking it, is couple therapy (Abudabbeh, 1996). It is theorized that because the institution of marriage is so important and divorce remains much less acceptable among Arab Americans, they are highly likely to be open to solutions for maintaining marriage, including seeking couple therapy. Couples have sought treatment because of differing expectations that result from two people not having had an opportunity to know each other before marriage. Other couples seek therapy to help with a specific issue such as a wife's suspicions about her husband spending time alone in his office or a husband who brought his wife to have the therapist convince her that he was not lying to her when he reassured her that she did not have cancer. One male who had been separated from his wife had begun a relationship with another woman. When the wife was ready for repairing their relationship, he found himself in a difficult situation as he had built a strong relationship with the new woman, but was not willing to give up the wife (the mother of his children) for the new one. He sought "advice" as to how to solve this problem.

CONCLUSION

The Arab American population is a multi-ethnic, multicultural, and multi-racial population. An initial intake assessment should identify the following: county of origin and region, religious affiliation, reason for immigration to the United States, socioeconomic status prior to immigration, and whether the country of origin was in any form of political turmoil.

The most common reasons for seeking treatment are history of serious mental illness, marital conflict, and trans-generational conflict. Treatment approaches that work most effectively are psychoeducational, relational, and cognitive-behavioral therapy. Depending on the country of origin, most of the traditional approaches utilized in the Western style of therapy have to be abandoned. Flexibility in selecting the treatment modality to fit the particular Arab American client and the family needs to be developed.

REFERENCES

Abudabbeh, N. (1996). Overview on Arab Americans. In I. M. McGoldrick, J. Giardano, & J. K. Pearce (Eds.), *Ethnicity and family therapy* (2nd ed.). New York: Guilford Press.

Abudabbeh, N. (1995). *Mental illness and the Arab culture: Clinical issues.* Paper presented at the American Psychiatric Association, 148th meeting, Miami, Florida.

Abudabbeh, N., & Nydell, M. (1993). Transcultural counseling and Arab Americans. In J. McFadden (Ed.), *Transcultural counseling: Bilateral and international perspectives* (pp. 262–284). Alexandria, VA: American Counseling Association.

Arab American Institute. (2003). *Arab American demographics.* Washington, DC: CIC.

Barkouki, A. S., & Winter, W. D. (1991). *Serving the mental health needs of Arab Americans.* Paper presented at the NAIM conference, Washington, DC.

Dwairy, M. A. (1998). *Cross-cultural counseling, the Arab-Palestinian case.* Binghampton, NY: Haworth Press Inc.

Hassoun, R. (1999). Arab-American health and the process of coming to America: Lessons from the metropolitan Detroit area. In M. W. Suleiman (Ed.), *Arabs in America: Building a new future* (pp. 157–176). Philadelphia: Temple University Press.

Hourani, A. (1970). *Arabic thought in the liberal age: 1798–1939.* London: Oxford University Press.

Meleis, A. (1991). Between two cultures: Identity, roles and health. *Health Care for Women International, 12,* 365–377.

Shabbas, A., & Al-Qazzaz, A. (Eds.). (1989). *Arab world notebook.* Berkley, CA: Najda.

Suleiman, M. W. (1999). *Arabs in America: Building a new future.* Philadelphia: Temple University Press.

U.S. Census Bureau. (2000). *Summary, file 4.* Washington, DC.

Zoghby, J. (2003). Report on survey of Arab American households. *Zoghby international poll* (commissioned by Arab American Institute). Washington, DC.

CHAPTER 12

An Afrocentric Approach in Working With African American Families

Valerie Borum

AN AFROCENTRIC CONCEPTION OF "STARTING WHERE THE CLIENT IS . . . "

> History, as nearly no one seems to know, is not merely something to be read . . . or even principally . . . the past . . . we carry it within us, are unconsciously controlled by it . . . and history is literally present in all that we do . . . it is to history that we owe our frames of reference, our identities, and our aspirations. James Baldwin (1979, p. 6)

For African Americans, the sense of belonging, the essence of who they are, and their right to assemble in collective and familial units is based on the color of their skin. To be African in America, or African American, is to somehow disrupt neatly sealed categories of what it means to be American—un-hyphenated, unmarked, and seemingly coming from no position or ethnicity (Ellison, 1970; Sartwell, 1998). Possessing African American ancestry has been a marker for imposing external limitations and a symbol of a definitive "outsider" or "racialized other" (Chennault & Dyson, 1998; Ellison, 1970; Sartwell, 1998). And yet, despite their exclusion as a unique (and misunderstood) ethnic group and their social status vis-à-vis a socially constructed notion of a "racial" hierarchy, there continues to be something unquestionably American about this ethnic group of historical and contemporary Africans in America. This point of view awakens a seemingly paradoxical possibility that "whatever else the true American is . . . is also Black" (Ellison, 1970, p. A7).

The above stance challenges the erroneous assumptions that American culture or what it means to be an American is somehow synonymous with White, Anglo-Saxon ancestry. An irrefutable part of this nation is grounded in the cultural, psychological, and material make-up of a distinctive African American heritage and motif (Bennett, 1993; Sertima, 1976). As a distinct historical, cultural, and ethnic group, African American families and communities have generally been represented and described in the literature along this continuum: a) their experiences living in a hostile environment dominated by White American ethnic groups, and b) their experiences stemming from their own distinct and internal cultural dynamics (Billingsley, 1968; Butler, 1992; English, 1991).

A prevailing misconception about African American culture, however, is the assumption that the "New World" experience eradicated all vestiges of a pan-African cultural tradition brought to this country as a result of deracination and U.S. enslavement (Akbar, 1981; Ani, 1994; Asante, 1990; Azibo, 1996; Kambon, 1996; Schiele, 1997). African Americans came to this country, albeit against their will, with rich and vibrant cultural traditions and cosmological worldviews. In fact, what is striking is the role enslavement, segregation, and exclusion from larger society has played in the retention of African traditions by African Americans. African Americans forged a distinct pan-ethnic culture consisting of many African ethnicities and languages, a strength of diversity that was commensurate with the traumatic challenges faced in the New World. This is an indication of the tenacity of culture and its potential reinterpretations to fit new and demanding realities faced in different physical and cultural environments (Akbar, 1981; Green, 1995; Kambon, 1996).

In working with African Americans in general, and African American families in particular, social workers and other helping professionals should be aware that African American families and communities need to be understood in the context of their very unique history in the U.S., that represents a far different history than that of any other ethnic group in America. For example, their unique journey (e.g., transatlantic slave trade/African Holocaust) entailed a set of circumstances that were directly and explicitly for the purpose of enslavement (Akbar, 1996; Green, 1995; Griffin, 1999).

As a result, African Americans are neither immigrants who willingly came to this country, nor indigenous to this land— although they were here before most ethnic Europeans and other ethnic groups (Bennett, 1993; Sertima, 1976). No other ethnic group shares this dilemma of being neither immigrant nor indigenous. Yet, this group has longed to develop their potential and power in an American environment free of false notions of Black inferiority, as well as overwhelming false notions of White supremacy, White racism, and oppression (cultural, economic, political, and social), in order to fulfill a desire for a deeper sense of their own humanity and that of the nation as a whole (Bennett, 1993; Ellis, 1983). Billingsley (1968) further argues that to deny African American history is to deny African American humanity.

WHAT IS AN AFROCENTRIC FRAMEWORK?

In order to further develop a model of practice grounded in a theoretical framework that is inclusive of African American historical, ethnic, and cultural significance, as well as diversity of concepts and perspectives when dealing with issues of culture and behavior patterns, a sociocultural framework, such as Afrocentricity, is required (Akbar, 1984; Asante, 1988; Collins, 1990; Dubois, 1908; Schiele, 2000). An Afrocentric framework emphasizes and assumes holism (Williams & Finger Wright, 1992), and is predicated on philosophical assumptions (e.g., worldview) generating from contemporary African America and traditional Africa (Akbar, 1981; Asante, 1990).

Afrocentricity's (also known as Africentricity or African-centered) overarching belief system (i.e., paradigm) and theoretical underpinnings recognize African American history and culture as the focal point in any analysis of people of African American descent. It is a theory of social change that epitomizes the political, economic, and cultural freedom of African Americans. Asante

(1990) suggests that Afrocentricity asserts that peoples of African descent are active, primary, and central agents in the making of their histories. This guiding principle of human agency acts as a filter in describing African/African American existence in America and throughout the Diaspora.

As a result, Afrocentricity has its own distinct attributes. For example, Afrocentricity's cosmological aspects, such as worldview, entail viewing reality from the perspective of interdependency, where all elements of the universe are interconnected. Its ontological aspects, such as the view of human nature, assume all elements of the universe (e.g., people, animals, inanimate objects, etc.) are spiritual—all elements are created from the same universal, spiritual substance. Epistemologically, a great deal of emphasis is placed on an affective way of knowing and obtaining information, while its axiological significance underscores interpersonal relationships as the highest value. Afrocentricity is a *philosophical ideology* (a way of living, thinking, and knowing) that places African American history, culture, and African heritage at the center of the lives of persons of African descent; therefore, Afrocentricity can be more accurately described as a "philosophical outlook determined by history" (Akbar, 1984; Asante, 1988, 1990).

AN AFROCENTRIC FRAMEWORK FOR UNDERSTANDING INTRA-GROUP DIVERSITY

When conducting a sociocultural analysis of African American families utilizing an Afrocentric approach, it can be assumed that different definitions and perspectives may exist within this group (Butler, 1995; English, 1991; Pinderhughes, 1995; Williams & Finger Wright, 1992). African American culture is not monolithic by any means and is characterized by considerable diversity (Butler, 1992; Drake & Cayton, 1945; English, 1991; Hamnerz, 1969). It would be quite unusual for this highly creative ethnic group not to express diversity within itself or between other ethnic groups.

The differences and variance in perspectives, characteristics, and lifestyles among African Americans are assumed to be based on the degree of retention of traditional African values and practices; varying levels of acculturation; and variation in socioeconomic statuses (Levine, 1977; Schiele, 1997; Williams & Finger Wright, 1992). Other synchronic variables or factors such as geographic origin, religious background, gender, sexual orientation, disability, multi-ethnicity, age/generation, and personality have also been assumed to play a role in differences and variance among African Americans (Billingsley, 1968; Boyd-Franklin, 1989; Devore & Schlesinger, 1996; Green, 1995).

Practitioners (and researchers), however, need to be aware that diversity within the African American community should not be overemphasized without a thorough understanding of these differences. African Americans, as a distinct ethnic group, have oftentimes been viewed in a dualistic manner (either/or), typical of Eurocentric cosmological conceptions of the world (Akbar, 1981; Asante, 1990). For example, intra-group diversity within *any* ethnic group does not negate a common or shared history, culture, identity, and experience. Likewise, African American diversity is an expression of a common theme and worldview based in the group's unique history, culture, identity, experience, struggle, and quest for liberation (Ellis, 1983; Paris, 1995).

The author has developed a template for conceptualizing individual diversity within, or intra-group diversity among African Americans by utilizing the familiar expression: the whole is always greater than the sum of its parts. The "whole" is broadly defined as African American culture, which entails a common or shared history, heritage, language, belief and value systems, customs, traditions, and products/artifacts of members of a specific ethnic group (Asante & Welsh-Asante, 1985; Bennett, 1993; Schweder & Levine, 1984). The "sum of its parts" refers to the diversity within this group, or synchronic variables such as age/generation, gender, sexual orientation, religion, geographic origin, personality, or personhood. All synchronic variables are understood and conceptualized within the context or "umbrella" of an ethnic group's culture—the whole.

The flip side of the previously mentioned dualism—either/or equation—is to incorrectly view culture as monolithic, or to use a "one size fits all" approach in working with African American families. Culture is neither static nor all encompassing, since ethnic groups coexist with other ethnic groups within national boundaries as well as a multitude of other physical environments, units of situation, and the cosmic world. As a result, what many in the social sciences and other fields of study fail to recognize is that concepts of culture (and their inherent diversity) are all variables— *not* constants. These concepts are not static or permanently fixed in time and space and should be viewed as dynamic and fluid in nature (Butler, 1992; Green, 1995; English, 1991).

In addition, contrary to many White Americans belief that there is no content in Whiteness or Europeaness in America, these concepts are *never* neutral. Ethnic groups who have become "White," tend to mistakenly view their intra-group diversity or their synchronic variables as interchangeable or synonymous with concepts of culture and ethnicity, when in fact, they are not. For example, one will see concepts of gender (read: White women), sexual orientation (read: White gay, lesbian, bisexual, and transgender), disability and/or deafness (read: White deaf community), and so on without an inclusion or understanding of the role that ethnicity and culture (the whole) plays in the conceptualizations of those synchronic variables (the sum of its parts). This mismatch in grounding White, Euro-American synchronic variables in the Black experience via African Americans' conceptualizations of their unique ethnicity and culture makes it difficult, if not impossible, for most Americans to understand and appreciate concepts of ethnicity and culture; it also facilitates Black disempowerment (hooks, 1989).

This occurs, in part, because of the binary logic (dualisms) found in Eurocentric worldviews, which results in a separation and disconnection of cultural and ethnic ideas, realities, and ultimately human beings. No longer whole, culturally distinct ethnic groups are placed and conceptualized within this dichotomy: cultural vs. culturally neutral, with culture and ethnicity as separate, isolated, and incomplete entities. As Sartwell (1998, p. 14) states regarding Eurocentric dualisms and their resulting incompleteness,

> . . . The primordial dualisms of the Western tradition are between mind and body, culture and nature, general and particular (and when you cut to the chase, these are *the same* dualism). The dualisms are inscribed in European languages or, constitutive of European languages.

Afrocentrically, concepts of ethnicity, culture, and intra-group diversity are viewed as a process (dynamic) and in *diunital* (both/

and) terms—underscoring the coexistence and interconnectedness of what seemingly appear to be opposites (Butler, 1992; Meyers, 1988). An Afrocentric framework subsequently assumes that acculturation is an adjustment process that does not occur quickly but rather over a period of time (Dove, 1996; Williams & Finger Wright, 1992). The process of adjustment in the United States, however, differs according to ethnic unit of situation and/or status of a group. For example, African Americans' adjustment in the U.S. has ironically been based on the perception and reception of African Americans collectively as a group, rather than the process of adjustment based on their intra-group diversity in individual personality or achievement. This occurs primarily because White Americans have defined and constructed racism, as an American phenomenon, in individual terms, even though if everyone were judged in individual terms, or by the content of their character and not by the color of their skin, there would be no racism (Bowser & Hunt, 1996; Hacker, 1995).

AFRICAN AMERICAN FAMILIES' HELP-SEEKING BEHAVIORS AND COPING MECHANISMS

In order to get a fuller picture of some of the cultural and ethnic differences among American families, African Americans, for example, often seek professional help and services, but they tend not to perceive these experiences as positive for three inter-related reasons. First, African American families often view social service agencies and their representatives (i.e., social workers) as firmly rooted in the systematic oppression of Black people. As a result, African Americans are often wary of services delivered by professionals, especially those from different ethnic backgrounds, due to past instances of racism and neglect by service providers (Boyd-Franklin, 1989; Gary, 1985; Martin & Martin, 1985; McAdoo, 1981; Pinderhughes, 1995; Solomon, 1976).

Second, African Americans receiving social services, as well as other services from helping professions, are often criticized for their parenting styles (e.g., discipline techniques/choices) and their family behavior patterns are often viewed as pathological and dysfunctional (Denby & Alford, 1996; Green, 1995; Pinderhughes, 1995). African American families' reactions and responses to this imposed "model of pathology" are oftentimes not quite understood by professionals, in light of their professional imposition of inadequate services, insults stemming from professional ignorance/arrogance, and/or lack of cultural, social, and economic support (Beazley & Moore, 1995; Lipsky, 1985; Stack, 1974). Families may walk away from these social service agencies feeling blamed for their victimization and their desire for culturally sensitive assistance (Boyd-Franklin, 1989; Lum, 1992; Pinderhughes, 1995).

Third, an appreciation and understanding of African American cultural patterns and strengths inherent in African American families are often ignored (Boyd-Franklin, 1989; Staples, 1971). For example, Browder (1996), Hines and Boyd-Franklin (1982), and Hill (1972) note that despite the problems that plague many African Americans, the African American family has developed distinctive strengths (e.g., flexible family roles, strong religious orientation, etc.) that have contributed to its survival. These families have developed strategies for coping effectively with the crises that every family inevitably confronts. These coping responses may vary from family to family, however, they often reflect an ethnic group's cultural milieu (Pinderhughes, 1995; White & Parham, 1990).

Why is an appreciation of African American families' sociocultural strengths crucial to social workers and to other helping professionals? An appreciation is required in understanding the responses to perceived situations, the parent/family-child relationship, and the necessity of preparing African American children to live in a multitude of environments, oftentimes hostile (Chestang, 1972; McAdoo & McAdoo, 1985). For example, researchers have been able to demonstrate that there are differences in observable parenting behavior among various ethnic groups. Although the parenting behaviors may seem identical, they actually have drastically different meanings and realties (Gonzales, Cauce, & Mason, 1996).

For example, Gonzales, Cauce, and Mason (1996) found that parenting behaviors (e.g., verbal discipline) among African American families were viewed as harsh and hostile by White American observers; however, African Americans, when viewing the exact same parenting behaviors, observed these behaviors as demonstrating warmth and love. Similarly, researchers have found that what appears to be "harsh" and "over-controlling" parenting by African American families living in high-risk communities (e.g., urban areas and predominantly White suburbs) actually correlates with healthy child outcomes, differing from research conducted with White American families (Baldwin, Baldwin, & Cole, 1990; Denby & Alford, 1996).

In addition, African Americans may also be raising their children with disabilities in this same larger hostile environment or high-risk communities—the incidence of disability is more prevalent among African Americans than any other ethnic group in America (Alston & Turner, 1994). African American families not only use the above parenting behaviors (and a vast array of others) with their children, they also rely heavily on spiritual means for coping and action. Spirituality represents a crucial reservoir that African American families can tap into for coping and handling the stressors involved in raising African American children with or without disabilities.

Although American families, in general, may share similar experiences, there are some that epitomize the importance of using spirituality. African American families often cope successfully in their parenting roles "by turning to God in their times of need and placing all problems in His hands" (Burton & Richardson, 1996, p. 141). Burton and Richardson (1996) also found that African American family caretakers often revealed that through faith and prayer they were able to cope and function in their roles as caretakers/parents. Take, for example, the following excerpts of African American families with children with disabilities (Borum, 2001):

> I was sitting in his (doctor's) office and he was talking to me, but then God was on the other side talking to me too! God was saying, "I can do anything!"

> I think my religious background has a lot to do with it. As I said earlier, if God didn't want it to be this way, it wouldn't have happened, so He gave me a child with a disability. I can deal with the situation and that has encouraged me to do everything for my child.

> I started walking and God told me all the things He would do for her. It will be rough, but He will take care of me and her, and I will be able to handle anything that came against me. God said, "I'll do anything but fail!"

> God—definitely! Without Him, where would we be? I give Him all the praise. He has been my strength, and I believe through Him my son will prosper.

The first few days were stressful. I had a lot of support, Bible study group, my faith was very strong and a lot of prayers were all very helpful. I got strength from God.

When I found out he (son) was deaf, I mean I was very upset. I crashed my car. I cried and then the next day I was like okay I wonder where I start or what do I do next? You know I had my grieving period. It's okay to let yourself grieve, but not too long, because you are losing time. You have to just do it. You can't give up on your child. You can't say, "Oh, he's disabled, he can't do this or he can't do that. He'll never do this." How do I know? My child might do anything . . . anything! You can't limit him, because society tries hard enough to limit him as it is.

The literature extensively reports spirituality as an integral and important aspect of African American cultural life that constitutes a significant part of their coping ability (Chatters & Taylor, 1989; Gerace & Noelker, 1990; Henderson, Mayka-Guiterrez, Garcia, & Boyd, 1993; Nichols, 1976; Thurman, 1975). According to Burton and Richardson (1996), spirituality serves as a primary strategy used by African American caretakers. Spirituality underscores the belief in and awareness of the interconnectedness of all human beings and elements in the universe (Schiele, 2000).

AFRICAN AMERICAN LANGUAGE AS A CONDUIT IN INTERPRETING SOCIAL CLASS

Researchers have been able to point out that practitioners, in particular, and researchers have a tendency to overrely on and uncritically use secondary sources and statistical differences of aggregates of African American populations without representative proportions from varying social classes (Kershaw, 1998; Stanfield, 1994; Hill, 1972). For example, the uncritical reliance on current conceptions of social class and their link to culturally relevant behavior among African Americans deem the use of Black English as evidence of "low income." The tendency of helping professionals and researchers to create unwarranted images based on class continues the practice of associating class correlates (e.g., education, income, occupation, region, urban, suburban, etc.) with lifestyles and values. This occurs because one forgets that education or income is only one correlate of social class and not class lifestyle as a construct. As Hill (1972) states in regard to what a practitioner/ researcher may assume in practice/research endeavors is that the practitioner/researcher:

> . . . really believes that all "middle-income" persons are "middle-class" and all "low-income" persons are "lower-class," and fails to realize that many low-income persons have "middle-class" values and life-styles, while many middle-income persons have "lower-class" values and life-styles. The belief in the homogeneity of life-styles and values of persons occupying similar socio-economic levels, which is so prevalent in the literature on social class, results partly from this merger of class life styles with their operational indicators. (p. 29)

The assumption that only "lower income" African Americans speak Black English or that Black English consists of only "slang" is yet another prevailing misconception. Black English, which the author refers to interchangeably as African American Language, is really an attempt on African Americans' part to capture the essence of the African American collective and personal mental contents of their shared reality. The intra-group variation found in African American Language is a reflection of the varying mental experiences of the group itself. The language of African Americans is a continuous evolution of shared experiences and symbols that have been agreed upon by its ethnic group members in order to express those shared and unique experiences. The "Standard English" language is incapable of reflecting the experiences, subtleties, and sensitivity in expressing rhythm, affection, creativity, and protest that characterize the life of African Americans (Asante & Welsh-Asante 1985; Butler, 1992).

African American language allows for much more flexibility, by the inclusion of highly meaningful nonverbal communication and expression via body language. This is a communication modality for the maintenance of expression, flow, and rhythm in dramatizing that which Standard English fails to communicate (Butler, 1995; Dodds-Standford, 1971; Salzmann, 1993; Smitherman, 1994, 1975). According to Butler (1992, p. 34), African American body language might be regarded as a "highly exquisite form of pantomime." In fact, African Americans grounded in this African American cultural worldview, this language, develop acute sensitivity to subtleties in intonation and expression as well as body language often unobserved by White American speakers. Consequently, African Americans are able to pick up unexpressed hostility and prejudice, even when carefully camouflaged, on the part of non-African Americans (Butler, 1992; Smitherman, 1994).

While most African American families are bilingual, capable of switching back and forth between languages to meet the necessary demands of the situation and/or to convey a specific meaning or tone, some African American families speak primarily Black English. Still other African American families are trilingual/multilingual, while still others may speak primarily Standard English (Gray & Nbyell, 1990; Salzmann, 1993). In fact, members in one family unit may cut across all domains of the above language continuum.

Some African American families may speak Black English with family members or friends, where personal and spirited matters are most often discussed. A conversation with a White professional (e.g., social worker), however, generally dictates a switch to Standard English because of most professionals' language limitations and the pejorative view most White professionals hold toward Black English, that is, unless they use the language in efforts to be "cool." This obligatory shift in language or the perceived cooptation of expressions and concepts grounded in the African American experience by professionals can be an emotional and political matter for African Americans, which professionals may be oblivious to. Furthermore, this obligatory switch to a different language worldview or the inauthentic responses on the part of professionals trying to be "cool," may also alter these families' capacity to discuss the important issues that prompted social services and early intervention services (Dillon, 1994; Gray & Nbyell, 1990; Jones, 1979; Salzmann, 1993).

Linguists concluded by the mid-1960s that Black English was a full-fledged language, but presenting this material to various helping professionals can lead to responses of disbelief and astonishment (Gray & Nybell, 1990; Taylor, 1998). If the various English languages are accorded different degrees of social prestige, Black English is among those that are least esteemed because of its primary association with African American "lower income," urban speakers (Smitherman, 1986, 1994).

McAdoo and McAdoo (1985) have been able to report that African American behavior is considered an abstract form of behavior as opposed to a concentration on concrete rules and standards. African Americans, thus, socialize and are socialized through a "tacit" conditioning process—a process by which group members pick up "modes, sequences, and styles of behavior" through their day-to-day encounters rather than through linear, directed modes of conditioning. For example, according to McAdoo and Mc-Adoo (1985):

> Black cultural styles are enacted by Black parents (and other family members and friends) and passed on to the children essentially because such are habitual forms of behavior, ingrained patterns of action, motifs that are displayed with such consistency and that help to provide an ambience so compelling that the child can pick them up through an unarticulated conditioning process. Black cultural motifs, thus, can get conditioned even as parents might belie what they articulate to be their values and child-rearing objectives. (p. 42)

Many philosophers have come to realize that languages, as vehicles of concepts, embody not only philosophical points of view, but they also influence philosophical thought. This means that, to some extent, the thoughts of the thinker are somewhat determined by the structure, grammar, and vocabulary of the language that this thinker uses. The ontology and logic are derived as a result of a worldview that then gives rise to a consideration of linguistic features. Thus, when one African American family member speaks Spanish, for example, she appears to be a different person—because her worldview has to shift in order to articulate the Spanish language using culturally appropriate philosophical underpinnings to assist the different language properties.

> I speak three languages, and I understand that my ability to speak three languages is an intellectual capacity. Clearly, you know, saying this is redundant because language is clearly intellect, but that it also gives you a different worldview, because when I am being Black it is a different worldview from when I'm being Latina. I have had people who say to me that when I speak Spanish, I am a different person than when I speak English. I have friends of mine who are French-speaking who say, "Wow, you are a different person!" So, I knew that this issue of learning different languages really expands you profoundly and profoundly. (Borum, 2001, p. 186)

In other words, different languages constitute and therefore require different logic systems and philosophical worldviews (Gyekye, 1987; Smitherman, 1994). Smitherman (1994, p. 2) suggests that African American Language crosses boundaries of synchronic variables, such as age, sex, religion, region, and even social class, because the language is derived from the same source of *lived/ shared* experiences, culture, and the philosophical assumptions that are embedded in those lived/shared experiences—worldview. Every language suggests or implies a worldview, a vision of the world (Henry, 1990; Smitherman, 1994). This epistemic approach affords one the opportunity to witness how *history, culture,* and *language* are important variables in an Afrocentric understanding of the complexity of African American families.

It must be noted, however, that the crossover of African American Language into "mainstream" America is problematic as a result of power differences (Butler, 1992; Smitherman, 1994). For example, as Smitherman (1994, p. 21) states, "Whites pay no dues, but reap the psychological, social, and economic benefits of a language and culture born out of a struggle and hard times." In fact, African American language and culture have actually turned into one of the most profitable and lucrative cultural product/ artifacts in the U.S. This gap must be closed. As Ralph Wiley (1991, p. 38) states in *Why Black People Tend to Shout,* "Black people have no culture because most of it is out on loan to white people. With no interest!" Although the British, Whites, Euro-Americans, and African Americans speak a "common" English language, "each has paid, and is paying a different price for this 'common' language, in which, as it turns out, they are not saying, and cannot be saying, the same things: They each have very different realities to articulate . . . " (Baldwin, 1979, p. A3).

Therefore, it is important for professionals to acquire a thorough understanding of both the cultural ecology of African American families and their own cultural ecology as helping professionals. Also, the natural language of practitioners (and researchers) is culturally embedded by a particular worldview and is present in every aspect of the helping process (e.g., problem identification, concepts, populations, models of practice, etc.). If the practitioner (or researcher) does not examine this culturally embedded linguistic variable, s/he will miss the impact of this methodology on every aspect of the helping process (Goodwin, 1990).

Afrocentricity is a powerful conceptual tool that can show how developing knowledge of a culture from the viewpoint of that culture can transform social work practice. Knowledge developed in this manner can enable various professions to work more vigorously for the empowerment of African American families. For example, Afrocentricity provides a framework from which to begin reorganizing ways in which culture, language, power, economics, knowledge, spirituality, and even family are locations of *both* privilege *and* oppression (Everett, Chipungu, & Leashore, 1991; McIntosh, 1993; Pinderhughes, 1995; Swigonski, 1996).

AN AFROCENTRIC DEFINITION OF MENTAL HEALTH AMONG AFRICAN AMERICANS

Mental health, like most culturally embedded concepts of functional behavior, is culturally bound. In other words, mental health is defined within the context of the culture within an ethnic group. Culture determines the parameters of mental health according to psychological orientation and behavioral manifestations of a specific ethnic group (Akbar, 1981; Asante, 1990; Azibo, 1996; Kambon, 1996; Myers, 1988). As a result, there can be no universal model of assumptions or values to determine the ontological perspective of what it means to be human. There can be no standard in defining "normal" behavior or human functioning (Akbar, 1996).

From an Afrocentric model of mental health, however, grounded in Afrocentric premises and underlying assumptions, the nature of humanity or human beings, in essence, is spiritual, with mental and physical attributes that are to be utilized for the development of the spirit (Akbar, 1990, 1991; Kambon, 1996). This is precisely one of the underlying reasons it is very problematic to define mental health in universal terms or across cultures. For example, from a Eurocentric perspective based in Euro-American history, traditions, culture, language, worldviews, etc., mental health infers the absence of mental illness or pathology and sanity by its absence of insanity. "Now that's insane to me," remarked Na'im Akbar, a seminal Afrocentric scholar and clinical psychologist, in 1981. It is important to remember that these Eurocentric ideas of mental health/mental illness are grounded in a dualistic view of the world (Akbar, 1981, 1996; Azibo, 1996).

Because Eurocentric cultural worldviews, in varying degrees, rely heavily on statistical models, for example, of human functioning, these ideas may appear culturally foreign to cultural/ethnic groups outside of this particularistic view of the world and human beings. As Josefowitz (1985, p. 78) suggests of White culture: "We emphasize the scientific method . . . we believe in cause and effect, and dualism: either/or, mind/body . . . the polarities. Numbers are meaningful to us." Thus, the statistical model is premised on subjective, particularistic, cultural notions of what constitutes mental health. For example, mental illness within this model is viewed as those behaviors that deviate from the norm or normative functioning. Mental health is then that behavior that constitutes and represents a norm (bell curve) or where most people fall within a statistical norm (Akbar, 1981, 1996; Azibo, 1996).

From this point of view, African Americans uniting for the express purpose of challenging and altering White supremacy (albeit false) and subsequent institutional arrangements would be considered to represent mental illness, while White racism would be considered to represent normalcy. Under this model, enslavement, lynching, repeated rape of Black women and Black female children by White men (married or not), the overrepresentation of African American men in the prison industry—"slave ships that don't move," and the continued exclusion of Black men from the labor market would not represent mental illness.

The point to be extracted from the above is that every concept or idea of order and disorder (or mental health and mental illness) is derived from the perspective and standpoint (cultural location or positionality) of the ethnic and cultural worldview of the observer. Concepts represent the foundation of any scientific method or model of mental health (Akbar, 1996; Ani, 1994; Azibo, 1996; Kambon, 1996; Kershaw, 1998; Stanfield, 1994). This is why Kershaw (1998) states that it is of vital importance to first operationalize the variables under study, so they can later be empirically tested via quantitative or qualitative methods. In other words, make sure that the underlying construct of every concept is grounded in the meanings that are of significance in the lives of African Americans or any other ethnic group—measurement equivalency. Because every idea has an owner, the owner's identity matters.

For example, several Afrocentric researchers, scholars, psychiatrists/psychologists, and social workers have developed a model of mental heath regarding African Americans. Within this model, psychopathology is considered a condition of distortion in the African American self-consciousness and the African American self-extension orientation. This condition is labeled Psychological/ Cultural Misorientation, and is said to be psychological in nature within the context of social and cultural reality.

Some of the "symptoms" of this disorder can be seen in African Americans who have a pseudo-European/Eurocentric self-consciousness—one that dominates the person's African American self-consciousness and personality. This African American person does not necessarily display any anxiety or confusion—at least within the context of Eurocentric consciousness—regarding his/her converted/distorted sense of identity and functioning. This occurs, in large part, because Eurocentric societal institutions encourage this psychopathological condition among African Americans. This condition, however, is considered to be a condition affecting African Americans, yet, within the context of Eurocentric American, societal systems, it "masquerades as functional normalcy" (Baldwin, 1984). In fact, many arrangements of American society socialize, indoctrinate, reinforce, and support psychological and cultural misorientation in African American families and communities (Akbar, 1996; Baldwin, 1984).

Because of the dualisms within the Eurocentric worldview, it is dualistically anti-African American in nature. Therefore, for an African American to take on this worldview via assimilation/ acculturation is to become anti-self and anti-peoplehood among his/her own ethnic group. Assimilation policies and procedures uphold false notions of White supremacy and Black inferiority— the African American worldview is a very powerful tool to counteract such false notions. This deflection of Black consciousness (e.g., we are all American/women/gay and lesbian, etc.—we are all the same) is actually a method that inhibits Black consciousness and liberation, while promoting and supporting the survival thrust of the Euro-American minority group—less than 20% of the world's population is of European descent (Bennett, 1993; Cress Welsing, 1991).

Take for example the plea of the following African American, female student studying at Yale University—a predominantly White university: "Why talk about freedom—why not just talk about sanity? We're trying to stay sane" (hooks, 1989, p. 67).

African Americans, particularly those in predominantly White universities and suburbs, are facing a crisis; however, not the kind of crisis typically viewed as such within the context of professional social work. This student is illustrating what many African Americans are experiencing living in the midst of what Nobles (1985, p. 26) describes as "white insanity" as well as experiencing "white fatigue syndrome/double consciousness"—the longing to be free of dualisms that associatively peg Blackness as negatively marked and Whiteness as positively unmarked (hooks, 1989; DuBois, 1965).

African Americans are forced to adopt this Eurocentric frame of reference, especially when this is the only or predominant frame of reference operating in societal institutions (e.g., universities). The push for assimilation is the result of White Americans usurping the concept "integration" and changing its meaning to assimilation in order to fit neatly within the Eurocentric survival thrust and worldview (Akbar, 1981). Dr. Martin Luther King, Jr., understood the concept of integration as the inclusion of the fully conscious African American—not as assimilation (King, 1969).

Prudhomme, an African American psychiatrist at Howard University, noted as early as 1938 that as African American families assimilate or acculturate into this Eurocentric framework of viewing the world and human beings, the greater the likelihood that African Americans will begin to display similar experiences and mental illnesses. Azibo (1996, p. 48) and Akbar (1984) state that mental illness among African Americans occurs because the definition of mental health is grounded in culture-bound characteristics of White males. These characteristics are aggressiveness, competitiveness, control, affectlessness, individualism, materialism, reductionism, independence, conflict, survival of the fittest, mastery and control of nature, patriarchy, and future orientation.

The value of individualism can disrupt African American familial and collective orientation—"I am because we are and because we are, therefore I am" (Mbiti, 1970). The African American sense of self is extended to include one's people; therefore, the notion of an "individual" who is separate and apart from others as an autonomous and self-contained being is considered a Eurocentric illusion—Afrocentrically, no such entity exists (Akbar, 1981; Asante, 1990). The family unit is considered the smallest unit of analysis/prevention/intervention. Hence, professionals encouraging autonomy and independence (i.e., separation) on the part of African American children may interfere with familial ties, equilibrium, and the goals of the family to extend self to include one's people and family unit. Many African American families place a high value on extended families as a vital source of support in child rearing, sharing of resources, and overall familial well-being. Thus, families may place the welfare of the family unit above the interests of one family member (Logan, 1996; Stack, 1974). This is in contrast to Eurocentric notions of a nuclear family, and as Josefowitz (1985, p. 77) explains regarding White culture: "We believe in rugged individualism. The individual is the primary unit of analysis."

Afrocentricity is a good place to start when answering the question: Where do we go from here as a nation when there is so much dependency on the oppression of African Americans?

> Race consciousness is *imposed* on black people in America; we will simply not let you forget that you are black . . . Now if you are operating in the white world and you are black, I do not have to tell you that all the white folks are intensely aware of your race at all times . . . Furthermore, we white folks cannot possibly *become* conscious of our race *except* in a situation in which black folks are conscious of their race, and hence are able to give voice to the racial constructions current in our culture. In virtue of our construction of ourselves, a construction that entails the erasure of that very construction, we are precisely the people who *could not* become conscious of our race on our own . . . this dualistic conception of race is absolutely required, and not only to produce certain desired economic and political results for white people (though certainly and centrally for that, too). It is required by the dualisms that dominate the Western tradition; that is, the specific forms of economic and political hegemony which we practice are articulated through what is essentially a metaphysical construction. (Sartwell, 1998, pp. 140–141, 14)

> Frederika Bremer, when reflecting upon her visit to America about 1850, gave this country a new thought in saying to Americans, "The romance of your history is the fate of the Negro." (Woodson, 1933, p. 139)

The above remains a continuous challenge and opportunity for social workers to work more effectively for the empowerment of African American families.

REFERENCES

Akbar, N. (1981). Cultural expressions of the African-American child. *Black Child Journal, 2*(2), 6–16.

Akbar, N. (1984). Africentric social sciences for human liberation. *Journal of Black Studies, 14*(4), 395–414.

Akbar, N. (1996). *Breaking the chains of psychological slavery.* Tallahassee, FL: Mind Productions & Associates.

Alston, R. J., & Turner, W. L. (1994). A family strengths model of adjustment to disability for African American clients. *Journal of Counseling & Development, 72*(4), 378–388.

Ani, M. (1994). *Yurugu: An African-centered critique of European cultural thought and behavior.* Trenton, NJ: Africa World Press, Inc.

Aponte, C. I. (1996). Cultural diversity course model: Cultural competence for content and process. *Acrete, 20*(1), 46–55.

Asante, M. K. (1988). *Afrocentricity.* Trenton, NJ: African World Press, Inc.

Asante, M. K. (1990). *Afrocentricity* (2nd ed.). Trenton, NJ: African World Press, Inc.

Asante, M. K., & Welsh-Asante, K. (1985). *African culture: The rhythms of unity.* London: Greenwood.

Azibo, D. A. (1996). *African psychology in historical perspective and related commentary.* Trenton, NJ: Africa World Press, Inc.

Baldwin, J. (1979, July 29). If Black English isn't a language, then tell me, what is? *New York Times,* p. A3.

Baldwin, A. L., Baldwin, C., & Cole, R. E. (1990). Stress-resistant families and stress-resistant children. In J. Rolf, A. S. Masten, D. Cicchetti, K. H. Neuchterlein, & S. Weintraub (Eds.), *Risk and protective factors in the development of psychopathology* (pp. 257–280). New York: Cambridge University Press.

Barker, S. F. (1957). *Induction and hypothesis: A study of the logic of confirmation.* Ithaca, NY: Cornell University Press.

Beazley, S., & Moore, M. (1995). *Deaf children, their families and professionals: Dismantling barriers.* London: David Fulton Publishers.

Bennett, L. (1993). *Before the Mayflower: A history of Black America.* New York: Penguin.

Bernal, M. (1987). *Black Athena: The Afroasiatic roots of classical civilization.* NJ: Rutgers University Press.

Billingsley, A. (1968). *Black families in White America.* Englewood Cliffs, NJ: Prentice Hall.

Borum, V. (2001). *Culture, disability, and the family: An exploratory study of African American parents with deaf and hard of hearing children.* Doctoral dissertation, Howard University, Washington, DC.

Bowser, B. P., & Hunt, R. G. (Eds.). (1996). *Impacts of racism on White Americans* (2nd ed.). Thousand Oaks, CA: Sage.

Boyd-Franklin, N. (1989). *Black families in therapy.* New York: Guilford Press.

Browder, A. T. (1996). *Survival strategies for Africans in America: 13 steps to freedom.* Washington, DC: The Institute of Karmic Guidance.

Burton, C. A., & Richardson, R. C. (1996). Following in faith: The study of an African-American caregiver. *Social Work and Christianity, 23*(2), 141–145.

Butler, J. P. (1992). *Of kindred minds: The ties that bind.* Rockville, MD: U.S. Department of Health and Human Services.

Carruthers, J. H. (1972). *Science and oppression.* Chicago, IL: The Kemetic Institute.

Chatters, L. M., & Taylor, R. J. (1989). Age differences in religious participation among Black adults. *Journal of Gerontology: Social Sciences, 44,* S183–S189.

Chennault, R. E., & Dyson, M. E. (1998). Giving Whiteness a Black eye. In J. L. Kincheloe, S. R. Steinberg, N. M. Rodriguez, & R. E. Chennault (Eds.), *White reign: Deploying Whiteness in America* (pp. 299–347). New York: St. Martin's Griffin.

Chestang, L. (1972). *Character development in a hostile environment.* Chicago: University of Chicago Press.

Collins, P. H. (1990). *Black feminist thought: Knowledge, consciousness, and the politics of empowerment.* New York: Routledge.

Cress Welsing, F. (1991). *The Isis papers.* Trenton, NJ: Third World Press.

Daly, A., Jennings, J., Beckett, B. O., & Leashore, B. R. (1995). Effective coping strategies of African Americans. *Social Work 40*(2), 241–248.

Dash, M. I. N., Jackson, J., & Rasor, S. C. (1997). *Hidden wholeness.* Cleveland, OH: United Church Press.

Denby, R., & Alford, K. (1996). Understanding African American discipline styles: Suggestions for effective social work intervention. *Journal of Multicultural Social Work, 4*(3), 81–98.

Devore, W., & Schlesinger, E. G. (1996). *Ethnic sensitive social work practice* (4th ed.). Boston: Allyn and Bacon.

Dillard, J. L. (1972). *Black english.* New York: Random House.

Dillon, D. (1994). Understanding and assessment of intragroup dynamics in family foster care: African American families. *Child Welfare, 73*(2), 129–139.

Diop, C. A. (1990). *The cultural unity of Black Africa.* Chicago: Third World Press. (Original work published 1959 as L'Unite Culturelle de l'Afrique Noire.)

Dixon, V. (1976). World views and research methodology. In L. King, V. Dixon, & W. Nobles (Eds.), *African philosophy: Assumptions and paradigms for research on Black persons.* Los Angeles: Fanon Center.

Dodds-Standford, B. (1971). *I, too, sing America: Black voices in American literature.* Rochelle Park, NJ: Hayden Book Company, Inc.

Dove, N. (1996). Education and culture. *Urban Education, 31*(4), 357–371.

Drake, C., & Cayton, H. (1945). *Black metropolis: A study of Negro life in a northern city.* New York: Harcourt, Brace, & World.

DuBois, W. E. B. (1908). *The Negro American family.* Atlanta: Atlanta University Press.

DuBois, W. E. B. (1965). *The souls of Black folk.* New York: New American Library, Inc.

Ellis, C. F., Jr. (1983). *Beyond liberation: The gospel in the Black American experience.* Downers Grove, IL: InterVarsity Press.

Ellison, R. (1970, April 6). What America would be like without Blacks. *New York Times,* p. A7.

English, R. E. (1991). Diversity of world views among African American families. In J. E. Everett, S. S. Chipungu, & B. R. Leashore (Eds.), *Child welfare: An Africentric perspective* (pp. 19–35). New Brunswick, NJ: Rutgers University Press.

Everett, J. E., Chipungu, S. S., & Leashore, B. R. (Eds.). (1991). *Child welfare: An Africentric perspective.* New Brunswick, NJ: Rutgers University Press.

Gary, L. E. (1985). Attitudes toward human service organizations: Perspectives from an urban Black community. *Journal of Applied Behavioral Science, 21*(4), 445–458.

Gerace, C. S., & Noelker, L. S. (1990). Clinical social work practice with Black elderly and their family caregivers. In Z. Harel, E. A. McKinney, & M. Williams (Eds.), *Black aged* (pp. 237–245). Newbury Park, CA: Sage.

Gonzales, N. A., Cauce, A. M., & Mason, C. A. (1996). Interobserver agreement in the assessment of parental behavior and parent-adolescent conflict: African American mothers, daughters, and independent observers. *Child Development, 67,* 1483–1497.

Goodwin, M. H. (1990). *He-said-she-said: Talk as social organization.* Bloomington, IN: Indiana University Press.

Gray, S. S., & Nybell, L. M. (1990). Issues in African-American family preservation. *Child Welfare League of America, 39,* 513–523.

Green, J. W. (1995). *Cultural awareness in the human services: A multi-ethnic approach.* Boston: Allyn and Bacon.

Griffin, P. R. (1999). *Seeds of racism: In the soul of America.* Cleveland, OH: The Pilgrim Press.

Guggenheim, L. (1993). Ethnic variation in ASL: The signing of African Americans and how it is influenced by conversational topic. *Communication Forum, 2,* 51–76. Washington, DC: Gallaudet University.

Gyekye, K. (1987). *An essay on African philosophical thought.* Philadelphia: Temple University Press.

Hacker, A. (1995). *Two nations: Black and White, separate, hostile, unequal.* New York: Ballantine Books.

Hamlet, J. D. (Ed.). (1998). *Afrocentric visions: Studies in culture and communication.* Thousand Oaks, CA: Sage.

Hamnerz, U. (1996). *Exploring the city: Inquiries toward an urban anthropology.* New York: Columbia University Press.

Henderson, N. J., Mayka-Gutierrez, M., Garcia, J., & Boyd, S. (1993). A model for Alzheimer's disease support group development in African-American and Hispanic populations. *Gerontologist, 3,* 409–414.

Henry, C. P. (1990). *Culture and African American politics.* Indianapolis, IN: Indiana University Press.

Hill, R. B. (1972). *The strengths of Black families.* New York: Emerson Hall.

Hines, P. M., & Boyd-Franklin, N. (1982). *Black families.* New York: Guilford Press.

hooks, b. (1989). *Talking back: Thinking feminist—thinking Black.* Boston, MA: South End Press.

Jones, D. L. (1979). African-American clients: Clinical practice issues. *Social Work,* 112–118.

Josefowitz, N. (1985). *You're the boss!* New York: Warner Books.

Kambon, K. K. (1996). The Africentric paradigm and African American psychological liberation. In D. A. Y. Azibo, *African psychology: In historical perspective and related commentary*. Trenton, NJ: Africa World Press, Inc.

Keller, J., & McDade, K. (1997). Cultural diversity and help-seeking behavior: Sources of help and obstacles to support for parents. *Journal of Multicultural Social Work, 5*(1/2), 63–78.

Kershaw, T. (1998). Afrocentrism and the afrocentric method. In J. D. Hamlet (Ed.), *Afrocentric visions: Studies in culture and communication*. Thousand Oaks, CA: Sage.

King, M. L., Jr. (1967a). *The trumpet of conscience*. San Francisco, CA: Harper and Row Publishers.

King, M. L., Jr. (1967b). *Where do we go from here: Chaos or community?* Boston, MA: Beacon Press.

Koch, L. M., & Gross, A. (1997). Children's perceptions of Black English as a variable in interracial perception. *Journal of Black Psychology, 21*, 215–226.

Levine, L. W. (1977). *Black culture and Black consciousness: Afro-American folk thought from slavery to freedom*. New York: Oxford University Press.

Lipsky, D. K. (1985). A parental perspective on stress and coping. *American Journal of Orthopsychiatry, 55*(4), 614–617.

Logan, S. (Ed.). (1996). *The Black family: Strengths, self-help, and positive change*. Boulder, CO: Westview Press.

Lum, D. (1992). *Social work practice and people of color: A process stage approach* (2nd ed.). Pacific Grove, CA: Brooks/Cole Publishing Company.

Martin, J. M., & Martin, E. P. (1985). *The helping tradition in the Black family and community*. Silver Spring, MD: National Association of Social Workers.

Martin, J. M., & Martin, E. P. (1995). *Social work and the Black experience*. Silver Spring, MD: National Association of Social Workers.

Mary, N. L. (1990). Reactions of Black, Hispanic, and White mothers to having a child with handicaps. *Mental Retardation, 28*, 1–5.

Mbiti, J. S. (1970). *African religions and philosophies*. Garden City, NY: The University of Chicago Press.

McAdoo, H. P. (Ed.). (1981). *Black families*. Beverly Hills, CA: Sage.

McAdoo, H. P., & McAdoo, J. L. (Eds.). (1985). *Black children: Social, educational, and parental environments*. Newbury Park, CA: Sage.

McCallion, P., & Matthew, J. (1997). Exploring the impact of culture and acculturation. *Family Relations, 46*(4), 347–358.

McDonald, T. P., Couchonnal, G., & Early, T. (1996). The impact of major events on the lives of family caregivers of children with disabilities. *Families in Society: The Journal of Contemporary Human Services*, 502–514.

McIntosh, P. (1993). White privilege: Unpacking the invisible knapsack. In V. Cyrus (Ed.), *Experiencing race, class, and gender in the United States* (pp. 209–213). CA: Mayfield Publishing Company.

Meyers, L. J. (1987). The deep structure of culture: Relevance of traditional African culture in contemporary life. *Journal of Black Studies, 18*(1), 72–85.

Meyers, L. J. (1988). *Understanding an Afrocentric world view: Introduction to an optimal psychology*. Dubuque, IA: Kendall/Hunt Publishing Co.

Morris, J. K. (1992). Personal power in Black mothers of handicapped sons. *AFFILIA*, 7(3), 72–92.

Nichols, E. (1976). *The philosophical aspects of cultural differences.* Unpublished manuscript.

Nobles, W. (1974). *A formulative and empirical study of Black families.* Washington, DC: U.S. Department of Health, Education and Welfare, Office of Child Development.

Nobles, W. (1985). *Africanity and the Black family.* Oakland, CA: Black Family Institute Publications.

Nobles, W. (1986). *African psychology: Toward its reclamation, reascension and revitalization.* Oakland, CA: Black Family Institute Publications.

Paris, P. J. (1995). *The spirituality of African peoples: The search for a common moral discourse.* Minneapolis, MN: Fortress Press.

Pinderhughes, E. (1988). Significance of culture and power in the human behavior curriculum. In C. Jacobs & D. D. Bowles (Eds.), *Ethnicity and race critical concepts in social work.* Silver Spring, MD: National Association of Social Workers.

Pinderhughes, E. (1995). Empowering diverse populations: Family practice in the 21st century. *Families in society: The Journal of Contemporary Human Services,* 76(3), 131–140.

Pinderhughes, E. (1997). Developing diversity competence in child welfare and permanency planning. *Journal of Multicultural Social Work,* 5(1/2), 19–38.

Prudhomme, C. (1938). The problem of suicide in the American Negro. *Psychoanalytic Review,* 25, 187–204, 372–391.

Roediger, D. R. (Ed.). (1998). *Black on White; Black writers on what it means to be White.* New York: Schocken Books.

Rogers-Dulan, J. (1998). Religious connectedness among urban African American families who have a child with disabilities. *Mental Retardation,* 36(2), 91–103.

Salzmann, Z. (1993). *Language, culture, and society.* Boulder, CO: Westview Press.

Sartwell, C. (1998). *Act like you know: African-American autobiography and White identity.* Chicago, IL: The University of Chicago Press.

Schiele, J. H. (1997). The contour and meaning of Afrocentric social work. *Journal of Black Studies,* 27(6), 800–819.

Schiele, J. H. (2000). *Human services and the Afrocentric paradigm.* Binghamton, NY: Haworth Press, Inc.

Schweder, R. A., & Levine, R. A. (1984). *Culture theory: Essays on mind, self and emotion.* New York: Cambridge University Press.

Sertima, I. V. (1976). *The African presence in ancient America: They came before Columbus.* New York: Random House, Inc.

Smitherman, G. (1975). *Black language and culture: Sounds of soul.* New York: Harper & Row.

Smitherman, G. (1986). *Talkin' and testifyin': The language of Black America.* Detroit, MI: Wayne State University Press.

Smitherman, G. (1994). *Black talk: Words and phrases from the hood to the amen corner.* New York: Houghton Mifflin Company.

Solomon, B. (1976). *Black empowerment: Social work in oppressed communities.* New York: Columbia University Press.

Stack, C. (1974). *All our kin: Strategies for surviving in a Black community.* New York: Harper & Row.

Stanfield, J. H. (1994). Ethnic modeling in qualitative research. In N. K. Denzin & Y. S. Lincoln (Eds.), *Handbook of qualitative research*. Thousand Oaks, CA: Sage.

Staples, R. (1971). *The Black family; Essays and studies*. Belmont, CA: Wadsworth Publishing Company.

Swigonski, M. E. (1996). Challenging privilege through Africentric social work practice. *Social Work, 41*(2), 153–161.

Taylor, O. (1997). The Ebonics debate: Separating fact from fiction. *Black Issues in Higher Education, 13*(24), 84–85.

Thomas, A., & Sillen, S. (1993). *Racism and psychiatry*. New York: Carol Publishing Group.

Thurman, H. (1975). *Deep river and the Negro spiritual speaks of life and death*. Richmond, IN: Friends United Press.

Thurman, H. (1976). *Jesus and the disinherited*. Boston: Beacon Press.

Wallace, B. J. (1980). *Black mothers' attitudes toward their disabled children*. Doctoral dissertation, Brandeis University, New York, New York.

Weaver, D. R. (1982). Empowering treatment skills for helping Black families. *Social Casework, 2*(1), 100–105.

White, J. L., & Parham, T. A. (1990). *The psychology of Blacks: An African-American perspective*. NJ: Prentice Hall.

Wiley, R. (1991). *Why Black people tend to shout!* New York: Penguin Books.

Williams, S. E., & Finger Wright, D. (1992). Empowerment: The strengths of Black families revisited. *Journal of Multicultural Social Work, 2*(4), 23–3.

Woodson, C. G. (1933). *The mis-education of the Negro*. Trenton, NJ: Africa World Press.

Yacobacci-Tam, P. (1988). Interacting with the culturally different family. *Volta Review, 89*(5), 46–58.

CHAPTER 13

Hispanic Families in the United States With Deaf and Hearing-Impaired Children

Idalia Mapp

The diagnosis of deafness or a hearing impairment in an infant or child can have a profound impact on the parents, who are likely to experience one or more negative reactions, such as stress, grief, anger, guilt, helplessness, confusion, depression, and anxiety (Bailey et al., 1999; Feher-Prout, 1996; Kampfe, 1989; Mapp, 2004a, 2004b; Mapp & Hudson, 1997; Moores, Jatho, & Dunn, 2001; Steinberg, 1991). In addition, when parents discover that their child has a hearing loss, they need to make many important decisions that can exacerbate anxiety and stress, such as how they will communicate with their child, whether they should provide their child with hearing aids or other assistive devices, whether to arrange for early intervention services, and where the child will go to school (Bennett, 1989; Cohen, 1993; Charles, Gafni, & Whelan, 1997; Stein, 1983; Steinberg et al., 2003).

Each key decision, in turn, implies still others that must be made. The decision about school, for example, includes related decisions about whether the child will be integrated into a mainstream classroom or segregated with other hearing-impaired children, and whether to arrange for the child to have special services to improve his or her hearing loss. Each decision the parents make, furthermore, invariably demands that they interact with personnel from government, the school system, or both. The same process applies to parental decisions about utilizing or accessing health care, social work, and other vital, bureaucratically structured service systems.

For Hispanic parents in America, as well as parents from other ethnic and racial minorities, the ability to cope with both negative cognitions and emotions and the demands of bureaucratic systems related to having a deaf or hearing-impaired child is often especially difficult. One major reason is that coping efficacy is inversely related to economic and educational status (Fujiura, Yamaki, & Czechowicz, 1998; Moores, Jatho, & Dunn, 2001). In addition, Hispanics in America commonly face barriers related both to communication difficulties and cultural traditions that impede contacting and dealing effectively with service professionals, such as beliefs about the benefits of folk cures and reliance on family members as opposed to professionals to cope with problems (Lian & Fantanez-Phelan, 2001; Mapp, 2004a; Steinberg et al., 2003). Because of these and other sociocultural factors that impede coping efficacy—such as family structure, immigration status, and alcohol abuse—social and professional supports are often crucial for Hispanic parents to surmount psychological and emotional impairments and resume normal functioning (Bailey et al., 1999; Meadow-Orlans, Mertens, Sass-Lehrer, & Scott-Olson, 1997; Reyes-Blanes, Correa, & Bailey, 1999).

Considering the above, the primary purpose of this chapter is to discuss and analyze, for Hispanic parents in the United States with deaf and hearing-impaired children, a) the specific psychosocial risks, needs, and problems they face, b) clinical assessment factors specific to them, and c) treatment approaches that would be expected to be most effective for these parents. To provide background and context to the discussion, a brief demographic profile of the Hispanic population in the United States is first presented.

DEMOGRAPHIC PROFILE

Although men and women from Spanish-speaking countries do not use the term "Hispanic" to describe themselves, most Americans use this verbal construct (or a synonym, "Latino") to collectively describe people from more than 20 countries—often with strikingly different cultures, governments, and histories—in South America, Central America, Spain, and the Caribbean. In the United States today, individuals of Hispanic descent are both the largest minority group—numbering more than 35 million individuals (12.5% of the population)—and the most rapidly increasing: their population in the U.S. has increased by nearly 13 million (36.5%) since 1990, when they numbered 22.4 million (U.S. Census Bureau, 2000, 2002). By 2050, Hispanics in America are projected to number 97 million, nearly one fourth of the total population (Centers for Disease Control, 2004).

Individuals of Mexican origin in the U.S. comprise almost two thirds of the Hispanic population, with the other two largest groups being from Puerto Rico and Cuba, numbering approximately 4 million and 1.5 million, respectively (U.S. Census Bureau, 2002). The remainder of Hispanics in the U.S. identify themselves as Argentinians, Colombians, Dominicans, Brazilians, Guatemalans, Costa Ricans, Nicaraguans, Salvadorians, Spaniards, Panamanians, and others.

Among U.S.-resident Hispanics, more than 900,000 (4.2%) have hearing impairments, while in America overall, there are 19,500,000 adults who are hard of hearing, including 990,000 children. Profoundly deaf children and adults number 350,000; of these, 65,000 are children. Approximately 45% of deaf children are from an ethnic/racial minority group, according to the Annual Survey of Deaf Children and Youth for 1999–2000 by the Gallaudet Research Institute (2004). Among them, the largest proportion is Hispanic (21%), followed by Black/African American (16%), compared with individuals identified as "White only, not Hispanic," who constituted 55% of deaf children and youth.

These figures show that Hispanics are overrepresented among the population of deaf and hard of hearing individuals in America. This is consistent with other disability statistics for the U.S., showing rates of disability as higher among low-income households—and Hispanic children with a disability living disproportionately in low-income, single-parent homes (Centers for Disease Control, 2004; U.S. Census Bureau, 2000). The poverty rates, for example, are 14% for Cuban Americans, 31% for Puerto Ricans, and 27% for Mexican Americans compared with 13.5% for all Americans

(Centers for Disease Control, 2004). Regarding education, only 56% of Hispanics at least 25 years of age have graduated from high school, compared with 83% of the total U.S. population. Academic achievement varies considerably among Hispanic subgroups, though; for example, 70% of Cuban Americans, 64% of Puerto Ricans, and 50% of Mexican Americans have graduated from high school (U.S. Census Bureau, 2002). To a great extent, these socioeconomic and educational data are inversely related to the lengths of residency of the respective groups in the United States, that is, individuals from Mexico and Puerto Rico, who have been here the longest, are, overall, the poorest and least educated Hispanic groups in America. This fact largely reflects the socioeconomic backgrounds of the individuals who migrate to the U.S. and their reasons for migration, for instance, to increase their standard of living, as in the case of Mexicans and Puerto Ricans, or to escape political persecution, as in the case of the first wave of Cuban immigrants during the 1960s. This issue and other demographic variables are discussed further at appropriate places throughout the chapter devoted to analysis of psychosocial risks and needs, clinical assessment factors, and treatment approaches for Hispanic parents in the U.S. with deaf or hearing-impaired children.

PSYCHOSOCIAL RISKS AND NEEDS OF POPULATION

The data just presented suggest that the changing demographics of deafness require special skills, sensitivities, and sociocultural information on the part of professionals who work with Hispanic parents of deaf or hearing-impaired children, since risk is embedded in the social and economic context of the nation. Hispanic American parents' access to systems of care for both themselves and their deaf or hearing-impaired children differs significantly according to a variety of socio-demographic factors, the same as for other sociocultural groups in America. These factors include, most importantly, socioeconomic status, immigration status, educational background, English language capabilities, and geographic locale. In general, Hispanic parents who live in cities (rather than rural areas), are middle class or above (rather than poor), have health insurance (rather than no health insurance), are proficient in the English language (rather than speak and understand only Spanish), have at least a high school education (rather than less than a high school education), and are here legally (rather than illegally) have the most access to care for their deaf and hearing-impaired children—including health care, mental health care, and social services.

To illustrate the effect of socioeconomic status on access to care, consider that 37% of Hispanics are uninsured, compared with 16% of all Americans (Centers for Disease Control, 2004). This high number for Hispanics is driven mostly by their lack of employer-based coverage—only 43% compared with 73% for non-Hispanic Whites. Medicaid and other public coverage reaches 18% of Hispanics.

Regarding language barriers to care, as recently as 1990 about 40% of Hispanics either did not speak English at all or did not speak it well. While the percentage of Spanish-speaking mental health professionals is not known, only about 1% of licensed psychologists who are also members of the American Psychological Association (2004) identify themselves as Hispanic. Moreover, there are only 29 Hispanic mental health professionals for every 100,000 Hispanics in the United States, compared with 173 non-Hispanic White providers per 100,000 (Centers for Disease Control, 2004).

Steinberg and colleagues (2003) found from an interview study that, despite the best intentions of professionals who serve the Hispanic community, there remains a significant divide in access to information. Materials written in Spanish were frequently offered, but appeared to be limited to general pamphlets translated from English, rather than materials written to be culturally relevant to Hispanic people.

In addition to the variables discussed above—related to language, socioeconomic status, educational attainment, and immigration status—other variables define risks for U.S.-resident Hispanics, including those of a personal nature, such as substance abuse behaviors and mental health status (Alvirez & Bean, 1976; Centers for Disease Control, 2004; Rodriguez & Santiviago, 1991). Regarding the former, although Hispanic Americans in general have rates of alcohol use similar to non-Hispanic Whites, Hispanic men have relatively high rates while Hispanic women have relatively low rates. Studies have also found that Hispanic youth in America experience proportionately more drug use than do non-Hispanic White youth (Centers for Disease Control, 2004). In addition, rates of substance abuse are higher among U.S.-born Mexican Americans compared to Mexican-born immigrants. Specifically, substance abuse rates are twice as high for U.S.-born Mexican American men than for Mexican-born men, but seven times higher for U.S.-born Mexican American women than for Mexican-born women (National Center for Health Statistics, 2004).

As for mental health status, while Hispanics in America have rates of mental illness similar to those of the general population, data suggest negative psychological and emotional effects due to American residency: for instance, adult Mexican immigrants have lower rates of mental disorders than Mexican Americans born in the United States, and adult Puerto Ricans living on the island tend to have lower rates of depressions than Puerto Ricans living in the U.S. (National Center for Health Statistics, 2004). In addition, many refugees enter the U.S. with trauma related mental and emotional problems. Refugees from Central America, for example, have experienced considerable civil war related trauma in their homelands. Studies have found rates of posttraumatic stress disorder among Central America refugee patients ranging from 33% to 60% (Gianaro, 2004).

Among Hispanic Americans with a mental disorder, fewer than 1 in 11 contact mental health specialists, while fewer than 1 in 5 contact general health care providers. As for the use of complementary therapies by Hispanic Americans, precise estimates do not exist. One study found that only 4% of the Mexican American sample consulted a *curandero, herbalista*, or other folk medicine practitioner within the past year, while percentages from other studies have ranged from 7% to 44%. The use of folk remedies is more common than consultation with a folk healer, and these remedies are generally used to complement mainstream care. One national study found that only 24% of Hispanics with depression and anxiety received appropriate care, compared with 34% of Whites. Another study found that Hispanics who visited a general medical doctor were less than half as likely as Whites to receive either a diagnosis of depression or antidepressant medicine (Centers for Disease Control, 2004).

CLINICAL ASSESSMENT FACTORS

When considering the delivery of clinical services to U.S.-resident Hispanic parents with deaf or hearing-impaired children, the sources of their psychosocial problems must be considered and assessed, including such factors as current life transitions and role changes, lack of environmental resources or supports, and developmental difficulties. In addition, one must also assess their coping capacities, strengths, and unique cultural characteristics, which can impact the diagnostic assessment and treatment process in clinical practice.

As the foregoing discussion has shown, Hispanics in the U.S. are a highly variegated group, differing greatly in terms of socioeconomic status, educational level, length of residency, immigration status, English language proficiency, and other factors that can affect their ability to cope with the stressors of having a deaf or hearing-impaired child. In addition, members of the different Hispanic groups enter the U.S. with differing degrees of psychosocial problems, often resulting from trauma in their homelands that led to the immigration to America.

The differences between Hispanic parents are profound both within and between groups. As a result, generalizations about factors that could affect clinical assessments should be made with great caution, especially as they refer to specific parents, who should be viewed as unique individuals, with their own personal histories and experiences that differentiate them from other individuals. The mental health history, religious orientation, level of trust in others, self-esteem, self-efficacy, ego strength, and identity conflict resulting from dual ethnic membership (Cohen, 1993) will differentiate one potential client from another, one family from another, and must enter into the clinical assessment at intake, along with other personal variables.

Steinberg and associates (1997), for example, examined the perceptions, attitudes, and beliefs about deafness and disability in nine Hispanic families with deaf children, aged 6–13 years, using in-depth interviews that focused on the families' experiences in adjusting to the child's hearing loss. The interviews emphasized, in particular, concepts of causation of deafness; communication with the deaf child; and perceptions of the accessibility of services. The findings showed that most parents expressed either positive or neutral feelings about deafness, and that their concepts of causation varied, with some parents attributing deafness to divine will, and others to heredity or physical insult. In addition, many parents reported that their extended families and communities stigmatized the deaf child.

When a deaf or hearing-impaired child is born to parents who do not cope well, the additional demands can lead to greater pressures on an already strained parent-child relationship. These conditions can lead to abusive or unavailable parenting. The negative impact on low-income, single, or unemployed parents with deaf children is often expected to be especially profound.

Apart from individuals differences, to the extent that clinicians understand the important cultural, sociological, demographic, and historical factors characteristic of each group of Hispanic parents, they can more sensitively and effectively identify and deduce factors likely to be sources of psychosocial problems. These factors include income, education, immigration status, length of residency in the U.S., geographic location, and ability to speak English, among others. Specifically, consider the following differences between the three largest Hispanic groups in America with deaf or hearing-impaired children: Mexicans, Puerto Ricans, and Cubans.

Mexicans as a group have been here since the 16th century, though they started migrating in large numbers at the end of the 19th century. They are generally poor, have low levels of formal education, vary greatly in their ability to speak English, are concentrated in California and other Western states (especially Texas, New Mexico, and Arizona), and many are illegal immigrants, especially those who have arrived recently to try to improve their socioeconomic status. Of the nearly 25 million Hispanics of Mexican birth or ancestry in the U.S., nearly 10 million live in California, and 5 million in Texas. It is difficult, however, to accurately ascertain how many Mexican Americans live in this country, since many of them are here illegally or have become assimilated and do not identify as Hispanic.

Puerto Ricans, unlike members of all other Hispanic groups, do not need special papers to enter the U.S., since citizenship was granted to them in 1917, when the island, a possession of the United States since 1898, gained more participation in its own government and obtained a Bill of Rights. Although Puerto Ricans are not formally acknowledged as "citizens," they are permitted to travel freely back and forth to Puerto Rico to keep connections with family and friends. Generally, they are poor compared with most Americans, have relatively low levels of formal education, and are often bilingual. Their primary reason for migration to the U.S. is economic, to improve their standard of living. Most Puerto Ricans live in New York City (about 2.5 million), though many reside in other states, especially Florida and Texas.

Cubans have been migrating here since the middle of the 19th century. Although there were perhaps 30,000 Cubans in the United States by 1958, they first arrived in large numbers in the 1960s, after Fidel Castro won the revolution in 1959 and established a revolutionary government. So the first modern group of Cuban immigrants were political refugees, who were welcomed with open arms by the United States government. They were generally middle class or wealthy, as they were attempting to protect their assets from being taken by the Castro regime. Over 1.1 million Cubans have left their homeland since then. Almost 90% of Cuban Americans live in four states: Florida, New Jersey, New York, and California, with the majority (60%) in Florida. Although Cubans number less than 5% of the overall Hispanic population in the United States, they have been singled out as a success story and viewed as a "model minority." Cuban Americans currently earn about 17% more than other Hispanic groups, although they still average 12% less than Anglos. Since the early 1960s, subsequent waves of Cuban refugees to the U.S., however, have not been as well off. Many of them since the 1980s, known as "*Marielitos*," have come from a lower socioeconomic background and are more racially mixed. Most recently—since the 1990s, when the Cuban economy began its *periodo especial* ("special period") after the disintegration of the Soviet Union and the end of aid to Cuba—the refugees here have often been very poor, and have risked their lives to get to the United States (Franklin, 1997; U.S. Census Bureau, 2000).

These differences among Hispanics in the U.S. are crucial for understanding and assessing their psychosocial risks, needs, and abilities to cope with having a deaf or hearing-impaired child. The between-group and within-group factors discussed above affect not only the parents' differential abilities to afford services, communicate with care providers, and reveal information about themselves honestly (especially in the case of illegal immigrants), but also their personal identities, beliefs about the efficacy of professional health care, and attitudes toward deafness, among many other factors.

Mapp (2004b) found, in a large literature review study, that Hispanic parents' task of coping is more difficult than may at first seem apparent for several reasons, especially their relatively low socioeconomic status and barriers associated with low levels of educational attainment and English language proficiency. As a result, Hispanic parents may need additional supports—including rarely or never utilized supports—because the literature shows that support services are more effective for families with higher education levels and higher socioeconomic status. The literature also shows other key variables affecting parents' coping procedures that should be considered in a clinical assessment, including the character of the parents, their attitude toward having a child, the degree to which they use denial, and the stress they experience resulting from communication problems.

Regarding the coping abilities and strengths of U.S.-resident Hispanic parents with deaf or hearing-impaired children, several studies (Skinner, Correa, Skinner, & Bailey, 2001; Steinberg et al., 2003) found that many parents cited their religious beliefs and faith in God as providing sustenance, hope, and guidance through the diagnostic period and as their child develops. Clergy, however, were infrequently mentioned as a source of support. Often a cogent decision-making style and analysis of cost-benefit ratios coexisted peacefully with trust that their faith in God would guide them to the best opportunities for their child; this was often closely related to their hope for their child's future.

Mapp and Hudson (1997) reported that Hispanic parents tended to adjust rather readily to their child's hearing loss, as they found lower levels of stress than expected among their research participants. The researchers speculated that this surprising finding could have resulted because the parents in the study had lived with this reality for some time, rather than recently learned about their child's hearing disability. The parents, therefore, may have had time to adjust, and learned to cope effectively with both the emotional and cognitive reactions to having a deaf or hearing-impaired child. Nonetheless, the findings from the study suggest that Hispanic parents have internal strengths that can and should be understood by clinicians and researchers, in order to devise effective treatment plans for them.

TREATMENT APPROACHES

Many Hispanic parents in the United States experience barriers to pursuing or using treatment services to help them cope with the stress, anxiety, depression, and other cognitive and emotional problems related to having a deaf or hearing-impaired child. The barriers differ, however, for different Hispanic groups and individuals within groups, because of cultural, social, economic, and other factors, discussed throughout the chapter. For this reason, professionals need specific knowledge to adequately address problems for members of this large, variegated community.

For one thing, lack of English language proficiency limits access to health care services, especially since there are relatively few relevant care professionals who speak Spanish in the U.S. Language difficulties are apt to most frequently occur in both poorer groups with lower degrees of formal education and newer immigrants who have yet to learn English. Various studies (Mapp, 2004a; Steinberg et al., 2003) have found that Hispanic parents who were unable to take full advantage of information and resources in English tend to experience a more narrow perspective of the options available, and a more limited perspective of prognosis and the future potential of their child. Also, regarding language related barriers, when Hispanic parents do not have adequate information—largely related to a lack of materials in Spanish—they are more likely to resist health care resources completely, because they find services to be threatening and inaccessible. As a result, they prefer to look to nonmedical and noneducational networks for support and information (Fischgrund, Cohen, & Clarkson, 1987).

Differences in immigration status also affect Hispanic parents' treatment-seeking behaviors. Parents who are in the U.S. illegally are unlikely to want to "access the system," reveal themselves within a bureaucratic context, and risk being jailed or deported. Even if they do initiate a care process, when talking with social workers, physicians, and government officials, they are unlikely to be as open or honest as they would be if they were here legally. Immigration status and language barriers also cause many Hispanic parents to underutilize support systems within a school system context (Bailey et al., 1999; Bennett, 1989). In the special education setting, parents of Hispanic heritage seldom participate in the development of their child's Individualized Educational Programs (Delgado, 1984; Stein, 1983).

Another barrier to pursuing and using services is health insurance, which relates to socioeconomic status and employment. Although many health insurance plans cover treatment services that would benefit Hispanic parents with deaf or hearing-impaired children, one third of Hispanic families in the United States do not have health insurance (National Center for Health Statistics, 2004). Thus, even if language and immigration status do not provide barriers to treatment, the inability to pay for services is a direct impediment to service use.

In addition to barriers associated with language, immigration, economic, health insurance, and educational status, other factors may prevent or limit the pursuit and use of treatment services among Hispanic parents in the U.S. They include geographic locale (city dwellers have more access to services than rural dwellers); beliefs about health, illness, and care providers (positive beliefs about the effectiveness of care providers and the possibility of cure are more apt to result in treatment-seeking behaviors); and attitudes about self-reliance, such as *machismo*, to the extent it manifests as an extreme belief in individualism that negates help from others, viewing help-seeking as weakness or inadequacy.

Because of the barriers to treatment, it is important that concerned care professionals and policy leaders devise strategies to help Hispanic parents in need to overcome the barriers, so that they may enter into the therapeutic helping process. This requires making such parents aware that help exists; providing materials that appeal to their literacy levels and cultural backgrounds; making treatment affordable, or even free, for poverty-level parents; and reaching out to them through media, churches, schools, and places of employment, among other ways, in the communities where they live. In order for this strategy to be successful, materials must be produced in Spanish as well as in English. The therapeutic process needs to be explained simply and clearly, emphasizing the benefits of therapy, using concepts designed for each specific cultural group that are consonant with their ways of understanding and viewing the world.

In this context, it is important to mention that materials should indicate awareness of psychological and emotional problems that are common in Spanish-speaking cultures. Culture-bound syndromes seen in Hispanic Americans include *susto* (fright), *nervios* (nerves), *mal de ojo* (evil eye), and *ataque de nervios*. Symptoms of an *ataque* may include screaming uncontrollably, crying, trembling, verbal or physical aggression, dissociative experiences, seizure-like or fainting episodes, and suicidal gestures (Malgady & Rodriguez, 1994; National Center for Health Statistics, 2004; Steinberg et al., 1997).

Public service "commercials" designed for television, radio, and government and private organizations concerned about Hispanics in the U.S. should subsidize print media that discuss when therapy is needed and could be beneficial. In addition, subsidies for treatment should be available in the community for parents who cannot afford treatment and do not have health insurance. Along with economic strategies to overcome barriers, Hispanic communities must have more Spanish-speaking therapists, and community members should be made aware that they exist and are readily available to provide assistance.

While there is much that is not known about the interplay of language with factors such as client characteristics, acculturation, and fluency levels, the recognition of the importance of culture and respect for language preference applies to Hispanic culture. Families interviewed by Steinberg and colleagues (2003) greatly valued the opportunity to converse in Spanish with a member of the community. From the findings, one could conclude that cultural matching may prove to be the crucial variable in interventions, and that trilingual interpreters would be well suited to handle the complex nature of translation and interpretation.

According to Janis and Mann (1977), even when parents and professionals speak the same language, the information presented may be misunderstood. A difference in the language spoken by professionals rendering care and families receiving the information may increase the chances for misunderstanding, difficulty, and stress.

There is evidence (Charles, Gafni, & Whelan, 1997) that Hispanic parents are aware of and value the higher quality of specialized services that are generally provided at no cost to families in the United States when compared with the vastly different quality and cost of services to deaf and hard of hearing children in their countries of origin. Some families admit to remaining in the United States, separating themselves from their country of origin and extended family, in order that their child may receive a wider array of services (Steinberg et al., 2003).

Based on the foregoing discussion, "What recommended psychotherapeutic approaches would best fit with Hispanic parents to decrease their distress and increase their well-being?" Few studies are available, unfortunately, on the response of Hispanics to mental health care. One randomized study found that members of low-income, Spanish-speaking families were more likely to suffer a significant exacerbation of symptoms of schizophrenia in highly structured family therapy than in the less structured case management. Several studies have found that bilingual patients are evaluated differently when interviewed in English as opposed to Spanish. One small study found that Hispanic Americans with bipolar disorder are more likely to be misdiagnosed with schizophrenia than are non-Hispanic White Americans (*Fact sheet: Latinos/Hispanic Americans*, 2004). Because of the complexity in diagnosis and treatment suggested by these few studies, it seems judicious to offer proposed treatment approaches with caution.

A solid starting point would appear to derive from the observation that many parents, from the time they learn their child is deaf or hearing impaired, begin a process of grieving, especially when the child is very young. They "mourn," in effect, the loss of the "perfect child" (Kampfe, 1989; Mapp, 2004a, 2004b). Therefore, grief counseling would be one recommended treatment approach for such parents, either alone or within the context of a support group, depending on diagnostic criteria at intake. Also, therapy should take into account that, because new parents naturally expect to have a healthy child in every respect, their disappointment can lead to depression or hostility against the child, among other negative reactions, and further harm the integrity of the family unit. Thus, social work intervention should focus on helping parents to resolve feelings about their child's deafness or other disability.

To the extent the parents are exhibiting signs of depression or extreme anxiety, or are exhibiting other *DSM* criteria associated with loss or disappointment, the therapy could be supplemented with an anti-anxiety or depression medication. The therapist should speak Spanish, if the parents are most comfortable with that language, especially since one's native language is the language in which emotions are best expressed (Harris, 1989).

In general, the reaction to learning that one's child is deaf or hearing impaired tends to be most acute initially, and then to subside over time, to one degree or another, as the parents learn to assimilate the reality of the experience. Thus, a short-term psychotherapeutic approach is suggested as a treatment modality, based on an interaction model between client and therapist. Long-term psychoanalytic or other therapeutic approaches are generally not suggested for Hispanic parents with deaf or hearing-impaired children. Cognitive-oriented therapies should be employed with more verbal and educated clients, whereas more empathic and behavior-oriented approaches should be the modality for clients with low levels of education and limited analytical skills.

Support groups would seem to be especially effective for Hispanic parents who have the fewest connections to family and friends, such as Cubans who cannot return to their homeland, where other family members may still reside. On the other hand, Puerto Ricans in the U.S. often have a constant connectedness to extended family, if they so desire to utilize it, as they are free to travel back and forth to their homeland. In addition, their family members may freely travel to visit them in the states. For Puerto Rican parents, therefore, support groups may be less necessary within the therapeutic context.

A study by Mapp and Hudson (1997) suggests that, as time passes, Hispanic parents of deaf and hearing-impaired children experience unexpectedly low levels of stress and develop the use of specific coping skills. Specifically, the researchers conducted a correlational study of 98 parents of children with hearing loss to determine the relationships among the parents' stress levels, their reported coping strategies, and the demographic characteristics of themselves and their hearing-impaired children. The study revealed that racial and ethnic group membership was significantly related to the degree of use of several coping strategies. Hispanics differed significantly from African Americans in that they made greater use of coping strategies, including confrontive strategies, distancing, self-control, social support, planful problem solving, and positive reappraisal. They also differed from other groups in the sample in their use of confrontive and planful problem solving coping strategies. Findings such as these could be used by therapists to help the parents strengthen the coping strategies they are inclined to use, as well as develop new ones appropriate for their specific situations.

Mapp (2004b) also found in a large literature review study that Hispanic parents coped by using one or more of the following coping mechanisms: avoidance, religious devotion, denial, faith, optimism, social support groups, economic assistance, medical technologies, psychotherapy, narratives, subcultural isolation, individual distancing, attribution of blame, fatalism, training courses, and rationalization. These findings show that Hispanic parents are open to a wide variety of potential approaches to healing, but that no parents used all possible methods. A goal of therapy, therefore, is to discover, for particular parents, what their coping predispositions are, and to work with those, at least as starting points, to develop an effective treatment strategy.

CASE VIGNETTES

Case 1

Puerto Rican parents living in Manhattan first began to suspect their baby boy had a problem when he was 18 months old, because he wasn't paying attention to or talking to them. They decided to take the boy to see a doctor in Puerto Rico, based on family recommendations, and because they felt the doctor would better "understand" what could be wrong with their boy, based on cultural familiarity. When the parents found out the boy was deaf, and would likely never hear or speak verbally, they felt extreme sadness—especially the mother—because she had been expecting a perfectly healthy child. Her sadness turned to depression, and the spouses were showing signs of marital strife. The father began drinking more heavily. They then talked to an uncle who lived in Queens, and he arranged for them to see an English-speaking social worker in New York, who could recommend treatment options. Soon, the parents were sent to see a psychotherapist who specialized in grieving, and was bilingual in English and Spanish. After 3 months of seeing the therapist, the parents' negative psychological and emotional symptoms began to lift, as they more fully came to understand and accept the reality of their new, unwanted situation.

Case 2

Mexican parents in the United States illegally, living in Texas, were frightened and confused when they began to suspect that their 3-year-old daughter had a hearing problem. They had little money, barely spoke English, and no close family connections in the U.S. whom they felt could help them. As a result, they avoided seeking professional help for several months after suspecting a problem, and relied heavily on folk treatments and especially religion to help them cope. They prayed incessantly but did not confide to their priest about their child's problem. At all costs, they wanted to avoid being detected by "the system," but they did not want to return to Mexico, for fear of being caught or not being able to reenter the U.S. A year or so later, when it became apparent their child's hearing and speech development were extremely subpar, they decided they must seek some sort of professional help. After asking around among friends in their local community, they were referred to a social worker in private practice who spoke Spanish and agreed to advise them *pro bono*. She arranged for them to see a private ear-nose-and-throat (ENT) specialist, who agreed to provide diagnostic services at a fee the parents could afford over time. He spoke only English, however. The father did not understand the term "deaf" initially, but he did understand the phrase "no hearing." Soon, the physician called in a nurse who spoke Spanish, to explain the condition to the parents, and provide materials in Spanish for them to read. They quickly realized that with their limited economic, educational, and language resources, along with their illegal immigration status, they would have an extremely difficult future ahead. For the time being, all they could do, they thought, was resign themselves to the fact that they would have to cope with the situation as best they could, on their own, drawing on their faith in God and internal, personal strengths.

SUMMARY

When parents learn their child is deaf or has a hearing impairment, they are likely to experience stress, grief, anger, guilt, helplessness, confusion, depression, or anxiety, among other negative cognitive and emotional reactions. At the same time, the parents must make important decisions that can heighten the anxiety and stress, involving communicating with their child, hearing aids or other assistive devices, arranging for intervention services, and schooling.

In the United States, Hispanics have a disproportionately high number of deaf and hearing-impaired children. Although U.S.-resident Hispanics are a highly variegated group, the great majority are from Mexico, with a significant number from Puerto Rico, and have high rates of poverty, low levels of formal education, and English language deficiencies, among other detriments that negatively impact coping efficacy. Many Mexicans and a minority of Cubans (the third largest Hispanic group in the U.S.) also are illegal immigrants. These social and cultural factors mainly contribute to the risks and problems Hispanics in the U.S. confront related to coping with the demands of having a deaf or hearing-impaired child. In addition, a substantial number of Hispanics from various countries enter the U.S. with differing degrees of psychosocial problems, often a result of the trauma in their homelands that led to their immigration to the U.S.

All of these factors must be clinically assessed, to determine the type of treatment approach that would be efficacious for Hispanic parents with deaf or hearing-impaired children. The barriers these parents face related to utilizing care services differ, however, for different Hispanic groups and individuals within groups. For this reason, professional care providers need specific knowledge about Hispanic subcultural groups in the U.S., as well as specific knowledge about particular parents seeking treatment, to adequately address problems for members of this large, variegated community.

To reach Hispanic parents in need and attract them to treatment, print materials must be produced in Spanish, in clear and readily understandable language, that shows awareness of the common culture-bound psychological and emotional problems experienced by members of Hispanic communities. In addition, television and radio outreach campaigns are vital; more Spanish-speaking therapists are needed; outreach programs are necessary in churches, places of employment, schools, and other community settings; and subsidies for poverty-level parents are critical. During the entire process of outreach, identification, and appeal, community leaders must put a personal "face" on the impersonal bureaucracies that, by and large, provide treatment services, in order to reduce the fears and anxieties Hispanic parents are apt to experience, especially those who are the least educated, affluent, and proficient in the English language.

In general, the reaction that parents experience when they first learn about their child's deafness or hearing impairment is a grief reaction, similar to the mourning process. Therapy should therefore be aimed at alleviating these acute symptoms, and should be planned to be short term. Cognitive-based and analytic therapies should be only used with the more verbal and highly educated parents, whereas therapies that are more empathic and behavior-oriented should be used with parents who are less verbal, analytical, and educated. Support groups would be most needed for parents who lack ready access to their extended families and friends, such as illegal immigrants and those who came here as political refugees.

Studies have shown that Hispanic parents utilize a wide variety of coping modalities, and that they increasingly adjust to having a deaf or hearing-impaired child over time. Therapists should become aware of the coping modalities of parents, both as unique individuals and as members of distinct sociocultural groups. These modalities must be used as a basis for creating a treatment plan that would be both culturally sensitive and specific to the unique needs of each particular parent.

REFERENCES

Alvirez, D., & Bean, F. D. (1976). The Mexican-American family. In C. H. Mindel & R. W. Haberstein (Eds.), *Ethnic families in America* (pp. 271–291). New York: Elsevier.

American Psychological Association. (2004). Retrieved from http://www.apa.org

Bailey, D., Skinner, D., Correa, V., Arcia, E., Reyes-Blanes, M., Rodriguez, P., Vazquez-Montilla, E., & Skinner, M. (1999). Needs and supports reported by Latino families of young children with developmental disabilities. *American Journal on Mental Retardation, 104*(5), 437–451.

Bennett, A. T. (1989). *Hispanic families and children in the special education intake process.* New York: The Lexington Center.

Centers for Disease Control. (2004). Retrieved from http://www.cdc.gov/omh/AMH/factsheets/mental.htm

Charles, C., Gafni, A., & Whelan, T. (1997). Shared decision-making in the medical encounter: What does it mean? (or it takes at least two to tango). *Social Science and Medicine, 44*(5), 681–692.

Cohen, O. (1993). Educational needs of African American and Hispanic deaf children and youth. In K. M. Christensen & G. L. Delgado (Eds.), *Multicultural issues in deafness* (pp. 45–67). New York: Longman Publishing.

Delgado, G. L. (1984). *The Hispanic deaf: Issues and challenges for bilingual special education*. Washington, DC: Gallaudet College Press.

Fact sheet: Latinos/Hispanic Americans. (2004). Retrieved from http://www.surgeongeneral.gov/library/mentalhealth/cre/fact3.asp

Feher-Prout, T. (1996). Stress and coping in families with deaf children. *Journal of Deaf Studies and Deaf Education, 1*(3), 155–166.

Fischgrund, J., Cohen, O., & Clarkson, R. (1987). Hearing-impaired children in Black and Hispanic families. *Volta Review, 89*(5), 59–67.

Franklin, J. (1997). *Cuba and the United States: A chronological history*. Melbourne, Australia: Ocean Press.

Fujiura, G., Yamaki, K., & Czechowicz, S. (1998). Disability among ethnic and racial minorities in the United States: A summary of economic status and family structure. *Journal of Disability Policy Studies, 9*(2), 111–130.

Gianaro, C. (2004). *Memories torment war refugees*. Retrieved from http://www.researchmagazine.uga.edu/spring2004/refugees.htm

Harris, P. L. (1989). *Children and emotion*. Oxford: Basil Blackwell.

Harry, B. (1992). Making sense of disability: Low-income, Puerto Rican parents' theories of the problem. *Exceptional Children, 59*(1), 27–40.

Janis, I., & Mann, L. (1977). *Decision-making: A psychological analysis of conflict, choice, and commitment*. New York: Free Press.

Kampfe, C. (1989). Parental reaction to a child's hearing impairment. *American Annals of the Deaf, 134*(4), 255–259.

Lian, M., & Fantanez-Phelan, S. (2001). Perceptions of Latino parents regarding cultural and linguistic issues and advocacy for children with disabilities. *Journal of the Association for Persons with Severe Handicaps, 26*(3), 189–194.

Malgady, R., & Rodriguez, O. (1994). *Theoretical and conceptual issues in Hispanic mental health*. New York: Krieger Publishing Company.

Mapp, I. (Ed.). (2004a). *Essential readings on stress and coping among parents of deaf and hearing-impaired children*. New York: Richard Altschuler & Associates, Inc./Gordian Knot Books.

Mapp, I. (2004b). *Stress and coping among African American and Hispanic parents of deaf and hearing-impaired children: A review of the literature*. Unpublished manuscript.

Mapp, I., & Hudson, R. (1997). Stress and coping among African American and Hispanic parents of deaf children. *American Annals of the Deaf, 142*(1), 48–56.

Meadow-Orlans, K., Mertens, D., & Sass-Lehrer, M. (2003). *Parents and their deaf children: The early years*. Washington, DC: Galluadet University Press.

Meadow-Orlans, K., Mertens, D., Sass-Lehrer, M., & Scott-Olson, K. (1997). *Support services for parents of children who are deaf or hard of hearing*. Presentation at Convention of the American Instructors of the Deaf (CAID)/Conference of Educational Administrators of Schools and Programs for the Deaf (CEASD) meeting: Pages of the Past . . . Chapters of the Future, Hartford, CT.

Moores, D., Jatho, J., & Dunn, C. (2001). Families with deaf members: American Annals of the Deaf, 1996 to 2000. *American Annals of the Deaf, 146*(3), 245–250.

Muñoz-Dunbar, R., & Stanton, A. (1999). Ethnic diversity in clinical psychology: Recruitment and admission practices among doctoral programs. *Teaching of Psychology, 26*(4), 259–263.

National Center for Health Statistics. (2004). Retrieved from http://www. cdc.gov/nchs/

Reyes-Blanes, M., Correa, V., & Bailey, D. (1999). Perceived needs of and support for Puerto Rican mothers of young children with disabilities. *Topics in Early Childhood Special Education, 19*(1), Special Issue: 62, 54–62.

Rodriguez, O., & Santiviago, M. (1991). Hispanic deaf adolescents: A multicultural minority. *The Volta Review, 93*(5), 89–97.

Skinner, D., Correa, V., Skinner, M., & Bailey, D. (2001). Role of religion in the lives of Latino families of young children with developmental delays. *American Journal on Mental Retardation, 106*(4), 297–313.

Stein, R. C. (1983). Hispanic parents' perspectives and participation in their children's special education program: Comparisons by program and race. *Learning Disability Quarterly, 6,* 432–439.

Steinberg, A. (1991). Issues in providing mental health services to hearing-impaired persons. *Hospital and Community Psychiatry, 42*(4), 380–389.

Steinberg, A., Davila, J., Collazo, J., Loew, R. C., & Fischgrund, J. E. (1997). A little sign and a lot of love . . . Attitudes, perceptions, and beliefs of Hispanic families with deaf children. *Qualitative Health Research, 7*(2), 202–222.

Steinberg, A., Bain, L., Li, Y., Delgado, G., & Ruperto, V. (2003). Decisions Hispanic families make after the identification of deafness. *Journal of Deaf Studies & Deaf Education, 8*(3), 291–314.

U.S. Census Bureau. (2000). *Profile of general demographic characteristics for the United States: 2000.* Washington, DC: U.S. Bureau of the Census.

U.S. Census Bureau. (2002, March). *Current population survey. Ethnic and Hispanic Statistics Branch, Population Division.* Retrieved from http://www.census.gov/ population/socdemo/hispanic

CHAPTER 14

Multicultural Dimension of the Third Shift: Employee, Mother, and Student

Susan Bair Egan

The role of student in the life of a woman is a role that is often neglected in the psychological assessment of women by professionals and by female students themselves. Because this role is taken on voluntarily and is usually time limited, the importance of the role strain and the stress it may cause may be overlooked in the treatment of women who are overwhelmed with additional responsibilities at home and work. Not much has changed since Hochschild (1989) found that when women are employed outside the home they are also largely responsible for homemaking and child care obligations, therefore working a "second shift." The "third shift" of being a student may take a toll on women's psychological and physical health, her marriage, her children, and her job or career.

Mental health professionals need to be aware of all of the roles a woman has and how she experiences each role. This chapter looks at some of the implications of the student role for women, with particular attention to race, ethnic, and cultural factors. As colleges and universities are creating more flexible programs that enable employees and parents to attend school on both undergraduate and graduate levels, and because of the importance of being competitive in the job force through education, a greater diversity is being seen in schools of higher education. It is this author's contention that the additional role of student is felt more strongly for women. This is supported by Home (1997a), who conducted a study on female graduate students with multiple roles and found that "these students face high costs and carry heavy responsibilities, and the limited available support is not always effective. Educators and researchers need to work together to devise strategies to enhance multiple-role management, while evaluating the usefulness of those strategies" (p. 345).

ROLE STRAIN AND SOCIAL SUPPORT

The impact that multiple roles have on women has been a topic in the literature for the past 30 years, the impetus being when women who were also wives and mothers entered the workforce in greater numbers. Role strain has been largely viewed from two different perspectives, role scarcity and role expansion. The scarcity view implies that multiple roles produce role strain and that this is harmful. Goode (1960) defined role strain as the difficulty an individual has in meeting given role demands. While in general, role strain is normal, it is his theory that total role obligations are over demanding. Since the individual cannot meet all demands, he or she struggles to make the role system manageable. To reduce role strain, individuals make decisions to enter or to leave a role relationship as well as to role bargain with others. Pearlin (1983) relates role strain to stress, believing that ordinary social roles cause strain if they are not satisfied, if they are in conflict with others, if they are in conflict with other roles held, where there is the unscheduled addition and loss of roles, and when roles are restructured. He states, however, that role strain depends on a person's disposition and the values and aspirations she brings to her role.

The expansion view implies that additional roles are beneficial. That is, rewards from one role can expand to others. Alternatively, multiple roles can buffer consequences of role failure or loss. For example, a student who earns a high grade on an assignment may feel more accomplished at her place of employment, or the loss of a job would be less traumatic if the role of student could be enhanced. It is also thought that the more roles a person holds, the higher her sense of self and purpose. Early theorists did, however, acknowledge that while multiple roles were beneficial, they were less beneficial for women than men (Gove, 1972; Marks, 1977; Sieber, 1974).

In a review of the research on role strain, Thoits (1987), however, wisely pointed out that the empirical evidence provides unqualified support for neither theory. Yet much of the research on multiple roles continues to be based in either the scarcity or expansion hypotheses. Added, however, is the examination of the quality of the roles held. Rather than counting the number of roles held when looking at role strain, what is important are the types of roles, the combination and complementarity of the roles, and how the roles are perceived (Baruch & Barnett, 1987; Greenberger & O'Neil, 1993; Piechowski, 1992; Simon, 1997).

Greenberger and O'Neil's study (1993) on the well-being of adults in multiple roles includes the dimensions of the degree of commitment individuals have to their roles, the level of demands their roles entail, the evaluations by individuals of their performance in work and family roles, their level of satisfaction in these roles, and the extent of their social support. In relation to the well-being of women, they found that job satisfaction and perceived support from their neighbors were associated with well-being. Marital and parental satisfaction were related to anxiety and depression but not to role strain. Role strain was evidenced in women who spent more time on work but felt greater dissatisfaction with their jobs, in women who felt their husbands and neighbors were unsupportive of their work and parenting efforts, and women who reported they were not living up to being a good wife.

Social support has been widely researched in the role it plays in mental health. Turner (1983) provides an extensive review of the literature and research on social supports and concludes that social support means many things to many people. He advocates, however, that all social supports not be seen as one entity. That is, social support should refer only to the experience or cognition of being supported by others, comprised of self-relevant information as processed and held by the individual. Emotional and perceived support is what is associated with psychological distress. Krahn (1993) conceptualizes social support as the supportive assistance from important others that addresses perceived needs. She underscores Turner's emphasis that there are different, unchangeable, dimensions of social support. Examination of the structure and functioning of the social support network as it relates to enacted support, perceived adequacy or satisfaction with support, content and sources of support, and characteristics that predispose one to accessing support is required.

In reference to students and social supports, a study by Malinckrodt and Leong (1992) attempted to identify the sources and types of social support that are most beneficial for graduate students in dealing with stress, particularly the graduate programs and family environments. They found that women report more stress, more stress symptoms, less support, and greater role strain than male graduate students, and therefore imply that there is increased role strain for women. A further exploration of social support in relation to multiple role women and the role of student will help inform the mental health professional in clinical assessments and treatment.

STUDENTS AND ROLE STRAIN

Paralleling the research on women as they entered the workplace, in the 1980s social work research began to look at the role of student who had either work or family responsibilities while attending school. Some studies found that part-time social work students did experience more role strain and stress than traditional students (Kramer, Mathews, & Endias, 1987; Patchner, 1983). However, other studies found no differences in stress levels (Fortune, 1987; Munson, 1984; Sales, Shore, & Bolitho, 1980). Koeske and Koeske (1989) studied social work students in the context of their role combinations rather than the number of roles held, grouping by full-time students with no jobs, full-time students with part-time jobs, and part-time students with full-time jobs. They found that full-time students with part-time jobs reported the greatest distress, having more demands and fewer resources. This was also the only group who reported that social support reduced symptoms of stress.

Role strain and the social work student was not found to any extent in the literature in the 1990s with the exception of the work of Home (1997a, 1997b). She did an extensive study of role demands, social support, role strain, and stress among female graduate students in multiple roles. She found that women with lower incomes, mothers of children under the age of 13, and women studying full time reported high role strain. Role demands, particularly student role demands, were a critical predictor of role strain. Flexible assignment dates and access to financial aid actually increased role strain for the women in this sample, two things that students ask for in helping them manage. Perhaps the accumulated work that comes from a flexible deadline and the strain of student debt are factors here. Distance education was the only institutional support that reduced student role demands in this study.

If the school or university itself is a form of social support for students, how can the institution best respond to the needs of students? Recommendations encompass responses from the university, the school of social work, faculty, and other supports (Brennan & Black, 1984; Kramer, Mathews, & Endias, 1987; Merdinger, 1991; Reeser, McDonald, & Wertkin, 1992). From the university, students look for support in terms of bookstore and library hours and child care. They request an increase in the amount of financial aid available and that the school be an advocate in the financial aid and scholarship process. From the social work school, students suggest a comprehensive orientation or a separate orientation for part-time students and their families that would include current students and alumni and focus on the stresses they will experience in the program. Some would like a lower number of required courses per semester or year. They want more flexibility in field placement and credit for work experience. From faculty, students want the ability to negotiate due dates, reduced assigned readings, respect for their input, an understanding of the personal implications of their decision to attend graduate school, and some control over their education. They would like faculty to vary their assignments and encourage student participation in the determination of assignments. Social supports include formally organized student support groups, the formalized support of other part-time students, stress management and time management workshops, and social functions for students with faculty and staff that would allow for formal and informal interactions, while being particularly sensitive to multiple role students when planning these activities.

Home (1997b) found that many female multiple role students had difficulty realistically assessing student role demands before beginning study, particularly underestimating time needed outside of class and fieldwork, as well as child care needs. She suggests that networking among multiple role women would help develop and maintain realistic expectations for themselves and their families. However, Babcock, Burpee, and Stewart (2001) studied social work students to help determine strategies they use to manage stress. Not one student in their sample, which included three schools of social work, reported that the use of stress reduction courses, time management workshops, or formal support groups would be helpful.

The literature reviewed here as well as literature in the field of education is strikingly void of distinctions in role strain or supports with regard to race and ethnicity. How these variables effect female students will be discussed next.

MULTICULTURALISM AND STUDENT ROLE STRAIN

Jackson (1997) did an extensive study on role occupancy and minority mental health. It is her belief that role experiences are not the same for all individuals, and while some attention in the literature has been given to gender differences, race and ethnicity has been ignored. She therefore examined the relationship between role occupancy—role accumulation, role status, and role combinations—and psychological well-being among African Americans, Mexican Americans, Puerto Ricans, and non-Hispanic Whites, and found that race/ethnicity clearly has an impact on mental health. It is interesting to note, particularly for this chapter, that she considered nine social roles in terms of role occupancy: worker, spouse, parent, sibling, son/daughter, friend, caregiver, group member, and churchgoer. Student is not a role included in this study. However, her results in terms of the role occupancy are helpful in understanding the effects of race and ethnicity on social roles. She found that non-Hispanic Whites and Mexican Americans experienced better psychological health from a higher number of roles than African Americans and Puerto Ricans, that all racial/ethnic groups benefited from the spousal role, and that going to church and having a sibling benefited all groups with the exception of Puerto Ricans. Caregiving is related to psychological distress for non-Hispanic Whites and African Americans. Belonging to an organization is related to better mental health for non-Hispanic Whites, yet is related to poorer mental health among African Americans and Puerto Ricans.

This author conducted a study in 1990 to better understand the influence of race and ethnicity in female graduate social work students with multiple roles (Egan, 1997). When social supports and coping with stress were explored, a pattern of racial and ethnic differences, as well as similarities, was seen.

Data were collected through a questionnaire of closed- and open-ended questions, as well as interviews. The sample consisted of 111 students with an age range of 22 to 58 years, 48% White, 28% African American, 22% Hispanic, and 2% Asian. Half of the students were in a couple relationship and over half did not have children. Of those with children, almost all had a least one child living at home. Students were asked about their motivation to attend graduate school, their social supports when they were considering attending school, and their supports while in graduate school. Responses about why they wanted to attend school were similar among the racial/ethnic groups. They wanted to gain more clinical skills and theoretical knowledge, advance their careers, help others, and promote self-growth and professionalism. Hispanic women made particular reference to planning to work with the Hispanic community. When considering graduate school, White women ranked their spouses as their strongest support, then friends, then supervisors and therapists. The African American women ranked spouses as their strongest support, then mothers, relatives, and friends. The Hispanic women ranked supervisors at work as their strongest support while considering applying to school, then spouses, mothers, and coworkers. It is significant to note that the African American women in this study found family in general to be their source of support, whereas Hispanic women found their support in the workplace, and neither African American nor Hispanics ranked a therapist as a source of support. Their supports in graduate school did not differ, but women from each group made friends while in graduate school who were a source of support. Also, whereas supervisors were ranked as the most supportive to the Hispanic women at the time of consideration for graduate school, they were not ranked as a main source of support while the students were in school. Although few women indicated that their children were sources of their support, when asked about them they expressed pleasure that their children were proud of them and that they were positive role models for their children. The women of color in particular expressed how important it was that they set examples for their children regarding the importance of education.

The students in this study were also asked to rank order their most stressful roles while in school. All experienced the student role as the most stressful—White, 38%, African American, 53%, and Hispanic, 58%. When the most stressful roles were analyzed only for the group of women who had children at home, the student role was still ranked first, then employee, and then wife/significant other.

The women were asked to wish for things that would facilitate their competency and comfort with their roles and responsibilities. Again, similarities and differences were seen in relation to race and ethnicity. Most women wished for more money but did so in relation to their schooling, that is, wanting more money to make their lives easier so they could complete their studies. They simply wanted to have the luxury of being a full-time student and not have to take out student loans. Most women wished for more time for family and for studying. White women wished for housekeepers and leisure time and vacations. Hispanic and African American women wished for child care, which is in contrast to their not mentioning their mothering role as one of their stressors.

It was evident from this study that even when a female graduate student has multiple roles, she views the role of student as the most stressful, regardless of the student's race or ethnicity, whether or not she is married and whether or not she has children at home. The study also challenged previously held assumptions about the needs of social work students in reference to special support groups. It was this author's contention that a support group based at school may be appealing only to White women, and although attempts to culturally diversify such a group may assuage liberal conscience, the group might be regarded as an irrelevant use of time by women of color who are working mothers. This goes against, however, findings that support groups for students of color can be beneficial (Capello, 1994; Wright, 1999).

To further understand students in multiple roles this author conducted another study of multiple role female students in 2002 at the same graduate school of social work. The focus in this study, however, was the use of supports from the family, the workplace, and the university. It was hypothesized that the use of supports would reduce role strain and that the patterns of the use of such support would differ based on race and ethnicity. It was found, however, that the higher the role strain experienced, the more the students used available supports. Differences were seen between White, African American, and Hispanic students.

The sample of 228 is comprised of continuing female graduate social work students holding at least one role other than the role of student—wife/partner, mother, caregiver, or employee. A questionnaire with closed- and open-ended questions was used to measure role demands, role strain, and use of supports.

Half of the sample is White, almost one third is African American, and 20% is Hispanic. The age range is 21 to 58 years with the mean of 36.5 years. Half of the students are in a relationship, with 40% married and 10% living with a partner. Almost 27% of the students live with their spouse and children and 24% live with spouse only. Fourteen percent live with parents and 12% are single parents. Approximately half of the sample has children and one third have at least two. Of the students with children, two thirds have at least one child under 13 years of age. A small number of these students, 17%, define themselves as caregivers, that is, assuming the primary responsibility for the daily tending, supporting, and monitoring of a relative (adult and/or child) who has physical, intellectual, emotional, or learning difficulties. Almost all of the students, 86%, are employed either full or part time. Two thirds of the students in this sample carry two or more roles in addition to student.

Students were asked about religiosity and health. Thirty-four percent indicate low religiosity, 41% moderate, and 19% high. Health was a major concern for few students, 4%, of some concern for 35%, and of no concern for the majority, 61%. Of the students in this sample, 34% reported a family income of less than $40,000, 18% an income between $41,000 and $60,000, 24% an income between $61,000 and $80,000, and 21% an income of over $81,000.

Three scales were used to measure role demands—family role demands, job-time demands, and student role demands. The family role demand scale assesses the perception of the intensity of family and caregiving demands. The job-time demand scale assesses work schedule flexibility, frequency of interrole conflicts, and irregular work demands. The student role demand scale asks how often the respondent is overwhelmed by student work.

Role strain was measured with three scales—role conflict, role overload, and role contagion. The role conflict scale includes items measuring respondents' perception of being "pulled apart" by different obligations, and items assessing how often specific conflict situations occur, such as conflicts between role pairs (student role vs. family or student role vs. employment). The role overload scale assesses the respondents' perception of having too much to do. The role contagion scale evaluates the extent to which respondents feel preoccupied with one role while performing another but mediated by "positive spillover," where strength in one role makes another role easier.

The sample was analyzed as a whole to determine perception of role demands and role strain. These students reported moderate amounts of family demands and employment demands, but somewhat higher student demands. The three role demand components were combined to make one Role Demand Scale. Overall, the perception of role demands was moderate; the mean score was 36.5, range 10–75. The three components of role strain were combined to create a Role Strain Scale. The students in this sample experienced moderate role strain; the mean was 54.4, range 24–89.

The students were asked to indicate if they used any of six specific supports offered by employers in relation to their student role, such as flex time to attend class or tuition reimbursement. The mean use was 3.2. Students were also asked if they used any of 37 specific services provided through the graduate school of social service or the university as a whole and the mean use of such services was 13.7, with a range of 3–36.

Further analyses determined that there were differences among the three ethnic/racial groups considered here in terms of number of roles, role demands, use of supports, and role strain. In this sample, there were no significant differences among the three groups in reference to age, living arrangements, number of children, age of children, number of dependent children, caregiver status, health concerns, number of roles held, religiosity, health, or supports from family and informal networks. There was significant difference in marital status, with African American students less likely to be married or living with a partner. The African American and Hispanic students are significantly more likely to be employed but they also have significantly less family income than White students.

On the Role Demand Scale and the Role Strain Scale, Hispanic students experienced significantly more role demands and role strain. Both African American students and Hispanic students used significantly more employment supports than did White students. Hispanic students used a significantly higher number of university supports than the African American and White students.

In this sample there was a high correlation of role strain and number of roles and role demands. It was hypothesized that the more a student used family and informal supports and services provided by her employer and the university, the less she would perceive her role demands and the less role strain she would experience. However, it was found that the more role demands and role strain experienced, the greater the use of these supports. Students with less income had fewer roles, but more role demands and made greater use of employment and university services. Those students with some or major health concerns experienced higher role demands and higher role strain.

Further analysis was done to see if race/ethnicity is a factor in the pattern of use of supports. The African American students with fewer roles used university supports to a greater degree. High role demands, high role strain, and their use of employment supports were also related to use of the university supports for this group. Hispanic students, the group in this sample that experienced significantly more role demands and higher role strain, also made more use of university supports. Yet lower income, health concerns, and fewer role demands were the factors directly related to such use. They did not make use of employment supports even though almost all of the students in this group were employed. White students in this sample made the least use of university and employment supports.

As an administrator in the graduate school, this author was surprised to find that the students who experienced more role strain made greater use of the university support services and that these students were the women of color. However, from the questionnaire it is seen that when women take advantage of the opportunities offered through the university and their employer, there are still consequences. Representative comments from some of the African American students who responded to the questionnaire are

"The most difficult part of my graduate education is the inconvenience of scheduling required classes. As a mother it puts strain on me and my family when I have to leave school late at night. Sometimes I only see my kids in the morning when I get them ready for school, because I return home when it's past their bedtime. Although my employer gives me release time to attend school, my caseload remains the same. I'm expected to work harder to catch up with what is done at work when I'm at school."

"Field work along with full-time job and a family to boot has at times made me feel inadequate in the choices I have had to make. As a single mother who is African American, my supports are limited. I have had to search harder to find programs for my son to be in and keep him on the right track. My job and school have been successful but my child and family are suffering."

"Being a wife, caseworker, and graduate student at the same time has made me aware of the strengths that I possess. Although there are times when it seems I can't go on, when I get back to class and have discussions with my peers, it makes me feel more encouraged."

Many African American women also commented on the need for a more diverse faculty and more courses dealing with cultural diversity. Many of the Hispanic women commented on the fact that English as their second language made the research and the writing of papers more of a challenge. Some specific comments from the Hispanic women are

"The difficulty stems from being a divorced parent, raising a child alone, trying to survive financially, having a demanding job, and trying to meet all the MSW requirements and excel in school. However, returning to school has been an asset to my life. School on Saturday is the highlight of the week because you learn new things, meet new people, and it justifies the daily life struggle. There are many times I feel overwhelmed because I also have a very sick elderly mother but I would not give up my studies. My student role has been very difficult but I am going to make it. At times it is very stressful but what keeps me going is the need for Spanish speaking mental health professionals—and my children and family."

"I'm the only one of 12 children who is working on a master's degree. I have the support of my family, however, it would make a difference if I could share my experiences with them. Being the youngest and going to school, I feel obligated to take care of my parents' needs, which most often conflict with my student obligations."

"My parents are divorced and each one of them spends approximately 3 months of each year with me, then they return to Mexico. During the time they stay with me, I am the primary caretaker in all matters—economic, health, etc. In addition, since my parents do not speak English they depend on me to take them out and provide entertainment. The 6 months they live with me I am very stressed."

As in this author's earlier study, the only students who said that support groups would be helpful were the White students. Some other comments from the White students follow:

"I fortunately do not find juggling school, work, family life, and my personal life to be highly stressful. Individually each role can have brief moments of becoming demanding, however, it is manageable. My friends, family, and coworkers have been supportive and available as I need them. I have found that when school, work, and my lifestyle have conflicts it is usually due to poor time management—no one to blame but myself."

"I am the parent of a special needs child and have had to juggle and manage a number of problems related to his physical and mental health and child care issues. In addition, I am the primary caretaker for my elderly disabled mother. During the course of my studies she became gravely ill and I needed to coordinate her care. I have felt a lot of conflict and have had to put my own needs last in order to juggle family, school, and job but I don't regret the path I have chosen. I believe in my goal."

"The MSW program is difficult but it's supposed to be difficult. Luckily I am recently married and have no children. I rely on my husband as much as I can. He's unemployed and has more time but he can't go to work for me or do my school work for me. Doing all of this is mentally draining. I get very emotional, cry at stupid things, and often shut down, feeling unmotivated, tired, and depressed. But that's what happens when you stretch yourself thin."

In a study of graduate social work students on cross-cultural conflicts, Hendricks (1993) found that such conflicts exist for students, and particularly for Hispanics. Although she did not focus on role strain, her findings support the studies by this author. Hendricks found that cross-cultural conflicts are perceived differently based on cultural identity, the amount of difference between the cultures at home and at school, and the student's coping strategies.

While these studies were conducted to gain a better understanding of students for social work educators, the implications are relevant to clinicians. An understanding of how the role of student is perceived by the student herself as well as by those in her support network in the context of race, ethnicity, and culture enhances assessment and assists in culturally competent interventions.

CLINICAL IMPLICATIONS

We live in an atmosphere where multitasking is admirable, even considered a strength. Because of this a woman may downplay the complexities of her multiple roles or not even realize the effect they are having on her mental health. Clinical assessment must take into consideration the woman's own view of her student role and how it is affecting others in her life. Cultural issues need to be at the forefront in this assessment. The clinician's personal and professional attitudes, beliefs, and knowledge will make psychotherapy effective (Vazquez, 1994).

It is important for the clinician to understand why the role of student was added. For some it may be the fulfillment of a lifelong dream while for others it may be a burdensome obligation.

Whatever the reason, completion of the education carries expectations of career change, career advancement, or increased income. The impetus behind the decision to go to school and the desired outcomes will provide insight into how the demands of the student workload are negotiated.

The perception of the woman's partner, children, and other family members needs to be determined. How education is viewed in respect to employment and family responsibilities will differ among racial and ethnic groups. If the family is proud of her accomplishments or if they are resentful of the time she spends at school or studying, this needs to be explored. The clinician can help the female student explain to her family why she is in school, her own expectations for study and ways to share with them what she is learning. If the student role is causing a strain in the marital relationship, this needs to be addressed as well. The female student's partner may have mixed emotions about her studies, particularly if they put an imbalance in their relationship in terms of college degree or income. Also, if she is the first in the family to earn an advanced degree this added pressure may be onerous.

The clinician should also explore the woman's adjustment to the student role. Whether she enjoys the challenge and stimulation of being a student, or feels uncomfortable because of gender, race, ethnicity, or age will lend insight into possible role strain. The student who is going to school after being widowed or divorced or the woman returning after raising a family will face different issues than a younger student. These women may be fearful of the unknown and have difficulty meeting others whose ideals may be different or who have more confidence in themselves (Herkelmann & Dennison, 1993). Also, efforts must be made to assess the advantages of the addition of the student role, as some women will experience greater independence, a more positive sense of self, and an expanded support network.

In addition, it is important to understand consequences if the woman must terminate her studies due to the financial burden, inability to adequately perform, or because of life events such as pregnancy or illness. Unfulfilled expectations as to what earning a degree would bring for the client as well as her family should be dealt with in treatment. Even when the termination is due to positive life changes such as a move or an addition to the family, the anticipated rewards of the degree may be mourned.

An action-oriented and ego supportive approach is a recommended treatment for multiple role women. The added demands of time and commitment that clinical treatment involves in the lives of already very busy women should be recognized (Freeman, Logan, & McCoy, 1987; Gibbs, 1984; McBride, 1990). In a study of university women in multiple roles, McBride (1997) concludes that the clinicians for these women need to be role models, showing that there can be a balance between concern for others with concern for self, therefore encouraging personal change within the context of social awareness.

The differences in the use of supports by race and ethnicity seen in this author's studies can help inform clinical assessment and treatment. While clinicians must be careful not to overgeneralize traits or characteristics to all people of a race or ethnicity, certainly, there must be recognition of the tensions and stresses of social, political, socioeconomic, and broader environmental conditions that clients in particular racial or ethnic groups face. Only in a cultural framework can assessment and treatment be effective (Boyd-Franklin, 2003; Comas-Diaz & Greene, 1994; Parham, 2002; Ho, Rasheed, & Rasheed, 2004; Sue, Ivey, & Pedersen, 1996).

Role overload is a common deterrent for African American women's engagement in treatment. Because they typically have so much to do, unless they really understand how therapy can be helpful, it is hard for them to commit themselves to it. It helps for the therapist to emphasize the woman's sense of being a survivor, her strengths, and her ability to find her own solutions. Also, because African American women tend to underrate the complexities of their lives because their older female relatives had it so much harder, clinicians must help them validate their own experiences (McGoldrick, Garcia-Preto, Hines, & Lee, 1989). Racial identity will be a central part of treatment for the African American. Both the difficulty of coping with racism and the richness of a woman's ethnic identity should be a routine part of treatment. For the client who is a student, the clinician must address the historical oppression that African Americans have faced in formal education (Allen, 1999; Greene, 1994).

Hispanic women are expected to be responsible for taking care of their home and children and often feel obligated to sacrifice themselves in order to accomplish this. Even when Hispanic women work outside the home, they are still expected to be submissive and passive in comparison to men. As their roles expand to the workplace or to school, they may have conflicted feelings about their traditional roles but not be able to verbalize this in treatment. However, the value that a Hispanic woman places on her family must be respected by the clinician, as an intervention that devalues traditional feminine roles or emphasizes a focus on the self could alienate the client from treatment (Falicov, 1998; McGoldrick et al., 1989). The mother-daughter bond is particularly strong in the Hispanic culture and daughters are not expected to leave home and become independent. Daughters who do pursue education may experience guilt or a sense of disloyalty for breaking with tradition and role expectation (Alvarez, 1999). In a study of Hispanic college students, brief counseling as a concise, action-oriented approach that incorporates a solution-focused approach within a limited time frame was found to be successful. Those who work with Hispanic students should help reduce the language barrier, add humor, and acquire knowledge of Hispanic background, history, and values (Cruz & Littrell, 1998). Hispanic students in higher education may have faced discriminatory treatment in school as children, particularly if they or their parents are immigrants and English is not their first language. An important part of clinical treatment is to help the female student understand how institutional racism is a factor in her self-esteem and identity. A person-in-environment approach that recognizes the many levels of challenges that Hispanics face and deals with justice issues is necessary for effective treatment (Zuniga, 2004).

Petersen (2000) states that women blame themselves for inadequacies regardless of the presenting problem. She recommends that clinicians assist women in separating the cultural definitions of women from their own self-definitions, help them see how they may have been solicited into certain patterns that they want to change, encourage self determination through the assessment of their cultural heritage, promote connections with a supportive environment, and help them recognize their strengths and use their own voices.

When more and more women are working a "third shift," clinicians must recognize implications of this additional role for the client and her family. The role demand and role strain will differ from woman to woman, but must be understood in their cultural context.

REFERENCES

Allen, I. (1999). Therapeutic considerations for African American students at predominantly white institutions. In Y. M. Jenkins (Ed.), *Diversity in college settings: Directives for helping professionals* (pp. 37–49). New York: Routledge.

Alvarez, M. (1999). Diversity among Latinas: Implications for college mental health. In Y. M. Jenkins (Ed.), *Diversity in college settings: Directives for helping professionals* (pp. 99–115). New York: Routledge.

Babcock, M. D., Burpee, M. R., & Stewart, T. G. (2001). Sources of stress and coping strategies of full-time MSW students. *Arete, 25*(2), 87–95.

Baruch, G. K., & Barnett, R. C. (1987). Role quality and psychological well-being. In F. J. Crosby (Ed.), *Souse, parent, worker: On gender and multiple roles* (pp. 63–73). New Haven: Yale University Press.

Boyd-Franklin, N. (2003). *Black families in therapy.* New York: Guilford Press.

Brennan, E. M., & Black, E. A. (1984). On finding a workable balance: The multiple roles of the part-time student. *Journal of Continuing Social Work Education, 3*(1), 19, 43–46.

Capello, D. (1994). Beyond financial aid: Counseling Latina students. *Journal of Multicultural Counseling & Development, 22*(1), 28–39.

Comas-Diaz, L., & Greene, B. (1994). *Women of color: Integrating ethnic and gender identities in psychotherapy.* New York: Guilford Press.

Cruz, J., & Littrell, J. M. (1998). Brief counseling with Hispanic American college students. *Journal of Multicultural Counseling & Development, 26*(4), 227–240.

Egan, S. B. (1997). Multicultural dimensions of the third shift: Employee, mother and student. In E. P. Congress (Ed.), *Multicultural perspectives in working with families* (pp. 76–88). New York: Springer Publishing.

Falicov, C. (1998). *Latino families in therapy: A guide to multicultural practice.* New York: Guilford Press.

Fortune, A. (1987). Multiple roles, stress and well-being among MSW students. *Journal of Social Work Education, 23*(3), 81–90.

Freeman, E. M., Logan, S., & McCoy, R. (1987). Clinical practice with employed women. *Social Casework: The Journal of Contemporary Social Work, 68*(7), 413–420.

Gibbs, J. (1984). Conflicts and coping strategies of minority female graduate students. In E. White (Ed.), *Color in a White society* (pp. 22–36). Silver Spring, MD: National Association of Social Workers.

Goode, W. (1960). A theory of role strain. *American Sociological Review, 25*, 483–496.

Gove, W. (1972). The relationship between sex roles, mental illness, and marital status. *Social Forces, 51*, 34–44.

Greenberger, E., & O'Neil, R. (1993). Spouse, parent, worker: Role commitments and role-related experiences in the construction of adults' well-being. *Developmental Psychology, 29*(2), 181–197.

Greene, B. (1994). African American women. In L. Comas-Diaz & B. Greene (Eds.), *Women of color: Integrating ethnic and gender identities in psychotherapy*. New York: Guilford Press.

Hendricks, C. O. (1993). Cross-cultural conflicts in social work education: The Latino experience. *Dissertation Abstracts International* (UMI No. 9328601).

Herkelmann, K., & Dennison, T. (1993). Women in transition: Choices and conflicts. *Education, 114*(1), 127–145.

Ho, M. K., Rasheed, J. M., & Rasheed, M. N. (2004). *Family therapy with ethnic minorities*. Thousand Oaks: Sage.

Hochschild, A. (1989). *The second shift: Working parents and the revolution at home*. New York: Viking.

Home, A. (1997a). Learning the hard way: Role strain, stress, role demands and support in multiple-role women students. *Journal of Social Work Education, 33*(2), 335–346.

Home, A. (1997b). The delicate balance: Demand, support, role strain and stress in multiple role women. *Social Work & Social Sciences Review, 7*(3), 131–143.

Jackson, P. B. (1997). Role occupancy and minority mental health. *Journal of Health and Social Behavior, 38,* 237–255.

Koeske, R. D., & Koeske, G. F. (1989). Working and non-working students: Roles, support and well-being. *Journal of Social Work Education, 25*(3), 244–256.

Krahn, G. (1993). Conceptualizing social support in families of children with special needs. *Family Process, 32,* 235–248.

Kramer, H., Mathews, & Endias (1987). Comparative stress levels in part-time and full-time social work programs. *Journal of Social Work Education, 23*(3), 74–80.

Malinckrodt, B., & Leong, F. T. L. (1992). Social support in academic programs and family environments: Sex differences and role conflicts for graduate students. *Journal of Counseling and Development, 70*(6), 716–723.

Marks, S. (1977). Multiple roles and role strain: Some notes on human energy, time and commitment. *American Sociological Review, 41,* 921–36.

McBride, A. B. (1990). Mental health effects of women's multiple roles. *American Psychologist, 45,* 381–384.

McBride, M. (1997). Counseling the superwoman: Helping university women cope with multiple roles. *Guidance and Counseling, 12*(4), 19–22.

McGoldrick, M., Garcia-Preto, N., Hines, P. M., & Lee, E. (1989). Ethnicity and women. In C. Anderson & F. Walsh (Eds.), *Women in families: A framework for family therapy* (pp. 169–199). New York: W. W. Norton.

Merdinger, J. (1991). Researching women students: Their ways of knowing. *Journal of Teaching in Social Work, 5*(2), 41–51.

Munson, C. E. (1984). Stress among graduate social work students: An empirical study. *Journal of Education for Social Work, 20,* 20–29.

Parham, T. (2002). *Counseling persons of African descent*. Thousand Oaks: Sage.

Patchner, M. (1983). The practitioner becomes a student: The stresses of transition. *Journal of Continuing Social Work Education, 2*(2), 21–23, 31.

Pearlin, L. (1983). Role strains and personal stress. In H. B. Kaplan (Ed.), *Psychosocial stress: Trends in theory and research* (pp. 3–32). New York: Academic Press, Inc.

Petersen, S. (2000). Multicultural perspective on middle-class women's identity development. *Journal of Counseling & Development, 78*(1), 63–72.

Piechowski, L. (1992). Mental health and women's multiple roles. *Family in Society, 73*, 131–139.

Reeser, L. C., MacDonald, F., & Wertkin, R. A. (1992). Enhancing student coping and modifying the stressful academic environment: Advice from students and faculty. *Journal of Teaching in Social Work, 6*(2), 87–97.

Sales, E., Shore, B. K., & Bolitho, F. (1980). When mothers return to school: A study of women completing an MSW program. *Journal of Education for Social Work, 16*, 57–64.

Sieber, S. (1974). Toward a theory of role accumulation. *American Sociological Review, 39*, 567–78.

Simon, R. (1997). The meanings individuals attach to role identities and their implications for mental health. *Journal of Health and Social Behavior, 38*(Sept.), 256–274.

Sue, D. W., Ivey, A. E., & Pedersen, P. B. (1996). *A theory of multicultural counseling and therapy*. Pacific Grove: Brooks/Cole.

Thoits, P. (1987). Negotiating roles. In F. J. Crosby (Ed.), *Spouse, parent, worker: On gender and multiple roles* (pp. 11–22). New Haven: Yale University Press.

Turner, R. (1983). Social support and psychosocial distress. In H. Kaplan (Ed.), *Psychosocial stress: Trends in theory and research* (pp. 105–155). New York: Academic Press.

Vasquez, M. J. (1994). Latinas. In L. Comas-Diaz & B. Greene (Eds.), *Women of color: Integrating ethnic and gender identities in psychotherapy* (pp. 114–138). New York: Guilford Press.

Wright, D. (1999). Group services for students of color. In Y. M. Jenkins (Ed.), *Diversity in college settings: Directives for helping professional* (pp. 149–167). New York: Routledge.

Zuniga, M. (2004). Latino needs: Flexible and empowering interventions. In L. Gutierrez, M. Zuniga, & D. Lum (Eds.), *Education for multicultural social work practice: Critical viewpoints and future directions* (pp. 185–199). Alexandria, VA: Council on Social Work Education.

Section Four

Challenging Practice Issues

CHAPTER 15

Working With HIV-Affected Culturally Diverse Families

Cynthia Cannon Poindexter

This chapter presents thoughts on social work with families in a multicultural society when HIV disease is added to the mix of challenges. Social workers are intricately linked to the struggles and solutions of the HIV pandemic. An effective and ethical social worker cannot remain ignorant of the facts about HIV or expect to avoid the issue in practice. HIV work is inherently compatible with the skills, knowledge, and values of social work—empowering disenfranchised, oppressed, and marginalized individuals, families, and groups (Shernoff, 1990). The National Association of Social Worker's (NASW; 2000) policy statement on HIV acknowledges both the uniqueness and the universality of the concerns of HIV-infected and HIV-affected persons; challenges us to address social justice, discrimination, and access to care; and calls on the profession to show strong leadership.

Throughout this chapter, "family" is not limited to those with biological or civil ties, but refers to whomever the person with HIV defines as significant and important in his or her life. It is typical in the HIV field to recognize not just persons who are kin, but also kindred—those linked through love even if not through

Acknowledgment: I am grateful to the HIV-infected persons and HIV-affected family members who have patiently taught me about their struggles and strengths. This chapter is written in memory of my friends and colleagues who have died of AIDS and in honor of those who live with HIV.

legalities (Matocha, 1992). A true family system may not resemble what is found in the traditional social science literature. I will use "relative" or "family of origin" when I am specifying that type of relationship.

Here I define HIV and suggest effects it can have on families; outline some of the concerns that tend to be common in HIV-affected families; give a few examples of unique stressors for African Americans, Latinos, and gay males; and offer recommendations. Throughout I draw on research and practice literature as well as my own experience. This overview is greatly restricted in scope, because it is impossible to discuss every variation of family, touch on every cultural group, or address every form of oppression. Space limitations preclude my specifically addressing families of Caribbean, Native American, Hawaiian, Asian, or Middle Eastern origins, for example. I am also not able to do justice to the intense and special needs of the families of those who are transgendered, in the sex industry, drug-affected, and/or homeless. I do not deal separately with the special needs of children, adolescents, women, or elders who are HIV-infected or HIV-affected. I do not address the intersection of sexual or domestic violence with HIV. There are many other omissions. I hope that by introducing some of the possible experiences, strengths, and needs of HIV-affected families, readers will be spurred to further exploration.

SCOPE AND SERIOUSNESS OF THE ISSUE

The human immunodeficiency virus (HIV) is an infectious retrovirus leading to an incurable life threatening condition known as HIV disease. The symptomatic end stage of the spectrum of HIV disease is known as AIDS (Acquired Immune Deficiency Syndrome). Persons living with HIV are also referred to as HIV-positive or HIV-infected; caregivers, family members, and other loved ones are called HIV-affected.

Because the retrovirus attacks and destroys the human immune system, the infected person over time becomes more susceptible to cancers and bacterial, viral, parasitic, fungal, and other opportunistic infections. Medications can do much to prevent and treat these dangerous conditions, but to date there is neither cure nor vaccine. HIV remains life threatening.

HIV is a planet-wide plague, a medical and social emergency unprecedented in our lifetimes. It is impossible to exaggerate its destructiveness. The way this retrovirus can burn through a human body, family system, community, or country is horrifying. Peter Piot, executive director of the United Nations AIDS project, said that this pandemic "has already spread further, faster, and to more devastating effect than any other in human history" (Piot, 2003, p. 1). It is unimaginable that any practicing social worker, regardless of setting, will not at some time work with HIV-infected persons and HIV-affected families as they struggle to cope.

Given the underreporting of HIV disease and the fact that not everyone with HIV knows that he or she is infected, it is impossible to know exactly how many people are living with HIV. The Centers for Disease Control (CDC) estimates that at the end of 2002 there were about 400,000 persons living with HIV in the U.S. It is likewise difficult to know how many HIV-affected families there are, but if we assume that each infected person has a circle of loved ones defined as "family," we can use that same estimate.

HIV, as is the case with many social and public health disasters, tends to run along the lines of oppression. Those most heavily affected tended to be in already stigmatized and marginalized groups. It is likely that social workers will be involved with families who have already been struggling daily with the effects of xenophobia, sexism, ageism, addiction phobia, classism, homophobia, religious intolerance, and racism. HIV stigma gets added to the layers of disenfranchisement and deepens the invisibility and neglect of society. All types of humans and all configurations of family systems are susceptible to HIV. Remember that HIV infection is not associated with any particular ethnic group, national origin, gender, socioeconomic class, age, or sexual orientation.

HIV is difficult to face and manage alone. Most persons with HIV must turn to an informal support network at some point in the illness for practical and emotional support. Unfortunately, persons with HIV sometimes still experience rejection from those they wanted to count on for care. Despite these relationship failures, however, people with HIV are often able to turn to their trusted social networks during those times when they need sustenance. HIV alters the life course of a family almost as profoundly as it does the HIV-infected individual (Wardlaw, 1994). Family members can be confronted with intense shock, fear, anxiety, anger, burden, losses, stigma, and isolation (Gordon-Garofalo, 2000). Although the significant persons in the life of someone with HIV may not be the primary focus of social service interventions, they are nevertheless in need of information, emotional support, and resources.

PSYCHOSOCIAL CONCERNS SHARED BY FAMILIES

Having HIV or loving someone who is infected is an experience about which we cannot generalize, because family responses to HIV depend on individual members, history, interaction, roles, values, beliefs, emotional patterns, boundaries, perceived route of HIV transmission, level of HIV knowledge, and inclinations regarding secrecy (Cates, Graham, Boeglin, & Tielker, 1990). Yet it is also true that HIV brings certain bio-psycho-social-spiritual concerns to individuals, couple, and families, regardless of group membership or history. Following is a brief discussion of managing HIV stigma, adjusting to a transformed reality, living with an unpredictable disease, care burdens, grief, and renewed meaning.

Management of Stigma and Privacy

HIV is at this time the most intensely stigmatized physical condition. HIV stigma, although it has lessened over the course of the pandemic, is still a virulent impediment to prevention, care, and treatment efforts targeted to persons with HIV and their families (Herek & Capitanio, 1993). Family members must make difficult decisions about whether to disclose the presence of HIV and to whom; these decisions are often made in stages, along a complex stigma continuum ranging from complete secrecy to complete disclosure (Powell-Cope & Brown, 1992).

Stigma can keep families locked behind a wall of secrecy, hiding their needs and feelings from their social environments. Because of stigma, HIV-affected family members can experience social isolation (McDonell, Abell, & Miller, 1991). The absence of support can increase the stress of family members, exacerbating the already weighty toll of HIV disease (Brown & Powell-Cope, 1993; Wardlaw, 1994). Isolation also causes hidden or disenfranchised grief (Brown & Powell-Cope, 1993; Dane, 1991; Doka, 1989). There results a cycle of nonsupport and a deepening of grief (Walker, Pomeroy, McNeil, & Franklin, 1996).

Stigma may effect who constitutes family after the diagnosis. Sometimes HIV-positive persons are reluctant to ask relatives for support because of sexual or drug disclosures that might be necessitated when an HIV diagnosis is revealed. When the person with HIV anticipates judgement, decreasing intimacy, negative interactions, or other interpersonal costs, he or she may be less likely to access support from relatives (Smith & Rapkin, 1996).

Crises, Stress, and an Altered Reality

Because of the uncertain trajectory of HIV disease, family members usually experience a volatile emotional roller coaster, filled with episodes of crisis (Cates et al., 1990; Matocha, 1992; Poindexter, 1997; Stulberg, 1998). HIV can tip the scales for families who are already dealing with the effects of poverty, substandard housing, dangerous neighborhoods, substance use, and mental health concerns, and can send them into a tailspin. Loved ones may be angry at the unfairness of the disease, at the person with HIV, at unhelpful or unresponsive social network members, or at the resulting secrecy and isolation. Loving someone with HIV may challenge or threaten a family member's long-held views about drug use, sexuality, illness, spirituality, death, safety, and relationships. Family members often find themselves painfully rethinking core personal, religious, or cultural beliefs in order to incorporate this new reality (Gant, 1996). Sometimes a person who has been estranged from the family reenters it when symptomatic HIV necessitates the receipt of financial, practical, or emotional support. Reintegration becomes a gigantic task, complete with struggles over autonomy and decision making (Cates et al., 1990).

Management of a Complicated Disease and Protocols

HIV disease is wildly unpredictable and the medication protocols are quite complex and often cause debilitating side effects. Persons with HIV are usually struggling to adhere to complicated regimens, manage side effects, and maintain wellness through nutrition, exercise, and complementary therapies. Health maintenance and adherence are greatly enhanced through support, acceptance, and encouragement. Family members are often heavily involved in the day-to-day—sometimes hour-to-hour—monitoring and enhancement of the person's health. Again, responses vary: some family members will seek and devour any information available, and others will find that their anxiety increases if they know too much.

Caregiver Stress

During episodes of illness, persons with HIV may need their family members to become caregivers. Family members may take over tasks for the person with HIV as that person's functioning and wellness vacillates, such as helping with legal and financial matters, procuring benefits and services, providing substantial emotional comfort, assisting with practical and logistical tasks (including personal care), and assisting in the maintenance of communication with others. Caregivers can be stressed as they try to address medical, financial, emotional, physical, and logistical needs. Caregiving can disrupt the normality regarding work, finances, housing, and relationships. Family members' emotional, financial, and physical well-being can be taxed as well (Leblanc, London, & Aneshensel, 1997; Wardlaw, 1994). HIV caregiving tends to negatively effect the caregiver's physical and emotional well-being, lessening the time he or she has to attend to health maintenance and stress management (LeBlanc, Pearlin, & Aneshensel, 1997; Stulberg, 1998).

HIV-affected relative caregivers tend to be female (Pequegnat & Stover, 1999) and/or midlife and older (Boyle, Ferrell, Hodnicki, & Muller, 1997; Nelms, 2000). Women and older persons tend to have multiple care responsibilities, and may be overburdened even though they are desirous of taking care of everyone in the family system. When a caregiver is also HIV-positive, particularly parents and/or partners, they report feeling increased stress, possibly due to concerns about their own uncertain health and futures, as well as fears that no one will be able to care for them (Folkman, Chesney, Cooke, Boccellari, & Collette, 1994; Mellins & Ehrhardt, 1994).

Multiple Losses and Grief

There are many sources of sorrow for the loved ones of persons with HIV. Family members might mourn the changing nature of their relationship with the sick person; developmentally unexpected losses and challenges; and the loss of the loved one's functioning, health, dreams, and future (Jankowski, Videka-Sherman, & Laquidara-Dickinson, 1996; Stulberg, 1998).

Many HIV-affected families have experienced or are anticipating multiple deaths (Wardlaw, 1994). When a child is diagnosed with HIV, the parents and other children may subsequently test positive as well (Reidy, Taggart, & Asselin, 1991; Wiener, 1998). When parents or grandparents are caring for HIV-infected or affected orphans, they are likely to already be grieving the death of a partner or adult child, as well as being intensely concerned for the health and future of the surviving minor children (Brabant, 1994; Joslin, 1995). The family's sense of well-being is permanently disrupted.

When families of choice are comprised of gay men or past or present drug users, there are often several people in the network who are HIV-infected. In these situations, when there are multiple infections in the care network, people may move between the roles of care recipient and caregiver. The burden of sadness in these networks may at times be unbearable.

Some HIV family members are serial caregivers, having provided HIV care to several friends or relatives (adults and/or children). These caregivers may be at high risk for burnout. Furthermore, when individuals and family members access HIV-related support services, they meet and get close to others whose lives are threatened or who are losing independence and facilities. It sometimes feels as if the accumulation of threat and loss is unbearable.

Meaning-Making and Spirituality

The above stressors are juxtaposed with increased meaning, strengthened relationships, enhanced spirituality, and personal growth as caregivers care for the person with HIV (Ayres, 2000; Carlisle, 2000; Davies & Stajduhar, 1998; Jankowski, Videka-Sherman, & Laquidara-Dickinson, 1996; Poindexter, 2001; Poindexter & Boyer, 2003; Reynolds & Alonzo, 1998; Ward & Brown, 1994; Wardlaw, 1994). Matters of the human spirit often become of great concern to HIV-affected families for two reasons. One, HIV challenges people to consider seriously the meaning and purpose of life and death. Two, families may be struggling with how to live with HIV within the framework of a formal religion that influences beliefs about disclosure, behavior, illness, death, gender roles, and rituals (Hoffman, 1996).

CONCERNS SPECIFIC TO GAY, LATIN, AND AFRICAN AMERICAN FAMILIES

In the U.S., African Americans, Latinos, and Gay men of all ethnic groups have been most heavily hit by HIV/AIDS. Some of the possible challenges of those family groups will now be highlighted. (Strengths of each group will be raised in the section on interventions.) Not only do these groups share a disproportionate burden of the pandemic, but the extreme oppression (racism, xenophobia, or homophobia) they have borne over time has exacerbated the effects of HIV, and vice versa.

Families of African Descent

From the beginning of the pandemic, people of African descent in the U.S. have been hugely disproportionately affected by HIV. Consistently, African Americans are 12% of the population, yet in 1982, a year after AIDS was documented, Blacks comprised 23% of the reported cases of AIDS. Now Blacks make up 40% of those with AIDS and 50% of those with HIV. Of the women with HIV in the U.S., 64% are Black (CDC, 2002).

HIV has furthered the incredible inequities faced by Blacks in the U.S. HIV has occurred within the historical context of forced violent immigration and enslavement, centuries of oppression and lynching, and continued punitive responses and victim blaming (Gant, 1996). In addition, the recent scientific evidence that HIV probably originated a century ago in Africa causes some people of African descent to resent the overt or covert implications of blame for the disease. Thus, when a social worker is addressing someone who has been raised in the U.S. and identifies African ancestry, it is counterproductive to ignore the probability of distrust, realistic paranoia, and increased desire for privacy. Faith-based organizations have acted as a double-edged sword, because individuals and caregivers have been able to find spiritual and emotional comfort there, but not necessarily the ability to be open about the presence of HIV (Gant, 1996; Poindexter, Linsk, & Warner, 1999). In addition, the general culture may render some people unseen and unheard, especially transgendered persons, sex workers, and men who have sex with men (Stewart, 2000).

Families of Latin and Central American Descent

Latins make up 13% of the U.S. population, but 19% of those with AIDS. As with all groups, it is dangerous to generalize about Latin communities because of the wide diversity of nationalities, origins, traditions, and cultures. Yet given that caveat, there are special barriers for many Latin families, who may be greatly concerned with lack of legal documentation, language and literacy barriers, length of residence, levels of acculturation and assimilation, unemployment, substandard housing, distrust of providers, poverty, and difficulty with accessing testing, services, and treatment (Paz, 2000). There is cultural hesitancy to seek support outside the extended circle of relatives, as well as a tendency to cope through spirituality and traditional curative practices rather than formal service systems (Abenis-Cintron, 1996; Lorenzo, 2002). There may be challenges related to discussing and practicing safer sex. Many Latinos and Latinas are aligned with Catholic doctrine, and thus may find it very problematic to negotiate condom use. Latin cultures tend to support homophobia; men may have sex with men but not openly identify as gay (Paz, 2000). Latin men who have sex with men may feel emotionally connected to their families of origin but may not be receiving support from them for their HIV-related challenges (Castro, Orozco, Aggleton, Eroza, & Hernandez, 1998).

Gay Male Families

AIDS was first identified in urban gay men who had access to physicians who could observe and report unusual infections and cancers. Gay men were among the hardest hit in the beginning, when there was no information about what caused the disease or how one was vulnerable, and there were no tests or treatments. Now men who have sex with men—including all ethnic groups and ages—are over 60% of the reported HIV incidence in the U.S. (CDC, 2002). The deaths in the gay community have been overwhelming, and the grief and burnout are legendary (Cad-well, 1998).

Homophobia predates the epidemic by centuries, but HIV has exacerbated its effects. Gay male couples, along with their extended families and children, suffer the double stigma of homophobia and HIV. HIV has greatly disrupted the normative development of gay men and their families over the last 2 decades. Gay partners are not easily accepted in the current political and cultural climate as "normal," or true families (Sipes, 2002; Wight, 2002). Nevertheless, gay male couples experience the same HIV-related stresses as anyone else, such as taking on caregiving tasks; learning to live with powerlessness, anger, fear, uncertainty, and grief; negotiating stigma, discrimination, and disclosure decisions; becoming educated about the complexities of HIV disease; maintaining relationships, hope, and communication; and making medical, pharmaceutical, and end-of-life decisions (Sipes, 2002). In addition, there may be some unique stressors for this group. Gay families often have a harder time accessing family-centered services, visiting loved ones in hospitals, getting time off work for caregiving or bereavement, or finding solace in their disenfranchised grief (Shernoff, 1997). Often gay men have a unique type of caregiving stress because they enter the caregiving role at a relatively young age and possibly less mature stage (Wight, 2002).

SOCIAL WORK RESPONSES

HIV-affected families of all configurations and origins need and deserve accessible supportive services from culturally competent professionals. McDonell, Abell, and Miller (1991) noticed that family members were more willing to provide HIV care when they had access to resources, social support, knowledge about HIV transmission, coping mechanisms, and ways to manage HIV stigma. Extrapolating implications from that list, it seems that social workers should strive to provide to families access to services and benefits, social networks, and information. They should assist them in honing their coping skills and competence, offer family counseling, and help them with decisions about disclosing the presence of HIV. Services are often formulated to focus on the person with HIV infection, as they should be. However, advocates, practitioners, and policy makers could better serve the person living with HIV if the family members were acknowledged, appreciated, and supported as well. Principles common across interventions are offered next, then specific supports vital in supporting HIV-affected families. Some vignettes as illustrations are included.

Practice Principles Common to All Interventions

Just as there are concerns in common to most HIV-affected families, there are social work principles common to all responses. They are awareness of HIV stigma, acknowledgment of the seriousness of HIV, assessment, strengths, allowing the family to self-define, cultural competence, and increasing access.

Stigma and Confidentiality

When a member of a family system discloses the presence of HIV, they are leaping across a dangerous chasm of fear, experience, and history to do so. The appropriate first response is to express your sense of honor and gratitude that you were trusted with this information. HIV-affected families are often extremely concerned about the maintenance of privacy and confidentiality, and the management of information. Social service providers cannot let down their guards in this regard. Social workers should explain confidentiality guidelines repeatedly, normalizing the family member's concerns about privacy, and help them problem-solve around difficult disclosure decisions. Practitioners should be even more careful than usual about asking permission to contact or involve anyone in someone's care (Babcock, 1998a).

Acknowledgment of HIV's Devastation

Whenever you discover that anyone—regardless of the relationship or setting—cares for or about someone with HIV, this should be a signal to acknowledge the inherent pain and struggle of the situation, invite the person to consider supportive counseling, and offer information about legal and benefits advocacy. Even if the person reports feeling balanced and in control in the moment, make a note to check in with them periodically, because that state of balance is sure to change. If you are working with a family—no matter what the presenting or prevailing issue is—if HIV is present, it should be acknowledged and dealt with as a family crisis. Even if the family of origin is currently estranged from the person with HIV, the specter of a stigmatized, infectious, life threatening disease is hovering over all the members of that system.

Assessment

A considered, individualized, enlightened, mutual ongoing assessment process—including both assets and needs—is vital in working with HIV-affected dyads and families. Wardlaw (1994) points out that it is difficult to generalize about what HIV-affected families may need because experiences vary so widely depending on the individual, the family, the culture, the resources available, and the disease course. In working with part of or all of a family system, especially a family of origin or extended family, assess and help them consider the following: beliefs, secrets, and overarching narratives; norms regarding relating, coupling, and parenting; gender, age, and caretaking roles; history of abuse or estrangement; patterns of communication; alliances and connections; scapegoating, conflicts, and disengagements; where they feel they are developmentally; boundary permeability within and outside the system; views of the family and each other; external pressures (finances and discrimination, for example), management of HIV stigma, and larger cultural identities. When working with gay male families, it is helpful to assess their history and comfort with disclosure of sexual orientation; the amount and nature of social support; and self-esteem and internalized homophobia (Cadwell, 1998; Derevenco & Frederick, 1999). Likewise, when working with families of African or Latin descent, consider how oppression and alienation is affecting their ability to access informal and formal support.

Strengths Perspective

Regardless of the struggles a family is experiencing, they have strengths. From assessment to termination, internal and external resources must be sought, acknowledged, and used. Rather than approaching families only with a deficit lens, we must also acknowledge their assets, resilience, and abilities. Anticipate that their core values may not be immediately or automatically evident to you, but they are there and are most likely allowing them to sustain themselves in the midst of intense stress. As you identify family and cultural values, align with the families in the use of these concepts to maximize support for the person with HIV and themselves. No matter how helpless and buffeted the family system feels in the face of the calamities of HIV, there are ways—however small—to regain some control. Help people to problem-solve, find ways to move and be active, adjust their expectations, and celebrate their successes. Remember that many families report a renewed sense of meaning and stronger connections within the crises of HIV; help them find and acknowledge those gifts.

Family Is Defined by the Family

It is important to refrain from assuming anything about what a family system is, who is included, or how they are affected. Many HIV-infected persons were estranged or alienated before HIV entered their lives—especially if they are transgendered, gay, addicted, sex workers, or incest survivors—and they already have an alternative network. Some persons are alienated from their relatives after they receive a diagnosis and must develop new families. Many have developed hybrid families, incorporating relatives as well as partner and friends (Wardlaw, 1994). A social worker serving persons with HIV may need to adjust his or her view to accommodate this broader definition. For instance, when the best friend of a person with HIV approaches a social worker for emotional or practical support around loving someone who is seriously ill, they should know that this is an HIV-affected family member, and guard against minimizing the emotional pain in that person's life.

In working with HIV-affected persons, not only will social workers need to accept who an individual defines as family, but to consider who the family system considers to be in the family. Questions such as these are appropriate: Who are your loved ones? Who is in your inner circle? Whom can you count on? Whom do you want to be involved in your care? Whom do you trust? There may be a "play sister" down the street who brings meals every day, an unrelated older woman who is involved in all family decision making, an unofficial foster son who is helping financially, a large strong network of gay friends who coordinate daily check-ins, or divorced parents who are together planning for the care of the person with HIV. You may find that fellow support group members are the only visitors to the hospital, that personal care is being given by a close-knit group of sex workers, or that a drug dealer has become the most dependable source of information about the ill person. The above scenarios are drawn from this author's personal experience. Never underestimate the power and significance of human connection in the midst of tragedy.

> Dee, a transgendered adolescent Black gay male, has been liv- ing on the street for several months. She sells sex periodically to pay for crack and food. When she collapses on the street one day, she is taken to an emergency room, admitted, and diag- nosed with AIDS-related pneumonia. Dee tells the social worker that she does not feel that she can reconnect with or access sup- port from her family of origin, who cut her off when she first be- gan acting on her transgendered identity. Because of her compromised health, she is concerned about living in doorways and in the cold weather. The foster care system proves to be a dead end, you can find no group homes to accept her, and homeless shelters are uncomfortable with the fact that she is male but living as a female. Dee and her family of choice—other homeless teenagers—figure out a way to set up housekeeping in a condemned building in the inner city, where they maintain in- termittent contact with you. Through their support, Dee is able to remain adherent to antiretroviral medication. When Dee be- comes incapacitated 2 years later, she is admitted to an HIV- related hospice facility, where she receives visits from her sup- port network until she dies.

Cultural Competence

Related to strengths-based practice is cultural competence. Cul- ture—a learned way of viewing and behaving in the world, that is held over time by a group of people—can encompass beliefs, norms, traditions, symbols, metaphors, artifacts, folklore, rituals, celebra- tions, art, dances, music, food, and apparel. Culture is often the way beliefs are organized (including those concerning wellness, illness, medication, medical care, and dying); moral, spiritual, and religious concepts are developed; ideas about gender, sexuality, parenting, and age are forged; behavior is structured; and life and death are made sense of. Culture also informs our notions about what is and is not a family, who should and should not be confided in, where and how help can be accessed, and who should care for the sick.

The economic, historical, and political realities of most ethnic groups comprise a double-edged sword because both major strengths and major strains are present: strengths that stem from their unique traditions, group identity and pride, and worldviews, and strains stemming from being misunderstood, marginalized, oppressed, and stigmatized. Because attitudes regarding affectional orientation, gender and family roles, disclosure of personal information, seeking help and medical treatment, and dealing with loss vary across cultural groups, it is vital that social workers strive to understand the specific beliefs and traditions of the HIV-affected person or family (Escobar, 1997; Weaver, 1999).

Cultural competence—or developing the skills to work with people from diverse backgrounds—is an ongoing journey, and it is not possible to fully arrive. Social workers must seek and acknowledge the multiple cultural identities within which people exist, guarding against thinking simplistically. As is the case with all social work skills, cultural competence is based on listening carefully and respectfully, eliciting necessary information, taking a strengths approach, working in partnership and collaboration, being reflexive about one's own biases, exploring the meaning that the beliefs and norms have in people's lives, and negotiating shared understanding and goals (Ka'opua, 1998). One can never take a "cookbook" approach to working with humans; it is not effective to use one's beginning knowledge of a culture to generalize those themes or norms to all individuals or families. Human beings are not easily categorized. Within all nationalities, ethnic groups, cultures, communities, and families, there is wide individual diversity. For the sake of discussion, people are categorized here, but bear in mind that people always occupy several groups at once and that it is always a mistake to believe that individuals, couples, and families can be understood only on the basis of membership in a community.

The dominant U.S. values of individualism and independence may not resonate with many cultures that are based on family and community cohesion and shared responsibility (Ka'opua, 2000, 2001; Murray-Johnson, 2001). Social workers should approach each person and family tentatively, without assumptions, and with the utmost respect for their possible fears about dishonoring the family, distrust of governmental or health authorities, adherence to non-Western or alternative medical treatments, and beliefs about the nature of illness, death, and the afterlife. Ask people how they identify and what that has to do with their self concept, beliefs, and decision making.

Sometimes workers see cultural values as barriers to getting things done; those same values can be pathways to success. Assess and use (but be careful not to overburden) already existing or naturally occurring informal support networks. Indigenous, faith-oriented, or self-help groups are either already providing HIV information and support, or they could be enlisted to do so (Gant, 1996). Cultural beliefs regarding faith and spirituality, interpersonal connections, family loyalty and unity, responsibility to others, traditional healing and health practices, health maintenance, group pride, and quality of life should not be seen only as impediments; they can be enlisted to positively influence adherence to pharmaceutical regimens and other healthful behavior changes (Baez, 1999; Escobar, 1997; Ka'opua, 2000; Stewart, 2000).

Recognize that additional stress can stem from differences between the family's health related beliefs and expectations of social service and health care professionals (Abenis-Cintron, 1996) and that adherence to medical care and protocols are heavily influenced by cultural beliefs and whether the social support system understands the need for treatment and supports the behavior change (Ka'opua, 2000). Finally, it is important when working with HIV-affected families, not to subscribe to the usual sexism and ageism that says it's the "job" of women and elders to provide this stressful care without support.

HIV disease itself can be viewed as a particular culture (Poindexter, 2000). Being confronted with HIV presents a family with a transformed worldview, a new and complicated language, and the necessity of rethinking previous notions of behavior, time, and support. Cultural competence does not only include considering the community, nation, region, or group with which the family identified before the diagnosis, but also this new confusing HIV world.

Increased Access to Services

HIV sometimes gets marginalized in the social service world. While specialized AIDS service organizations are vital, it is also imperative that every social worker and every agency be prepared to recognize, talk about, make referrals for, and support HIV-affected families. Organizations focusing on specific populations—whether based on immigrant status, ethnicity, religion, gender, age, identified problem, health status, or sexual orientation—must be prepared to address HIV. Sometimes services must be taken to where the family is. When the family system is in the midst of taking care of one or more persons impaired with HIV disease, it is very difficult to leave the home for services. In this circumstance, home visits for case management and counseling are required. Furthermore, services should be based in neighborhoods where the most highly affected families live. Agencies should offer language interpretation in addition to case managers fluent in the relevant languages, as well as information translated, back-translated, and checked that it makes sense culturally.

Community-based advocacy and service organizations are often well equipped to support HIV-affected families, because they are already trusted, connected, and culturally competent. However, they tend to have less access to traditional funding sources. This inequity can be addressed through targeted capacity-building programs, providing assistance with grant writing and fund development, and forming interagency and other collaborative efforts to strengthen the chances of gaining entry to foundations and government funders.

Specific Interventions

There are many services from which HIV-affected families may benefit; below are discussed some of the most common: individual, couple, and family counseling; case management, concrete services, and referrals; support groups; and bereavement support.

Individual Counseling Regarding the Family System

When working with HIV-positive individuals, it is useful to view them as members of a family system. Even if the person feels completely alone and without support, there is a network of some kind in his or her past that is influencing current feelings and thoughts. When a person with HIV—no matter their ethnicity, age, gender, skin color, affectional orientation, nationality, religion, or ability—seeks assistance with disclosing to his or her family and asking them for acceptance and support, the social worker should do careful mutual problem solving that takes into account family history and attitudes, cultural expectations and beliefs, and the individual's experiences and worries.

Sometimes a person with HIV requests counseling because the HIV diagnosis has dredged up painful issues regarding family dynamics or failures. Anger about histories of substance use, incest, abuse, neglect, and abandonment often threaten to consume the person with HIV when he or she is struggling to face the end of life. When a person is looking at a future of needing financial, emotional, or logistical support, it is often terrifying to consider asking an estranged or dysfunctional family for help. Giving up some autonomy to people who tend to be controlling and critical is frightening; needing care from those who once neglected or abused you sometimes feels like the worst possible fate. Sometimes a person with HIV seeks support or problem solving as they strive to reconnect with estranged members of the family of origin or choice—perhaps because his or her health has worsened, s/he needs more practical or personal assistance, or because s/he wishes to forgive or seek acceptance. A social worker can be a valuable partner in this very frightening process.

HIV counseling is often different from traditional counseling, that is, an organized set of acts carried out by a therapist. More likely there is more intense, continuous engagement, listening, and rapport building, with more fluid boundaries. In the face of intense suffering, social workers are called upon to be more present, accessible, and genuine than in more typical situations (Stewart, 2003).

> Gilda is a 27-year-old White woman who has just tested HIV-positive while in a drug treatment facility. The trauma of having HIV triggers overwhelming rage about the childhood she experienced with an alcoholic mother and abusive father. She becomes immobilized, obsessing about her unwillingness to rely on her parents as she gets sick. She feels that her recovery is in jeopardy because of her despair. She enters into individual counseling in order to have a safe place to talk about her anger and depression, with the goal of eventually being able to approach her family of origin with forgiveness and ask them for support and care.

Couples Counseling

Couples counseling should be offered to HIV-affected straight and gay partners. It is especially difficult for gay couples to find culturally competent counselors, so it is vital that social workers help them find appropriate resources. Partners often find that their shared experience, relationship goals and roles, and emotional well-being are greatly affected by the HIV diagnosis and roller coaster of HIV disease. Relationships may be disrupted, endangered, or destroyed. Sometimes when HIV enters the relationship after the couple has committed to a relationship, one member of the couple may blame the other. Sometimes couples who have previously separated reunite in order to provide care for one or both of them.

In counseling, the pre-HIV relationship, single and dual response to the diagnosis, and avoided topics should be explored. The couple may want to work on increasing trust, forgiveness, or empathy. They may want to find ways to negotiate decisions about legal issues, health care, safer sex, and end-of-life care. They may need to work on intimacy and over-caregiving issues, improve communication, deal with the management of stigma and disclosure, discuss relationships with families of origin, plan for the future of children, or mediate the stress that HIV has placed on their relationship (Remien & Smith, 1999; Shelby, 1998). In addition, individual counseling may be appropriate if one or both partners wish to talk about their unique sources of pressure or grief.

A form of couples counseling can be offered to a caregiver and care recipient even if they are not partners. Sometimes parents, children, siblings, or friends can benefit from dyadic counseling with the person with HIV so they can work on mutual empathy and communication.

Anna is a 65-year-old widowed Latina who requests counseling because she and her son Luis are experiencing much tension at home. Luis is a 40-year-old gay man who recently moved in with her when he became incapacitated with AIDS. Luis seems to be angry about dying, unwilling to connect with other people, and depressed over his loss of job, home, and independence. Anna experiences his alternate rages and withdrawals as hostile and frightening. After several individual counseling sessions, Anna begins to have more empathy for Luis's experiences and is able to engage in some constructive self-care. The social worker also offers in-home counseling to Luis, and he eagerly accepts. Anna and Luis move on to joint counseling, expressing their fears and sorrows to each other. They find they are able to listen and communicate better and are less reactive to each other.

Family Counseling for Coping and Adjustment

HIV-affected families may not seek traditional family therapy (Cates et al., 1990), because of stigma, shame, being engulfed with caregiving tasks, and the necessity of focusing primarily on the HIV-infected persons. They are probably in a crisis mode, not interested in examining their family dynamics or history. These families are often in need of resources, support, and advocacy, however, so it is the social worker's responsibility to develop and deliver more creative forms of family-centered intervention. Families often benefit from social work support to reduce their isolation, make decisions about disclosure and help-seeking, problem-solve around caregiving conflicts, incorporate painful emotions, access community resources that are acceptable to them, learn about HIV care, and improve family functioning (Mellins & Ehrhardt, 1994; Smith & Rapkin, 1996). Social workers can also help family members understand the importance of pharmaceutical and medical interventions, as well as complimentary health maintenance, and help them encourage their loved ones without nagging them or over-caretaking (Ka'opua, 2001). When a family member is ill with HIV, other members tend to think about end-of-life decisions and try to prepare for the possibility of death, even if the person with HIV is not desirous of discussing those eventualities with them (Stajduhar, 1997).

Case Management, Crisis Intervention, Concrete Services, and Referrals

Comprehensive case management that incorporates effective and timely crisis intervention, arranging for services and benefits, and making appropriate referrals is imperative for many families. Case management must be supportive, educational, empowering, and respectful. Case management helps people manage crises, stigma, illnesses, and medication adherence. Case managers coordinate service providers, provide information, and help people access legal services, medical care and medications, financial benefits, and religious support (Chernesky & Grube, 1999; Poindexter, 1997).

Often couples and family members will need referrals to attorneys to develop living wills, wills, and durable powers of attorney; to physicians to address their own health and stress concerns; to psychotherapists to address chronic or acute mental health concerns; and/or to pastoral counselors or clergy persons to talk about spiritual concerns. HIV-affected families often need practical assistance with child care, personal care, housekeeping, respite care, home health care, nutrition, transportation, benefits, and medical care. When the HIV-positive person is critically ill, loved ones may need assistance with accessing and managing insurance and public benefits, making decisions about care and treatment, advocating within service systems, broaching painful subjects with their ill loved one, and acknowledging fears and ideas about dying (Babcock, 1998b). Even when a family presents emotions or dynamics as the major concern, what environmental supports they might want to access in the present and future should be assessed. Recognize that caregivers are likely to be more concerned about the persons with HIV and likely to neglect their own physical and mental health. Social workers can gently suggest ways for the caregiver to stay healthy as well, facilitating linkages when they are ready.

Dave is a 42-year-old Jewish gay man who is estranged from his family of origin. His family of choice—his lover Carlos and a dozen friends—constitute a strong care network. They take turns stopping by to see him when he is ill, preparing meals and cleaning the house. Dave is uncomfortable accessing social services, but over time Dave becomes incontinent, bed-bound, and is in agonizing pain, and his lover and friends feel less able to take care of his personal needs. Feeling overwhelmed, Carlos calls a social service agency to request help with figuring out what to do. After a family conference with Dave, Carlos, and three close friends, a social worker helps them arrange for home health care, home delivered meals, and help with pain management.

Support Groups

Family members of adults and children with HIV often find much solace, social support, and practical benefit when they meet with their peers. They find validation and solutions as they speak of fear, grief, medical crises, child-rearing and caregiving challenges, stigma management, and anger. They share information on treatments and community resources, exchange tasks and visits, or arrange for telephone check-ins (Aronstein, 1998; Kreibick, 1993).

　　Note that HIV caregivers may be reluctant to join a group because of confidentiality concerns or may drop out because of lack of time, transportation, or child care; the death of the care recipient; or the overload of pain when hearing other people's stories (Crandles, Sussman, Berthaud, & Sunderland, 1992). Social workers should be sensitive to the fact that group experiences are not appropriate for everyone, but offer them and try to maximize their accessibility and benefit.

Bereavement Counseling

HIV at this time remains a life threatening incurable illness, so every HIV-infected family eventually faces the decline and death of their loved one. A family member can never be fully prepared for a terminal illness or death, no matter how many years they have known about the HIV diagnosis. Fearing the worst is one thing; having your worst fears confirmed is quite another. Because of funding restrictions, family members often lose social services when the person with HIV dies. It is important, however, that they access support for their grieving if they desire it. Bereavement support can be offered to individuals, couples, families, or groups.

Bereavement counseling can also be useful before the death of the ill person, because anticipatory grief can be overwhelming and debilitating. Loved ones are often peeling a metaphorical onion of sorrow. Loving someone with HIV is stressful in and of itself; providing financial or personal support constitutes another layer; and having several HIV caregiving experiences is a higher level. Grief overload or caregiving burnout should be looked for, and helping the person develop ways to stay afloat is important as well.

Kamya (2000) lists these possible concerns for family members in need of bereavement support: grief over past, present, or future losses; trauma concerning multiple losses; bewilderment over out-of-time losses; survivor guilt; meaning-seeking and spirituality; secret or disenfranchised grief; seeking healing and hope; and bereavement overload. Note that disenfranchised or secret grief—common with HIV—can lead to a more complicated bereavement. For example, men whose male spouses have died from HIV are at particular risk for unsuccessful or complicated bereavement. Their sadness is worsened by a lack of social support and acceptance of their loss. Gay widowers are likely to experience social isolation, depression, confusion, anger, and sorrow (Shernoff, 1997; Sowell, Bramlett, Gueldner, Gritzmacher, & Martin, 1991).

HIV-affected individuals and families are often comforted by finding ways to express—together and separately—what has been important about their lives together, how they want their time remembered, what might ease the dying; how to acknowledge lost dreams, hopes, and plans; and what is desired to mark the death. These are extraordinarily painful discussions for loved ones to have with each other, and it is common for people to avoid these subjects, even when they are close and accustomed to being able to talk about almost anything. Sometimes it is easier to confide wishes and fears to someone outside the family system; social workers sometimes assume the role of listener and facilitator. Often people will find a measure of solace or clarity through keeping journals, writing poetry, putting together scrapbooks, making audio or video tapes for children being left behind, writing letters expressing gratitude or love, planning the memorial service together, bequeathing significant objects and possessions; or deciding where memorial donations will be sent. HIV-positive parents can be encouraged to think about permanency planning for their children in the event of their disability or death, offering resources for legal and financial planning and helping to find second families (Taylor-Brown & Wiener, 2000). It is unrealistic to expect that all family systems will reach the point where real, honest, respectful conversations can occur regarding what members have meant to each other and how they want to be remembered, but to the extent that people can be helped toward this end, the less regret they have about things left unsaid or undone.

CONCLUSION

Readers may be left feeling helpless and overwhelmed, because HIV is not an easy issue to face. Yet I hope that the discussion of social work responses generates empowerment and activism, because that is the only antidote to this pandemic. This chapter cannot end without acknowledging the special intensity of this work, and urging self-care. When social workers enter the HIV arena—an extraordinarily intense, challenging, and sad field of practice—boundaries can become more fluid than formal training prepares one for. In the HIV field, social workers—whether HIV-negative or positive—meet colleagues, volunteers, advocates, and friends who have HIV, and in this way HIV enters your world in a personal way. Sometimes social workers become part of the family system, the care team for someone with HIV. In these circumstances, the social worker connects with, values, loses, and grieves for people with HIV. Professional distance is a myth. Losses must be acknowledged and addressed even when they occur within the work context.

REFERENCES

Abenis-Cintron, A. (1996). Stressors, coping strategies, and family adaptation of inner-city Latino caregivers with human immunodeficient children. *Dissertation Abstracts International: Section B: The Sciences & Engineering, 56*(9-B), 5156.

Aronstein, D. (1998). Organizing support groups for people affected by HIV. In D. M. Aronstein & B. J. Thompson (Eds.), *HIV and social work: A practitioner's guide* (pp. 293–302). New York: Haworth.

Ayres, L. (2000). Narratives of family caregiving: The process of making meaning. *Research in Nursing and Health, 23,* 424–434.

Babcock, J. (1998a). Involving families and significant others in acute care. In D. M. Aronstein & B. J. Thompson (Eds.), *HIV and social work: A practitioner's guide* (pp. 101–108). New York: Haworth.

Babcock, M. (1998b). Bereavement work in the acute care setting. In D. M. Aronstein & B. J. Thompson (Eds.), *HIV and social work: A practitioner's guide* (pp. 109–122). New York: Haworth.

Baez, E. (1999). Spiritual issues and HIV/AIDS in the Latino community. In M. Shernoff (Ed.), *AIDS and mental health practice: Clinical and policy issues* (pp. 117–124). New York: Haworth.

Boyle, J. S., Ferrell, J. A., Hodnicki, D. R., & Muller, R. B. (1997). Going home: African-American caregiving for adult children with human immunodeficiency virus disease. *Holistic Nursing Practice, 11*(2), 27–35.

Brabant, S. (1994). An overlooked AIDS affected population: The elderly parent as caregiver. *Journal of Gerontological Social Work, 22*(1/2), 131–145.

Brown, M. A., & Powell-Cope, G. (1993). Themes of loss and dying in caring for a family member with AIDS. *Residential Nursing Health, 16*(3), 179–191.

Cadwell, S. (1998). Providing services to gay men. In D. M. Aronstein & B. J. Thompson (Eds.), *HIV and social work: A practitioner's guide* (pp. 411–430). New York: Haworth.

Carlisle, C. (2000). The search for meaning in HIV and AIDS: The carers' experience. *Qualitative Health Research, 10*(6), 750–765.

Castro, R., Orozco, E., Aggleton, P., Eroza, E., & Hernandez, J. J. (1998). Family responses to HIV/AIDS in Mexico. *Social Science & Medicine, 47*(10), 1473–1484.

Cates, J. A., Graham, L. L., Boeglin, D., & Tielker, S. (1990). The effect of AIDS on the family system. *Families in Society: The Journal of Contemporary Human Services* (April), 195–201.

Centers for Disease Control and Prevention. (2002). *Division of HIV/AIDS Prevention, Basic Statistics*. Retrieved from www.cdc.gov.hiv/stats.htm

Chernesky, R. H., & Grube, B. (1999). HIV/AIDS case management: Views from the frontline. *Care Management Journals, 1*(1), 19–28.

Crandles, S., Sussman, A., Berthaud, M., & Sunderland, A. (1992). Development of a weekly support group for caregivers of children with HIV disease. *AIDS Care, 4*(3), 339–351.

Dane, B. O. (1991). Anticipatory mourning of middle-aged parents of adult children with AIDS. *Families in Society: The Journal of Contemporary Human Services* (February), 108–115.

Davies, B., & Stajduhar, K. I. (1998). Palliative care at home: Reflections on HIV/AIDS family caregiving experiences. *Journal of Palliative Care, 14*(2), 14–22.

Derevenco, M., & Frederick, R. (1999). Internalized homophobia in the psychotherapy of gay men with HIV/AIDS. In M. Shernoff (Ed.), *AIDS and mental health practice: Clinical and policy issues* (pp. 179–186). New York: Haworth.

Doka, J. D. (1989). *Disenfranchised grief*. New York: Lexington.

Escobar, E. E. (1997). Psychosocial themes in Latino families affected by AIDS. *Dissertation Abstracts International Section A: Humanities & Social Sciences, 57*(8-A), 3560.

Folkman, S., Chesney, M. A., Cooke, M., Boccellari, A., & Collette, L. (1994). Caregiver burden in HIV-positive and HIV-negative partners of men with AIDS. *Journal of Consulting and Clinical Psychology, 62*(4), 746–756.

Gant, L. M. (1996). HIV/AIDS caregivers in African-American communities: Contemporary issues. In V. J. Lynch & P. A. Wilson (Eds.), *Caring for the HIV/AIDS caregiver* (pp. 55–71). Westport, CT: Auburn House.

Gordon-Garofalo, V. (2000). Social work treatment with caregivers: Taking care of them so they can take care of their loved ones. In V. Lynch (Ed.), *HIV/AIDS at year 2000: A sourcebook for social workers* (pp. 107–122). Boston: Allyn and Bacon.

Herek, G. M., & Capitanio, J. P. (1993). Public reactions to AIDS in the United States: A second decade of stigma. *American Journal of Public Health, 83*(4), 574–577.

Hoffman, M. A. (1996). *Counseling clients with HIV disease: Assessment, intervention and prevention*. New York: Guilford Press.

Jankowski, S., Videka-Sherman, L., & Laquidara-Dickinson, K. (1996). Social support networks of confidants of people with AIDS. *Social Work, 41*(2), 206–312.

Joslin, D. (1995). Older adults as caregivers in the HIV/AIDS epidemic. *Coalition on AIDS in Passaic County Winter newsletter*. Wayne, NJ: Coalition on AIDS in Passaic County.

Kamya, H. (2000). Bereavement issues and spirituality. In V. Lynch (Ed.), *HIV/AIDS at year 2000: A sourcebook for social workers* (pp. 242–256). Boston: Allyn and Bacon.

Ka'opua, L. (1998). Multicultural competence. In D. M. Aronstein & B. J. Thompson (Eds.), *HIV and social work: A practitioner's guide* (pp. 51–64). New York: Haworth.

Ka'opua, L. S. (2000). Beliefs, support, and adherence to antiretroviral regimens among Hawaiians living with HIV. *Dissertation Abstracts International Section A: Humanities & Social Sciences, 61*(4-A), 1613.

Ka'opua, L. S. (2001). Treatment adherence to an antiretroviral regime: The lived experience of native Hawaiians and kokua. *Pacific Health Dialog, 8*(2), 290–334.

Kreibick, T. (1993). Caretakers' support group. In C. Levine (Ed.), *A death in the family: Orphans of the HIV epidemic.* New York: United Hospital Fund.

LeBlanc, A. J., London, A. S., & Aneshensel, C. S. (1997). The physical costs of AIDS caregiving. *Social Science Medicine, 45*(6), 915–923.

LeBlanc, A. J., Pearlin, L. I., & Aneshensel, C. S. (1997). The forms and mechanisms of stress proliferation: The case of AIDS caregivers. *Journal of Health and Social Behavior, 38*, 223–236.

Lorenzo, F. (2002) Bereavement issues to consider for Latino children whose parents die of AIDS. In R. Perez-Koenig & B. Rock (Eds.), *Social work in the era of devolution: Toward a just practice* (pp. 120–134). New York: Fordham University Press.

Matocha, L. K. (1992). Case study interviews: Caring for persons with AIDS. In J. F. Gilgun, K. Daly, & G. Handel (Eds.), *Qualitative methods in family research* (pp. 66–84). Newbury Park, NJ: Sage.

McDonell, J. R., Abell, N., & Miller, J. (1991). Family members' willingness to care for people with AIDS: A psychosocial assessment model. *Social Work, 36*(1), 43–53.

Mellins, C. A., & Ehrhardt, A. A. (1994). Families affected by pediatric Acquired Immunodeficiency Syndrome: Sources of stress and coping. *Journal of Developmental and Behavioral Pediatrics, 15*(3), S54–60.

Murray-Johnson, L. P. (2001). Addressing cultural orientations in fear appeals: Promoting AIDS-protective behaviors among Mexican immigrant and African American adolescents and American and Taiwanese college students. *Journal of Health Communication, 6*(4), 335–359.

National Association of Social Workers. (2000). *NASW Policy Statement: AIDS/HIV.* Washington, DC: Author.

National Center on Social Policy and Practice. (1991). *Beyond medicine: The social work response to the growing challenges of AIDS.* Washington, DC: National Association of Social Workers.

Nelms, T. P. (2000). The practices of mothering in caregiving an adult son with AIDS. *Advanced Nursing Science, 22*(3), 46–57.

Paz, J. (2000). Latinos and HIV. In V. Lynch (Ed.), *HIV/AIDS at year 2000: A sourcebook for social workers* (pp. 97–106). Boston: Allyn and Bacon.

Pequegnat, W., & Stover, E. (1999). Considering women's contextual and cultural issues in HIV/STD prevention research. *Cultural Diversity & Ethnic Minority Psychology, 5*(3), Special issue: HIV/AIDS and ethnic minority women, families, and communities, 287–291.

Piot, P. (2003, March). Speech to the 59th session of the United National Commission on Human Rights, Geneva, Switzerland.

Poindexter, C. (1997). In the aftermath: Serial crisis intervention with persons with HIV. *Health and Social Work, 22*(2), 125–132.

Poindexter, C. (2000). Common concerns: Social and psychological issues for persons with HIV. In V. Lynch (Ed.), *HIV/AIDS at the year 2000: A sourcebook for social workers* (pp. 178–187). Boston: Allyn & Bacon.

Poindexter, C. (2001). "I'm still blessed": The assets and needs of HIV-affected caregivers over fifty. *Families in Society: The Journal of Contemporary Human Services, 82*(5), 525–536.

Poindexter, C., & Boyer, N. C. (2003). Strains and gains of grandmothers raising children in the HIV pandemic. In B. Berkman & L. Harootyan (Eds.), *Social work and health care in an aging world: Informing education, policy, practice, and research* (pp. 227–244). New York: Springer Publishing.

Poindexter, C., Linsk, N., & Warner, S. (1999). "He listens . . . and never gossips": Spiritual coping without church support among older, predominantly African-American caregivers of persons with HIV. *Review of Religious Research, 40*(3), 230–243.

Powell-Cope, G. M., & Brown, M. A. (1992). Going public as an AIDS family caregiver. *Social Science Medicine, 34*(5), 571–580.

Reidy, M., Taggart, M. E., & Asselin, L. (1991). Psychosocial needs expressed by the natural caregivers of HIV infected children. *AIDS Care, 3*(3), 331–343.

Remien, R., & Smith, R. (1999). Couples of mixed HIV status: Therapeutic and policy issues. In M. Shernoff (Ed.), *AIDS and mental health practice: Clinical and policy issues* (pp. 265–284). New York: Haworth.

Reynolds, N. R., & Alonzo, A. A. (1998). HIV information caregiving: Emergent conflict and growth. *Research in Nursing and Health, 21,* 251–260.

Shelby, D. (1998). Disrupted dialogues: Working with couples. In D. M. Aronstein & B. J. Thompson (Eds.), *HIV and social work: A practitioner's guide* (pp. 183–202). New York: Haworth.

Shernoff, M. J. (1990). Why every social worker should be challenged by AIDS. *Social Work, 35*(1), 5–8.

Shernoff, M. (1997). *Gay widowers: Life after the death of a partner.* New York: Haworth Press.

Sipes, C. S. (2002). The experiences and relationships of gay male caregivers who provide care for their partners with AIDS. In B. J. Kramer & E. H. Thompson (Eds.), *Men as caregivers: Theory, research, and service implications* (pp. 151–189). New York: Springer Publishing.

Smith, M. Y., & Rapkin, B. D. (1996). Social support and barriers to family involvement in caregiving for persons with AIDS: Implications for patient education. *Patient Education and Counseling, 27*(1), 85–94.

Sowell, R. L., Bramlett, M. H., Gueldner, S. H., Gritzmacher, D., & Martin, G. (1991). The lived experience of survival and bereavement following the death of a lover from AIDS. *Image, 23*(2), 89–94.

Stajduhar, K. I. (1997). Loss and bereavement: HIV/AIDS family caregiving experiences. *Canadian Journal of Nursing Research, 29*(4), 73–86.

Stewart, P. (2000). HIV/AIDS issues among African Americans: Oppressed, gifted, and Black. In V. Lynch (Ed.), *HIV/AIDS at year 2000: A sourcebook for social workers* (pp. 50–65). Boston: Allyn and Bacon.

Stewart, P. (2003). Supportive counseling for women with HIV[?] In D. J. Gilbert & E. M. Wright (Eds.), *African-American woman and AIDS: Critical responses* (pp. 205–219). Westport, CT: Praeger.

Stulberg, I. (1998). Clinical issues for families. In D. M. Aronstein & B. J. Thompson (Eds.), *HIV and social work: A practitioner's guide* (pp. 223–246). New York: Haworth.

Taylor-Brown, S., & Wiener, L. (2000). Parents and their children: Planning in the face of uncertainty. In V. Lynch (Ed.), *HIV/AIDS at year 2000: A sourcebook for social workers* (pp. 66–78). Boston: Allyn and Bacon.

Walker, R. J., Pomeroy, E. C., McNeil, J. S., & Franklin, C. (1996). Anticipatory grief and AIDS: Strategies for intervening with caregivers. *Health and Social Work, 21*(1), 49–57.

Ward, D., & Brown, M. A. (1994). Labor and cost in AIDS family caregiving. *Western Journal of Nursing Residency, 16*(1), 10–25.

Wardlaw, L. A. (1994). Sustaining informal caregivers for persons with AIDS. *Families in Society: The Journal of Contemporary Human Services, 75*(6), 373–384.

Weaver, H. N. (1999). Through indigenous eyes: Native Americans and the HIV epidemic. *Health & Social Work, 24*(1), 27–34.

Wiener, L. (1998). Counseling parents and children with HIV. In D. M. Aronstein & B. J. Thompson (Eds.), *HIV and social work: A practitioner's guide* (pp. 315–326). New York: Haworth.

Wight, R. G. (2002). AIDS caregiving stress among HIV-infected men. In B. J. Kramer & E. H. Thompson (Eds.), *Men as caregivers: Theory, research, and service implications* (pp. 190–212). New York: Springer Publishing.

CHAPTER 16

Evidence-Based Marriage and Family Treatment With Problem Drinkers: A Multicultural Perspective

Meredith Hanson
Yvette M. Sealy

Alcoholism and other forms of problem drinking are health and social problems that affect members of all societal groups. It is estimated that 8 million people in the United States are alcohol dependent, and another 5.6 million people are alcohol abusers (Johnson, 2003). The enormity of these numbers suggests that either their own history of alcohol abuse, or that of a relative, has affected adversely at least 50% of all adults. For example, 25% of all children and adolescents have been exposed to the negative effects of alcohol use through contact with an alcoholic parent (Fromme & Kruse, 2003; Johnston, O'Malley, & Bachman, 2003; Windle, 2003). Approximately 50% of all clients seeking help from mental health professionals experience problems associated with their own drinking or that of a family member (Drake & Mueser, 1996). Well over two thirds of all social workers encounter clients with alcohol- or other drug-related problems (O'Neil, 2001).

The risk of developing alcohol-related difficulties is not the same for all population groups, and problem drinking has differential consequences for members of different cultural communities. National survey data reveal that among the four main ethnic minority groups in the U.S., both current drinking and heavy drinking are most prevalent among American Indians, Native Hawaiians, and Alaska Natives, and lowest among Asian Americans and Pacific Islanders. Hispanics and African Americans have problem drinking rates between these extremes, with Hispanics having higher problem rates than African Americans (National Institute on Alcohol Abuse and Alcoholism [NIAAA], 2002; Substance Abuse and Mental Health Services Administration [SAMHSA], 2003). Among adolescents, African Americans appear to have some of the lowest rates of alcohol problems, while Hispanic adolescents have some of the highest rates of heavy drinking.

Among all ethnic and cultural groups men drink more often than women, and they tend to consume larger quantities of alcohol when they drink (NIAAA, 2002; SAMSHA, 2003). The gap between the drinking rates of men and women has narrowed over the past 30 years (Morell, 1997; Straussner, 2001). Despite drinking less than men, women experience disproportionately more problems associated with drinking (Straussner & Zelvin, 1997).

Cultural norms and values are key determinants of the differences in drinking patterns among members of different communities. American Jews have lower rates of both abstinence and alcohol-related difficulties than do members of other cultural groups. African American and other Black women have higher rates of abstention than Caucasian women. Hispanic and Asian/ Pacific Islander women have even higher abstention rates than Black and Caucasian women. Within the Hispanic and Asian/ Pacific Islander culture traditional values discourage alcohol use by women. Although some women in these groups still consume alcohol, the quantity is usually lower than that consumed by women of other ethnic groups (Caetano, Clark, & Tam, 1998).

Age, degree of acculturation, marital status, and employment status also help to explain variations in drinking patterns. Young adults have the highest rates of alcohol consumption and problems associated with use. Employed women drink more frequently, but consume less alcohol than do unemployed women. Likewise, women with lower incomes drink less often than women of higher socioeconomic status, but drink more alcohol when they drink.

Married women and men tend to have lower rates of alcohol-related problems than unmarried women and men.

Findings about the association between acculturation and drinking patterns are mixed. In general, as members of ethnic minority groups become more acculturated to the "dominant" U.S. culture, their drinking patterns and problems seem to become more like those of this dominant culture. This seems to be the pattern among Asian immigrants, for example (Westermeyer, 1997). However, in some cases "acculturative stress" associated with language differences, poverty, loss of homeland, and racial discrimination may account for the higher levels of alcohol use among less acculturated individuals. Depression and anxiety are common psychological responses to stress, and excessive drinking may be an accompanying behavioral response (Caetano, 1987; Caetano et al., 1998; Randolph, Stroup-Benham, Black, & Markides, 1998).

TREATMENT FOR MEMBERS OF SPECIFIC ETHNIC AND CULTURAL GROUPS

Despite the fact that problem drinking has a differential impact on members of particular ethnic and cultural groups, with few exceptions, empirically supported interventions for drinking related problems have not been validated for different cultural and ethnic groups. Thus, the research literature provides little persuasive evidence that members of different cultural and ethnic communities either benefit or do not benefit from specific intervention approaches.

Two alcohol prevention programs and one treatment model have been evaluated to determine the effectiveness of culturally sensitive versions for the populations in question (NIAAA, 2002). Modified versions of the Strengthening Families Program (SFP) have been found to be effective in reducing family problems and alcohol use among urban and rural African Americans and urban Hispanics (Kumpfer, 1998). Likewise, a school-based Life Skills Training (LST) program designed to help adolescents cope with social pressures to drink and use other drugs has been modified to take into account the cultural heritages of inner-city African American and Hispanic youth. Researchers found that, although both the standard LST program and the modified version yielded significant decreases in drinking by Hispanic and African American youth, participation in the modified program was associated with a significantly greater reduction in drinking (Botvin et al., 1995). A version of the Community Reinforcement Approach (CRA), a well validated alcoholism treatment package that is designed to alter environmental and family contingencies that reinforce and sustain drinking behaviors (Meyers & Miller, 2001), was modified to include American Indian traditions. The modified version was found to be successful in helping Navajos in New Mexico achieve abstinence (Miller, Meyers & Hiller-Sturmhofel, 1999; NIAAA, 2002).

The small number of validated culturally sensitive treatment approaches for people affected by alcohol problems has led many experts to call for more research and understanding of the impact of family and community values on alcohol use and treatment seeking (e.g., Yalisove, 2004). Others have proposed clinically derived treatment approaches for members of specific ethnic groups (e.g., Amodeo, Robb, Peou, & Tran, 1996). Still others have called for a greater awareness of practical, attitudinal, and other barriers that may limit access to treatment by members of different cultural and social groups (e.g., Durrant & Thakker, 2003). Each of these arguments has merit. We suggest that, in addition, social workers should use an evidence-based practice (EBP) paradigm to adapt existing empirically validated treatment approaches so that they are more responsive to the needs, circumstances, and value preferences of members of specific cultural and ethnic communities.

EVIDENCE-BASED PRACTICE

Evidence-based practice (EBP), developed initially in medicine as "a new paradigm for . . . practice" in the early 1990s (Evidence-Based Medicine Working Group, 1992), has spread rapidly to other human service and health fields. According to Kirk and Reid (2002), EBP (what they refer to as research-based practice) represents a culmination of the influence of science on direct social work practice. EBP complements Epstein's (2001) notion of practice-based research (PBR) in which "research-inspired principles" and tactics are used "within existing forms of practice to answer questions that emerge from practice in ways that inform practice" (p. 17).

The most widely disseminated definition of EBP is that it involves a practitioner using clinical expertise and experience to blend the best external research evidence, client values and preferences, and clinical state and conditions to make practice decisions (Gambrill, 2003; Haynes, Devereaux, & Guyatt, 2002; Sackett et al., 2000). It is a collaborative approach to social work practice in which clients and practitioners (and often other concerned constituents) share decision-making power.

Two fundamental principles guide EBP. First, "evidence" may be drawn from any empirical observation about the relation between events. As such, evidence is hierarchical ranging from unsystematic observations extracted from clinical experience to systematic reviews of controlled clinical trials and "randomized controlled trials" of particular interventions with specific clients (Guyatt et al., 2000; Guyatt et al., 2002). Second, evidence by itself is never sufficient to make clinical decisions (Guyatt et al., 2002). Clinical judgments should reflect not only the best available evidence, but also personal, professional, and societal values and resources. As Haynes and colleagues (1996) argue, in particular practice situations client preferences, as well as clinical expertise and constraints, may override the best evidence from systematic research findings. McNeece and Thyer (2004) suggest more forcefully that once a practitioner presents a client with information about the costs and benefits of different intervention options, the final decision on how to proceed rests with the client.

An evidence-based approach to decision making in practice involves five steps (Cournoyer, 2004; Sackett et al., 2000):

(1) Problems and challenges that emerge in practice are transformed into searchable questions about a client's condition, intervention options, and/or prognosis. The questions should be client- and problem/need-focused. They must be specific enough to yield useful information about what social workers can do to help their clients achieve the outcomes they desire.

(2) Using key words and other sources a social worker searches the literature (e.g., journals, bibliographic databases, and books) to locate evidence for effective interventions that address the questions posed in the first step. A key aspect of this step is

determining the type of evidence needed to answer the questions. While many authorities suggest that systematic reviews of controlled clinical trials provide the best evidence for evaluating intervention related questions (e.g., Gray, 2004), other sources of evidence, including systematic case studies, may also provide valuable information (e.g., Epstein, 2001; Nathan, 2004).

(3)   Once relevant literature has been located a social worker must evaluate the quality of the evidence. The validity of the findings—especially their generalizability—must be determined. In addition, the clinical significance and utility of the findings must be assessed. Over and above the statistical significance of the findings, practitioners must determine if effect size is large enough to have clinical meaning and if interventions are described precisely enough to be replicated in practice (e.g., Cournoyer, 2004; Edwards & Steinglass, 1995).

(4)   When social workers have located evidence that is valid and meaningful, while fitting the constraints of their practice situations, they should discuss the evidence and various options with clients. This is the point where clinical expertise may be most crucial as social workers help clients arrive at informed decisions and as they tune into clients' preferences and concerns. It is in applying the best evidence in their practice that skilled clinicians use their expertise and experience to adapt the evidence and to improve its "goodness of fit" with clients' preferences and beliefs, their clinical conditions, and the practice contexts (e.g., Nock, Goldman, Wang, & Albane, 2004).

(5)   The final step in the process involves social workers evaluating the effectiveness of an evidence-based intervention with particular clients. As Cournoyer (2004) observes, "by itself, nomothetic information is insufficient. [One] also require[s] ideographic evidence that . . . practices are effective for the clients . . . actually serve[d]" (p. 187). Social workers may use single-system designs, standardized evaluation tools, and/or group designs to make this determination. The central idea from an EBP perspective is that ultimately the utility of any evidence is based on its relevance for particular practice situations.

FAMILY INVOLVEMENT IN ALCOHOLISM
TREATMENT: AN EVIDENCE-BASED APPROACH

Over the past half century the weight of the empirical evidence and comprehensive reviews of the alcohol treatment literature suggest that family and social network involvement are associated with beneficial treatment outcomes (e.g., Copello & Orford, 2002; Corcoran & Thomas, 2000; Edwards & Steinglass, 1995; McCrady, 1989; Meyers & Miller, 2001; Miller & Wilbourne, 2002; Miller, Wilbourne, & Hettema, 2003; O'Farrell, 1993; O'Farrell & Fals-Stewart, 2003; Smith & Meyers, 2004; Steinglass, 1976; Vaughn & Howard, 2004). The evidence seems strongest for involving family members to engage problem drinkers, especially unmotivated ones, into treatment (Edwards & Steinglass, 1995; O'Farrell & Fals-Stewart, 2003; Smith & Meyers, 2004). Interventions to teach effective communication and problem-solving skills also seem useful in reducing the overall level of family stress and problem drinking once a drinker has entered treatment (Edwards & Steinglass, 1995; Miller et al., 2003; O'Farrell & Fals-Stewart, 2003). Finally, multidimensional family treatment, which includes interventions aimed at improving parent-child communication and parental understanding of adolescent substance use, has been found to be among the most effective treatments for adolescent substance abuse (Vaughn & Howard, 2004).

While family involvement in the therapeutic process is beneficial, its impact "is differentially felt" (Edwards & Steinglass, 1995). First, outcomes are somewhat better when men are the problem drinkers than when women have the drinking problems. Second, outcomes are more positive when family members have greater social and emotional investment in their relationships. Third, when family members agree that drinking is a problem that must be addressed and they are supportive of treatment their involvement is more helpful. Fourth, a family member's own substance abuse problem limits her/his ability to help another person resolve an alcohol-related problem. Finally, a history of domestic violence should preclude involving a spouse to engage an unresponsive problem drinker (e.g., Thomas & Agar, 1993).

Although none of the reviews cited above address cultural and ethnic factors systematically, by adopting an EBP perspective social workers can use their findings to assist members of different cultural groups. A case example is informative.

Engaging an "Unmotivated" Problem Drinker

A 40-year-old Puerto Rican woman (Concerned Spouse, CS) sought the assistance of a social worker in a mental health clinic. According to the CS, her husband, a 42-year-old clerical worker, drank heavily, often spending his paycheck on drinking. The CS said that her husband drank to intoxication about three to four times per week, he missed work due to drinking, he was in danger of losing his job, and he had begun to drink in the mornings before breakfast. As a result, the family was behind in its bills. In addition, the couple's teenage children were embarrassed by their father's behavior. They rarely brought friends home, and their schoolwork was suffering. The CS said that she felt distressed, "I don't talk to my friends as much. I also do not like to call his job and say he is sick because he is hung-over." The CS added that her husband did not believe that he had a drinking problem and that they argued frequently about the drinking.

The CS sought professional help before only to be told by a counselor that she was "co-dependent" and overly concerned about the drinking. The counselor advised her to give her husband some literature on alcoholism and let him decide whether or not to seek treatment. The CS said she took this advice, which only angered her husband more. She also expressed amazement that someone would think that her concern about her family was a problem (i.e., that she was codependent). She asserted, "I have a responsibility for my family. That is the way I was raised." The social worker believed that it was apparent from the CS's response that the counselor had not fully assessed her cultural values relative to her role in the family (e.g., "I have a responsibility for my family. That is the way I was raised."). Further, the CS should not have been advised to disengage and provide her husband with alcoholism literature without additional assessment and discussion about this strategy.

The social worker completed a social history and assessment and determined that the CS was very committed to her marriage and family ("I love my husband and children. Leaving my husband is not an option."), that she had no history of substance abuse, that she had a strong support network (family, friends, and church), and that there was no history of physical family violence ("We argue, but my husband has never threatened the children or me. When he drinks, he withdraws into his own shell.").

The social worker scheduled a follow-up meeting with the CS to discuss different intervention options.

Transforming the Problem Into Searchable Questions

Transforming the problem encountered in this case situation into searchable questions requires a social worker to include words or phrases like "family member," "spouse," "unmotivated," "uncooperative," "reluctant," "engage," "problem drinker," and/or "alcoholic" in the questions. Two searchable questions are: "What, if any, intervention strategies are effective in working with spouses to engage unmotivated problem drinkers into treatment?" "What types of spousal interventions—such as making demands or using less harsh responses—are most helpful in engaging reluctant alcoholics into treatment?"

Conducting a Literature Search

A hierarchical conception of evidence suggests that professionals should determine first if systematic reviews of the research literature, including reviews of controlled clinical trials, exist (Gray, 2004; Guyatt et al., 2000). Fortunately, a number of systematic reviews examine research on family involvement to engage reluctant or uncooperative problem drinkers (e.g., Edwards & Steinglass, 1995; O'Farrell & Fals-Stewart, 2003; Smith & Meyers, 2004).

Edwards and Steinglass (1995) conclude that family involvement is very effective in motivating problem drinkers to enter treatment and possibly reduce their alcohol consumption even before they enter formal treatment. O'Farrell and Fals-Stewart's (2003) analysis of 10 controlled studies involving "unmotivated" drinkers supports this conclusion. They add that coping skills training aimed at helping concerned family members understand their own motivations and disengage from the problem drinker's behavior, Al Anon involvement, and strategies to promote change in the drinker's behavior have all led to reduced emotional distress among concerned family members (see also, Smith & Meyers, 2004; Thomas, 1994; Thomas & Agar, 1993).

O'Farrell and Fals-Stewart (2003) found that approaches that relied on more aggressive confrontation by family members did not fare well in two systematic studies (Liepman, Nirenberg, & Begin, 1989; Miller, Meyers, & Tonigan, 1999). While most of the family members who completed the intervention training succeeded in getting problem drinkers into treatment, less than one third of the families completed the training. Loneck and colleagues (1996), who also studied this type of "hard" confrontational method, found similar results, but added that even when they entered treatment the drinkers did not necessarily complete it or benefit from it (see also, Miller, Meyers, & Tonigan, 1999). In a related study, Loneck and colleagues (1995) found that a focus on the negative impact of drinking on family members and concerned others (rather than on the drinker) was indirectly associated with acceptance of treatment by the drinker.

Although controlled clinical trials usually do not examine the differential contribution of treatment components on outcome, an examination of the studies cited above, as well as other literature (e.g., Smith & Meyers, 2004; Thomas & Agar, 1993), suggests that social workers who wish to involve family members to help problem drinkers enter treatment should target the following areas:

(1) Family members must be educated about the nature of alcoholism and problem drinking so that they can understand more fully the factors that contribute to excessive drinking and that may impede cessation of drinking.

(2) Social workers should focus not only on the drinker's behaviors but also on the family members themselves. Effective family interventions help family members to disengage somewhat from the drinker and his/her behaviors, find other social supports (e.g., Al Anon group involvement; family support), and enrich their own lives (e.g., engaging in hobbies and activities that they enjoy, which they may have discontinued due to the drinker's behavior).

(3) Successful interventions help family members learn how to communicate their concerns to problem drinkers more effectively, while at the same time communicating their love and support (e.g., learning assertiveness and conflict resolution skills).

(4) Family members must be helped to learn how to give positive feedback for desirable (e.g., sober) behavior, rather than responding only to the drinking behavior (e.g., through nagging and complaining behavior).

Evaluating the Quality and Clinical Utility of the Evidence

Family involvement studies generally have not been examined to determine the differential benefit of family involvement to engage problem drinkers from different ethnic and community groups. Many of the study samples have been ethnically diverse, however, and none of the studies have reported differential findings associated with ethnicity. For example, Hispanic persons made up over one third of the sample in one study, and ethnicity was not a factor that affected outcome (Miller, Meyers, & Tonigan, 1999).

Two approaches that involve family members to engage reluctant problem drinkers have described interventions sufficiently to enhance their clinical utility; these are Community Reinforcement Approach and Family Treatment (CRAFT; Smith & Meyers, 2004) and Unilateral Family Therapy (Thomas, 1994; Thomas & Agar, 1993; Thomas & Santa, 1982). The developers of CRAFT have produced a highly practical treatment manual that thoroughly describes intervention responses, includes treatment forms and scales, and provides case illustrations, making the approach readily replicable and adaptable to client preferences and the constraints of practice situations.

Discussing the Evidence and Intervention Options With Clients

Once the social worker has completed an examination of the evidence, she must discuss the findings and different intervention options with the client. In the case situation presented above the social worker can feel confident in informing the CS that there are ways she can be assisted and that Hispanic individuals have found them to be useful (e.g., in the case of CRAFT). It will be important to underscore with the CS the time commitment involved (10–12 meetings), her responsibilities, and changes she may need to make (e.g., disengaging from her husband a little and focusing on other aspects of her life; learning new ways to speak with her husband). The social worker may also discuss the more aggressive confrontational approaches that have been evaluated. Although outcomes with these latter approaches have not been as positive as with less aggressive approaches, it may be important for the CS to have this information in making her decision and in understanding why some of her past responses to her husband's drinking have not produced the results she desired. The outcomes the CS can expect include less familial stress, her husband considering treatment, and changes in his drinking pattern.

In discussing intervention options with the CS, the social worker must be mindful of the values, beliefs, and cultural practices that are prominent in Puerto Rican communities. As was pointed out in the case example (p. 346), the first counselor apparently was not sensitive to these values and practices. Consequently, the CS may have been alienated from the helping process and the intervention strategy, itself, did not seem to be appropriate. The social worker must strive to understand the specific value preferences, wishes, and circumstances of the CS. The CS's strong commitment to her family, which is consistent with Puerto Rican values and traditions, is an important factor that will help her sustain her efforts. The importance of family, one's responsibility to family, and the adverse impact of the husband's drinking behavior on his family may also be important factors to emphasize in efforts to mobilize him to seek assistance. Discussion with the CS should explore social supports that are available and acceptable (e.g., her church). It also should examine communication styles and discussion topics that the CS is willing to undertake with her husband.

Evaluating the Intervention's Effectiveness With Particular Clients

When the social worker evaluates the intervention's effectiveness, she must keep in mind the multiple targets of family intervention. Although the presenting concern was the husband's drinking, other intervention targets include family stress (as reflected in the CS's statements and the children's behavior) and the CS's behavior (changes in communication patterns; her efforts to disengage and enrich her life). Each of these areas should be examined to ascertain the intervention's impact. The most desirable outcome would be that the husband entered treatment and eliminated the drinking problem. However, even if this outcome were not attained, intervention could be successful if the CS's stress was lowered, family functioning improved, and the family members learned more adaptive ways to live with a problem drinker.

The success of family involvement can be measured by examining whether or not the CS completes the treatment. In addition, by using a single-case study design with baseline and follow-up behavioral measures, scales to measure mood and distress, and clinical observation, a social worker can determine the extent to which target goals are reached. As she uses similar family interventions with other clients, a social worker can also draw on aggregate data to assess the value of family involvement with her clients.

CONCLUSION

In this chapter we have illustrated how an evidence-based practice paradigm can be used to assist families that are experiencing alcohol-related difficulties. While the specific case example applied the EBP paradigm to family involvement to motivate a reluctant problem drinker to enter treatment, EBP principles are equally applicable to marriage and family treatment once a problem drinker has entered treatment, and to situations involving adolescent substance abuse.

Marriage and family treatment to assist people with drinking problems generally have not been validated for members of particular ethnic and cultural groups. Thus, we do not know if they are particularly beneficial for members of different communities or if they are contraindicated. Until more research is conducted to assess the effectiveness of family involvement in the treatment of drinking problems in different ethnic and cultural groups, it is probably wise to use approaches that have general evidence of efficacy with the assumption that these approaches are most likely to generalize.

When using validated treatment approaches it is critical for social workers to be culturally sensitive. That is, they must be aware of values, beliefs, norms, and practices that characterize different ethnic communities, both in terms of alcohol consumption and in terms of marital and family roles and responsibilities. In addition, social workers must clarify how cultural and community norms are experienced by the clients with whom they are working. By appreciating the views, beliefs, and preferences of their clients and demonstrating a genuine interest in those preferences, social workers will be in position to adapt empirically validated treatments to the needs and circumstances of clients from all ethnic and cultural groups. Responsible professional practice requires the use of empirically sound intervention options. It also requires social workers to work collaboratively with clients to help them select intervention options that not only have the best prospects of success but also are acceptable to them.

REFERENCES

Amodeo, M., Robb, N., Peou, S., & Tran, H. (1996). Adapting mainstream substance-abuse interventions for Southeast Asian clients. *Families in Society*, 77, 403–413.

Botvin, G. J., Schinke, S. P., Epstein, J. A., Diaz, T., & Botvin, E. M. (1995). Effectiveness of culturally focused and generic skills training approaches to alcohol and abuse prevention among minority adolescents: Two-year follow-up results. *Psychology of Addictive Behaviors*, 9, 183–194.

Caetano, R. (1987). Alcohol use and depression among U.S. Hispanics. *British Journal of Addiction*, 82, 1245–1251.

Caetano, R., Clark, C. L., & Tam, T. (1998). Alcohol consumption among racial/ethnic minorities: Theory and research. *Alcohol Health & Research World*, 22(4), 233–238.

Copello, A., & Orford, J. (2002). Addiction and the family: Is it time for services to take Notice of the evidence? [Editorial]. *Addiction*, 97, 1361–1363.

Corcoran, J., & Thomas, C. (2000). Family treatment with adult substance abuse. In J. Corcoran (Ed.), *Evidence-based social work practice with families: A lifespan approach* (pp. 369–394). New York: Springer Publishing.

Cournoyer, B. R. (2004). *The evidence-based social work skills book*. Boston: Allyn and Bacon.

Drake, R. E., & Mueser, K. T. (1996). Alcohol-use disorders and severe mental illness. *Alcohol Health and Research World*, 20(2), 87–93.

Durrant, R., & Thakker, J. (2003). *Substance use and abuse: Cultural and historical perspectives*. Thousand Oaks, CA: Sage.

Edwards, M. E., & Steinglass, P. (1995). Family therapy treatment outcomes for alcoholism. *Journal of Marital and Family Therapy*, 21, 475–509.

Epstein I. (2001). Using available clinical information in practice-based research: Mining for silver while dreaming of gold. In I. Epstein & S. Blumenfield (Eds.), *Clinical data-mining in practice-based research* (pp. 15–32). New York: Haworth Press.

Evidence-Based Medicine Working Group. (1992). Evidence-based medicine: A new approach to teaching the practice of medicine. *Journal of the American Medical Association*, 268, 2420–2425.

Fromme, K., & Kruse, M. (2003). Socio-cultural and individual influences on alcohol use and abuse by adolescent and young adults. In B. Johnson, P. Ruiz, & M. Galanter (Eds.), *Handbook of clinical alcoholism treatment* (pp. 26–36). Philadelphia, PA: Lippincott Williams & Wilkins.

Gambrill, E. (2003). Evidence-based practice: Sea change or the emperor's new clothes? [Editorial]. *Journal of Social Work Education, 39,* 3–23.

Gray, G. E. (2004). *Concise guide to evidence-based psychiatry.* Washington, DC: American Psychiatric Publishing, Inc.

Guyatt, G. H., Haynes, R. B., Jaeschke, R. Z., Cook, D. J., Green, L., Naylor, C. D., et al. (2000). Users' guide to the medical literature XXV: Evidence-based medicine: Principles for applying the users' guides to patient care. *Journal of the American Medical Association, 284,* 1290–1296.

Guyatt, G., Haynes, B., Jaeschke, R., Cook, D., Greenhalgh, T., Meade, M., et al. (2002). Introduction: The philosophy of evidence-based medicine. In G. Guyatt & D. Rennie (Eds.), *Users guides to the medical literature: A manual for evidence-based clinical practice* (pp. 3–12). Chicago: AMA Press.

Haynes, R. B., Devereaux, P. J., & Guyatt, G. H. (2002). Physicians' and patients' choices in evidence based practice. [Editorial]. *British Medical Journal, 324,* 1350.

Haynes, R. B., Sackett, D. L., Gray, T. M., Cook, D. J., & Guyatt, G. H. (1996). Transferring evidence from research to practice: 1. The role of clinical care research evidence in clinical decisions. [Editorial]. *ACP Journal Club, 125*(3), A14, 1–4.

Johnson, B. (2003). Epidemiology of alcoholism. In B. Johnson, P. Ruiz, & M. Galanter (Eds.), *Handbook of clinical alcoholism treatment* (pp. 2–9). Philadelphia: Lippincott Williams & Wilkins.

Johnston, L. D., O'Malley, P. M., & Bachman, J. G. (2003). *Monitoring the future national survey results on drug use, 1975–2002: Vol II. College students and young adults ages 19–40.* (NIH Pub, No. 03-5376). Bethesda, MD: National Institute of Drug Abuse.

Kirk, S. A., & Reid, W. J. (2002). *Science and social work: A critical appraisal.* New York: Columbia University Press.

Kumpfer, K. L. (1998). Selective prevention interventions: The Strengthening Families Program. In R. S. Ashery, E. B. Robinson, & K. L. Kumpfer (Eds.), *Drug abuse prevention through family interventions* (NIDA Research Monograph 177, pp. 160–207). Rockville, MD: National Institute on Drug Abuse.

Liepman, M. R., Nirenberg, T. D., & Begin, A. M. (1989). Evaluation of a program designed to help family and significant others to motivate resistant alcoholics into recovery. *American Journal of Drug and Alcohol Abuse, 15,* 209–221.

Loneck, B. M., Banks, S. M., Coulton, C. J., Kola, L. A., Holland, T. P., & Gerson, S. N. (1995). Stress and outcome in the alcoholism intervention: A preliminary investigation. *Alcoholism Treatment Quarterly, 13*(2), 33–42.

Loneck, B. M., Garrett, J. A., & Banks, S. M. (1996). A comparison of the Johnson Intervention with four other methods of referral to outpatient treatment. *American Journal of Drug and Alcohol Abuse, 22,* 233–246.

McCrady, B. S. (1989). Outcomes of family-involved alcoholism treatment. In M. Galanter (Ed.), *Recent developments in alcoholism: Treatment research* (Vol. 7, pp. 165–182). New York: Plenum.

McNeece, C. A., & Thyer, B. A. (2004). Evidence-based practice and social work. *Journal of Evidence-Based Social Work, 1*(1), 7–25.

Meyers, R. J., & Miller, W. R. (Eds.). (2001). *A community reinforcement approach to addiction treatment.* New York: Cambridge University Press.

Miller, W. R., Meyers, R. J., & Hiller-Sturmhofel, S. (1999). The community reinforcement approach. *Alcohol Research and Health, 23*(2), 116–121.

Miller, W. R., Meyers, R. J., & Tonigan, J. S. (1999). Engaging the unmotivated in treatment for alcohol problems: A comparison of three strategies of intervention through family members. *Journal of Consulting and Clinical Psychology, 67,* 688–697.

Miller, W. R., & Wilbourne, P. (2002). Mesa Grande: A methodological analysis of clinical trials of treatments for alcohol use disorders. *Addiction, 97,* 265–277.

Miller, W. R., Wilbourne, P. L., & Hettema, J. E. (2003). What works? A summary of alcohol outcome research. In R. K. Hester & W. R. Miller (Eds.), *Handbook of alcoholism treatment approaches: Effective alternatives* (3rd ed., pp. 13–63). Boston: Allyn and Bacon.

Morell, C. (1997). Women with depression and substance abuse problems. In S. L. A. Straussner & E. Zelvin (Eds.), *Gender and addictions* (pp. 223–242). Northvale, NJ: Aronson.

Nathan, P. E. (2004). The evidence base for evidence-based mental health treatments: Four continuing controversies. *Brief Treatment and Crisis Intervention, 4,* 243–254.

National Institute on Alcohol Abuse and Alcoholism. (2002). Alcohol and minorities: An update. *Alcohol Alert, 55,* 1–4.

Nock, M. K., Goldman, J. L., Wang, Y., & Albano, A. M. (2004). From science to practice: The flexible use of evidence-based treatments in clinical settings. *Journal of the American Academy of Child and Adolescent Psychiatry, 43,* 777–780.

O'Farrell, T. J. (Ed.). (1993). *Treating alcohol problems: Marital and family interventions.* New York: Guilford Press.

O'Farrell, T. J., & Fals-Stewart, W. (2003). Marital and family therapy. In R. K. Hester & W. R. Miller (Eds.), *Handbook of alcoholism treatment approaches: Effective alternatives* (3rd ed., pp. 188–212). Boston: Allyn and Bacon.

O'Neil, J. V. (2001, January). Expertise in addictions said crucial. *NASW News,* p. 1.

Randolph, W. M., Stroup-Benham, C., Black, S. A., & Markides, K. S. (1998). Alcohol use among Cuban-Americans, Mexican-Americans, and Puerto Ricans. *Alcohol Health & Research World, 22*(4), 265–269.

Sackett, D. L., Straus, S. E., Richardson, W. S., Rosenberg, W., & Haynes, R. B. (2000). *Evidence-based medicine: How to practice and teach EBM* (2nd ed.). London: Churchill Livingstone.

Smith, J. E., & Meyers, R. J. (2004). *Motivating substance abusers to enter treatment: Working with family members.* New York: Guilford Press.

Steinglass, P. (1976). Experimenting with family treatment approaches to alcoholism, 1950–1975: A review. *Family Process, 15,* 97–123.

Straussner, S. L. A. (2001). Ethnocultural issues in substance abuse treatment: An overview. In S. L. A. Straussner (Ed.), *Ethnocultural factors in substance abuse treatment* (pp. 3–28). New York: Guilford Press.

Straussner, S. L. A., & Zelvin, E. (Eds.). (1997). *Gender and addiction.* Northvale, NJ: Aronson.

Substance Abuse and Mental Health Services Administration. (2003). *Overview of findings from the 2002 National Survey on Drug Use and Health.* Office of Applied Studies, NHSDA Series H-21, DHHS Publication No. SMA 03-3774. Rockville, MD: Author.

Thomas, E. J. (1994). Evaluation, advanced development, and the unilateral family therapy experiment. In J. Rothman & E. J. Thomas (Eds.), *Intervention research: Design and development for human service* (pp. 267–295). New York: Haworth Press.

Thomas, E. J., & Agar, R. D. (1993). Unilateral family therapy with spouses of uncooperative alcohol abusers. In T. J. O'Farrell (Ed.), *Treating alcohol problems: Marital and family interventions* (pp. 3–33). New York: Guilford Press.

Thomas, E. J., & Santa, C. A. (1982). Unilateral alcohol therapy for alcohol abuse: A working conception. *American Journal of Family Therapy, 10,* 49–58.

Vaughn, M. G., & Howard, M. O. (2004). Adolescent substance abuse treatment: A synthesis of controlled evaluations. *Research on Social Work Practice, 14,* 325–335.

Westermeyer, J. (1997). Native Americans, Asians, and new immigrants. In J. H. Lowinson, P. Ruiz, R. B. Millman, & J. G. Langrod (Eds.), *Substance abuse: A comprehensive textbook* (3rd ed., pp. 712–716). Baltimore: Williams & Wilkins.

Windle, M. (2003). Alcohol use among adolescent and young adults. *Alcohol Research & Health, 27*(1), 79–85.

Yalisove, D. (2004). *Introduction to alcohol research: Implications for treatment, prevention, and policy.* Boston: Pearson Education, Inc.

CHAPTER 17

The Impact of Ethnicity and Race on the Treatment of Mothers in Incest Families

Virginia C. Strand

S exual abuse of children has been the subject of numerous professional publications since the beginnings of the 1980s, but only in the 1990s has more attention been paid to the correlates between ethnicity, race, and sexual abuse. We know a lot more than previously about the prevalence and impact of child sexual abuse in terms of its relationship to race and ethnicity. Freeman and colleagues (2001) found in a community sample of women sexually abused as children that White women were more likely than African American or Hispanic women to have been abused in childhood. Feiring, Coates, and Taska (2001) explored the impact of victimization in childhood in a cohort of African American, Hispanic, and White children. They found that Hispanic children were more likely to be abused by a parent figure that had been in the home for a year or more, and that there were lower levels of perceived primary caregiver support in these Hispanic families than in others. Children from White families were more likely to make internal attributions for abuse and demonstrated a higher level of shame than Hispanic or African American child victims. Shaw and associates (2001) also investigated the impact of sexual abuse on Hispanics and African Americans. His findings resonated with those of Feiring, Coates, and Taska, in that he found that perpetrators in Hispanic families were more likely to be fathers or stepfathers. Hispanic mothers were more likely than African American counterparts to see their families as being confused regarding family values and rules.

Romeo and associates (1999), in a study of the occurrence of sexual abuse in a community sample of Latina women, found that one third reported an incidence of victimization. Ramos, Koss, and Russo (1999) explored the definitions and values of rape and sexual abuse using a focus group with Mexican American women. Their findings suggest that keeping silent about sexual abuse is a major cultural norm. This may contribute to underreporting in studies aimed at estimating prevalence for sexual abuse among Hispanics. In a study of Asian and Pacific Island refugees, Ima and Hohm (1991) found that sexual abuse was less common than physical abuse.

Johnson and Young (2003) found in their study that poor, young African American women were in general at high risk for sexual abuse, and Jasinski, Williams, and Siegel (2000) found that a history of childhood sexual abuse in young, urban African American women predicted heavy alcohol use in adulthood. These findings are consistent with those of Marcenko, Kemp, and Larson (2000), who found that child sexual abuse in an urban sample of low-income women correlated with adult drug use and psychological distress in adulthood.

The impact of culture has, of course, enormous implications for intervention and ongoing treatment. The increasing variety of different racial and ethnic groups in this society makes it important for practitioners to heighten both their appreciation of differences and their level of skill in interventions with clients with ethnic or racial backgrounds different from their own. Indeed, as Cardemil and Battle (2003) emphasize, to be effective, therapists need to move beyond appreciation to actively incorporate dialogues about diversity in their sessions with clients.

The purpose of this chapter is to highlight ethnic differences and to show how sensitivity to those differences, as well as knowledge about the dynamics of child sexual abuse, can enhance the ability to engage in a meaningful way with the mother in the incest family. The focus is specifically on engagement of the mother at the time immediately following a report of child sexual abuse. The chapter explores some of the dynamics that emerge as one works with families from other than the dominant European American culture. Before looking specifically at three distinct ethnic or racial groups, however, two issues are addressed. The first is that of common transference reactions for clients of color working with White therapists, and the second is the dynamics that characterize the mother in the incest family.

THEORETICAL CONSIDERATIONS

Common Transference and Countertransference Reactions

When the clinician is White, it is important to assume that racial and ethnic barriers will exist between the therapist and a client of color due to the social context in which we all live and work. The author presumes that clients of color, to a greater or lesser degree, experience a White therapist as a member of a dominant group and themselves as members of a subordinate group. Social class, educational background, and life experiences will, of course, mediate the degree to which an individual experiences being part of a subordinate group.

In practice, there are significantly more Caucasian American mental health professionals than professionals from other ethnic and racial groups. The formal mental health system is staffed primarily by White clinicians who do not share the same ethnic and racial characteristics, knowledge, or experiences of the clients they serve (Vargas & Willis, 1994). This is also true in the subspecialty of those working in the area of child sexual abuse. Caucasian American clinicians are by definition part of the dominant culture and as such share in privileges that may be invisible to them and taken for granted. It is often difficult for one in a dominant culture to see how these privileges can become a cause for frustration or engender feelings of helplessness in the minority client (McIntosh, 2001). One of the first steps in becoming culturally competent is to become aware of the values and biases in one's own culture (Kaufman & Love, 2004), and for the European American this means understanding the notion of White privilege.

The work of Jean Baker Miller (1991) sheds some light on issues regarding the relationship between dominant and subordinate groups in general. Although she was writing in the context of males to females, her principles are applicable to the situation under discussion. Dominant groups tend to act in particular ways with subordinate groups. There is a) a tendency to act destructively toward subordinate groups, b) a tendency to restrict the range of activities and even reactions of subordinate group members, c) discouragement of the full and free expression of their experiences, and d) a tendency to characterize members falsely and then to describe their situation as normal (Miller, 1991, p. 183). One result for members of the subordinate group is to engender anger, that often must be suppressed or deflected. The subordinate often develops complex psychological reactions and tendencies, including self-perceptions that one is weak and unworthy and has "no right" to be angry. To appease a member of the dominant group a subordinate may also act especially compliant, submissive, or passive.

The implication for the White therapist working with women of color is the need to recognize not only that the therapist may hold typical stereotypes regarding clients from different racial and ethnic groups, but also that clients will bring a particular transference reaction to the work based on their life experience in mainstream culture dominated by norms and values affiliated with being Caucasian (Abney, Yang, & Paulson, 1992; Cardemil & Battle, 2003; Lee, 2004; Thompson, Brazile, & Akbar, 2004). For example, Cardemil and Battle (2003) identify a common perception about mental illness among Asian clients that effects how they view mental health services. Mental illness is understood in many Asian cultures through the lens of achieving a balance between yin and yang, and by the influence of supernatural causes. Behavior in the therapy session may be open to misinterpretation if the therapist is not sensitive to such cultural influences. Sue (1990) reports that Japanese and Mexicans may avoid eye contact as a form of respect. If that is misinterpreted as shyness or guardedness, it may adversely affect the therapeutic alliance. African Americans have been found to want less interpersonal distance than Caucasian Americans, and may interpret the need for more interpersonal space on the part of a European American therapist as aloofness (Cardemil & Battle, 2003). Pinderhughes (1989) has pointed out that the European American therapist may inadvertently minimize or deny the impact of racism on them, and emphasizes that is important that the therapist be sensitive to the reality of racism for the client. The findings of Thompson and colleagues (2004) underscore the need for compassion, as their findings indicate that some African American clients feel that therapists are insensitive to their needs.

Given the above, it is not unusual for clients of color to bring to the encounter with a therapist feelings of anger, mistrust, passivity, or dependence based on their subordinate group experience. It is the job of the clinician to be careful not to misconstrue these as abnormal and mislabel as pathological what may be a very multidetermined response. In addition, women of color have unique needs, encumbered as they are with the double burden of racism and sexism (Gutierrez, 1990), being members of two subordinate groups in American society. When the confounding variable of incest is added to the mix, the situation becomes incredibly complex for the woman of color who is also the mother of a sexually abused child. It becomes crucial for the therapist to be sensitive to the multiple forces at work in her life, particularly at the time of the crisis of disclosure, and to take these into consideration when making an assessment and developing an intervention plan.

Secondary Victim Dynamics in the Mother in the Incest Family

It is helpful to have a conceptual framework by which to understand the reactions of the mother of a sexually abused child. As the author has outlined elsewhere (Strand, 2000), it can be useful to understand the reaction of the mother to the disclosure of sexual abuse as that of a secondary victim to trauma. There is a growing recognition that intrafamilial sexual abuse, and particularly the *disclosure* of that abuse, may have a traumatic impact on the mother as well as the child. Newberger and colleagues (1993) found that mothers interviewed shortly after disclosure scored significantly higher on a global symptomatology index than the mean for a normal population. Timmons-Mitchell and associates (1996) found that their sample of mothers whose children had recently disclosed sexual abuse scored significantly higher on two different measures for posttraumatic stress than did women in the normative sample for these measures. In their work with four mothers whose children had recently disclosed sexual abuse, Green and colleagues (1995) found that these mothers responded to the disclosure of sexual abuse with a number of symptoms associated with posttraumatic stress disorder, including the flooding of intrusive memories, the reexperiencing of painful affects, hyperarousal, and psychic numbing. Carter (1993) found high levels of shock, guilt, anger, shame, and traumatic symptoms in a sample of mothers of sexually abused children, and noted that the trauma was more severe in cases in which the mother's husband was the perpetrator.

Other recent research on the non-offending mother underscores the heterogeneity among mothers and the need for clinicians to develop differential responses (Crawford, 1999). Allaggia (2002) reports on the results of a grounded study aimed at identifying factors related to the mother's reaction following a disclosure of sexual abuse and found that reactions are complex. Of particular relevance was the finding that the initial response on the part of the mother may be quite different from the enduring response.

While Myer noted as early as 1984, (based on her study of 43 mothers), that the mothers in incest families should not be considered a monolithic group but in fact reflect as much diversity as any other population, her results and the subsequent research by others has only slowly been integrated into clinical practice (Myer, 1985). Massat and Lundy (1998) have added to our understanding of the factors affecting the non-offending mother's reactions at disclosure. They explored the reasons for mother's differential reactions, hypothesizing that it may be due to mother's perceived loss. Findings from their study reveal that over 50% experienced the loss of intimacy with the perpetrator, a change of residence, loss of income, and family dissatisfaction. There are significant "costs," therefore, to non-offending mothers that may in some cases influence the mother's degree of supportiveness following disclosure.

Importantly, findings about the mother's reaction at disclosure consistently indicate that most mothers believe and protect their child, although ambivalence is still characteristic of some (Elliot & Carnes, 2001). Bolen and Lamb (2004) theorize, however, that the ambivalence of the non-offending mother needs to be reconceptualized and viewed as a normative reaction when the costs of disclosure are high. This is consistent with the notion of the mother as a secondary victim, in that ambivalence can be understood as the effect of the traumatic impact of disclosure.

There exists a useful conceptualization in the literature (Finkelhor & Browne, 1985) regarding the impact of sexual traumatization that is helpful in understanding the mother's reaction. Finkelhor and Browne (1985) have outlined four dynamics as being typical of the response of the child victim. These are traumatic sexualization, betrayal, stigmatization, and powerlessness. The mother is affected similarly to the child. In terms of sexual traumatization the mother often experiences the disclosure as a threat to her sexual identity. Because sexuality is such a core aspect of self-esteem and of personality, this threat is significant. In the author's experience, mothers typically blame themselves for the offender's sexual contact with a child, especially if they have been living with the perpetrator until the intervention by an outside authority. They tend to view the cause of the incestuous relationship as their own sexual inadequacy, rather than as an inadequate and destructive response by their partner.

The mother's feelings of self-blame may be only partially apparent at the time of interface with initial investigative staff and rarely articulated because of the mother's sense of guilt. If one considers that the disclosure of sexual abuse outside the family results in an intervention by child protective services and/or law enforcement agencies, the mother is by definition in crisis. The response of initial investigative staff, usually paraprofessionals who are ill trained and lacking in understanding of incestuous family dynamics, is often to blame the mother. Support for this dynamic comes from recent research. McCallum (2001) reports that mothers feel blamed, scared, and fearful following disclosure. Hill (2001) found that feelings of guilt and failure as a parent were particularly strong in a group of non-offending mothers. This then feeds into the self-derogatory attitude the mother may already be experiencing.

The guilt and self-blame experienced by the mother, not only for the reasons outlined above but also because of her feelings of failure as a mother (particularly if the child has made a clear and factual disclosure to someone outside the family) contributes to the dynamic of stigmatization identified above. The author has known of many situations in which the mother, following a disclosure that has also been made public (e.g., through a newspaper report), will not shop at her usual places, will change banks and churches, and avoid close friends and family whom she would be ashamed to confide in lest they also blame her. Mothers often talk about being afraid to confide in close friends or family members because they worry that they will not understand, will question the child's truthfulness, or will attack the mother for failure to "see what was going on."

Therefore, at a time of crisis, when crisis theory teaches that support and the opportunity to verbalize the details surrounding the crisis are vital, the mother may isolate herself from her major sources of emotional support. The lack of opportunity to process the trauma contributes to her being immobilized. She may appear unable to take actions outsiders feel would be "normal" for a "good mother" to undertake under the circumstances. It is no wonder the mother often appears, particularly to the untrained observer, as if she is ineffective, unproductive, or dependent. From the author's point of view, this is often the result of feeling overwhelmed by events swirling around her and the lack of time to process information that has upset the foundation of her existence. Again, the results of recent studies support these dynamics. Both McCallum (2001) and Hill (2001) found that mothers are fearful, alienated, and isolated following a disclosure, and unsure where to turn for support.

In addition to the sexual traumatization and stigmatization, the mother often feels betrayed as well. To learn that her partner, with whom she may have been sexually active until the time of the disclosure (or even after), has been involved sexually with her child engenders an enormous sense of anger. She is often then struggling internally with the two emotions of self-blame (as noted above) and rage. For women who have been socialized to turn rage inward, the feelings of guilt and self-blame often win out. The rage, when it is expressed, may be deflected to secondary sources such as the intervention system, as Solin (1986) has written about, or to the child or children who made the disclosure.

The child may additionally become a target for the mother's rage because she feels betrayed by the child for telling someone outside the family. This heightens the mother's sense of failure as a mother—"Why didn't my child tell me?"—and in her confusion and inability to process the material flooding her, she may communicate her rage to her child(ren) out of this sense of betrayal.

The last dynamic, powerlessness, is usually present for the mother (McCallum, 2001) as well as for the child. She may feel as if the foundation on which her life was built has collapsed. Many mothers have been struggling with problems in relationships with their partners, but rarely do they know or expect that he will be sexually involved with their children, particularly at the same time that he is sexually involved with them. This sense of help-lessness is exacerbated by an intervention that forces a mother to choose between having her child(ren) placed in out-of-home care and separating from her husband. In fact, some control over her life has been taken out of her hands, and she feels understandably powerless.

These dynamics are viewed as guidelines for the therapist in engagement, assessment, and treatment planning. Implicit in this framework is the premise that the disclosure of sexual abuse by a spouse or partner is a crisis and that all four dynamics (sexual traumatization, stigmatization, betrayal, and powerlessness) will operate in the woman's life to some extent regardless of her preexisting personality structure. The mix will be different for each woman, and the degree to which one or more of the dynamics become salient will depend on the woman's psychological vulnerabilities and the nature and duration of her relationship with her child and partner. If the woman is a survivor of childhood sexual abuse herself, the traumagenic dynamics noted above may be particularly significant, as she may be dealing both with her own history and with the issues as a mother of a sexually abused child.

IMPLICATIONS FOR WOMEN OF COLOR

The author's thesis is that the dynamics of stigmatization and powerlessness are often heightened for women of various ethnic and racial backgrounds because of a somewhat different relationship between men and women in other cultural groups and because of their relationship to the mainstream culture. As Cardemil and Battle (2003) and McIntosh (2001) have discussed, the expectations and orientation of a White therapist and a client of color may be very different. For example, for women of Hispanic (particularly Puerto Rican) background, the double standard for men and women may be even stronger than it is in the mainstream culture (Comas-Diaz, 1989). The family is held in great esteem, and the role of men and women is culturally prescribed. For example, a "good" women is patient and forbearing, and the home is viewed as the appropriate center of her world. Men are the economic providers, and men need to prove their virility through domination of women. Women are supposed to show respect to men, and there is an emphasis on what is good for the family rather than good for the individual. Children are taught to respect their elders and to show deference in all social situations. Family members do not like to take problems outside the family, and informal solutions are often preferred over the interface with formal organizations (Comas-Diaz, 1989; McKinley, 1987).

Consequently, one can see how a Hispanic woman who learns of suspected incest on the part of her spouse or partner would be particularly vulnerable to a sense of shame. Disclosure threatens the entity of the family, threatens the alleged perpetrator's "manhood," makes family matters public, and places the child in the position of challenging an elder's authority. All of these are counter to the role expectations for the Hispanic family member.

The Asian woman is vulnerable for many of the same reasons. As with the Hispanic family, the Asian woman is viewed as the nurturer and caretaker, and she assumes responsibility for what happens to the children (Chin, 1983; Chen, Sullivan, & Shibusawa, 2003). The man is seen as the head of the family, and his authority would be viewed by the child as paramount. A difference is the emphasis on the community and family, as opposed to the individual, as the organizing principle of society. This accentuates the sense of belonging and obligation to the family and concomitantly the sense of personal obligation to the family. This is manifest in the desire to maintain family harmony (Bradshaw, 1994). In addition, Asian families tend to have wide kinship networks, and their reactions will influence the mother's response, making her sensitive to criticism and to taking actions that might invoke a negative reaction from the family.

Saving face is an important part of the culture (Sato, 1980), and seeking mental health services may be avoided out of a desire not to shame the family (Tsui, 1985). The motivation to save face would mitigate against revealing a secret as shameful as sexual abuse, especially if it was the woman's sexual partner who had molested her child. In addition, reticence to seek outside help may be influenced by the belief that distress is caused by a failure of will as well as by adherence to the cultural mandate to suffer in silence (Sue, 1990).

African American mothers, with the particular history of Black Americans in this culture, bring their own sense of vulnerabilities, which may make it difficult for them to trust mental health providers. As Boyd-Franklin (1989) has pointed out, the White therapist often has to earn the trust of Black clients. Unlike other groups, attribution of trust and respect for an authority figure such as a therapist is not as typical because of the specific history of oppression and racism for Black Americans.

There is evidence that African American families already utilize formal mental health systems less often than Whites when referred specifically for treatment of sexual abuse (Haskett, Nowlan, Hutchinson, & Whitworth, 1991). It has also been documented that African American subjects are more likely to use informal helping networks for personal problems, rather than turning to professionals (Chatters, Taylor, & Neighbors, 1989; Neighbors & Jackson, 1984).

It is more likely that an African American mother will encounter a White therapist than not. At some level there is mistrust of the dominant group, which will tend to increase the woman's inclination to keep her thoughts and feelings to herself and avoid being shamed in front of a group member who she may feel does not understand her. This guardedness and suspicion about whether the White therapist can really be helpful should be understood as a healthy adaptation to the reality of living in a racist society (Cardemil & Battle, 2003). Greene (1994) identifies this as a process of "armoring," a psychological mechanism manifest in both behavior and cognition whereby the African American woman prepares herself for interaction with another if there is the potential for racism. The therapist who is sensitive to this possibility can address the issue and may be able to prevent the mother from cutting herself off from a source of support where she can process her feelings. As noted above, if she does not allow herself to verbalize her reactions, it may increase her sense of shame, guilt, and stigmatization.

CASE EXAMPLES

The following examples illustrate how some of these dynamics were played out in three different cultures. The cases are based on ones from the author's practice, and particulars have been changed to protect the identity of the clients. In some instances different circumstances have been coalesced into one case to highlight a particular dynamic.

A Hispanic Family

The first case involves a Hispanic family. Mr. and Mrs. L. were recent immigrants from El Salvador. Mr. L. had come first to the United States, shortly after the birth of his second child, Joseph. At the time of the report to Child Protective Services, his oldest daughter, Victoria, was 5 and his son, Joseph, was 3½. Mrs. L. had not been married to Mr. L. until after the birth of Victoria. She had come to the country only about 1 year before the report and did not speak English, although she understood the language somewhat.

A day care provider made the initial report, based on observations of Victoria's behavior in day care. She was exhibiting age-inappropriate sexual behavior and language. Upon investigation and evaluation, both Victoria and Joseph made statements about their father having molested them. He had reportedly fondled their genitals and inserted his finger and penis into the rectums of both children.

Following the disclosure, the children were removed from the home, as Mrs. L. did not believe the accusations against her husband. Her children did not make any statements to her, and her husband denied the abuse. She was therefore unwilling to separate from him. The question becomes, was there anything about her cultural background that might contribute to the apparent inability to be protective? On closer examination, one can see how her background as well as her recent immigrant status in this country might make her hesitate to contradict her husband.

Mrs. L. had grown up in a traditional Catholic family. She was the youngest of five children. Her mother had been the primary caretaker and was respectful and obedient to her father, a dominant and hardworking man who was rarely home due to his job responsibilities. Mr. L. was much like her father. Mrs. L. stayed home with the children, and as noted above, had not learned English. Neither did she know how to drive. Her relationship with Mr. L. was characterized by deference to him and his opinions. Because sexual contact with children was a taboo subject and certainly counter to how a man like her husband would exhibit virility, the thought of his having been sexual with her children was beyond her comprehension.

Mrs. L., therefore, was understandably dependent on her husband for emotional support and social direction. She was not independently mobile and could not even manage the logistics to buy groceries and other necessities. She was also suspicious of formal organizations, and the family's brief encounter with the local social services department when they had been receiving income maintenance support at an earlier time had made her particularly suspicious of this agency. In addition, Victoria and Joseph were not talking to her or repeating the statements they had made to the intervention team, and Mrs. L. was suspicious of that team's accurate understanding of her children. Much as she did not want to lose custody of her children, she felt that she had no choice.

In this case the children were out of the home for a number of months, until the family court had intervened and adjudicated Mr. L. as a sexual offender. He had agreed to go to treatment, and in the early work with the father and mother their therapists set up a dialogue between them. In these sessions, Mr. L. was helped to tell Mrs. L. specifically what he had done to the children. Hearing this directly from him enabled Mrs. L. to move beyond her denial. She separated from him while he completed treatment, and the children were allowed to return to live with her.

An Asian Family

The second case involves an Asian family. Mr. and Mrs. N. had been in this country for about 7 years when their oldest daughter Kim, age 11, made a statement to her guidance counselor at school about her father touching her sexually. In addition to father, mother, and Kina, there was also a 7-year-old son, Ron. Mrs. N.'s mother lived with the family, and Mr. N.'s brother and sister-in-law owned and jointly operated the family business. The brother and sister-in-law, who did not have any children, often ate meals with the N. household.

Upon disclosure, Mr. N. was asked to leave the house, which he did. Mrs. N. and her family were in a panic. Kina's initial statements had been that her father fondled her vagina, buttocks, and breasts under and on top of her clothing. After the first disclosure to the guidance counselor, she began to minimize the actions and only made statements to the Child Protective Services (CPS) worker about her father touching her buttocks. She began to say that he only slapped her buttocks on the top of her clothing. The family insisted that this kind of touch was typical of their culture and also minimized the possibility of abuse.

Mrs. N., like Mrs. L., did not speak any English, and CPS had to rely on interpreters in their conversations with her. She appeared very frightened and unsure of herself. She denied to the worker that her husband could have been capable of the behavior he was accused of, saying that he worked late almost every night and sometimes slept over at the business if he was very busy. Because she did not work, she was home with her daughter and believed that she would have known if there were any inappropriate contact between her daughter and her husband.

Later in treatment a different story would emerge concerning the mother's awareness of a problematic relationship between the husband and daughter, but at the time of disclosure and in the period following, she had difficulty admitting this to herself and was not about to confide in a stranger. It is significant that early on in the intervention the relevance of cultural dictates overrode other considerations. For example, in her culture, the importance of saving face at all costs contributed to her siding with her husband against the outside, bureaucratic organization at the time of the initial report. Her husband had initially denied the allegations, and the importance of respecting his authority made it difficult for her to question him, let alone share such a shameful event, if true, with someone not only outside the family but outside the culture.

In addition, her wide kinship network, on which she was used to relying at times of crisis, discouraged her from believing the allegations. They insisted that even if Kina had made some statements, it was because she did not get along with her father. They pointed to the sibling rivalry and her jealousy of her younger brother, whom the father did in fact favor. The fact that Kina withdrew the more serious allegations after the CPS intervention that resulted in the removal of her father added to the mother's ability to deny the allegations.

An African American Family

With the third mother, Mrs. M., one sees how traditional values in the African American family interacted with the reaction to a report of suspected child sexual abuse. Mrs. M. was 28 at the time that her 11-year-old daughter Tamara made a disclosure at school about her mother's fiancé, Mr. F. He had been living with the family for about a year and was the father of Mrs. M.'s youngest child, who was 7 weeks old at the time of the report to CPS. In addition to Tamara and the baby, Ms. M also had three other children, a girl aged 6, a girl aged 4, and a boy aged 2. She was living on public assistance and not working.

The report to CPS had come about because Tamara had left a letter at school that her teacher found. In this letter she had written about how she did not like Rupert (her mother's fiancé) because of the way he talked to her and touched her. She wrote that he bought her clothes, sneakers, and other things she wanted that her mother could not afford. The letter said that Rupert had promised to buy her a kitten, and she really wanted that, but she did not want him to keep coming into her bed at night and bothering her.

Tamara and her mother did not have a good relationship. Tamara resented the pressure that her mother put on her to baby-sit and was tired of taking care of her siblings and doing housework. She had been skipping school, which infuriated her mother, partly because the school kept calling her and she felt that the school held her responsible. She was worried that they would file a neglect petition because of Tamara's absence from school. Tamara denied that anything inappropriate was happening when she was questioned by CPS. Mrs. M., already stressed by the birth of a new child and anticipating, finally, the security that marriage would bring, was particularly reluctant to entertain the suspicions of sexual abuse brought against Rupert.

Like many African American women, Mrs. M. had experienced a truncated life cycle (Hines, 1992), beginning with parenting in her teenage years (age 17), before she had completed her own adolescence or had had a chance to form her own sense of identity. Three different men had fathered her first four children, none of whom had been employed and two of whom had been serious substance abusers. The fact that the father of her newest baby was employed and offering marriage was an enormous opportunity for her. It was also typical of a pattern for lower income African American families, in which the woman first marries after having children and not necessarily the father of all of her children, resulting in the formation of a step-family. When Tamara denied the allegations, it was easy for Mrs. M. to ignore them, given her poor relationship with her daughter and the stronger relationship with her fiancé. This case illustrates how Mrs. M.'s dependence on her partner, poor relationship with her daughter, and suspicion of the intervention systems interacted to create suspicion on her part about the validity of the alleged sexual abuse.

SUMMARY OF IMPLICATIONS FOR TREATMENT

In all of the above cases, patience, sensitivity to cultural norms, and empathy were important in the ultimate successful engagement of the mothers. For all women of color, it is important to attend to the match between the therapist's orientation and expectations of therapy and those of the client. Many clients continue to feel shame, embarrassment, and fear over seeking help outside the family. They may lack knowledge about how services operate, there are often language barriers, and lack of informal support for the utilization of formal mental health structures. Much of this was true for the three clients described above. Because Hispanic, African American, and Asian clients tend to rely as much, if not more, on informal systems of helping, it is incumbent on the professional to take time to orient the client to the formal helping structure and to anticipate conflicts for the client in using the formal structure. It is also important to underscore that sharing emotional problems outside the family, especially for Asian women but also for Hispanic and Black Americans, may be uncomfortable (Abu-Ras, 2003; Cardemil & Battle, 2003).

The therapist should be careful not to view reluctance necessarily as resistance. It is also helpful to remember that Asian American cultures, the Chinese in particular, tend to view emotional difficulties as having a physical cause and may want to seek alternative remedies (e.g., assistance from a herbalist) for the emotional difficulties they or family members are experiencing (Cardemil & Battle, 2003; Crystal, 1989). Again, it is wise to be cautious about immediately viewing this as resistance.

As McIntosh (2001) and Thompson and associates (2004) have noted, the ethnocentric view of most White middle-class clinicians may lead them to mischaracterize reactions of African Americans generally. The tendency to label actions as a consequence of poor impulse control may reflect a lack of awareness on the part of White clinicians of the extent to which stimuli operating in the lives of average urban Black Americans constantly test self-control. Additionally, institutional racism has devalued African American women while at the same time idealizing their White counterparts (Greene, 1994).

Another variable at work for many women of color is their immigration status, as was the case for Mrs. L. This may play a part not only in fear of connection to formal systems if they are undocumented but also in the degree to which they are acculturated. Because many Asian, Latin American, and Caribbean countries hold more rigid sex role orientations than does mainstream American culture (Comas-Diaz, 1989; Custis, 1990; Lorenzo & Adler, 1984), a newer immigrant may hold more traditional views. This will affect the degree to which she feels she can accept a challenge to her husband or partner, as well as the degree to which she feels comfortable being engaged with the formal helping system. Again, this was the case with Mrs. L.

Certain strategies that have been found to be helpful with women of color mesh with what has been found helpful in working with mothers of sexually abused children. One such strategy is that of an empowerment approach, where strengths are emphasized and validated. Gutierrez (1990) and Comas-Diaz (1989) both stress that the promotion of competence, adaptation, and flexibility in role relations are helpful. For the mother in an incest family, who may be separated from her husband as a result of CPS intervention and/or dealing with the world of work for the first time, this emphasis—particularly in expanding role flexibility—is important.

Although extended family members may be extremely helpful, some authors (McCallum, 2001) stress the importance of the carefully planned involvement of such members, keeping in mind that many extended families may discourage the use of mental health agencies in general. For an issue like sexual abuse, that may be regarded as shameful not only for the individual mother but for the family, this advice is especially pertinent. In the case of Mrs. N., the extended family was actively discouraging involvement with the formal mental health system, forming an additional impediment to the engagement of Mrs. N. in therapy.

One strategy that has been especially useful for both women of color and mothers of sexually abused children is that of group therapy. McKinley (1987) describes the successful use of group psychotherapy for Hispanic women. The benefits include the ability to learn self-reliance, which may help to counter a culturally induced norm toward passivity and dependency. It can also support the development of self-assertion and provide for a correctional emotional experience. Similarly, Olarte and Masonick (1985) found group therapy helpful for Hispanic women for issues surrounding acculturation, family conflicts, and children's performance. The latter issue is often a salient one for mothers of sexually abused children, who are struggling to parent children who may be exhibiting emotional and behavioral disturbances. The power of the support and guidance gained from such a group can be invaluable. This was true for Mrs. L. and Mrs. M., but Mrs. N., the Asian client, remained more comfortable with individual treatment.

In conclusion, it has been suggested here that mothers of sexually abused children face common dilemmas and manifest common reaction patterns in response to the crisis of disclosure of sexual abuse by a partner or spouse. For women of color, certain of these typical reactions, especially those of stigmatization, shame, and powerlessness, may be heightened by their status in mainstream American culture. For the therapist, White or non-White, it is important not only to be familiar with the dynamics presented by mothers of sexually abused children but also to incorporate culturally sensitive interventions into practice.

REFERENCES

Abney, V. D., Yang, J. A., & Paulson, M. J. (1992). Transference and countertransference issues unique to long-term group psychotherapy of adult children molested as children. *Journal of Interpersonal Violence, 7*, 559–569.

Abu-Ras, W. M. (2003). Barriers to services for Arab immigrant battered women in a Detroit suburb. *Journal of Social Work Research and Evaluation, 4*(1), 49–66.

Allaggia, R. (2002). Balancing acts: Reconceptualizing support in maternal response to intra-familial child sexual abuse. *Clinical Social Work Journal, 30*(1), 41–56.

Bolen, R. M., & Lamb, J. L. (2004). Ambivalence of non-offending guardians after child sexual abuse disclosure. *Journal of Interpersonal Violence, 19*(2), 185–211.

Boyd-Franklin, N. (1989). *Black families in therapy.* New York: Guilford Press.

Cardemil, E. V., & Battle, C. L. (2003). Guess who's coming to therapy? Getting comfortable with conversations about race and ethnicity in psychotherapy. *Professional Psychology: Research and Practice, 34*(3), 278–286.

Carter, B. (1993). Child sexual abuse: Impact on mothers. *Affilia: Journal of Women and Social Work, 8*(1), 72–90.

Chatters, L. M., Taylor, R. J., & Neighbors, H. W. (1989). Size of informal helper network mobilized during a serious personal problem among Black Americans. *Journal of Marriage and the Family, 51,* 667–676.

Chen, S., Sullivan, N. Y., Lu, Y. E., & Shibusawa, T. (2003). Asian Americans and mental health services: A study of utilization patterns in the 1990s. *Journal of Ethnic and Cultural Diversity in Social Work, 12*(2), 19–42.

Chin, J. L. (1983). Diagnostic consideration in working with Asian Americans. *American Journal of Orthopsychiatry, 53*(1), 100–109.

Comas-Diaz, L. (1989). Culturally relevant issues and treatment implications for Hispanics. In D. R. Koslow & E. Salett (Eds.), *Crossing cultures in mental health* (pp. 31–48). Washington, DC: Society for International Education Training and Research.

Crawford, S. L. (1999). Intrafamilial sexual abuse: What we think we know about mothers and implications for intervention. *Journal of Child Sexual Abuse, 7*(3), 55–72.

Crystal, D. (1989). Asian Americans and the myth of the model minority. *Social Case Work, 70,* 405–413.

Custis, P. A. (1990). The consequences of acculturation to service delivery and research with Hispanic families. *Child and Adolescent Social Work Journal, 7*(2), 147–159.

Elliot, A. N., & Carnes, C. N. (2001). Reaction of non-offending parents to the sexual abuse of their child: A review of the literature. *Child Maltreatment, 6*(4), 314–331.

Feiring, C., Coates, D. L., & Taska, L. S. (2001). Ethnic status, stigmatization, support and symptoms development following sexual abuse. *Journal of Interpersonal Violence, 16*(12), 1307–1329.

Finkelhor, D., & Browne, A. (1985). The traumatic impact of child sexual abuse: A conceptualization. *American Journal of Orthopsychiatry, 55*(4), 530–541.

Freeman, R. C., Parillo, K. M., Collier, K., & Rusek, R. W. (2001). Child and adolescent sexual abuse history in a sample of 1,490 women sexual partners of injection drug-using men. *Women and Health, 34*(4), 341–349.

Green, A. H., Coupe, P., Fernandez, R., & Stevens, B. (1995). Incest revisited: Delayed post-traumatic stress disorder in mothers following the sexual abuse of their children. *Child Abuse & Neglect, 19*(10), 1275–1282.

Greene, B. (1994). African American women. In L. Comas-Diaz & B. Greene (Eds.), *Women of color: Integrating ethnic and gender identities in psychotherapy* (pp. 10–29). New York: Guilford Press.

Gutierrez, L. M. (1990). Working with women of color: An empowerment perspective. *Social Work, 35*(2), 149–153.

Haskett, M. E., Nowlan, N. P., Hutchinson, J. S., & Whitworth, J. M. (1991). Factors associated with successful entry into therapy in child sexual abuse cases. *Child Abuse and Neglect, 15,* 467–476.

Hill, A. (2001). "No one else could understand": Women's experiences of a support group run by and for mothers of sexually abused children. *British Journal of Social Work, 31*(3), 385–397.

Hines, P. M., Garcia-Preto, N., & McGoldrick, M. (1992). Intergenerational relationships across cultures. *Families in Society, 73*(6), 323–338.

Ima, K., & Hohm, C. F. (1991). Child maltreatment among Asian and Pacific Islander refugees and immigrants: The San Diego experience. *Journal of Interpersonal Violence, 6*, 267–285.

Jasinski, J. L., Williams, L. M., & Siegel, J. (2000). Childhood physical and sexual abuse as risk factors for heavy drinking among African American women: A prospective study. *Child Abuse and Neglect, 24*(8), 1061–1071.

Johnson, H. D., & Young, D. S. (2003). Addiction, abuse and family relationships: Childhood experiences of five incarcerated African American women. *Journal of Ethnicity in Substance Abuse, 1*(4), 29–47.

Kaufman, M., & Love, D. (2004). Recent trends in multicultural practice: Implications for practice teaching and field education. *Journal of Practice Teaching, 4*(3), 29–53.

Lee, W. M. (2004). Therapeutic considerations in work with biracial girls. *Women and Therapy, 27*(1–2), 203–216.

Lorenzo, M. K., & Adler, D. A. (1984). Mental health services for Chinese in a community mental health center. *Social Casework, 65*(10), 600–614.

Marcenko, M. O., Kemp, S. P., & Larson, N. C. (2000). Childhood experiences of abuse, later substance use, and parenting outcomes among low-income mothers. *American Journal of Orthopsychiatry, 70*(3), 316–326.

Massat, C. R., & Lundy, M. (1998). Reporting costs to non-offending parents in cases of intrafamial child sexual abuse. *Child Welfare, LXXVII*(4), 371–388.

McCallum, S. (2001). Non-offending mothers: An exploratory study of mothers whose partners sexually assaulted their children. *Violence Against Women, 7*(3), 315–334.

McIntosh, P. (2001). White privilege: Unpacking the invisible knapsack. In P. S. Rosenberg (Ed.), *Race, class and gender in the United States: An integrated study* (5th ed., pp. 163–168). New York: Worth Publishers.

McKinley, V. (1987). Group therapy as a treatment modality of special value for Hispanic patients. *International Journal of Group Psychotherapy, 37*(2), 255–268.

Miller, J. B. (1991). The construction of anger in women and men. In J. V. Jordan, J. Kaplan, A. Miller, J. Stiver, & J. Surrey (Eds.), *Women's growth in connection* (pp. 181–197). New York: Guilford Publications.

Myer, M. H. (1985). A new look at mothers of incest victims. Special issue: Feminist perspectives on social work and human sexuality. *Journal of Social Work and Human Sexuality, 3*(2–3), 47–58.

Neighbors, H. W., & Jackson, J. S. (1984). The use of informal and formal help: Four patterns of illness behavior in the Black Community. *American Journal of Community Psychiatry, 12*, 629–644.

Newberger, C. M., Gremy, I. M., Waternaux, C. M., & Newberger, E. H. (1993). Mothers of sexually abused children: Trauma and repair in longitudinal perspective. *American Journal of Orthopsychiatry, 63*(1), 92–102.

Olarte, S. W., & Masonik, K. (1985). Benefits of long-term group therapy for disadvantaged Hispanic outpatients. *Hospital and Community Psychiatry, 36,* 1093–1097.

Pinderhughes, E. (1989). *Understanding race, ethnicity, and power: The key to efficacy in clinical practice.* New York: Free Press.

Ramos, L. L., Koss, M. P., & Russo, N. F. (1999). Mexican American women's definition of rape and sexual abuse. *Hispanic Journal of Behavioral Sciences, 21*(3), 236–265.

Romeo, G. J., Wyatt, G. E., Loeb, T. B., Vargas Carmona, J., & Solis, B. M. (1999). The prevalence and circumstances of child sexual abuse among Latina women. *Hispanic Journal of Behavioral Sciences, 21*(3), 351–365.

Sato, M. (1980). Concept of shame and the mental health of Pacific Asian Americans. *Exploration in Ethnic Studies, 3*(1), 3–11.

Shaw, J. A., Lewis, J. E., Loeb, A., Rosado, J., & Rodriguez, R. A. (2001). A comparison of Hispanic and African American sexually abused girls and their families. *Child Abuse and Neglect, 25*(10), 1363–1379.

Solin, C. A. (1986). Displacement of affect in families following incest disclosures. *American Journal of Orthopsychiatry, 56,* 570–576.

Strand, V. (2000). *Treating secondary victims: Intervention with the non-offending mother in the incest family.* Thousand Oaks, CA: Sage.

Sue, D. W. (1990). Cultural-specific strategies in counseling: A conceptual framework. *Professional Psychology: Research and Practice, 21,* 424–433.

Thompson, V. L., Brazile, A., & Akbar, M. (2004). African Americans' perceptions of psychotherapy and psychotherapists. *Professional Psychology: Research and Practice, 35*(1), 19–26.

Timmons-Mitchell, J., Chandler-Holtz, D., & Semple, W. E. (1996). Post-traumatic stress symptoms in mothers following children's reports of sexual abuse: An exploratory study. *American Journal of Orthopsychiatry, 66*(3), 463–467.

Tsui, A. M. (1985). Psychotherapeutic considerations in sexual counseling for Asian immigrants. *Psychotherapy: Theory, Research and Practice, 22,* 357–362.

Vargas, L. A., & Willis, D. J. (1994). New directions in the treatment of ethnic minority children and adolescents. *Journal of Clinical Child Psychology, 23,* 2–4.

CHAPTER 18

Multicultural Social Work Practice With Immigrant Victims of Domestic Violence

Patricia Brownell
Eun Jeong Ko

S ince the 1970s, social workers, along with lawyers, grassroots advocates, and progressive government officials and lawmakers, have sought legislative, regulatory, and procedural remedies to protect the safety and well-being of women who are domestic violence victims (Schechter, 1982). While the initial beneficiaries of these efforts were women and their children with citizenship status, advocates recognized that domestic violence victims without citizenship status remained at grave risk of continued abuse and exploitation, disadvantage in child custody contests, and deportation. The purpose of this chapter is to examine domestic violence and social work practice with immigrant women in a multicultural context.

Impressive social and legal remedies were achieved for victims of domestic violence in the beginning of the women's movement. However, legislative and regulatory changes were critically needed for domestic violence victims with immigrant and refugee status to ensure their ability to access needed social welfare services and public benefits such as income support, health care, employment, education, housing, and personal social services. In addition, social workers were challenged to develop new models of intervention and practice that addressed the needs of immigrant domestic violence victims.

Domestic violence has been a concern of social workers and social reformers since the early days of the social work profession. In the late 19th century, the social response was to attempt to remove children from families where there was wife battering (Brace, 1872). The social work profession began with charity organization and settlement house workers assisting poor urban immigrants (Gordon, 1988). This mission to assist people of diverse cultures obtain needed resources, services, and opportunities remains with the profession today, as reflected in the National Association of Social Workers (NASW) Code of Ethics (NASW, 1996).

The NASW Code of Ethics provides guidance for the professional social worker to practice in a culturally competent manner. Section 1.05 of the Code is entitled Cultural Competency and Social Diversity. This section defines culturally competent social work practice as social workers' understanding culture and its function in human behavior and society, having a knowledge base about their clients' culture, demonstrating competence in the provision of services that are sensitive to clients' culture and differences among people and cultural groups, and understanding cultural diversity and oppression (NASW, 1996). Cultural awareness is defined as an understanding that an individual has different cultures, defined as races, religions, gender, ages, and physical disabilities (Ferrer, 1998). Domestic violence is a significant social problem in the United States. It is essential for social workers to detect and address domestic violence given its prevalence and consequences. Education and training for social workers should address the impact on race, ethnicity, culture, and immigration status: This enhances the ability of practitioner to offer more culturally responsive services (Davis, 2003).

DEMOGRAPHIC PROFILE OF IMMIGRATION IN THE UNITED STATES

The 2002 U.S. Census Bureau's March Current Population Survey (CPS) reports that 11.5% of U.S. residents were foreign born (Schmidley, 2003). Of these, 7.3% were noncitizens and 4.2% were naturalized citizens. There were 32.5 million foreign-born persons living in the U.S., of which about 63% or 20.5 million were noncitizens. Estimates from the latest CPS identify the largest proportion of the noncitizen population (60.3%) as Latin Americans, with the next largest (19.4%) as Asian (U.S. House of Representatives, 2004).

An estimated 8–9 million immigrants are undocumented, without any legal immigration status. Each year thousands of immigrant women who are married to United States citizens or lawful permanent residents (LPR) enter the United States (Raj & Silverman, 2002). Domestic violence occurs across ethnicity, gender, religion, age, and socioeconomic status (Kwong, 2002; Orloff, 2001; Rothwell, 2001). For battered immigrant women, immigrant status, lack of support, the language barrier, and low economic status add significant obstacles to their ability to terminate an abusive relationship (Orloff, 2001; Raj & Silverman, 2002; Rothwell, 2001; Romkens, 2001). In the second half of the 19th century and early 20th century, most immigrants came from European countries (Schmidley, 2003). The profile of immigrants has changed in the last century to include those from Africa, East and South Asia, and Central and South America. In 1890, 87% of foreign-born Americans came from Europe, compared with 1% from Asia and 1% from Latin America. In 1990, the change in immigration demographics compared with 100 years earlier was dramatic: the proportion of immigrants from European countries dropped to 22%, while the proportion of immigrants from Latin America increased to 43%, and the proportion of immigrants from Asia increased to 25% (Gibson & Lennon, 1999). The cultures, languages, familial expectations, and social service utilization patterns are different for newer populations of immigrants than for immigrants in the past.

DEFINITIONS

Domestic Violence

Domestic violence is defined as a social problem in which one's property, health, or life are endangered or harmed as a result of intentional behavior by another family member or significant other (Barker, 1995). Domestic violence is defined by state statue and penal code. For example, the State of Massachusetts defines domestic violence as actual or attempted physical harm, fear of imminent serious physical harm, or nonconsensual sex perpetrated by a current or former spouse, boyfriend, girlfriend, or fiancé, a current or former roommate or housemate, a blood relative, a current or former relative by marriage, or a person with whom the victim has had a child. This definition may vary from state to state.

According to the U.S. Bureau of Justice Statistics (1995), 1 million women suffer nonfatal violence at the hands of an intimate partner every year. Among victims of domestic violence, 28% of all violence against women is perpetrated by partners (U.S. Bureau of Justice Statistics, 1994). Around the world, at least one in every three women has experienced physical, sexual, or other type of abuse in their lifetimes (www.info@womenslaw.org, 2003). Domestic violence also has severely affected children. Each year, an estimated 3.3 million children are exposed to violence by family members against their mothers or female caretakers (American Psychological Association, 1996).

Domestic violence is believed to be more prevalent among immigrant women than among women who are U.S. citizens, and the majority of immigrants in the United States are women with children (Orloff & Little, 1999). Immigration status, coupled with gender and race, may place women and their children at increased risk of being trapped in an abusive situation because of their vulnerability within a family relationship and their social isolation within their communities (Orloff & Little, 1999).

Immigration Status

While male immigrants may also be victims of violence, including domestic abuse, the focus of this chapter will be on immigrant women victims of domestic violence. Terms related to immigration and refugee status are defined here. An immigrant is a noncitizen who was born in a country other than the United States, and remains in the U.S. with or without lawful admission for temporary or permanent resident status, as defined by the U.S. government. Immigrants with documentation that enables them to remain in the U.S. pending citizenship proceedings have qualified immigrant status. Others may have entered the U.S. with work, student, or other temporary visas or permits: these may have current or expired status (Drachman, 1995).

Immigrants without any formal immigrant status or history of formal immigrant status are referred to as non-documented immigrants. Refugees include those who are outside their country of origin and are unable to return to that country because of persecution or a well-founded fear of persecution. Refugee status is determined by the U.S. government, based on assessment of level of risk of return based on race, religion, nationality, membership in a particular social group, or political opinion (U.S. Department of Homeland Security, 2004). For the purposes of this discussion, noncitizen domestic violence victims will be identified as immigrants regardless of their immigration status, unless otherwise specified.

Domestic Violence and Immigration

Domestic violence advocates have broadened the definition of domestic violence for immigrant battered women. Categories of domestic violence and abuse related to immigrant women include emotional abuse, economic abuse, sexual abuse, use of coercion and threats, using children, using citizenship or residency privilege, intimidation, isolation and minimizing, blaming, and denying the abusive acts. Battering is also defined as the use of coercive behavior (physical, sexual, or psychological) by a man against his intimate cohabitating partner to force her to do what he wants her to do regardless of her own needs or desires, rights, or best interests (Ferrer, 1998).

Advocates argue that these categories of abuse have special potency for immigrant women, because perpetrators can lie about immigration status as a form of emotional abuse, threaten to report any paid work to the Immigration and Naturalization Service (now the Bureau of Citizenship and Immigration Services or BCIS) as a form of financial abuse, threaten to report the woman to the government if she refuses sex, threaten to report her or her children to the BCIS, fail to file papers to legalize her immigration status, hide or destroy important papers such as passports, not allow her to learn English, and try to convince her that she is a burden and the source of blame for the abuse. It should be noted here that the INS has been renamed the Bureau of Citizenship and Immigration Services (BCIS) and is part of the U.S. Department of Homeland Security (Carey, 2003).

Not every woman married to a U.S. citizen or lawful permanent resident is sponsored for legal status by her spouse. In abusive relationships, spouses who are citizens or lawful permanent residents may not file immigration documents on behalf of their spouses (Dutton, Orloff, & Hass, 2000). Several studies have shown that women whose status depends on their spouse are at higher risk of becoming victims of domestic violence than others (Kwong, 2002; Orloff, 2003; Orloff, 2001). Constant fear of deportation bars immigrant women from terminating abusive relationships. The abusers often use their victims' immigration status to control them (Romkens, 2001; Sitowski, 2001).

RISKS AND NEEDS OF IMMIGRANT DOMESTIC VIOLENCE VICTIMS

Immigrant battered women experience economic, social, and legal problems that are unique to their legal and cultural status in the United States. In the U.S., there is pride in diversity and multiculturalism (Wallace, 1999). However, new refugees, immigrants, and other minority groups often face misunderstanding and confusion when American traditional values conflict with their beliefs and customs. Immigrants may also experience conflicts with civil and criminal justice systems.

Patriarchy and belief in fate may make women feel they cannot control violence, and women from war torn countries may not recognize familial violence. Recent immigrants face multiple stressors, including pressures to assimilate. Conflicts between batterers who attempt to enforce traditional gender roles and their victims who want to take advantage of educational opportunities can escalate into domestic violence. Pressures on victims to present their ethnic immigrant community in a positive light by not reporting or speaking out about the abuse, and dependence on their batterers because of their immigration status, are also salient factors (Mills, 1998).

Barriers to protective services for immigrant domestic violence victims include those of gender, cultural norms, and fear of deportation. When people immigrate to other countries, they bring their cultural norms and values with them. Within the context of different norms and values, the behavior and philosophy of immigrant women toward domestic violence are differently expressed (Narayan, 1995; Raj & Silverman, 2002). Unlike Western culture, that encourages women to preserve equality and be independent, some other cultures may expect women to be subordinate and obedient to their husbands (Ho, 1990; Orloff, 2001; Song & Moon, 1998).

Data gaps in research on domestic violence include insufficient information on violence against women of color (Crowell & Burgess, 1996). Recent immigrants remain underrepresented in survey samples: reasons such as cultural and language barriers, fears of deportation, and fears of affecting relatives' applications for immigration have been cited as reasons for this oversight. There is a paucity of research on the effects of acculturation on domestic violence risk factors for women in similar immigrant populations (Crowell & Burgess, 1996).

Nondocumented Battered Women

Many nondocumented women may refuse to seek help for fear of being deported, according to the National Women's Abuse Prevention Project (1988). This may be because their country of origin has laws protecting husbands who beat their wives and deportation may place a nondocumented battered woman at risk of further abuse by family members on whom she would be dependent for support. It may also be because of the felt need of the victim to protect the interests of her family.

Maria married an American citizen and left an impoverished life in South America to live with her husband in the United States. She and her husband had three children, who were provided with material advantages they would not have had in her country of origin. Her husband never applied for citizenship status for her, and continually abused her. Maria refused to press charges or leave him, however, for fear that she would either lose her children to him or be forced to return to her country of origin, where they would live the same impoverished life she had escaped.

In this case, the fact that Maria's husband never petitioned for her green card permits him to keep her in virtual slavery. She is in a vulnerable position if she tries to leave her husband and he reports her to the BCIS. Her status also precludes her from receiving public assistance and creates barriers to her obtaining a job that could enable her to support herself and her children.

Some options exist for social workers who service immigrant women who are domestic violence victims. They include working collaboratively with agencies that provide information and access to benefits and services to special ethnic populations in their language as well as English; legal service agencies that specialize in immigration law and advocacy; and domestic violence shelters and nonresidential domestic violence programs. Most shelters and domestic violence programs, even if they receive government funding, will provide crisis services to domestic violence victims and their children regardless of citizenship status.

Nondocumented battered women are among the most difficult to assist. In addition to the psychological problems such women may have to address, formidable social problems can create practical difficulties as well. Resources like the National Center for Immigrants' Rights are available to provide information for social workers who are assisting nondocumented women address issues of domestic abuse. Social interventions, in addition to clinical interventions and education, are critical to the success of nondocumented women in freeing themselves from battering situations. According to Mills (1998), however, racial and cultural factors are concerns in social work practice with domestic violence victims. It is important for social workers to understand how immigrant women from different cultural backgrounds may experience domestic violence and face different barriers to ensuring their safety.

Latina Battered Women

Rios, in her paper entitled *Double Jeopardy: Cultural and Systemic Barriers Faced by the Latina Battered Woman* (n.d.), stresses the need for domestic violence workers to understand and respect the cultural differences presented by Latina battered women, and—at the community level—to advocate against those institutional factors, such as lack of social justice, that negatively impact on the Latino community, as well as other communities of color. A comparison of Anglo and Latino family values and structure reveal major differences that have important implications for effectively serving Latina battered women (Rios, n.d.).

In the Latino culture, individuals are seen first and primarily as members of the family, and family members are expected to actively work toward its unity and preservation. However, the Latino culture is also characterized by a patriarchal family structure and the expectation that traditional gender roles will be strictly adhered to. Consequently, the Latino woman is expected to be family identified: her sense of identify and self-esteem is linked to her perceived ability to fulfill the ideal of the self-sacrificing mother and wife. These factors, according to Rios, make it difficult for the Latina battered woman to take action against abuse by seeking judicial or police protection, or assistance through a shelter or family service agency. She is accustomed to subordinating her needs on behalf of her family, even at the risk of her own personal safety. Also, her sense of identity is so linked with her role of wife and mother that she may consider herself a failure if she takes action to break up her family.

These concerns may be supported and reinforced by family, friends, and community, and the victim may be urged to give the relationship another chance. Religious beliefs in the sanctity of marriage can provide another barrier. Service providers must acknowledge the conflicts engendered by a Latina woman's decision to confront the battering situation. This is compounded by Latinos' historical experience of oppression by the police and criminal justice system, which are viewed with suspicion. The lack of bilingual and culturally sensitive social workers can further alienate the Latina victim of family violence, should she choose to reach out for assistance in spite of the internal and structural barriers she faces in doing so.

Bonilla-Santiago (2002) provides an overview of cultural barriers and social service and legal needs of Latina battered women. A study conducted with Latina women demonstrated that most receive little or no assistance or protection from police, legal aid, welfare, mental health, or counseling services due to cultural and language barriers. Also, because Latina women are women from Latin America, Cuba, Mexico, Dominican Republic, Central America, and South America, their differing immigration statuses complicate policy and practice issues. Many Latina women are isolated and trapped in violent homes (34% experience some form of violence). Their perceptions of physical and psychological abuse also differ from Anglo and other women.

Studies on domestic violence among immigrant populations have found a high incidence of abuse against immigrant women by spouses and partners. In one study, 48% of Latina women reported increased violence by a partner since immigrating to the United States (Dutton et al., 2000). Cultural, social, and structural explanations are proposed for this. Language barriers may limit an immigrant domestic violence victim's ability to understand and negotiate service and immigration systems, question social expectations and community pressures, and access financial resources independent of their partner or spouse (Orloff & Little, 1999).

An exploratory study examined the influence of ethnic group membership and socioeconomic status on the coping strategies of women victims of partner abuse, comparing Mexican American and Anglo women. Only socioeconomic status significantly predicted successful coping strategies on the part of the victims in the study, suggesting that class and access to economic resources may be more significant than country and culture of origin in empowering battered women to achieve safe and violence free lives for themselves and their children (Fernandez-Esquer & McCloskey, 1999).

Asian Battered Women

Asian and Asian Pacific Americans may respond differently to domestic violence, based on the meaning they assign to their experiences of abuse (Tjaden & Thoennes, 2000). Asian women are often taught that in their roles as wives and mothers, they are responsible for keeping the family unit together under all circumstances (Kwong, 2002). In a domestically violent situation, women are often blamed for causing instability in their family by not conforming to the social norms and their native culture (Ho, 1990; Orloff, 2001). For example, Korean culture supports male dominance in the family, and women are considered inferior to them (Song & Moon, 1998). One aspect of cultural and ethnic heritage that is common across cultures is the inferior status of women. One study of Korean American families found that male dominant couples were four times more likely to engage in wife abuse (Kim & Sung, 2000). These findings are similar to a study of Vietnamese couples (Bui & Morash, 1999). Wife abuse in these cultures is compounded by economic stress (Kurst-Swanger & Petrosky, 2003).

According to Lee and Au (1998), there is a need to address lack of knowledge about female victims from diverse ethnic/racial backgrounds as well as men who batter them. Prevalence of spouse abuse in the Chinese community is not available. Within the Chinese immigrant population there is an unfounded myth that abuse doesn't occur, because Chinese women underutilize formal services. In fact, there are culturally specific influences on spouse abuse in the Chinese community. For example, Confucianism suggests that the traditional Chinese sense of self is rooted in relationships with significant others in the family, primarily, and there is a de-emphasis on independence from the traditional family system (Yick, 2000). Women are encouraged to internalize values about endurance and submission to maintain the collective existence and family harmony. As a result, women face tremendous pressures in trying to break abusive cycles in their families. The family name is expected to be protected at all costs. Contextual factors, including immigration status, exacerbate these pressures.

Chinese men may use immigration status to psychologically threaten their female partners and keep them subservient in an abusive situation. Nondocumented Chinese women are a vulnerable group as they are new immigrants without language, social skills, financial independence, and knowledge of American culture. Lacking refugee status creates an additional barrier. Women may get jobs more easily (such as low paying garment work), and men may resent this: redistribution of power within the family can cause tension. Social isolation and immigration status further limits women's help-seeking behavior. They may need culturally sensitive social services and shelter, and access to language translation. Most choose to stay with their abusers, so access to couple therapy is also important. Community education, especially for the men, is another important intervention strategy (Lee & Au, 1998).

Eastern European Battered Women

Russian Jewish immigrants were granted asylum in large numbers during and after the cold war. This recent large scale immigration parallels that of the 19th century and has resulted in newly created ethnic enclaves in large urban centers like New York. Judaism teaches that the Jewish home is a Mikdash Me'at, a holy space, and traditionally, Jewish women are responsible for domestic tranquility (Cramer, 1990). One identified barrier to battered immigrant Jewish women seeking help is a deep sense of shame, leading them to minimize or redefine the abuse to avoid humiliation. Another is the lack of services that meet the specific needs of Jewish battered women: shelters with kosher facilities, and arrangements with Jewish educational institutions where children can continue their education and observance of non-Christian holidays.

Lack of multilingual staff and fear of anti-Semitism by non-Jewish staff may also create reluctance on the part of Jewish women to seek services in battered women's shelters. Alternatively, they may also feel constrained in seeking services from a Jewish agency, out of fear that their community will find out they have been battered. Effective service delivery to this population includes some provision for kosher cooking utensils, access to a Rabbi, and the opportunity to select a Jewish or non-Jewish counselor, if desired. Advertising services for victims of domestic violence through temples, sisterhoods or women's organizations in temples, Hadassah, B'nai B'rith, Rabbis, Hillel, and Jewish community centers can be useful for outreach.

It is important to recognize that the actual dynamics of battering in Jewish families are the same as in non-Jewish families, although there is some evidence that Jewish women tend to stay in battering relations longer than non-Jewish women and those seeking shelter may be older than non-Jewish women. According to Cramer (1990), key factors in serving Jewish victims of domestic violence are understanding the meaning of family in Jewish life and the deep humiliation Jewish women often feel about being battered.

Indian and South Asian Battered Women

Domestic violence against women is an issue that many Indian Americans refuse to acknowledge as a problem within their community by contending it only occurs within poor, uneducated families (Gupta, 1992). Women advocates within the Indian immigrant community suggest that this is not the case. The story of Sita, heroine of the Indian epic *Ramayana*, mythologizes the self-immolating woman who becomes the "ideal woman" through her continuous efforts to prove herself worthy of her husband, Ram (Gupta, 1992). It is this feminine model of subjugation that female Indian children are taught to emulate.

While the dynamics of domestic violence are not unique in the Indian immigrant community, Indian battered women face additional problems due to immigration status, level of acculturation, and culturally insensitive mainstream organizations that create barriers to obtaining needed assistance (Gupta, 1992). Traditional arranged marriages create patrilocal joint family households that make Indian women vulnerable to abuse by extended family members as well as spouses. Often the Indian woman's family of origin will not extend assistance once she is married as she is not considered their concern anymore.

According to Gupta (1992), social stigma and pressure from the larger Indian community not to break up the family constitute significant deterrents to women reaching out for assistance through the formal service network. In recent years, a number of Indian and South Asian women have organized their own service network, including shelter services, to assist battered women in their communities. SAKHI, a New York based women's support group, is one of a number of organizations that have formed out of the Indian and South Asian communities to assist battered women and their families.

International Perspectives on Domestic Violence: Implications for Social Work with Immigrants in the U.S.

Summers and Hoffman (2002) provide a cross-cultural comparison of domestic violence, which the authors state is a global problem. This includes overviews of domestic violence in 13 countries, including the United States. Studies of women who are domestic violence victims in native countries of origin can provide insight into cultural barriers faced by women from these countries who have immigrated to the United States.

Yoshihama (1998) reports that a Japanese nationwide study conducted in 1992 raised consciousness about physical and psychological abuse. A link between spouse abuse, child abuse, and abuse during pregnancy is reported with some frequency. Battered women in Japan sought help through women's centers and the health system. However, they didn't always seek help through formal systems, as they considered domestic violence a private and shameful matter. The belief that battered women caused their abuse limits access to services. Japanese women interpreted abuse somewhat differently than in other cultures (overturning the dinner table; having liquid thrown at them to "purify" them—considered psychological abuse). One third of female murder victims in Japan are killed by intimate partners. Findings from focus groups with battered women in Japan suggest that they experience a web of entrapment with little hope of escape (Yoshihama, 2002). Victim blaming by family, friends, and professionals, and lack of assistance programs and police protection exacerbate the feeling of entrapment.

REMEDIES

The U.S. Census Bureau reports that the number of immigrants in the United States has increased significantly within the past 2 decades (U.S. Census Bureau, 2000). It further estimates that by the year 2015 more than half the people in the United States will be from a non-Western European background (U.S. Census Bureau, 1988). This dramatic increase in immigrants from developing countries has spurred an interest on the part of the social work profession in developing assessment tools and intervention techniques to facilitate ethnicity-sensitive practice.

A notable example is the *culturagram* developed by Congress (1994, 2002), a family assessment tool developed for use by social workers to individualize families from diverse cultures, assess the impact of those cultures on family members, and facilitate empathy and ability to empower culturally diverse clients. More information on the culturagram can be found in chapter 1. While professional social workers have increasingly acknowledged the growing cultural diversity of the client population (Brownell & Congress, 1998), this has not always translated into the development of specialized interventions for clients with socially stigmatizing problems such as domestic violence.

Four categories of remedies are discussed here, including three categories of remedies or interventions that have evolved out of social work practice with victims of domestic violence: social interventions, clinical interventions, and empowerment oriented interventions that often utilize the criminal justice system as part of an intervention strategy. Legislative remedies are discussed as a fourth category in relation to access to needed benefits and services for immigrant domestic violence victims. Each present opportunities and challenges for immigrant women and their social workers.

Social Remedies

Social interventions for victims of domestic violence focus on practical problem solving for battered women and their families. While short-term interventions are crisis oriented, longer term interventions are intended to assist the victim to live independently apart from the abuser. Examples include both residential and nonresidential services.

> Mrs. L., who emigrated from China a year ago, was kept a virtual prisoner in the home by her husband and her mother-in-law, who forced her to do housework and care for all the family members as well as her children. She was beaten by her mother-in-law as well as her husband if she refused to comply with their demands. The victim, Mrs. L., experienced both physical and emotional abuse, and may be eligible for crisis counseling and case management services that include linkage and referrals to language appropriate social and health services. Mrs. L. may also require assistance in relocating to a shelter residence that provides safety and transitional housing services.

Residential services encompass all the shelter service models that have evolved to provide temporary safe havens for victims of domestic violence and their families fleeing a battering situation. They are considered the most extreme of the victim-centered interventions: victims entering a shelter system must not disclose their whereabouts to anyone, not even their closest relatives. They are also considered to be the most effective in protecting women and their children who are threatened by harm from their batterers. Currently, specialized shelters are primary resources for women and children seeking protection from domestic violence (Dziegielewski, Resnick, & Krause, 1996).

Case management services are available for domestic violence victims through the shelters, which provide a maximum amount of time limited security for residents, or in the community. Nonresidential services for victims of domestic violence may include emergency hotline services, assistance with relocation, accessing emergency cash and other resources, and crisis counseling (Loring,

1994; Walker, 1994). Longer term social interventions may include income support for battered women and their children, re-housing, and job training. Public assistance is an important resource for some battered women and their families; it remains to be seen whether welfare reform initiatives that include block grants to states will eliminate this important safety net.

Most social interventions have built-in barriers for domestic violence victims from nondominant cultures. Shelters may not include multilingual staff. Those that are funded by public dollars may exclude nondocumented immigrants. Nonresidential programs may not offer culturally sensitive services or hire workers who are multilingual, although this is deemed essential for effective shelter-based interventions (Coley & Beckett, 1988). Victims of domestic violence from immigrant communities may not know about available services or understand how to obtain access to them.

Nondocumented immigrants could have an even more difficult time using long-term social interventions. Public assistance is not an option for them, housing may be too expensive to afford, and employment is difficult to obtain without exploitation. Social workers who work with immigrant women may find it useful to know how to make referrals to any organizations serving discrete immigrant communities. For example, in New York City, New York Agency for New Americans (NYANA) serves Russian and Central European immigrants, SAKHI specializes in working with South Asian and Indian Women, and The New York Asian Women's Center serves the Chinese community. One dimension of multicultural practice with victims of domestic violence is an in-depth knowledge of resources available to immigrants of all ethnic groups in the geographic area served.

Many cultures do not recognize domestic violence, and immigrants' countries of origin may not have laws that define and set criminal and civil penalties for domestic violence. As a result, women and their children from these cultures may face abusive situations alone without adequate support or knowledge of legal protections. Stressful living conditions in the United States, including language barriers and economic hardship, foster violence and discourage battered immigrant women from leaving their abusive partners (Orloff, 2001; Song & Moon, 1998).

Fear of deportation also impacts the help-seeking behavior of domestic violence victims. If the battered women are nondocumented immigrants, there are less likely to contact the police than victims who are U.S. citizens or permanent residents (Orloff, 2003). Legal protection and accessibility to public assistance are essential in order for battered immigrant women to escape from domestic violence situations (Dutton et al., 2000; Orloff & Kaguyutan, 2001). While immigrant domestic violence victims have access to fewer remedies than citizens, some services and interventions exist that are targeted specifically to immigrants and refugees. All immigrants regardless of status are eligible for emergency medical services reimbursable under the federal Medicaid program. Other remedies include clinical or counseling services, legal and law enforcement strategies, and information and referral services.

Advocacy groups provide extensive information on social and legal services available for immigrant battered women on the internet. Manuals with information on services and benefits offer information on all aspects of service provisions to immigrant battered women (Orloff & Little, 1999). These include overviews of domestic violence and immigrant women; cross-cultural issues; legal and policy issues in immigration cases and domestic violence; access to public benefits; and model programs. Other web-based information sources examine various immigration statuses of newcomers to the United States and discuss influences on service provision, access, and use, including service needs, and immigration legislation and its implication for services (Drachman, 1995).

Clinical Remedies

Clinical interventions, developed as part of family service agencies by social workers influenced by the medical profession and psychiatry, moved social workers away from the activist tradition of Jane Addams and Florence Kelley. However, the women's movement of the 1970s began to influence clinical social workers to move away from traditional clinical interventions and begin to incorporate empowerment strategies into their practice (Gondolf, n.d.). Practice with immigrant battered women brings new challenges to professionals to develop culturally competent practice modalities. As the case example of Mr. and Mrs. D. illustrates, immigrants engage in acculturation at different rates. This can cause tension to develop within families and between couples.

> Mr. and Mrs. D. sought counseling from an Indian therapist in their community. Mrs. D. complained Mr. D. had become abusive, both emotionally and physically, since they emigrated from India. Mr. D. countered that Mrs. D. had changed since coming to the United States. In India, she had been compliant and a good and respectful wife. In America, she began to become more independent and to demand greater freedom and autonomy.

This speaks to the need for a family therapist who is culturally sensitive. Traditional psychoanalytic interventions have not been found to be effective with victims of domestic violence. Classical psychoanalysis defines victims of domestic violence as masochistic: they are assumed to be receiving some gratification from the battering situation. Critics suggest that the traditional psychoanalytic approach to treatment of domestic violence victims promotes a "blame the victim" approach that encourages self-blame in victims.

While some feminist practitioners such as Shainess (1984) have reframed it to be more applicable to women who are victims of domestic violence, psychoanalytic thinking is also grounded in Western European culture and thought. As such, it may have little meaning for domestic violence victims from developing countries, eastern cultures, or communities of color. Family therapy is a controversial treatment modality for couples experiencing domestic violence. According to the American Medical Association, couples counseling or family intervention is generally contraindicated in the presence of domestic violence and may increase the risk of serious harm (National Center on Women & Family Law, Inc., 1993).

Family systems theory has been criticized as inappropriate for use with couples where there is active battering (Rodning, 1988). In this approach, the family is looked upon as a system, and battering as a symptom of a dysfunctional system. No member is assigned blame: the victim is viewed as an active participant in the abusive situation. The abuser, in this model, can avoid responsibility for the abusive actions by claiming provocation or a desire to maintain the homeostasis of the family system. For immigrant families from cultures that emphasize the responsibility of the woman to maintain family stability at all cost, this approach could reinforce internalized cultural values encouraging her to remain in the abusive situation for the good of the family.

However, some therapists have claimed success in using conjoint family therapy to treat couples together where domestic violence results from marital conflict (Geller, 1992). The premise for this is that when a couple is seen together, they are treated "as a dynamic unit whose patterns of reactions are interdependent" (Geller & Wasserstrom, 1984, p. 35). Further, cultural background and ethnic identity can create barriers to help-seeking, particularly for immigrant couples experiencing domestic violence, and once a decision to seek help has been made, conjoint family therapy may be the only form of intervention the couple is willing to accept. While some practitioners support couple therapy for families where domestic violence is a factor, many therapists are adamantly opposed to couples being treated together when there is active battering. Reasons include the danger posed to both victim and therapist, and the concern that the hope of a "cure" will dissuade the victim from heeding danger signs or seeking protection when necessary.

Crisis intervention models of treatment are utilized both in domestic violence shelter settings as well as in community-based treatment for victims of domestic violence (Dziegielewski et al., 1996). In a crisis, people respond to traumatic events according to their individual personality traits, coping mechanisms, and cultural values. The crisis intervention model suggests that in the face of emotional and physical abuse, victims can learn new coping mechanisms and problem solving skills.

Cognitive and behavioral approaches have been identified as effective short-term treatment modalities for victims of domestic violence (Dziegielewski et al., 1996). They can also be utilized to assist the victim in addressing the abusive situation within the preferred cultural context. One example of a cognitive-behavioral approach is rational emotive therapy (RET), which seeks to assist clients to address emotional disturbances and improve life situations by targeting irrational belief systems.

According to Robin, DiGiuseppe, and Kopec (1994), RET is the treatment modality of choice when doing cross-cultural therapy or counseling. RET encourages the client to maintain his/her cultural reality and provides a basis for examining and challenging long cherished cultural assumptions only when they lead to dysfunctional emotions, behaviors, and consequences. It also provides clients with the tools to comprehend the link between beliefs, emotions, and behaviors but does not force clients to think, feel, or behave like members of the dominant culture in order to change (Robin et al., 1994).

Feminist therapy models have been developed specifically to address the empowerment of women (Bricker-Jenkins & Hooyman, 1986). For example, survivor therapy, developed by Walker (1994), is an example of an intervention model intended to respond to the problems of battered women. It is based on the treatment approaches of both feminist therapy theory and trauma theory. By analyzing power and control factors in an abusive relationship, survivor therapy treats victims of violence by focusing on their strengths, a practice known as strengths-based therapy by social workers.

This model takes into account the woman's sociopolitical, cultural, and economic context, reflecting the dimensions of the nested ecological theory proposed by Dutton (1994). It also explores victims' coping strategies and assists them in building new ones, using many techniques from cognitive and behavioral therapeutic models. As a feminist model of psychotherapy, it explicitly incorporates the feminist therapist's goal of uncovering and respecting each client's cultural and experiential differences as an ethical guideline (Lerman & Porter, 1990).

Objectives of feminist therapeutic intervention models include the empowerment of clients using strategies to assist the abused partner redefine herself or himself as a survivor (not a victim). They also seek to enhance feelings of competence, strength, self-worth, and independence from the abuser (Walker, 1994). The feminist therapeutic models, as well as crisis intervention and cognitive-behavioral models like RET, seek to assist victims of domestic violence with the immediate crisis, as defined by the client, as well as to develop a new life philosophy that is based on empowerment and strength, not victimization.

Even feminist therapists may sometimes work with immigrant couples, particularly those who are self-referred. According to Lipchik (1994), if the identified problem is a lack of understanding of the laws governing family violence and both members of the couple are willing, the abusive husband may be referred to a batters group as a way to learn about male/female relations in American culture and the legal ramifications of spouse abuse. This may be included as part of an intervention strategy if an assessment finds the couple is not knowledgeable about this country's laws against physical abuse. This represents part of a solution focused approach that can assist the special needs of some immigrant families whose members are in different stages of assimilation and acculturation. For other family violence situations and particularly for those involving a nondocumented partner who is the victim of abuse, the issues are much more problematic.

A contextual perspective that recognizes the impact of cultural variables on a battered women's response to battering as well as other situational factors is essential to effective assessment and intervention strategies (Petretic-Jackson & Jackson, 1996). In addition, the effectiveness of clinical interventions depends in part on the ability of social workers and clients to verbally communicate. Even if clients can understand English, misinterpretations of meanings—mediated by cultural values—can result in the failure of the social worker to assist a client with whom she or he does not share a common culture.

Legal Remedies and the Criminal Justice System

The criminal justice system was perceived by domestic violence advocates in the 1970s as not demonstrating responsiveness to abuse of women. Increasingly, domestic violence advocates advocated for stronger protection of victims and punishment of perpetrators of abuse. Laws were passed to increase protections and sanctions in domestic violence situations. Again, however, many immigrant domestic violence victims were unable or unwilling to utilize these protections due to their ambiguous relationship with immigration and the law. This is another reason why social workers serving immigrant domestic violence victims need to work closely with immigrant lawyers or in an interdisciplinary social work and law setting.

Since the 1960s, the family court system has provided some protection and redress for victims of domestic violence through orders of protection and adjudication of family disputes. In addition, federal, state, and local funding has been appropriated for services to domestic violence victims and their families, obtained through the criminal justice system. While to date, most domestic violence service dollars have targeted victims and their families, attention is increasingly focusing on treatment for batterers as well. These treatment modalities range from mandatory arrest and court-ordered counseling to peer group support similar to the Alcoholics Anonymous (AA) model. Success with any of the available modalities for batterers has been intermittent, at best, and subject to mitigating circumstances (National Institute of Justice, 2003).

Remedies available through the criminal justice system may not be useful for immigrant battered women. In immigrant communities, both husband and wife may be unaware of laws that prohibit abuse of one spouse by another. The nondocumented domestic violence victim may not want to utilize the criminal justice system, out of concern for exposure to BCIS. The court system may be intimidating or confusing to new immigrants, who may have difficulty communicating in English.

Domestic violence situations involving immigrant domestic violence victims present special challenges for social workers and advocates. The immigration issues at stake may require the services of an immigration attorney knowledgeable about domestic violence and immigration.

Social workers and immigration attorneys collaborating on cases involving the court system should make every effort to ensure that translators, if used in the court proceedings, are unbiased and knowledgeable about the domestic abuse situation. Translators should also be familiar with language dialects used by the victims, if applicable. Victims and their children may be especially vulnerable to efforts on the part of the abusers to seek deportation of victims as a way of gaining custody of their children and using the court system to assert their power and control.

Legislative Remedies

Most of the social, legal, medical, and income services and benefits available to immigrant domestic violence victims in the United States are defined by federal and state laws and regulations, and funded through legislative appropriations at the federal, state, and local levels of government. Social workers who serve immigrant women in social service, legal, medical, and other settings must be knowledgeable about these laws and regulations to undertake effective assessments and work with victims to plan and implement effective safety strategies. Social workers must know how to work collaboratively with attorneys who specialize in immigration law and domestic violence. Finally, social workers are in excellent positions to identify service gaps and unmet needs of immigrant battered women, and the consequences of these on the well-being of immigrant battered women and their children. By providing legislative testimony and sharing the stories of their clients in a manner that protects confidentiality while highlighting needs for policy change, social workers can influence policy changes that improve and even save lives.

Social welfare policies can affect access to services and benefits in the United States for immigrant women who are domestic violence victims. These include the Violence Against Women's Act (VAWA I) of 1994; the Personal Responsibility and Work Opportunity Reconciliation Act (PRWORA) of 1996; the Illegal Immigrant Reform and Immigrant Responsibility Act (IIRIRA) Act of 1996; and the Violence Against Women's Act (YAWA II) of 2000. Each of these federal laws changed conditions under which immigrant battered women may be able to leave a battering situation and obtain social welfare services and benefits without facing deportation and separation from their families.

Violence Against Women Act 1994

As a first systematic attempt to address the issue of domestic violence, the Violence Against Women's act (VAWA) (Title IV of the Violent Crime Control and Law Enforcement Act of 1994—P. L. 103-322) was passed in 1994 with bipartisan support Recognizing the significance of domestic violence as a serious problem, Congress passed the Violence Against Women Act (VAWA) in 1994 to prevent domestic violence and also to promote the well-being of domestic violence victims. Congress also recognized that many U.S. citizen or lawful permanent resident spouses abuse their battered spouses and use their immigration status as a weapon to control them (Kwong, 2002; Orloff, 2001).

In order to provide relief to battered immigrant women by providing more opportunities for them to acquire legal status, Congress included protections for battered immigrant and children under VAWA 1994 (VAWA I) (Kwong, 2002; Orloff, 2001; Raj & Silverman, 2001; Orloff & Kaguyutan, 2001). VAWA I provided avenues for battered immigrant women to obtain lawful permanent residency without relying on their abusive spouses to file the document (Orloff, 2001; Kwong, 2002).

Personal Responsibility and Work Opportunity Reconciliation Act (1996)

The Personal Responsibility and Work Opportunity Reconciliation Act of 1996 (PRWORA—P. L. 104-193), Title I, created the Temporary Assistance to Needy Families, a block grant program that replaced Aid to Families and Dependent Children, a federal cash grant entitlement program for poor families with dependent children enacted originally as part of the Social Security Act of 1935. In Title I and other titles of the PRWORA, immigrant eligibility was narrowed for federal and state welfare benefits, food stamps, Medicaid, and cash grant public assistance. Welfare reform has affected more than 500,000 legal immigrants who received federal benefits including SSI and food stamps (Orloff & Little, 1999).

With the leadership of the late Senator Paul Wellstone (D-MN) and Senator Patty Murray (D-WA), an amendment to ease eligibility requirements for domestic violence victims was passed and incorporated into the Act as the Family Violence Option (FVO). However, many immigrants (both documented and non-documented), including victims of domestic violence victims, are barred from applying for these benefits for five years after entering the United States is the entry date was August 26, 1996—the date of the signing of this legislation by President Clinton—or later.

PRWORA does allow certain categories of qualified immigrants to receive public assistance, assuming they also meet other categorical and financial requirements. The categories of qualified immigrants include lawful permanent residents, refugees and asylees, persons granted conditional entry into the U.S., aliens paroled into the U.S. for at least one year, and women and children who have been battered or subjected to extreme cruelty by a U.S. citizen or lawful permanent resident and have a VAWA approved pending family based petition on file with the INS (now BCIS).

Illegal Immigrant Reform and Immigrant Responsibility Act (1996)

After the enactment of the PRWORA, Congress recognized the double jeopardy for battered immigrant women receiving financial assistance (Orloff, 2001; Orloff & Kaguyutan, 2001; Kwong, 2002). Previously undocumented battered immigrant women were not able to access public benefits because they were not "qualified immigrants."

Under the Illegal Immigrant Reform and Immigrant Responsibility Act of 1996 (IIRIRA—P. L. 104-208), Congress enacted a remedy by granting immigrant women access to the welfare safety net by enabling them to apply for qualified immigrant status. This was based on the recognition of the crucial role that economic independence plays in enabling battered immigrant women to extricate themselves from domestic violence (Orloff, 2001; Orloff & Little, 1999).

Violence Against Women Act 2000

Included in the Victims of Trafficking and Violence Protection Act of 2000 is a section, Division B—Violence Against Women's Act of 2000, Title V—Battered Immigrant Women (P. L. 106-386) that reauthorizes and amends the Violence Against Women's Act of 1994. The amendments to VAWA I that were incorporated into VAWA II included improved access to cancellation of removal, suspended deportation, and other immigrant protections for domestic violence victims. It also permitted programs funded by grants under VAWA to be used for immigration assistance to immigrant victims of domestic violence. Finally, it removed the United States residency requirement, and established a new category of visa, the U-visa, for victims of serious crimes related to domestic violence, stalking, and sexual assault (Kwong, 2002; Orloff & Kagunuyan, 2001).

Implications for Social Work Practice

The cultural diversity of American society has stimulated the growth of social work models of practice since the inception of the profession in the 19th century. Service delivery to victims of domestic violence was an integral part of family services among the profession's forerunners in the charity organization and settlement house movement. Charity organization agents serving the urban immigrant communities addressed problems of domestic violence, although in the early days of social work, this was done as part of the prevailing "child saving" mission.

Early social work reformers were also maternalists, and advocated against domestic abuse and for prohibition and women's pensions in order to achieve their (White middle-class) goal of assisting women to remain in the home caring for their children (Gordon, 1995). Their clients were immigrant women, often from rural areas in their countries of origin, who were forced to cope with the harshness and uncertainties of urban industrial life. Early social workers rarely attempted to empathize with the subjects of their ministrations, instead projecting values that were often quite alien to their female clients and advice that was often counterproductive.

However myopic these early reformers were regarding the problems facing immigrant families of the progressive era, they fought hard for solutions to social problems that affected all women. As social work began to turn inward in the 1920s, it began to look for solutions to social problems in psychotherapeutic techniques. The civil rights era and the women's movement of the 1960s and 1970s brought social workers back to a politicized and structural perspective in relation to social problems, including that of domestic violence.

At the beginning of the 21st century, the social work profession is responding to the globalization of social issues and the widespread immigration of families from cultures significantly different from the dominant European American culture, by developing multicultural approaches to working with clients. To address the problem of domestic violence within a multicultural context, social workers must develop a multidimensional understanding of the victim in relation to her/his family, community, and culture of origin, as well as intrapsychic processes. The ecological model of social work practice suggests intervention strategies that represent a synthesis of social and psychological techniques. It also requires a broad knowledge base and understanding of domestic violence victims from different cultures and their responses to new and existing service systems and modalities. Since the 1960s, social work has been struggling toward a multicultural model of service delivery that better reflects the basic tenet of social work practice: begin where the client is. The 20th century feminist movement—although begun by White middle-class professionals—has also reached immigrant communities of color.

Research by social workers into domestic violence as a multicultural phenomenon can yield important information about characteristics of abuse in immigrant communities, barriers to service utilization, and successful practice models. This is a recognized gap in knowledge about domestic violence and how it affects immigrant women in the United States. Lack of access to study subjects has made this a difficult area of study. However, researchers are beginning to learn more about immigrant domestic violence victims through targeted surveys (Yoshihama, 2000; Yick, 2000) and in-depth interviews (Yoshioko, Gilbert, El-Bassel, & Baig-Amin, 2003).

The elimination of domestic violence by one adult family member against another—a key issue in the 20th century women's movement—has challenged activists and social workers alike to evolve culturally sensitive models of service delivery. This reflects a new respect for diversity, as well as the commitment to reach underserved populations that have been isolated by language and culture. In doing so, social work is challenged to continually incorporate culturally sensitive values and techniques, in order to remain vital, relevant, and effective into the 21st century.

Culturally competent social work practice with immigrant victims of domestic violence requires professional social workers to be knowledgeable about social welfare and immigration policies, including federal and state laws and regulations. The ability of an immigrant domestic violence victim to ensure safety for herself and her children, as well as avoid deportation and possible separation from her children, rests on the informed application of existing policies by her service providers and advocates in her community.

The highly technical nature of many of these processes as defined by law and regulation require interdisciplinary collaboration between social workers and attorneys experienced in welfare and immigration law. Often, however, a social worker will be the first professional contact for an immigrant battered woman who seeks assistance through a medical facility, family service agency, or victims service program. This makes it essential that social workers have sufficient understanding of social welfare and immigration laws to enable them to provide support and empowerment, as well as interdisciplinary referrals as needed for legal counsel and advocacy, to immigrant clients who are victims of domestic violence.

The gaps and flaws in existing social welfare and immigration laws and regulations can mean continued danger and hardship for many immigrant battered women and their families. Section 6.04 of the NASW Code of Ethics states that "social workers should be aware of the impact of the political arena on practice and should advocate for changes in policy and legislation to improve social conditions in order to meet basic human needs and promote social justice" (NASW, 1996, p. 27). Social workers can use clinical interventions to assess, treat, and empower clients who are victims of domestic violence to leave an abusive relationship and seek safety for themselves and their children. However, as long as legal barriers remain, clients will have difficulty achieving the safety and stability essential to their well-being. By engaging in social action and change through political advocacy, social workers can enable and empower their clients to achieve their treatment goals through access to needed benefits, services, and legal protections.

Social workers need to understand social welfare policies and the implications for practice so that they can empower clients to access needed services for themselves and their families, and to learn how to influence and shape relevant policies to better serve their clients. Policy practice is an important dimension of social work practice (Jansson, 1999). The ethical responsibility for professional policy practice is stated in the NASW Code of Ethics under Section 6: Social Workers Ethical Responsibility for the Broader Society. This section emphasizes the social worker's responsibility not only to promote the general welfare of society and advocate for the fulfillment of basic human needs, but also to engage in social and political acts to promote social justice for all (NASW, 1996).

According to Jansson (1999), policy practice is defined as efforts to influence social policy development, enactment, implementation, and assessment. Policy advocacy is defined as a form of policy practice that is focused on assisting populations lacking power to effect social and political change on their own. Policy practice and advocacy on behalf of immigrant domestic violence victims transcend controversies within social work about whether the profession should focus on the needs of individuals or the larger society. Social work practitioners who engage in clinical or administrative practice or research with this population must become effective policy practitioners to ensure the best possible service outcomes for their clients.

CONCLUSION

New immigrants remain as vulnerable today as they were over a century ago. In spite of the growing interest and understanding of the need to ensure culturally competent and sensitive social work practice, there is still a dearth of knowledge about the incidence and prevalence of domestic violence among immigrant women and communities of color. Even more essential is a systematic study of the impact of existing services and interventions on victims of domestic violence from cultures other than the dominant European American culture, and the need for changes in the service delivery system.

Many immigrants are from developing countries with cultures and languages significantly different from mainstream America. The influx of immigrants from Asia, South Asia, and Spanish-speaking countries like Puerto Rico and Central and South America, represent communities of color that are often marginalized in American society. Case examples of battered women from Asia, Eastern Europe, and India, as well as the nondocumented in general, illustrate the difficulties of their obtaining needed services in the United States. An understanding of how different immigrant communities view domestic violence can help social workers begin to reformulate their practice, advocate for policy changes, and formulate effective responses to assist battered immigrant women.

REFERENCES

American Psychological Association. (1996). *Violence and the family: Report of the American Psychological Association Presidential Task Force on Violence and the Family*. Washington, DC: Author.

Barker, R. L. (1995). *The social work dictionary*. Silver Springs, MD: National Association of Social Workers.

Bonilla-Santiago, G. (2002). Latina battered women: Barriers to service delivery and cultural considerations. In A. R. Roberts (Ed.), *Handbook of domestic violence intervention strategies: Policies, programs, and legal remedies* (pp. 464–471). New York: Oxford University Press.

Brace, C. L. (1872). *The dangerous classes of New York, and twenty years' work among them*. Silver Springs, MD: National Association of Social Workers.

Bricker-Jenkins, M., & Hooyman, N. (1986). *Not for women only: Social work practice for a feminist future*. Silver Springs, MD: National Association of Social Workers.

Brownell, P., & Congress, E. P. (1998). Application of the culturagram to empower culturally and ethnically diverse battered women. In A. R. Roberts (Ed.), *Battered women and their families: Intervention strategies and treatment programs* (pp. 387–404). New York: Springer Publishing.

Bui, H. N., & Morach, M. (1999). Domestic violence in the Vietnamese immigrant community: An exploratory study. *Violence Against Women, 5*(7), 769–795.

Carey, C. (2003). *Immigration assistance for battered immigrant women: Self-petitions and battered spouse waivers.* New York: Asian Women's Center.

Coley, S. M., & Beckett, J. O. (1988). Black battered women: Practice issues. *Social Casework* (October), 483–490.

Congress, E. (1994). The use of culturagrams to assess and empower culturally diverse families. *Families in Society: The Journal of Contemporary Human Services, 531*–540.

Congress, E. (2002). Using culturagrams with culturally diverse families. In A. Robert & G. Greene (Eds.), *Social work desk reference* (pp. 57–61). New York: Oxford University Press.

Cramer, L. (1990). Recommendations for working with Jewish battered women. *National Coalition Against Domestic Violence (NCADV)* (Fall), 4–5.

Crowell, N. A., & Burgess, A. W. (1996). *Understanding violence against women.* Washington, DC: National Academy Press.

Davis, F. S. (2003). Social work response to domestic violence: Encouraging news from a new look. *Affilia, 18*(2), 177–191.

Drachman, D. (1995). Immigration statutes and their influences on service provisions, access, and use. *Social Work, 40*(2), 188–197.

Dutton, D. G. (1994). *Domestic violence.* Manitoba, Canada: University of Manitoba Press.

Dutton, M. A., Orloff, L., & Hass, G. A. (2000). Symposium Briefing Papers; Characteristics of help-seeking behaviors, resources and service needs of battered immigrant Latinas: Legal and policy implications. *Georgetown Journal on Poverty Law & Policy, 7*(2), 245–305.

Dziegielewski, S. F., Resnick, C., & Krause, N. B. (1996). Shelter-based crisis intervention with battered women. In A. R. Roberts (Ed.), *Helping battered women: New perspectives and remedies* (pp. 159–171). New York: Oxford Press.

Fernandez-Esquer, M. E., & McCloskey, L. A. (1999). Coping with partner abuse among Mexican American and Anglo women: Ethnic and socio-economic influences. *Violence and Victims, 14*(3), 293–310.

Ferrer, D. V. (1998). Validating coping strategies and empowering Latina battered women in Puerto Rico. In A. R. Roberts (Ed.), *Battered women and their families: Intervention strategies and treatment programs* (2nd ed., pp. 483–511). New York: Oxford University Press.

Geller, J. A. (1992). *Breaking destructive patterns.* New York: Free Press.

Geller, J. A., & Wasserstrom, J. (1984). Conjoint therapy for the treatment of domestic violence. In A. R. Roberts (Ed.), *Battered women and their families: Intervention strategies and treatment programs* (1st ed., pp. 33–48). New York: Springer Publishing.

Gibson, C., & Lennon, E. (1999). *Technical Paper 29: Table 2. Region of birth of the foreign-born population: 1850 to 1930 and 1960.* U.S. Bureau of the Census, Washington, DC: Internet Release date: March 9, 1999.

Gondolf, E. W. (1997). *Assessing women battering in mental health services*. Thousand Oaks, CA: Sage.

Gordon, L. (1988). *Heroes of their own lives: The politics and history of domestic violence*. New York: Viking Press.

Gordon, L. (1995). *Pitied but not entitled: Single mothers and the history of welfare*. New York: Free Press.

Gupta, V. M. (1992). The weakest link: Domestic violence in our community. *The Indian-American* (June), 42–44.

Ho, C. K. (1990). An analysis of domestic violence in Asian American communities: A multicultural approach to counseling. *Women and Therapy, 9*(1), 129–150.

Jansson, B. S. (1999). *Becoming an effective policy advocate: From policy practice to social justice*. Pacific Grove: Brooks/Cole.

Kim, J. Y., & Sung, K. (2000). Conjugal violence in Korean-American families: A residue of cultural tradition. *Journal of Family Violence, 15*(4), 331–345.

Kurst-Swanger, K., & Petcosky, J. L. (2003). *Violence in the home: Multi-disciplinary perspectives*. New York: Oxford University Press.

Kwong, D. (2002). Removing barriers for battered immigrant women: A comparison of immigrant protections under VAWA I & II. *Berkeley Women's Law Journal, 17*, 137–152.

Lee, M., & Au, P. (1998). Chinese battered women in North America: Their experience and treatment. In A. R. Roberts (Ed.), *Battered women and their families: Intervention strategies and treatment programs* (2nd ed., pp. 448–482). New York: Oxford University Press.

Lerman, H., & Porter, N. (1990). The contribution of feminism to ethics in psychotherapy. In H. Lerman & N. Porter (Eds.), *Feminist ethics in psychotherapy* (pp. 5–13). New York: Springer Publishing.

Lipchik, E. (1994). Therapy for couples can reduce domestic violence. In K. Swisher & C. Wekesser (Eds.), *Violence against women* (pp. 154–163). San Diego, CA: Greenhaven Press.

Loring, E. (1994). *Emotional abuse*. New York: Free Press.

Mills, L. G. (1998). *The heart of intimate abuse: New interventions in child welfare, criminal justice, and health settings*. New York: Springer Publishing.

Narayan, U. (1995). Male-order brides: Immigrant women, domestic violence and immigration law. *Hypatia, 10*(1), 104–119.

National Association of Social Workers. (1996). *NASW code of ethics*. Washington, DC: National Association of Social Workers.

National Center on Women & Family Law, Inc. (1993). *Couples counseling and couples therapy endanger battered women: Item No. 62*. New York: National Center on Women & Family Law.

National Institute of Justice. (2003). *Do batterers programs work? Two studies*. Washington, DC: United States Department of Justice, NCJ 200331.

National Women's Abuse Prevention Project. (1988). Special issues facing the undocumented woman. *The Exchange, 2*(3), 10–12.

Orloff, L. (2001). Lifesaving welfare safety net access for battered immigrant women and children. *William & Mary Journal of Women and Law, 7*(3), 597–657.

Orloff, L. (2003). *Concerning New York City executive order*. Federal Document Clearing House Congressional Testimony. Retrieved April 3, 2003, from http://80-web.lexix.com.avoserv.library.fordham.edu/universe/doc

Orloff, L., & Little, R. (1999). Public benefits access for battered immigrant women and children. In L. E. Orloff, *Somewhere to turn: Making domestic violence services accessible to battered immigrant women* (Chapter 11). Retrieved February 3, 2003, from http://www.vawnet.org/vnl/library/general/BIW99-cll.html

Orloff, L. E., & Kaguyutan, J. V. (2001). Offering a helping hand: Legal protections for battered immigrant women: A history of legislative responses. *American University Journal of Gender, Social Policy and the Law, 10*(1), 95–183.

Petretic-Jackson, P. A., & Jackson, T. (1996). Mental health interventions with battered women. In A. R. Roberts (Ed.), *Helping battered women: New perspectives and remedies* (pp. 188–221). New York: Oxford Press.

Raj, A., & Silverman, J. (2002). A violence against immigrant women: The roles of culture, context and legal immigrant status on intimate partner violence. *Violence Against Women, 8*(3), 367–398.

Rios, E. A. (n.d.). *Double jeopardy: Cultural and systemic barriers faced by the latina battered woman.* Unpublished paper.

Robin, M., DiGiuseppe, R., & Kopec, A. M. (1994). *Using rational-emotive therapy with culturally diverse clients.* Presented at the Third European Congress of Psychology, Tampere, Finland, July 7, 1993.

Rodning, S. A. (1988). Victim: Family systems and feminist perspective. *Affilia, 3*(3), 83–97.

Romkens, R. (2001). Law as a Trojan horse: Unintended consequences of rights-based interventions to support battered women. *Yale Journal of Law and Feminism, 13*(2), 265–290.

Rothwell, L. (2001). VAWA 2000's retention of the "Extreme Hardship" standard for battered women in cancellation of removal cases: Not your typical deportation case. *Hawaii Law Review, 23,* 555.

Schechter, S. (1982). *Women and male violence: The visions and struggles of the battered women's movement.* Boston: South End Press.

Schmidley, D. (2003). *The foreign-born population in the United States: March 2002.* Current Population Reports, P20-539, U.S. Census Bureau, Washington, DC (see p. 441).

Shainess, N. (1984). *Sweet suffering: Woman as victim.* New York: Bobbs-Merrill.

Sitowski, L. R. (2001). Congress giveth, congress taketh away, congress fixith its mistake? Assessing the potential impact of the battered immigrant women protection Act of 2000. *Law and Inequality Journal, 19*(2), 259–305.

Song, Y. I., & Moon, A. (1998). The domestic violence against women in Korean immigrant families: Cultural, psychological, and socioeconomic perspectives. In Y. I. Song & A. Moon (Eds.), *Korean American women: From tradition to modern feminism* (pp. 161–174). West Port, CT: Greenwood Publishing Group, Inc.

Summers, R. W., & Hoffman, A. M. (2002). Introduction. In R. W. Summers & A. M. Hoffman (Eds.), *Domestic violence: A global view* (pp. xi–xvi). Westport, CT: Greenwood Press.

Tjaden, P., & Thoennes, N. (2000). *Full report of the prevalence, incidence, and consequences of intimate partner violence against women. Findings from the National Violence Against Women Survey.* Washington, DC: National Institute of Justice, Grant 93-IJ-0012.

U.S. Bureau of Justice Statistics Special Report. (1994). *National crime victimization survey, violence against women* (NCJ-145325).

U.S. Bureau of Justice Statistics Special Report. (1995). *Violence against women: Estimates from the redesigned survey* (NCJ-154348).

U.S. Bureau of the Census. (1988). *Projection of the population of the United States by age, sex and race, 1988 to 2080. Current population reports (series P-25, no. 1018).* Washington, DC: U.S. Government Printing Office.

U.S. Department of Homeland Security. (2004). *DHS organization: Department components.* Retrieved from www.dhs.gov

U.S. House of Representatives. (2004). *Green book: Background material and data on the programs within the jurisdiction of the Committee on Ways and Means.* Washington, DC: U.S. Government Printing Office.

Walker, L. (1994). *Abused women and survivor therapy.* Washington, DC: American Psychological Association.

Wallace, H. (1999). *Family violence: Legal, medical, and social perspectives.* Needham Heights, MA: Allyn & Bacon.

Yick, A. G. (2000). Domestic violence beliefs and attitudes in the Chinese American community. *Journal of Social Service Research, 27*(1), 29–51.

Yoshihama, M. (1998). Domestic violence in Japan: Research, program developments, and emerging movements. In A. R. Roberts (Ed.), *Battered women and their families: Intervention strategies and treatment programs* (2nd ed., pp. 405–447). New York: Oxford University Press.

Yoshihama, M. (2000). Reinterpreting strength and safety in a socio-cultural context: Dynamics of domestic violence and experiences of women of Japanese descent. *Children and Youth Services Review, 22*(3/4), 207–229.

Yoshihama, M. (2002). Breaking the web of abuse and silence: Voices of battered women in Japan. *Social Work, 47*(4), 389–414.

Yoshioko, M. R., Gilbert, L., El-Bassel, N., & Baig-Amin, M. (2003). Social support and disclosure of abuse: Comparing South Asian, African-American, and Hispanic battered women. *Journal of Family Violence, 18*(3), 171–180.

CHAPTER 19

Suicide Attempts by Adolescent Latinas: Strategies for Prevention and Intervention

Sandra G. Turner
Carol P. Kaplan

L atinos are considered the fastest growing ethnic group in the United States. Recent projections indicate that by the year 2020, Latino adolescents will account for 25% of the youth population in the United States. They are at risk for many problems due to the stresses of poverty, immigration, and acculturation (Calderon, 1998). According to the Centers for Disease Control (2002) female high school students were significantly more likely to have attempted suicide than male high school students. The rate for Hispanic adolescent girls was the highest of any group studied. They were significantly more likely to have made a suicide attempt (12.1%) than African American female students (8.8%), or White female students (7.9%). Although the attempts are seldom lethal, the existence of this phenomenon places young Latinas at increased risk for death and serious injury, whether intentional or accidental.

The authors previously developed an integrative model for understanding this elevated rate of suicide attempts among Latina teens. The model proposed that attempts were related to the interaction of sociocultural, familial, developmental, and psychological factors, including family functioning, adolescent development, and girls' relationships with their mothers (Zayas, Kaplan, Turner, Romano, & Gonzalez-Ramos, 2000; Zimmerman, 1991). The authors focused on the significance of the mother-daughter relationship. Ng (1996), Razin and colleagues (1991), and Zayas and Dyche (1995) found that female Hispanic teens who attempted suicide had lived fewer years with their fathers than those who did not.

Recent studies of adolescent girls' development suggest that they need to retain a sense of connection at the same time that they are striving to separate and become more independent (Jordan, 1998). A mutual relationship in which girls perceive that their mothers are interested, empathic, available, and responsive to them is key to successfully negotiating this task. Mutuality in intimate relationships has been shown to foster self-disclosure, emotional resilience, positive coping strategies, and social support, and to diminish social isolation (Genero, Miller, Surrey, & Baldwin, 1992). Adolescent girls whose relationships are characterized by dominance and inflexibility rather than mutuality feel a chronic sense of stress (Powell, Denton, & Mattson, 1995; Zimmerman, 1991).

Adolescents who make suicide attempts tend to have one or all of the following: depression and depressive symptoms, low self-esteem, inadequate cognitive and social problem solving skills, poor coping skills, and poor impulse control (Campbell, Milling, Laughlin, & Bush, 1993; Kovacs, Goldstein, & Gatsonis, 1993; Rotheram-Borus, Trautman, Dopkins, & Shrout, 1990; Spirito, Francis, Overholser, & Frank, 1996; Wagner & Cohen, 1995; Wagner, Cole, & Schwarzman, 1995). One study found that when adolescent suicide attempters were compared with non-attempters, there were no differences in parent education, parent occupation, living with one parent or two, or levels of anxiety (Rotheram-Borus et al., 1990).

The integrative model hypothesized that in addition to a low level of mother-daughter mutuality, the families of female adolescent Hispanic suicide attempters would have a high degree of conflict and lack of understanding between parents and adolescents (Zayas et al., 2000). Families of all suicidal adolescents tend to have a dysfunctional family environment (e.g., low cohesiveness and adaptability, familial and marital conflict and violence, low parental support and warmth, and impaired parental psychological functioning), and this may affect the family's ability to help vulnerable adolescents (Fremouw, Callahan, & Kashden, 1993; King, Raskin, Gdowski, Butkus, & Opipari, 1990; Wagner & Cohen, 1995). When parents are authoritarian, adolescents may be outwardly more obedient and conforming, but generally have poorer coping skills and lower self-esteem (Dornbusch, Ritter, Leiderman, & Fraleigh, 1987). Canino (1982) found that well-functioning Puerto Rican families in the United States, despite holding to traditional sex roles, were flexible in their interactions with each other, their daughters, and their environments.

The authors subsequently conducted an exploratory study to investigate factors that are associated with the disproportionate incidence of suicide attempts among adolescent Latinas (Turner, Kaplan, Zayas, & Ross, 2002). This chapter will describe our research findings, present an illustrative case study, and propose strategies for both prevention and intervention with adolescent Hispanic girls who are at risk for suicide attempts.

EXPLORATORY STUDY OF SUICIDAL ADOLESCENT LATINAS

The authors studied 31 adolescent Hispanic girls who were receiving mental health services in the New York metropolitan area. Fourteen girls had attempted suicide in the previous 5 years and 17 had never attempted suicide. The two groups of girls had similar demographic profiles. The majority were born in the U.S. of parents who immigrated from Puerto Rico or the Dominican Republic, and lived only with their mothers in poor or working class communities. They were all attending school, and their average age was 14.7 years.

We hypothesized that girls who did not make suicide attempts would have higher levels of mutuality in their relationships with their mothers than those who did make attempts. We also expected that the non-attempters would have a greater repertoire of effective coping skills. We anticipated that girls who did not make attempts would have lower levels of depression, higher self-esteem, and more balanced family functioning. We defined a suicide attempt as any attempt at self-injury, whether or not the adolescent consciously intended to die (Sudak & Rushforth, 1993).

The authors administered the following measures to the 31 girls in the study:

1. A Background Demographic Information Questionnaire.
2. The Mutual Psychological Development Questionnaire (Genero et al., 1992). This measures the daughter's perception of the degree of her mother's responsiveness, interest, and empathy toward her as well as her own toward her mother.
3. The KIDCOPE (Spirito, Stark, Williams, & Guevremont, 1989; Spirito et al., 1996) measures the cognitive and behavioral coping strategies of distraction, social withdrawal, cognitive restructuring, self-criticism, problem solving, emotional regulation, emotional expression, wishful thinking, social support, blaming others, and resignation. Strategies are grouped according to whether they are negative or positive.
4. The Beck Depression Inventory II (Beck, Steer, & Brown, 1996). This scale assesses affective, cognitive, motivational, vegetative, and psychosomatic elements of depression.
5. The Rosenberg Self-Esteem Scale (Rosenberg, 1965, 1979), which measures the self-acceptance aspect of self-esteem.
6. FACES II (Olson, Portner, & Bell, 1982; Olson & Tiesel, 1991), which measures the adolescent's perception of the family environment in terms of cohesion and adaptability vs. conflict and rigidity.
7. The Short Acculturation Scale (Marin, Sabogal, Marin, Otero-Sabogal, & Perez-Stable, 1987), which assesses adolescents' acculturation to U.S. society, primarily through questions about preferences in use of language and friends.

RESULTS OF STUDY

Mother-daughter mutuality had a significant protective effect with adolescent Hispanic girls who were receiving mental health treatment. Girls who had a higher level of mutuality with their mothers felt that their mothers would listen and not just criticize or dismiss them when they talked about things that mattered to them. These girls were significantly less likely to have made a suicide attempt than girls with a lower level of mutuality. Even though the teens were all in outpatient mental health treatment, those who perceived their mothers to be understanding, empathic, and involved with them had not made suicide attempts, in contrast to those who did not perceive their mothers in this way.

The ability to use positive coping strategies under stress was also protective. In order to assess coping strategies, using the KIDCOPE, we presented the following vignette: "You want to spend more time going out with your friends. Your parents don't want you to go out with these friends, and want you to spend more time at home. Now your friends have called to invite you to a party and you know your parents will probably say no. You are wondering what to do." Possible responses included: "I blamed myself for causing the problem"; "I talked to others about ways to solve the problem"; "I kept wishing this had never happened." Those girls who were able to employ strategies such as problem solving, social support, emotional regulation, and cognitive re-structuring were significantly less likely to have made a suicide attempt than those who more often used negative strategies such as blaming others, wishful thinking, or withdrawal. Girls who made suicide attempts were able to occasionally employ positive strategies. However, when under stress they appeared to revert to negative strategies.

Although they were not significant, we found strong relation-ships among some of the other variables. For example, a strong relationship existed between the level of mother-daughter mutual-ity and the levels of both self-esteem and depression. Girls with higher perceived mutuality tended to have higher self-esteem and lower depression. We also found that girls who described their families as both flexible and cohesive tended to have higher self-esteem and lower depression than girls who thought their families were rigid and conflictual. For example, girls who felt that their families were cohesive and flexible reported that family members were supportive of each other, discussed problems together, and felt that discipline was fair. The following is a case study of a female Hispanic adolescent who attempted suicide.

CASE STUDY

Iris, of Puerto Rican and Dominican parents, was born in the U.S. At the age of 13 she made a suicide attempt and went into treatment in a mental health clinic after a brief hospitalization. She had made the attempt by ingesting over-the-counter medication that she had found in her apartment, but she suffered no medical consequences. The precipitating event was her mother's decision to leave her father because of his periodic physical abuse of her. Iris had two older brothers who were living out of the home. She and her mother, a nurse, lived together, and they had little contact with any extended family. Exceptionally bright and an "A" student, Iris was very pretty but very serious and looked older than her age. She was able to relate well and had a couple of good friends. She stated that she intended to go college and then to law school, a goal that seemed well within her reach.

Iris's mother, Jacqueline, loved her very much, was proud of her, and focused especially on her continued academic success. She worried that Iris might fall prey to negative influences in the neighborhood and wanted her to stay home. She had a very difficult time listening to her daughter discuss feelings about even ordinary adolescent problems or dilemmas. Because her two older sons had not done well in school and often got into trouble, she invested all her hopes, energy, and money in Iris. She herself had been raised in an authoritarian and dysfunctional family, from whom she was now estranged. Not surprisingly, in view of Jacqueline's authoritatian parenting style, Iris was similarly becoming estranged from her. Iris told the social worker that she could never discuss anything with her mother because she usually became agitated and angry. She described her mother becoming furious at small mistakes such as losing a sweater in school.

The worker attempted to facilitate communication between Iris and Jacqueline by having conjoint sessions with them. Encouraged to listen to her daughter, Jacqueline could not do it for very long before becoming agitated. The worker initiated sessions alone with her, which likewise failed to increase her capacity for empathy and understanding. She herself had grown up the hard way, and believed that Iris should be "strong" just as she was. Iris became increasingly convinced that it was useless to talk over problems with her mother. Aside from the social worker, Iris did not confide in anyone. When she and her mother were at home together she locked herself in her room.

In the second year of treatment, when she was 14, Iris started sneaking out with a friend to hang out with boys on nights when her mother was at work. She insisted that this was the only way to see boys because her mother did not allow her to have even telephone contact with them. She soon became sexually active. The worker facilitated her getting birth control, but suspected that Iris did not always use it. Her main emotional involvements were with boyfriends. Her relationship with her mother deteriorated further; they began having fights, and her grades began to slip. Jacqueline, frustrated and angered by Iris, was unaware of her acting out and remained focused mainly on her school performance and behavior at home. Iris distanced herself more and more, which made Jacqueline so angry that on one occasion she hit her beloved daughter.

When Iris reported to a school guidance counselor that her mother had hit her, Child Protective Services was called. As a result, the social worker made another attempt to engage Jacqueline in counseling. However, she felt so wounded by the experience of being reported, that her attitude became even more defensive. She felt that she worked hard to give Iris everything, and could not understand her "ingratitude." Mother and daughter lived in an angry truce, with minimal meaningful contact. At the same time, Iris grew increasingly involved with an older boy, Sergio, who had significant problems of his own. She successfully concealed the intensity of the relationship from Jacqueline, but often in sessions spoke longingly of wanting her mother to like and approve of Sergio. Yet she refused to consider the worker's suggestion of talking about it with her mother, insisting that Jacqueline would just get furious.

At 15 Iris no longer spoke of college and law school. Instead, she dreamed of marrying Sergio. When he broke up with her she was devastated and made another suicide attempt by ingesting pills. She was hospitalized, this time for several weeks. The hospital social worker, recognizing the urgent need for improved mother-daughter communication, attempted to facilitate this in conjoint sessions. Because of her fear for Iris, Jacqueline made an effort to participate, and the hospital social worker saw them together several times. She encouraged her to listen to Iris when she talked about her feelings, and she also prompted Jacqueline to tell Iris of her sadness that they were not closer. Jacqueline finally told Iris of her love and hopes for her.

When Iris was discharged, her regular therapist worked with her and her mother separately for several sessions. The initial focus with Jacqueline was to encourage her to express her feelings of sadness and fear about Iris. The worker helped her to accept Iris's desire to go out with her friends and have boyfriends as a normal adolescent desires and needs. The work with Iris focused on getting her past her anger to connect with her longing to confide her feelings to her mother the way she had as a younger child. No longer feeling "shut out" by Iris, Jacqueline was increasingly able to listen to her daughter without criticizing or getting angry at her. After 6 weeks of working with them individually, the therapist saw them together as well, and gradually mother and daughter started to talk to each other more about feelings and problems. The therapist observed more positive interactions between them.

Gradually Iris's grades improved and she started to feel better about herself. With increased freedom and support from her mother, she began to make better choices about friends and boy-friends. When she felt stressed, she now began to use newly acquired coping skills such as problem solving, and ask for support from her mother and her friends. She started to see a boy who had positive goals, and Jacqueline actually liked him. Mother and daughter began doing things together and they could be seen laughing together frequently. Sessions ended after 6 months, and the therapist maintained sporadic contact with the family. At last report when Iris was 17, she was applying to college, and had several good friends and a part-time job.

PREVENTION AND INTERVENTION IMPLICATIONS

Iris and her mother were eventually able to develop a level of mutuality in their relationship, but the case suggests that prevention and intervention efforts on the part of school personnel may have prevented her suicide attempts and the family's subsequent pain. If her middle school teachers had been alert to her distress over the separation of her parents and the deteriorating relationship with her mother, they might have brought her to the attention of a guidance counselor or social worker, and she may have gotten help sooner.

As we saw, however, Iris was not the only one in her family who needed help. Jacqueline did not understand the importance of active and empathic listening with her daughter, but rather regarded her motherly role in an authoritarian light. For parents in general, and for Hispanic parents in particular, parent education and training might have enabled Jacqueline to appreciate the importance of being responsive to and understanding of her daughter, and to learn strategies to put these principles into practice. Such parent education should begin as early as possible, but certainly by middle school, when children are beginning to resist parent authority and some parents respond by becoming more rigid. For Hispanic parents who feel frightened by mainstream U.S. adolescent norms, culturally sensitive programs about normal adolescent development, both in the schools and the community, would be valuable.

Suicide attempts represent an extreme method of coping with stress. Adolescents who attempt suicide typically have weak coping strategies (Spirito et al., 1996). Teaching teens and pre-teens positive coping skills in schools, after-school programs, and other community venues may not only prevent suicide attempts but may also foster better adjustment and higher self-esteem. After-school programs can also offer informal mentoring and group supports for better coping. As part of parent education, coaching parents to help their children use problem solving, social support, and other effective techniques when they find themselves in stressful situations is essential for helping teens become resilient and well-functioning (Wolchik et al., 2000).

Returning to the treatment of Iris and Jacqueline, the hospital social worker did not work with Iris alone, but recognized that improving the mother-daughter relationship was essential for helping Iris. The social worker enabled Jacqueline to empathize with her daughter as well as to express her own softer feelings and her hopes for Iris, not just anger and criticism. The inpatient and outpatient social workers collaborated in continuing this approach; and in addition to seeing Iris and Jacqueline individually, they also saw them together. This eventually resulted in Iris beginning to trust and confide in her mother, which made both of them much happier and raised Iris's self-esteem. The relationship had become one of mutuality rather than antagonism.

In her individual work with Iris, the outpatient therapist focused on helping her develop strategies for coping with stress. Instead of acting on suicidal impulses when she had a problem in school, felt rejected by a friend or a boy, or disagreed with her mother, Iris learned to use cognitive restructuring and turned to her mother for problem solving and support, now that she felt confident that her mother would really listen and engage in a constructive dialogue. She also turned to her friends for support. Positive coping approaches had also been taught to Jacqueline, so that in addition to listening to her daughter she was able to coach her in coping more effectively.

SUMMARY

This chapter has discussed the risk factors for suicidal behavior among Hispanic adolescent girls, and some of the influences that are thought to play a role in the elevated rate of attempts among this group. It has also presented the case of a suicidal adolescent Latina. The authors believe, based upon their review of the literature, exploratory research, and clinical experience, that prevention and intervention efforts with adolescent Hispanic girls should emphasize fostering mutual relationships of mothers and daughters as well as strengthening girls' coping strategies. The case of Iris illustrates interventions that were effective after a suicide attempt. However, we have also proposed that gatekeepers who work with adolescent Latinas, such as school personnel, can be important in preventing suicide attempts. Staff in after-school programs and community mentors could also play a role in prevention. All of these efforts can contribute to reducing the number of suicide attempts among Hispanic adolescent girls.

REFERENCES

Beck, A. T., Rush, A., & Shaw, E. (1979). *Cognitive therapy of depression*. New York: Guilford Press.

Beck, A. T., Steer, R. A., & Brown, G. K. (1996). *Beck Depression Inventory-II manual*. San Antonio, TX: The Psychological Corporation.

Campbell, N. B., Milling, L., Laughlin, A., & Bush, E. (1993). The psychosocial climate of families with suicidal pre-adolescent children. *American Journal of Orthopsychiatry, 63*(1), 142–145.

Calderon, M. (1998). Adolescent sons and daughters of immigrants: How schools can respond. In K. Borman & B. Schneider (Eds.), *The adolescent years: Social influences and educational challenges* (pp. 65–87). Chicago: University of Chicago Press.

Canino, G. (1982). Transactional family patterns: A preliminary exploration of Puerto Rican female adolescents. In R. E. Zambrana (Ed.), *Work, family and health: Latina women in transition* (Monograph no. 6, pp. 27–36). New York: Fordham University, Hispanic Research Center.

Centers for Disease Control. (2002). Youth risk behavior survey. *Morbidity and Mortality Weekly Reports, 51*(SS04), 1–64.

Dornbusch, S. M., Ritter, P. L., Leiderman, P. H., & Fraleigh, M. J. (1987). The relation of parenting style to adolescent school performance. *Child Development, 58*, 1244–1257.

Fremouw, W., Callahan, T., & Kashden, J. (1993). Adolescent suicidal risk: Psychological, problem solving, and environmental factors. *Suicide and Life-Threatening Behavior, 23*, 46–54.

Genero, N. P., Miller, J. B., Surrey, J. & Baldwin, L. M. (1992). Measuring perceived mutuality in close relationships: Validation of the mutual psychological development questionnaire. *Journal of Family Psychology, 6*(1), 36–48.

Jordan, J. (1998). *Toward connection and competence*. Wellesley, MA: Stone Center Publications.

King, C. A., Raskin, A., Gdowski, C. L., Butkus, M., & Opipari, L. (1990). Psychosocial factors associated with urban adolescent female suicide attempts. *Journal of the American Academy of Child and Adolescent Psychiatry, 29*, 289–294.

Kovacs, M., Goldstein, D., & Gatsonis, C. (1993). Suicidal ideation and childhood-onset depressive disorders: A longitudinal investigation. *Journal of the American Academy of Child & Adolescent Psychiatry, 32*, 8–20.

Marin, G., Sabogal, F., Marin, F. V., Otero-Sabogal, R., & Perez-Stable, E. (1987). Development of a short acculturation scale for Hispanics. *Hispanic Journal of Behavioral Studies, 9*, 183–205.

Ng, B. (1996). Characteristics of 61 Mexican American adolescents who attempted suicide. *Hispanic Journal of Behavioral Sciences, 18*, 3–12.

Olson, D. H., Portner, J., & Bell, R. Q. (1982). FACES II: Family adaptability and cohesion evaluation scales. *Family social science*. St. Paul, MN: University of Minnesota Press.

Olson, D. H., & Tiesel, J. (1991). FACES II: Linear Scoring and interpretation. *Family social science*. St. Paul, MN: University of Minnesota Press.

Powell, J. W., Denton, R., & Mattson, A. (1995). Adolescent depression: Effects of mutuality in the mother-adolescent dyad and locus of control. *American Journal of Orthopsychiatry, 65*(2), 263–273.

Razin, A. M., O'Dowd, M. A., Nathan, A., Rodriguez, I., Goldfield, A., Martin, C., et al. (1991). Suicidal behavior among inner-city Hispanic adolescent females. *General Hospital Psychiatry, 13*, 45–58.

Rosenberg, M. (1965). *Society and the adolescent self-image*. Princeton, NJ: Princeton University Press.

Rosenberg, M. (1979). *Conceiving the self*. New York: Basic Books.

Rotheram-Borus, M. J., Trautman, P. D., Dopkins, S. C., & Shrout, P. E. (1990). Cognitive style and pleasant activities among female suicide attempters. *Journal of Consulting and Clinical Psychology, 58*(5), 554–561.

Spirito, A., Francis, G., Overholser, J., & Frank, N. (1996). Coping, depression, and adolescent suicide attempts. *Journal of Clinical Child Psychology, 25*(2), 147–155.

Spirito, A., Stark, L. A., Williams, C., & Guevremont, D. (1989). Common problems and coping strategies I: Findings with normal adolescents. *Journal of Abnormal Child Psychology, 17,* 201–212.

Sudak, H. S., & Rushforth, N. B. (1993). Suicide. In M. I. Singer, L. T. Singer, & T. M. Anglin (Eds.), *Handbook for screening adolescents at psychosocial risk* (pp. 189–233). New York: Lexington Books.

Turner, S., Kaplan, C., Zayas, L., & Ross, R. (2002). Suicide attempts by adolescent Latinas: An exploratory study of individual and family correlates. *Child and Adolescent Social Work Journal, 19*(5), 357–374.

Wagner, B. M., & Cohen, P. (1995). Adolescent sibling differences in suicidal symptoms: The role of parent-child relationships. *Journal of Abnormal Child Psychology, 22*(3), 321–337.

Wagner, B. M., Cole, R. E., & Schwarzman, P. (1995). Psychosocial correlates of suicide attempts among junior and senior high school youth. *Suicide and Life-Threatening Behavior, 25*(3), 358–372.

Wolchik, S., West, S., Sandler, I., Tein, J., Coatsworth, D., Lengua, L., et al. (2000). An experimental evaluation of theory-based mother and mother-child programs for children of divorce. *Journal of Consulting and Clinical Psychology, 68*(5), 843–856.

Zayas, L. H., & Dyche, L. A. (1995). Ethnic issues in the treatment of Hispanic adolescent suicide attempters. In J. K. Zimmerman & G. M. Asnis (Eds.), *Treatment approaches with suicidal adolescents* (vol. 12, The Einstein Psychiatry Monograph series, pp. 203–218). New York: John Wiley.

Zayas, L., Kaplan, C., Turner, S., Romano, K., & Gonzalez-Ramos, G. (2000). Understanding suicide attempts by adolescent Hispanic females. *Social Work, 45*(1), 53–65.

Zimmerman, J. K. (1991). Crossing the desert alone: An etiological model of female adolescent suicidality. In C. Gilligan, A. G. Rogers, & D. L. Tolman (Eds.), *Women, girls, and psychotherapy: Redefining resistance* (pp. 223–240). New York: Haworth Press.

Section Five

Conclusion

CHAPTER 20

Spirituality and Culturally Diverse Families: The Intersection of Culture, Religion, and Spirituality

Zulema E. Suárez
Edith A. Lewis

Given the vast diversity within and between families, the existence of 19 major world religions that are subdivided into 270 large religious groups, and an estimated 34,000 separate Christian groups in the world, writing about religion and spirituality in culturally diverse families is daunting (Barrett et al., 1982). The United States is the most religious and one of the most diverse and most changing nations in the world (Eck, 2001, p. 5). However, the increasing complexity of our society and emerging research supporting the importance of spirituality in health and healing (Pargament, 1997; Pargament, Maton, & Hess, 1992) require that social workers have some understanding of the cultural, spiritual, and religious dimensions of people's lives (Canda & Furman, 1999; Hodge, 2003). While it is unrealistic to write about specific ethnic families and their complex spiritual and religious practices, knowledge about cultural and religious worldviews and religious and spiritual trends in the United States can inform and guide social work with families.

We start the chapter by providing an overview of contemporary religious trends in the United States to show its rich diversity and the changes that are taking place in people's religious and spiritual identification. After providing this demographic context, we look at the interrelation between ethnicity and religious identification. To better understand some recent changes in the spiritual-religious lives of U.S. Americans, we examine the distinction between religion and spirituality. Once used interchangeably, these terms have different meanings in today's world. From there, we explore religious and cultural worldviews, their interrelationship, and how these influence our feelings and behaviors. Finally, we discuss the implications for practice with ethnically diverse families.

Before we look at the distribution in the country, there is an important caveat to bear in mind while reading this chapter: We are only providing a gross overview of religions in the United States since we are lumping several denominations under the umbrella term Christianity. Religions often have different movements, resulting in vast differences within and between denominations. For example, Christianity consists of four groups: Evangelical, Catholic, Mainline, and Orthodox (Hodge, 2003).

RELIGIOUS TRENDS IN THE UNITED STATES

Although the majority of U.S. Americans identify with a specific religion, contemporary religious and spiritual trends reveal a changing and increasingly diverse and complex society. According to the 2001 American Religious Identification Survey (ARIS), the most comprehensive survey of its kind, the majority of Americans (81%) identify with a specific religion, with the overwhelming number of these, 76.5%, identifying as Christian (Kosmin, Mayer, et al., 2001). Slightly over half of Christian adults identify as Protestant with about a quarter identifying as Catholic, and 8% are other non-Catholic. The largest growth within the Christian population, however, has not been in the established religious denominations, but in the Evangelical movement. The number of Christian denominations considered "traditional" have been declining for decades.

At the same time, the United States is undergoing significant changes in religious identification, and the overall number of Christians living in this country is declining—from 86% in 1990 to 76.5% in 2001 (ARIS). If current trends continue, by 2042, non-Christians will outnumber Christians in the United States. While the number of adults (14.1%) who identify as spiritual but do not have a religion affiliation, also known as "spiritual but not religious" (Fuller, 2001), has more than doubled since 1990, the number of people who belong to non-Christian religions is also rising. For example, although the number of people adhering to Judaism has dropped to 2.8 million of the population from 3.1 million in 1990, the number of other groups classifying themselves as non-Christians has increased from about 5.8 million to about 7.7 million. According to the ARIS (2001) survey, the number of Muslims has more than doubled since 1990 (from 527, 000 to 1,104 million), even though it is difficult to get accurate estimates of this population. Buddhists constitute 0.5% of the population while Unitarian/Universalist and Hindus comprise less than 0.5% of the country (0.3 and 0.4% respectively).

Another phenomenon taking place in the United States is the increase of mixed religion marriages (ARIS, 2001). Almost a quarter (28 million) of married or domestic partner couples were in mixed religion households. Interestingly, Episcopalians (42%) and Buddhists (39%) were the groups most likely to be in a mixed religion family. Religious groups least likely to intermarry included Mormons and groups like some Baptists (the survey does not identify which), members of the Churches of Christ, Assemblies of God, members of the Evangelical movement, and those adhering to the Church of God.

In this section, we saw that although the United States is an overwhelmingly Christian country, this is quickly changing due to an increase in the number of people with no religious identification and in non-Christian groups. However, while traditional or mainline Christian churches are losing membership, the Evangelical movement within Christianity is growing (see Hodge, 2003). Given these changes, it may not be surprising that almost a quarter of all people in the United States are living in mixed religion households. Next, we look at the relationship between race, ethnicity, and religious identification.

RACE, ETHNICITY, AND RELIGIOUS IDENTIFICATION

Although the role of race has been key in the establishment of religions and/or denominations in this country (e.g., the African Methodist Episcopal (AME) church, the Amish), social scientists still often confuse the external status of race with the internal, or self-ascribed status of ethnicity. We wish to make this distinction clear at the outset, as the literature on this topic must be understood within the context of the definitions of race and ethnicity used by the researchers.

There is a strong interconnection between race, ethnicity, and religious affiliation (Canda & Furman, 1999). For example, there are close associations between ethnicity and religious beliefs in groups like the Amish, Mormons, Jews, American Hindus and Buddhists, and Arab American Muslims (Canda & Furman, 1999). Because of the close link between culture and religion, these groups may intentionally or unconsciously maintain a boundary between themselves and outsiders. Indeed, there is still considerable segregation according to religion with Sunday morning service being the most segregated hour in the United States, according to social scientists and many theologians (ARIS, 2001).

Given the interrelationship between race and religion, it is not surprising that several mainline denominations in the United States are predominantly White. Over 90% of Lutherans, Presbyterians, Mormons, and Congregational/UCC are White, as are adherents to Reformed, Conservative, and Orthodox Judaism. Episcopalians/Anglicans closely follow with 89% White membership. Catholics in the United States are predominantly from White (64%) or Latino (29%) backgrounds with fewer than 5% African American (ARIS, 2001). Although Baptists are also primarily White, close to a third are African American with only 6% Latino, other, and Asian. Interestingly, Muslims seem to be the most diverse with 34% Asians, 27% Blacks, 15% Whites, and 10% Hispanics. Under 2% of the total sample, Native Americans have a religious profile similar to White, non-Hispanic Americans with

20% identifying as Baptist, 17% as Catholic, and 17% indicating no religious preference. Only 3% indicated a primary identification with an "Indian" or tribal religion.

At the same time, the relationship between ethnicity and religion is weakening. This is especially evident among Jews and Latino groups. Only 53% of adults classifiable as Jewish identify with Judaism as a religion. The remaining 47% indicated that they had Jewish parentage, were raised Jewish, or considered themselves Jewish. Although Hispanic groups have been predominantly Roman Catholic (57% of adults), 22% reported their religion as one of the Protestant denominations, 5% indicated some other religious identification, and 12% denied having a religion (ARIS, 2001, p. 8).

In this section, we saw that the relationship between race, ethnicity, and religion is so strong that despite advances made in the Civil Rights Movement, churches are still segregated. This relationship, however, is beginning to weaken.

SPIRITUALITY VS. RELIGION

Although before the 20th century, the terms religious and spiritual were often interchangeable, they have assumed distinct meanings in a contemporary society where modern intellectual and cultural forces have accentuated the difference between "private" and "public" life (Fuller, 2001). Moreover, the advent of scientific and biblical scholarship, and cultural relativism has challenged educated Americans' blind loyalty to the traditions of established religious institutions, causing them to question existing orthodoxies (Fuller, 2001; Borg, 2003).

Since spirituality is difficult to define (Canda & Furman, 1999; Richards & Bergin, 1997), a composite of different definitions provides a working understanding of the concept. According to Canda and Furman (1999), "Spirituality refers to the fundamental aspect of what it is to be human—to search for a sense of meaning, purpose, and moral frameworks for relating with self, others, and the ultimate reality" (p. 37). Richards and Bergin (1997, p. 13) define spirituality as "those experiences, beliefs, and phenomena that pertain to the transcendent and existential aspects of life (i.e., God or a Higher Power, the purpose and meaning of life, suffering, good and evil, death, etc.)." Although spirituality may be expressed through religion or independently, today, many associate spirituality with "private" or personal belief and religion with the public realm of institutional membership, participation in formal rituals and adherence to official denominational doctrine.

Richards and Bergin (1997) view religion as a subset of spirituality. According to the authors, "Religious expressions tend to be denominational, external, cognitive, behavioral, ritualistic, and public. Spiritual experiences tend to be universal, ecumenical, internal, affective, spontaneous, and private. It is possible to be religious without being spiritual and spiritual without being religious" (p. 13). Although religious has to do with theistic beliefs, practices, and feelings often expressed institutionally, denominationally, and personally, this is not always the case. For example, a person may pray and read the Bible, living his/her life according to his/her understanding of scripture, but not belong to a religious institution. According to a *USA Today*/Gallup Poll (2002), an increasing number of Americans (33%) consider themselves to be spiritual but not religious, while 50% consider themselves religious and 10% neither spiritual nor religious. Although research shows that many people attempt to integrate elements of religion and spirituality, people who identify as religious have higher interest in church participation and commitment to orthodox beliefs (Fuller, 2001). Hence, although the terms spiritual and religious are interrelated, they are different.

WORLDVIEWS AND VALUES

The cultural life of all societies is shaped and directed by worldviews—beliefs about the universe and the nature of reality that provide answers about the meaning of life and about the most daunting questions about the human condition (Wager, 1977, as cited in Richards & Bergin, 1997, p. 51). Whether or not we are aware of our worldviews, they influence our behavior, our conceptions of nature and of our place in the world, and our interpersonal relationships. Worldviews also include affective-cognitive elements that are inextricably blended and vary on a continuum from explicit to implicit (Papajohn & Spiegel, 1975). Indeed, in many societies, members do not always draw a clear line between their culture and way of life (Papajohn & Spiegel, 1975) and Western researchers' concept of religion. Hence, to understand families culturally and spiritually, awareness of the existence of diverse worldviews is essential. Although cultural and spiritual-religious worldviews are interrelated, anthropologists and social scientists have approached these separately (see Richards & Bergin, 1997).

RELIGIOUS WORLDVIEWS

According to Dilthey (as reported in Richards & Bergin, 1997), although there are a variety of religious belief systems in the world, these can be subsumed under three major types of worldview that guide people in their quest for answers to their existential and metaphysical questions. Following we briefly summarize naturalism, idealism of freedom, and objective idealism.

Naturalism posits reality as a physical system accessible only through the five senses (Wagar in Richards & Bergin, 1997). The "good life" is the pursuit of happiness and power and the idea of mechanistic determinism tends to override freedom of will. Rationalism, positivism, existentialism, Marxism, and secular humanism are provided as examples of this worldview. The United States as a secular, industrialized country that has placed its faith in science and technology adheres to a naturalist view. However, given the overwhelming number of Christians in this country and the influence of religious worldviews in our public debates, some question whether we are Christian rather than secular. Despite the separation of church and state in the U.S., the motto "In God We Trust" is printed on all our currency. Positivism (i.e., if it cannot be measured it does not exist) may explain the reverence in our society and in universities for science and empirical research that validate our physical reality. Others argue that every experience in this world cannot be accessed through the five senses and that there is an "inner life" for all matter. Each of these examples recognizes the diversity in this worldview.

Idealism of freedom takes a subjective view of reality in which human beings have free will, and is grounded in a transcendental spiritual realm. The "good life" is defined as obedience to conscience or divine will and upholds moral freedom. In other words, as Mahatmas Gandhi and Rev. Dr. Martin Luther King, Jr. demonstrated with their practice of satyagraha, or nonviolence, people facing injustice can either respond in kind, or exercise their moral freedom by choosing to "love their enemies" to bring about the change they seek (McGreal, 1995). Western or monotheistic world religions like Judaism, Christianity, Islam, Zoroastrianism, and Sikhism exemplify this worldview.

Finally, objective idealism avoids the dualism in idealism of freedom by proclaiming the unity and divinity of all that is and uniting determinism and indeterminism. In this worldview, dichotomies in thinking (things are black or white, we are either dead or alive) are absent. Things are not seen as opposites of each other but as part of a whole that encompasses reality. For example, in this belief system, we cannot understand white without understanding black and how they interact with each other nor can we know life without knowing death, as exemplified by the popular Yin and Yang symbol. The Eastern religions Buddhism, Hinduism, Jainism, Shintoism, Confuscianism, and Taoism are examples of this worldview.

The ability of religions to recognize the similarities they have with one another is only possible when the "other's" divinity can be recognized. Although according to Dilthey (cited in Richards & Bergin, 1997), these worldviews have traditionally rivaled each other in providing alternative answers to the major questions of life, many people combine elements of these three types to form their own unique worldview that draws upon and transcends the prevailing views of the major religions.

CULTURAL WORLDVIEWS

As spirituality is concerned with finding the meaning and purpose of life, the suffering that befalls us, and moral and interpersonal frameworks for relating to others, cultural value systems also include moral standards and mores for living as well as motivation and patterns of interpersonal behavior. Cultural anthropologists have synthesized the variations in existential judgments and systems of belief, such as those found in various religious orientations, philosophies, and science with other cultural patterns to give us a better understanding of unique and universal cultural patterns (Papajohn & Spiegel, 1975). Although generalizations based on observations of one culture cannot be universally applied, some scholars argue that there is a fundamental universality to human problems, and societies have found similar answers for some of these existential challenges (Papajohn & Spiegel, 1975).

Building on the work of Kluckhohn and Strodtbeck (1961), Papajohn and Spiegel (1975) present a classification for understanding people's worldviews across cultures. This model of value orientations has three underlying assumptions. First, the number of existential problems to which all peoples must find solutions is finite since we all live and die, and live in families and communities, no matter what our ethnic and racial background. Second, although there is variability in people's responses to these problems, there is a limited, non-random range of possible solutions. For example, since death is universal, we all must grieve. How that happens may be different not only between ethnic groups but also within. This was evident when one of the authors ran an immediate loss group for Dominican women. Whereas people from rural areas of the Dominican Republic included the community in their mourning rituals, the urban women in the group were more private and resented opening their homes for community members to mourn with them. Third, although there will be a dominant profile of value orientations composed of the most highly valued orientations, there will also be variant orientations that are universal. Hence, although as noted earlier, the naturalist worldview is dominant in Western countries like the United States, Christian and other values also permeate our personal and public lives.

According to Papajohn and Spiegel's model, four major problems have challenged people across places and times. What is the modality of activity (Activity Orientation)? What is the modality of human beings' relationship to other human beings (Relational Orientation)? What is the temporal focus of human life (Time Orientation)? What is the relationship of humans to nature (Human Nature Orientation)? The responses to these questions are complex and reflect all the value orientations simultaneously. Hence, the authors caution the reader from interpreting these tendencies literally. For the sake of simplicity, however, we examine these orientations separately.

The activity orientation question refers to humans' mode of self-expression in activity and includes at least three possibilities: being, being-in-becoming, and doing. Cultures with a being orientation prefer spontaneous expression in activity of impulses and desires. This does not mean, however, that people are not censored from acting on aggressive or negative impulses since all societies have a moral code, although these may vary. People with this orientation tend to live in the present instead of planning and anticipating the future. The focus of activity is not development, but the "is-ness" of the personality and the spontaneous expression of that "is-ness." For example, a person with this orientation may be late to a class or an appointment with a social worker if they happen to bump into a friend along the way, since the chance encounter may override the planned event. This is not to say that the person does not value the planned activity, however; s/he is just being spontaneous. Some non-Western societies such as India or Latin American countries are considered to have a dominant being orientation.

Although the being-in-becoming, like the being orientation, is concerned with what the human being is instead of what s/he can accomplish, the idea of development is paramount in this orientation. Hence, the being-in-becoming orientation is the kind of activity that strives for the development of an integrated and whole personality. People who identify as "spiritual but not religious" view spirituality as a journey linked to spiritual growth and development (Fuller, 2002). Hence, they will read extensively and will attend workshops and retreats that will enhance their growth.

The doing preference characterizes American society, according to Papajohn and Spiegel (1975). This orientation stresses activity that is goal oriented and leads to measurable accomplishments. The more we do the more we will achieve. This is important since an individual's worth in this society is determined primarily on his/her past and future accomplishments more so than by their virtues. Consistent with the naturalist value for measuring, degrees and stock portfolios gain significance over kindness and compassion, abstract concepts that cannot easily be quantified. Hence, for the most part, the pursuit of money and status is revered above personal and spiritual development. This value is in contrast to Confucianism (objective idealism worldview), that holds that inner virtue and proper conduct is the path to personal and social harmony (Richards & Bergin, 1997).

The second human problem, according to this conceptual framework, addresses interpersonal relationships (Papajohn &

Spiegel, 1975). This orientation also has three subdivisions: lineal, collateral, and individualistic. Although all societies pay attention to all three principles in relations, it is a matter of emphasis. In Shintoism, as an example of a lineal and objective idealism worldview, "Loyalty and fulfilling one's duty to family, ancestors, and traditions as important" (Richards & Bergin, 1997, p. 70).

Collateral relationship patterns consist of a network of horizontal extended relationships consisting of large family systems that include blood and fictive kin since humans do not stand alone, but as part of a web (Papajohn & Spiegel, 1975). Therefore, children are trained to depend on the family network and to be obedient. Family loyalty is exchanged for caretaking throughout the person's life. Latin American families tend to nurture collateral relationships.

Individualism is a dominant American middle-class value (Papajohn & Spiegel, 1975). From early on, children are raised to be independent and to exercise self-control. They are also trained to experience separation from the family as normal by, for example, going to day care and summer camp (Papajohn & Spiegel, 1975). Under this value orientation, adults make decisions based on their individual self-interest as opposed to considering the needs of the extended family network. This value is consistent with a naturalist worldview.

Three preferences characterize human beings' place in time, the third existential problem. All societies deal with a past, present, and future, but they vary greatly according to which dimension they make dominant. Earlier we said that cultures with a being orientation value spontaneity and living in the present. Since values and religious worldviews are interrelated, this time orientation is also evident in religious thought. For example, most North American Christians, according to Marcus Borg (2003), a Lutheran theologian, "see[s] the Christian life as centered in believing now for the sake of salvation later—believing in God, the Bible, and Jesus as a way to heaven" (p. xiii). An emerging paradigm in Christianity, however, sees Christian life as a relationship with God that transforms life in the present (p. 15)." Hence, rewards come from being in relationship with God in the present, not from the afterlife (the future). As a relatively young country, the United States emphasizes a future orientation that will bring bigger and better things.

The fourth human problem is human beings' relationship to nature. The three-point range in this orientation is subjugation-to-nature, harmony-with-nature, and mastery-over-nature. Euro-centric scholars with a doing orientation often misinterpret the subjugation-to-nature orientation to mean that people who adhere to this orientation are fatalistic about the weather, illness, and death—implying passivity before the forces of nature and giving up without a fight. Our interpretation is different. We see subjugation-to-nature as knowing when to surrender to forces greater than we are when things are beyond our control. In Taoism this is known as we-wei, the principle of passive action that states that one should not resist, confront, or defy (Richards & Bergin, 1997). Ironically, in American culture we try to outwit nature via medical technology and meteorology and we have allowed the medical community to medicalize natural changes in our bodies such as childbirth, menopause, aging, and dying.

The harmony-with-nature orientation does not separate humans from nature since they are both seen as being part of the same whole (objective idealism). This orientation is more characteristic of Eastern or non-industrialized countries and of Native American populations who see humans as being one with the natural environment. For example, Native American shamans see Earth as a living organism, a belief common among many tribes, and encourage their clients' connections to natural forces (Krippner & Welch, 1992). The Asian religion Shintoism views spirituality "as feelings of appreciation and closeness to nature and enjoyment of life" (Richards & Bergin, 1997, p. 70). To Native Americans and women who practice women's spirituality, the Earth Mother is sacred and should not be exploited or pillaged. This knowledge may help us to better understand why Julia Butterfly Hill lived in a giant redwood tree named Luna for 2 years to protect it from the ax and to raise consciousness about saving these magnificent trees (see for example, Fitzgerald, 2002; Spretnak, 1994; Starhawk, 1987).

Mastery-over-nature, a third way of conceptualizing this relation, is consistent with a naturalist worldview. According to this view, human beings can overcome and exploit natural forces, confident that the resources used can be replenished or that alternatives for them will be discovered and utilized. This orientation is dominant in industrialized countries like the United States and is evidenced by our destruction and exploitation of the natural environment for material and scientific gains, according to some scholars. Since as a country, we do not share a harmony-with-nature view, we will cut down forests to build housing developments and shopping malls, while defiling grounds that are sacred to people who have a harmony-with-nature orientation.

The fifth common human problem deals with innate human nature. Are human beings evil, good, or some combination of good and evil (neutral or a mixture of both)? Whether these are changeable or unchangeable increases this threefold classification to six possibilities. Human beings can be considered evil and unalterable or evil but redeemable. According to Richards and Bergin (1997), many Christians see humans as being evil because of the fall of Adam and Eve, but as alterable through God's grace. Hindus see humans as being divine, while Shintoism sees them as inherently good and unalterable. This may explain why Hinduism does not provide a binding moral code for its followers. Other societies see humans as being good and corruptible since they have free will (some Christians, some Muslims, Sikhs, and followers of Zoroastrianism, to name a few). Others view humans as an unalterable mixture of good and evil. Since religions for the most part provide a way out of our state of suffering and imperfection, this may be a secular value. Finally, some hold that humans are a mixture of both good and evil but this is subject to influence. In other words, we are a mixture of light (good) and darkness (innocent misunderstanding or evil). According to Pema Chödrön, a Western Buddhist monk, the Buddha taught that

> there is a kind of innocent misunderstanding that we all share, something that can be turned around, corrected, and seen through, as if we were in a dark room and someone showed us where the light switch was. It isn't sin that we are in a dark room. (1991, p. 13)

In the preceding section, we examined the importance of religious and cultural worldviews in human behavior. Although people do not generally distinguish between their way of life and their worldviews, understanding the existence and importance of worldviews can help us understand the feelings and behaviors of people who are different from us.

SUMMARY AND IMPLICATIONS

In this chapter, we have attempted to highlight some of the issues to consider when working with families while acknowledging the role of spiritual or religious traditions in their lives. Using Papajohn and Spiegel's (1975) conceptual framework and the ARIS survey (2001), we have identified the following "lessons" of importance for this work.

There are as many intra-religious differences as there are interreligious differences. Given the large number of Christian denominations, Jewish, and Muslim traditions in the U.S., we cannot make assumptions about the religious beliefs or practices of clients since there are vast differences within and between the different subgroups of the major religious traditions (Canda & Furman, 1999). For example, among Christians, Lutherans may belong to the Missouri Synod, Wisconsin Synod, or Evangelical Lutheran Church in America (ELCA). The differences between these groups are so great that the Wisconsin and Missouri Synods will not share the communion table with ELCA Lutherans because they consider them too liberal. At the same time, other non-Lutheran reform traditions such as the Episcopal Church U.S.A. are in full communion with ELCA Lutherans because of an ecumenical partnership. Therefore, we need to learn from the clients about their Christian affiliation and traditions. We must be especially careful not to impose our understanding of the requirements of that tradition on our clients, even with those who are nominally in the same religious traditions as we are.

The diversity between and within religious groups in the U.S. has grown such that it is no longer enough to view the country as a Christian nation. At the same time, the United States is still numerically Christian from primarily Mainline and Catholic denominations, and the number of non-Christians and Evangelical Christians is rapidly increasing. Given current anti-Muslim sentiment, and that most Evangelicals are disproportionately drawn from minority groups like women, the poor, and others who have been denied power, we must attend to issues of religious freedom and social justice (Canda & Furman, 1999; Hodge, 2003).

We need to be clear about the ways in which these traditions are being ignored in our public social lives, and how as social workers we may be contributing to the oppression of these groups.

We must also bring forth into the public limelight the needs of these religious minorities, highlighting the strengths of their different traditions. For example, in many parts of the country it is not uncommon to see Muslim workers bring their prayer mats to the workplace, find a quiet place in the building, and do their daily prayers. Even 2 decades ago, that would have been unheard of. In cities such as Detroit, Michigan, the presence of large numbers of Muslims have influenced change so that their religious needs are being addressed.

Further, the Peace Alliance Foundation (formerly the World Renaissance Alliance), made up of several spiritual traditions, has organized prayer circles throughout the country for citizens to gather with their neighbors and identify ways to individually and collectively work toward peace nationally and in the world. The alliance, built around a 12-step model, is another current example of the way religious and spiritual traditions are beginning to blend for the purposes of further social justice.

Because the number of people without a religious identification is also markedly rising, we need to bear in mind that just because a client does not indicate a religious preference on an intake form, it doesn't mean s/he is not spiritual or even religious. It may be that they have multiple spiritual orientations like the "spiritual but not religious," or may adhere to at least one major religious category such as Christian, combined with other traditions such as Buddhism or Jainism (Canda & Furman, 1999). Since multiple orientations would not be represented in a standard agency intake form, social workers should ask clients to tell them about their spiritual traditions without referring to a specific religion.

Because people differ in their ways of understanding themselves and others, partly because of their socialized ways of viewing human behavior, it is useful to stop and determine the differences and similarities between the client and the worker when attempting to address religion and spirituality in practice. Using the Papajohn and Spiegel (1975) and the Dilthey typologies, the social worker can generate useful dialogue, leading participants to using mutually understandable terminology in their communication.

Finally, given the rise in mixed religion marriages, families and couples can benefit from acknowledging the differences in their spiritual and religious traditions so that conflicts can be managed effectively. McGoldrick, Giordano, and Pierce (1996) in their work across ethnic backgrounds identify the conflicts that may arise for mixed ethnicity families over when to celebrate a holiday, child-rearing practices, and how to mourn their dead. For example, if one spouse's tradition is to celebrate on the eve of a holiday while the other's is to celebrate during the actual day, this seemingly minor difference can cause repeated conflicts among these couples. By helping mixed religion (and sometimes mixed ethnicity) couples identify the differences in their cultural and religious worldviews and traditions, social workers can help them gain insight about this conflict without judging each other's traditions. From that exploration, a new way of integrating both members of the couple's traditions can be established and shared with other members of the extended family.

REFERENCES

Barrett, D., Kurian, G., & Johnson, T. (2001). *World Christian encyclopedia: A comparative survey of churches and religions—AD 30 to 2200* (2nd ed.). New York: Oxford University Press.

Barrett, D., Kurian, G., et al. (2001). *World religion encyclopedia: A comparative survey of churches and religions—AD 30 to 2200*. New York: Oxford University Press.

Borg, M. J. (2003). *The heart of christianity: Rediscovering a life of faith*. San Francisco: Harper Collins.

Canda, E. R., & Furman, L. D. (1999). *Spiritual diversity in social work practice: The heart of helping*. New York: The Free Press.

Chödrön, P. (1991). *The Wisdom of no escape and the path of loving-kindness*. Boston: Shambhala Classics.

Eck, D. L. (2001). *A new religious America: How a "Christian country" has become the world's most religiously diverse nation*. San Francisco: Harper Collins.

Fitzgerald, D. (2002). *Julia butterfly hill: Saving the redwoods*. Brookfield, CT: Millbrook Press.

Fuller, R. C. (2001). *Spiritual, but not religious: Understanding unchurched America*. Oxford University Press.

Grossman, C. (2002, March 7). Charting the unchurched in America. *USA Today*.

Hodge, D. R. (2003). The challenge of spiritual diversity: Can social work facilitate and inclusive environment? *Families in Society, 84*, 348–358.

Kluckhohn, F. R., & Stodtbeck, F. L. (1961). *Variations in value orientations*. New York: Harper and Row.

Kosmin, B. A., Mayer, E., et al. (2001). *American religious identification survey 2001*. New York: Graduate Center of the City University of New York.

Krippner, S., & Welch, P. (1987). *Spiritual dimensions of healing: From native shamanism to contemporary health care.* New York: Irvington Publishers, Inc.

Krippner, S., & Welch, P. (1992). *The spiritual dimensions of healing: From native shamanism to contemporary health care.* New York: Irvington Publishers, Inc.

McGoldrick, M. J., Giordano, J., & Pearce, J. K. (1996). *Ethnicity and family therapy.* New York: Guilford Press.

McGreal, I. P. (Ed.). (1985). *Great thinkers of the eastern world: The major thinkers and the philosophical and religious classics of China, India, Japan, Korea and the world of Islam.* New York: Harper Collins.

McGreal, I. P. (1995). *Great thinkers of the Eastern world: The major thinkers and the philosophical and religious classics of China, India, Japan, Korea, and the world of Islam.* New York: Harper Collins.

Papajohn, J., & Spiegel, J. (1975). *Transactions in families: Resolving cultural and generational conflicts.* Landham, MD: Jason Aronson Inc.

Pargament, K. I. (1997). *The psychology of religion and coping: Theory, research and practice.* New York: Guilford Press.

Pargament, K. I., Maton, K. I., & Hess, R. E. (Eds.). (1992). *Religion and prevention in mental health: Research, vision, and action.* New York: Haworth Press.

Richards, P. S., & Bergin, A. (1997). *A spiritual strategy for counseling and psychotherapy.* Washington, DC: American Psychological Association.

Spretnak, C. (Ed.). (1994). *The politics of women's spirituality: Essays by the founding mothers of the movement.* New York: Anchor Books Doubleday.

Starhawk. (1987). *Truth or dare: Encounters with power, authority, and mystery.* San Francisco: Harper Collins.

CHAPTER 21

Ethical Issues and Future Directions

Elaine P. Congress

Family therapy is often the most value conflicted and ethically challenging of therapies, namely because family therapy often evokes strong countertransference feelings in the practitioner. Although professionals may not have had the same experiences as their individual clients, almost all family therapists share a similar experience with their clients, as the former have also grown up in families. Often family therapists must guard against imposing their own values on families with whom they work. Practitioners' beliefs about families may be very influenced by their own individual experiences and cultural background. Research suggests that even highly experienced third or fourth generation clinicians may still be powerfully affected by their own cultural background (McGoldrick, 1998). Ethical practice with culturally diverse families necessitates that clinicians understand their own cultural background before undertaking work with families from different cultures (Congress, 1999; McGoldrick, Almeida, Preto, & Bibb, 1999).

The current National Association of Social Workers (NASW) Code of Ethics (1999) speaks to the need for social workers to understand their clients and "to demonstrate competence in the provision of services that are sensitive to clients' cultures and to differences among people and cultural groups" (NASW, 1999, p. 9). The culturagram (Congress, 1994, 2002) discussed in chapter

1 can help clinicians better understand their own cultural background, as well as those of their clients.

In the last 25 years, clinicians have increasingly focused on values, ethical issues, and dilemmas in work with individual clients (Congress, 1999; Lowenberg, Dolgoff, & Harrington, 2000; Reamer, 1999). There has been some attention in the literature to family therapy from a multicultural perspective (Estrada & Haney, 1998; Akamatsu, 1995; Odell, Shelling, Young, Hewitt, & Abate, 1994; McGill, 1992). Despite an attempt to integrate a social justice perspective into a family therapy program with a focus on cultural diversity (McGoldrick et al., 1999), attention to ethical issues in work with families has been minimal (Congress, 1997). A review of literature indicates only two books on ethics in family therapy (Huber, 1994; Waldron-Skinner & Watson, 1987) and nothing on ethical practice with culturally diverse families. The current NASW Code (1999) includes only one reference to family work and that only in terms of confidentiality.

Although most family therapists believe in self-determination and confidentiality, how are these values translated into ethical practice? How does family therapy affect self-determination? Are individual family members and the family as a whole able to freely determine their own behavior or is a certain type of behavior considered "bad" or "dysfunctional"? These questions may be particularly relevant for the family from a cultural background very different from that of the practitioner. The clinician often assumes the role of expert "knower," evaluating the family in terms of his or her perception rather than understanding the family through each member's perception (Laird, 1995). Narrative therapy emerges as a value-based model that requires the therapist to not begin family therapy with any preconceived understanding of the family, and to permit each family member to tell his or her own story. Allowing families to tell their own cultural stories (McGill, 1992), using genograms in a multicultural perspective (Estrada & Haney, 1998), developing family culturagrams (Congress, 1994, 2002), and using postmodernist approaches (Donavan, 2003) seem to maximize self-determination.

The importance of family relationships to culturally diverse families has been stressed (McGoldrick, 1998). Family therapists from cultures that stress an individualist approach must guard against viewing a family from a culture that stresses family connectiveness as too "enmeshed" if family members seem very close to each other. For example, a mother who must have her adolescent children accompany her shopping or is reluctant to allow her child to attend an out of state college may be described as not establishing appropriate boundaries by encouraging her adolescents to separate and individualize. A family in which older children are asked to care for younger children or to work in family businesses may be seen as exploitative of children. The family therapist must avoid labeling families from different cultures as dysfunctional because they favor a more collective *modus operandi* than the practitioner.

An important question is how much family therapy promotes individual self-determination. Often the family therapist is faced with a situation in which the goals of different family members conflict. For example, one spouse may see family therapy as a means to strengthen a marriage, while the other spouse envisions family therapy as helping them move toward separation and divorce. What goal does the family therapist promote? The family therapist may be asked to support one member's right to self-determination over the other, especially if there is conflict. How does a family therapist make decisions of this type? Family therapists must struggle with maintaining their own objectivity. At times family therapists may find themselves supporting what is familiar to them from their own background and experience. Family therapists who believe that families should stay together and that all areas of conflict can be resolved, are more likely to support the spouse who wants to continue the relationship. Family therapists who see separation and divorce as valid options for seriously conflictual relationships may tend to support the spouse who wants to terminate the relationship.

Often ethical dilemmas arise in helping families reconcile conflicts. How should the family therapist intervene when family conflicts arise around acculturation differences? It is well known that children and adolescents, possibly because of their greater association with the American educational system and peer culture, often become acculturated faster than their parents. This may lead to family conflict, especially during adolescence. How does the family therapist support individual self-determination when adolescent clients seek more association with peers and activities outside the home, while parents maintain that adolescents should primarily pursue home and family responsibilities? This conflict may be challenging for family therapists raised and trained within an American culture that usually views peer contacts outside the home as part of normal adolescent development. These therapists must avoid allying themselves with adolescents in the family they see, lest they lose the adults within the family. On the other hand, family therapists from a similar culture as the family often run the risk of supporting the parents and thus losing the children. Family therapists must strive to maintain a focus on the total family system and not ally with any one member or subgroup of the family.

Confidentiality is often a challenging issue for the family therapist. Practitioners often have differing opinions as to what information should be kept confidential and from whom. Some believe that whatever is discussed during individual sessions should be kept confidential, while others maintain that whatever is shared individually must be discussed by the family as a whole (Corey, Corey, & Callahan, 2002). Informing clients about the agency's policy in regard to handling individual communication in family work is considered ethical practice (NASW, 1999).

The NASW Code of Ethics addresses the importance of confidentiality in family work by stressing that the therapist "should seek agreement among [families] concerning each individual's right to confidentiality and obligation to preserve the confidentiality of information shared by others" (NASW, 1999, p. 11). Clients should be informed, however, that confidentiality can not be guaranteed.

The handling of confidentially is especially challenging for those who work with families from cultures who have a very different understanding of confidentiality. In a previous article on culturally diverse children this author noted that often children and parents from different cultures have a very different concept of confidentiality than the prevailing social work value of confidentiality (Congress & Lynn, 1994.) Neither children nor adults believed that group leaders would keep confidential information shared in group sessions. Healy (2001) notes that in Africa often extended families and community networks are involved in working with families, which mitigates a strict definition of confidentiality. African families, as well as those from other countries that favor a more collective approach, may question the American concept of confidentiality. Increasingly we work with families from many parts of the world that have a family community approach to problem solving that contrasts with the prevailing American concept of maintaining individual confidentiality.

Since I wrote the first edition of *Multicultural Perspectives in Working with Families*, I have become increasingly aware of how much the United States NASW Code of Ethics and the way we work with families is based on an Anglo Saxon perspective. Even compared to the codes of other developed countries, the provisions about confidentiality in the U.S. Code of Ethics are the most comprehensive and include the most specific practice situations. (Congress & McAuliffe, in press). The focus on strict confidentiality is particularly challenging at a time during which more and more families come from diverse backgrounds. Professionals must continually struggle with promoting confidentiality with families for whom the concept has limited meaning. Often a dilemma arises between enforcing American concepts of confidentiality and being sensitive to cultural differences in the use of confidentiality. The International Federation of Social Workers' (IFSW) Ethical Standards (2004) represent an attempt to develop ethical standards for social workers around the world. The Standards make a general statement about confidentiality, that social workers should maintain confidentiality about people who use their services except when there is "a greater ethical requirement" (such as the preservation of life) (IFSW, 2004, p. 1). It is interesting to note that this international standard uses an individualist approach to confidentiality and does not recognize a more collective perspective in providing social work services. There is a statement, however, that social workers should also adhere to the codes of their respective countries, that does provide for cultural differences in the use of confidentiality.

Although rights to privacy and confidentiality are stressed in American culture in general and social work practice in particular, these values may not have the same meaning for families from different cultures. For example, undocumented families may be reluctant to talk with family therapists. They may fear that practitioners whom they view as unknown authority figures possibly associated with government, may share information about them with immigration officials, thus leading to deportation. This may be particularly true now, as subsequent to 9-11 and the passing of the Patriot Act, there is greater government scrutiny of those who are not American citizens. Even if the family has legal status, past oppression and discrimination experienced by family members may make them reluctant to share information with outsiders (family therapists) from different cultural backgrounds.

All families have different ways of communicating and sharing personal information. In some families there is very open communication (perhaps too open) between family members. Other families have many secrets, kept confidential especially from children. Not only do family therapists have different ways of handling confidentiality, but also different families handle confidentiality in different ways. Some families from a similar cultural background may handle confidentiality in a similar way; others may approach confidentiality in a way unique for the family. It is necessary for the family therapist to explore a family's unique beliefs about privacy, confidentiality, and maintaining secrets. The family therapist must then be careful not to impose his or her own beliefs about maintaining secrets in family therapy. For example, a family therapist who insisted that there be no secrets in family therapy, and then insisted that an unemployed father discuss his feelings of inadequacy in a family session alienated the father and the family never returned for additional sessions.

Different family members may have different understandings about confidentiality. Parents from cultures that believe that adolescents should share openly their beliefs and behaviors and not maintain secrets may be in conflict with their adolescents influenced by American teenage culture, who may want to hide personal information from other family members. Recent court decisions that support adolescents' right to confidentiality for health care decisions may also affect family therapy with families from diverse backgrounds.

Informed consent is considered essential for ethical social work practice (NASW, 1999). Because of the vulnerability of many poor multicultural clients, the use of informed consent has been seen as strengthening and empowering to families from diverse backgrounds (Palmer & Kaufman, 2003). Furthermore, informed consent is a required component for evidence-based social work. Informed consent can occur, however, only if clients and families understand the nature of the treatment they will receive.

How can the family therapist facilitate informed consent with families from diverse cultural and linguistic backgrounds? Family therapists must be able to communicate with families in a language they can understand. This points to the need for family therapists to speak in the same language as the families whom they see. This is often challenging given the diversity of languages spoken by American immigrant families.

Using children as interpreters can be problematic, as communication can be distorted and parent's power within the family can be threatened. An example of distorted communication occurred when a social work student asked a 10-year-old daughter to inquire of her mother how she felt. The mother spoke for 10 minutes. At the end the daughter interpreted her mother's response as, "She says she feels fine." Another, perhaps more troubling, communication problem occurred when a 15-year-old boy with behavior problems was asked to interpret for his parents when they came for a family session. By using the adolescent as an interpreter the tenuous power relationships in a family were weakened even more.

Even if the therapist is able to communicate in the language of the family, ensuring informed consent can be problematic. Whereas informed consent can occur with parents, how much informed consent do children have? This is an issue in all family therapy, but may be more acute in families from cultures in which children are not seen as having rights. Family therapy can be affected by parents who have not explained to children why they are coming for therapy and furthermore do not see the need for family therapy. The ethical family therapist must strive to enable all members of a family to exercise informed consent. The purpose of family therapy may have to be explained in a way that children and those not familiar with family therapy can understand.

What new trends have influenced family therapy in the 21st century? Mental health treatment has already been greatly affected by a managed care model and one can predict that family therapy services will continue to be provided in a managed care environment. The impact of managed care on family therapy will be a focus on more short-term solution focused models of treatment. This may be very effective with immigrant families who have limited resources and want treatment that is time limited with very specific treatment objectives.

The trend toward managed care also necessitates a specific focus on clear goals and objectives that will appeal to culturally diverse families who want to see clear results within a limited amount of time. The current focus on evidence-based treatment is also conducive to family therapy with families from different cultural backgrounds. A major tenet of evidence-based family therapy is that the therapist must identify to the client the focus of treatment and specific means by which treatment goals are to be achieved.

With the current focus on managed care, there is concern that family therapy is not always reimbursable. There is no accepted diagnostic system for families comparable to the *DSM IV*, which is used to measure individual dysfunction and symptomatology. A challenge is that mental health family treatment often involves billing at full rate for the primary client (identified patient) and billing for other family members as collaborative visits.

Evidence-based practice is conducive to family therapy with diverse families. First, an exploration of client values is conducted. This is essential in work with families that may have a different value system from that of the therapist. A second major component is the need for informed consent so that the family may choose from different family therapy models. As stated previously, this is challenging given the diversity of cultural backgrounds and languages. Some culturally diverse families may rely on the therapist as the expert and not want to choose among different options. Also, the therapist may believe that s/he is the expert and knows what model would work best with the family. A third major component of evidence-based practice that is firmly supported by the Code of Ethics is that social workers should only rely on models that have proven to be effective. This is challenging as there has been limited research on the effectiveness of the different family models, and even less research on the effectiveness of different family therapy models with clients from different cultural backgrounds.

However, practice wisdom, an important component of evidence-based social work, suggests that family work would be advisable with people from diverse cultures that favor a collective approach to resolving problems. Family therapy seems particularly appropriate when families seek treatment as a group, in contrast to the many Americans who seek individual treatment. One challenge, however, might be that those families from cultures in which there is a male dominated hierarchy within the family may be resistant to therapy in which each member has an equal voice, and there is an expectation that each is open in discussing feelings and problems.

The United States, similar to other countries around the world, is becoming increasingly culturally diverse. In New York City 40% of the population is foreign born, for the United States as a whole, the average percentage of foreign born is 20% (U.S. Census Bureau, 2000). Because of increased poverty and violence, many communities where new immigrants live are currently under siege and can provide only limited support to their residents. One can predict that this situation will not improve very soon with cutbacks in financial and social service resources for poor people. Culturally competent family treatment that focuses on strengthening families provides much support for families in a challenging social environment.

Family therapists work more and more with families from many different cultural backgrounds. Also, as many people from diverse cultural backgrounds seek professional education, one can predict that family therapists will increasingly come from diverse cultural backgrounds. There is some evidence to suggest, however, that it has been difficult to attract and retain trainees of color, as "family therapy is not the world in which they are familiar . . . though their own values are very family oriented" (McGoldrick et al., 1999, p. 194). Other explanations that McGoldrick and colleagues offer for the limited number of trainees of color is that many from non-White backgrounds view the family therapy field as White dominated, and secondly, therapists of color must contend with many life stresses that may prevent them from pursuing specialized training in family therapy.

One anticipates that this will change as more people of color move into the middle class and seek professional education. Many begin to work with families after pursuing a masters in social work. Currently the Council on Social Work Education (CSWE) reports that approximately 20% of graduating MSW students are from other than White cultural backgrounds (Lennon, 2002). The focus in social work education is to prepare students for culturally competent practice with families, as well as individuals, groups, and communities. In the years to come, an increasing number of families from diverse cultural backgrounds will be able to receive culturally competent family therapy from professional social workers.

REFERENCES

Congress, E. (1994). The use of culturagrams to assess and empower culturally diverse families. *Families in Society, 75*(9), 531–540.

Congress, E. (Ed.). (1997). *Multicultural perspectives in working with families.* New York: Springer Publishing.

Congress, E. (1999). *Social work values and ethics: Identifying and resolving professional dilemmas.* Belmont, CA: Wadsworth.

Congress, E. (2002). Using culturagrams with culturally diverse families. In A. Roberts & G. Greene (Eds.), *Social work desk reference* (pp. 57–61). New York: Oxford University Press.

Congress, E., & Lynn, M. (1994). Group work programs in public schools: Ethical dilemmas and cultural diversity. *Social Work in Education, 16*(2), 107–114.

Congress, E., & McAuliffe, D. (in press). Social work ethics: Professional codes in Australia and the United States. *International Social Work.*

Corey, G., Corey, M., & Callahan, P. (2002). *Issues and ethics in the helping professions.* Pacific Grove, CA: Wadsworth Publishing Company.

Donavan, M. (2003). Family therapy beyond post modernism: Some consideration on the ethical orientation of contemporary practice. *Journal of Family Therapy, 25,* 285–306.

Estrada, A., & Haney, P. (1998). Genograms in a multicultural perspective. *Journal of Family Psychotherapy, 9*(2), 55–62.

Healy, L. (2001). *International social work: Professional action in an interdependent world.* New York: Oxford University Press.

Huber, C. (1994). *Ethical, legal, and professional issues in practice of marriage and family therapy.* New York: Merrill.

International Federation of Social Workers. (2004). *Ethical standards.* Geneva: Author.

Laird, J. (1995). Family centered practice in post modern era. *Families in Society, 76*(3), 150–160.

Lennon, T. (2002). *Statistics on social work education in the United States: 2000.* Silver Springs, MD: Council on Social Work Education.

Lowenberg, F., Dolgoff, R., & Harrington, D. (2000). *Ethical decisions for social work practice.* Itasca, IL: F. E. Peacock Publishers, Inc.

McGill, D. W. (1992). The cultural story in multicultural family therapy. *Families in Society, 73*(6), 339–349.

McGoldrick, M. (1998). *Revisioning family therapy: Race, culture, and gender in clinical practice.* New York: Guilford Press.

McGoldrick, M., Almeida, R., Preto, N. G., & Bibb, A. (1999). Efforts to incorporate social justice perspectives into a family training program. *Journal of Marital and Family Therapy, 25*(2), 191–210.

National Association of Social Workers. (1999). *Code of ethics.* Washington, DC: NASW Press.

Odell, M., Shelling, G., Young, K., Hewitt, D., & Abate, L. (1994). The skills of the marriage and family therapist in straddling multicultural issues. *American Journal of Family Therapy, 22*(2), 145–155.

Palmer, N., & Kaufman, M. (2003). The ethics of informed consent: Implications for multicultural practice. *Journal of Ethnic and Cultural Diversity in Social Work*, *12*(1), 1–26.

Reamer, F. (1999). *Social work values and ethics*. New York: Columbia University Press.

U.S. Census Bureau. (2000). Retrieved from http://factfinder.census.gov/home/saff/main.html?_lang=en

Waldron-Skinner, S., & Watson, D. (1987). *Ethical issues in family therapy*. London: Routledge and Kegan Paul.

Index

Springer Series on Social Work

Albert R. Roberts, PhD, Series Editor

Advisory Board: Gloria Bonilla-Santiago, PhD, Barbara Berkman, PhD, Elaine P. Congress, DSW, Gilbert J. Greene, PhD, Jesse Harris, DSW, C. Aaron McNeece, DSW